THE OPTIONAL MATRIMONIAL PROPERTY REGIME

THE OPTIONAL MATRIMONIAL PROPERTY REGIME

The Franco-German Community of Accrued Gains

Maria Giovanna Cubeddu Wiedemann (ed.)

intersentia
Cambridge – Antwerp – Portland

Intersentia Publishing Ltd.
Sheraton House | Castle Park
Cambridge | CB3 0AX | United Kingdom
Tel.: +44 1223 370 170 | Email: mail@intersentia.co.uk

Distribution for the UK:
NBN International
Airport Business Centre, 10 Thornbury Road
Plymouth, PL6 7 PP
United Kingdom
Tel.: +44 1752 202 301 | Fax: +44 1752 202 331
Email: orders@nbninternational.com

Distribution for the USA and Canada:
International Specialized Book Services
920 NE 58th Ave. Suite 300
Portland, OR 97213
USA
Tel.: +1 800 944 6190 (toll free)
Email: info@isbs.com

Distribution for Austria:
Neuer Wissenschaftlicher Verlag
Argentinierstraße 42/6
1040 Wien
Austria
Tel.: +43 1 535 61 03 24
Email: office@nwv.at

Distribution for other countries:
Intersentia Publishing nv
Groenstraat 31
2640 Mortsel
Belgium
Tel.: +32 3 680 15 50
Email: mail@intersentia.be

The Optional Matrimonial Property Regime. The Franco-German Community of Accrued Gains
Maria Giovanna Cubeddu Wiedemann (ed.)

ISBN 978-1-78068-224-2
D/2014/7849/55
NUR 822

British Library Cataloguing in Publication Data. A catalogue record for this book is available from the British Library.

PREFACE

European family law can be a fascinating topic. The family law of each Member State is different, and it is a challenge in Europe to try to use the law to achieve practical solutions to the problems encountered by national and transnational couples. The solutions proposed should also be regarded as providing guidance and helping to resolve future issues.

The genesis of this book lies in a project regarding property relations between spouses, which was presented for the first time at the *Tagung der Wissenschaftlichen Vereinigung für das Familienrecht* in Potsdam, Germany.

The Franco-German Agreement on the establishment of an optional matrimonial property regime, which became law in both countries in 2013, is the first attempt at unifying substantive matrimonial property law in Europe. The innovations included in the Agreement may be useful for the adoption of the same instrument in different states.

This study promotes the spread of the Franco-German regime on a European and international level. The Agreement's added advantage is to offer a joint instrument that does not require the parties to give up their domestic laws. The contents and specifics of the joint optional property regime can be better understood by comparison with domestic regulations in France and Germany. The importance of this is showcased through a comparison of German, Swiss, Italian and Dutch matrimonial property regimes.

Due to the increasing mobility of persons within the European Union it is considered desirable that other Member States accede to the Agreement. To promote this, the book provides a short commentary on the law, accurate and timely translations of the normative text, the memoranda and explanatory reports, as well as the German implementing legislation, in English, Italian and Spanish.

The book is, in a broad sense, also intended to assist lawyers in helping spouses to enter into matrimonial agreements. It will also be of considerable interest to policy-makers and economists concerned with family law. European family law can also be an enjoyable and rewarding topic to study and I hope this book will be useful, not only in revision and in question-answering techniques, but also in providing students with enthusiasm for the subject.

ACKNOWLEDGEMENTS

Many people have helped in the preparation of this book, both directly and (even) more indirectly.

Above all, I am indebted to Prof. em. Dr Dr h.c. mult. Dieter Henrich whose enquiring mind and enthusiasm are always an inspiration and Dr Jens Scherpe for his constant friendliness and willingness to help.

I would like to express my gratitude to colleagues Prof. Marella Magris and Prof. Helena Lozano Miralles whose comments and suggestions have assisted in the translations. I am very grateful to all those who translated and reviewed a sample part of this book and provided some very useful remarks, Dr Bernadette Chaussade-Klein, Avv. Dr Maria Virginia Maccari and Dott. Elisa Sgubin, Dott. Daniele Orlando, Thomas Feige and Michaela Kolb. I also extend my appreciation to Prof. Dr Albert Lamarca. As always, any further comments or suggestions would be welcome.

Financial support has been received from the *Dipartimento di Scienze giuridiche, dell'Interpretazione, del Linguaggio e della Traduzione*, University of Trieste. I am very thankful to the Director Prof. Paolo Pittaro who has been extremely helpful with guidance for the contribution. My thanks go also to Ann-Christin Maak-Scherpe of Intersentia, who was loving and supportive beyond measure during the publication of the book.

Maria Giovanna Cubeddu Wiedemann
Trieste, February 2014

CONTENTS

LIST OF CONTRIBUTORS

Prof. Maria Giovanna Cubeddu Wiedemann
University of Trieste, Italy

Prof. em. Dr Dr mult. h.c. Dieter Henrich
University of Regensburg, Germany

TRANSLATIONS

French

Dr jur. Bernadette Chaussade-Klein
Wissenschaftliche Angestellte, Law Faculty, University of Munich, Germany

English

Prof. Marella Magris
Associate Professor in German Language and Translation, University of Trieste, Italy

Dott. Daniele Orlando
PhD candidate in Translation Studies, University of Trieste, Italy

Italian

Avv. Maria Virginia Maccari
PhD in European Private Law, University of Trieste, Italy

Dott. Elisa Sgubin
PhD candidate in European Private Law, University of Trieste, Italy

Spanish

Prof. Helena Lozano Miralles
Associate Professor in Spanish Language and Translation, University of Trieste, Italy

Thomas Feige
Degree in Translation and Interpreting, University of Salamanca, Spain

Michaela Kolb
Degree in Translation and Interpreting, Cologne University of Applied Sciences, Germany

LIST OF ABBREVIATIONS

BGB	Bürgerliches Gesetzbuch (German Civil Code)
BGBl.	Bundesgesetzblatt
B.W.	Burgerlijk Wetboek (Dutch Civil Code)
cat. CC	Code civil de Catalunya (Catalunya Civil Code)
CEFL Principles	Principles of European Family Law Regarding Property Relations between Spouses
(CE) Recommendation (89)	(CE) Recommendation (89) on Contributions Following Divorce of January 1989
(CM) Recommendation (81) 15	(CM) Recommendation (81) 15 of 16 October 1981 on the rights of spouses relating to the occupation of the family home and the use of the household contents
EGBGB	Einführungsgesetz zum Bürgerlichen Gesetzbuche (Introductory Act to the German Civil Code)
fr. CC	Code civil français (French Civil Code)
Hague Convention 1978	Convention on the Law Applicable to Matrimonial Property Regimes of 14 March 1978, entered into force in 1992
it. CC	Codice civile italiano (Italian Civil Code)
LPartG	Lebenspartnerschaftsgesetz (Civil Partnership Act)
Rome III	Council Regulation (EU) No 1259/2010 of 20 December 2010 implementing enhanced cooperation in the area of the law applicable to divorce and legal separation
Rome IV	Proposal for a Regulation on jurisdiction, applicable law and the recognition and enforcement of decision in matters of matrimonial property regimes (COM (2011) 126/2)
sp. CC	Código civil español (Spanish Civil Code)
ZGB	Zivilgesetzbuch (Swiss Civil Code)

PART I
INTRODUCTION

THE OPTIONAL MATRIMONIAL PROPERTY REGIME

Maria Giovanna CUBEDDU WIEDEMANN and Dieter HENRICH

CONTENTS

I. EUROPEAN LEGISLATION, DOMESTIC LAWS AND JOINT RULES

Within the European Union (EU), family law is governed in a variety of ways. The search for European solutions to provide an adequate response to the gradual increase of marriages between people of different nationalities and people not living in their state of origin has been going on for some time. A harmonization of the substantive family law of the individual states in its entirety cannot be attempted due to the distinct traditions and cultures of those states. Consider the difficulties faced by the EU in their effort to harmonize the rules of jurisdiction and applicable law in matters of divorce and separation,[1] or of jurisdiction, applicable law and the recognition and enforcement of decisions in matters of matrimonial property regimes.[2] These projects, part of a broader plan of European codification, stalled not only because of divergent rules on conflicts of law, or because of the difficult issues regarding various criteria of the applicable law such as domicile or citizenship, but above all because of the foreseeable multiplicity of models of marriage or divorce.

The harmonization process in family law, however, is now undoubtedly underway. The concern lies with finding appropriate instruments and methods. One common approach is drawn from the Franco-German Agreement on the optional matrimonial property regime of the community of accrued gains,[3] which has recently become law in both countries. This project – assumed on the occasion of the 40th anniversary of the *Elysée-Vertrag* between Germany and France – which relates to the regulation of an optional property regime common to both jurisdictions, aims to address the difficulty of establishing the applicable law in transnational relationships and the obstacles that the community of property regime creates in the credit sector, as well as the desire for a more prompt resolution of disputes. At the proposal of German Minister for Justice Leutheusser-Schnarrenberger, on 13 January 2010, the German Government consented to the Agreement.[4] "Cosmopolitanism does not reveal itself only in ideas, but also and especially in life projects" ("*Weltoffenheit zeigt sich nicht nur in Einstellungen sondern auch und gerade in Lebensentwürfen*").[5] The reasons given by the German Minister for Justice for the Agreement concerned several aspects of family law, all related to the gradual increase of marriages between people of different nationalities and, more generally, the movement of persons: "the answers by private international law are often complex and differ from state to state. An ever growing Europe needs clear and flexible solutions for weddings that do not stop at national borders and in front of the membership of a State".[6]

---

1 Council Regulation (EU) No 1259/2010 of 20 December 2010 implementing enhanced cooperation in the area of the law applicable to divorce and legal separation (Rome III Regulation).

2 Council of the European Union, *Proposal for a Regulation on jurisdiction, applicable law and the recognition and enforcement of decision in matters of matrimonial property regimes* (COM (2011) 126/2 Def.) (Rome IV Regulation): see Martiny, Die Kommissionsvorschläge für das internationale Ehegüterrecht sowie für das internationale Güterrecht eingetragener Partnerschaften, Praxis des Internationalen Privat- und Verfahrensrechts, 2011, 4th revised text, Interinstitutional File 2011/0059 (CNS) of 20 December 2012, No. 18045/12.

3 *Abkommen zwischen der Bundesrepublik Deutschland und der Französischen Republik über den Güterstand der Wahl-Zugewinngemeinschaft/Accord entre la Republique fédérale d'Allemagne et la République francaise instituant un régime matrimonial optionel de la participation aux acquêts.*

4 *Pressemitteilung der Bundesjustizministerin* of 13 January 2010, at <www.bjm.de>.

5 *Ibid.*

6 *Ibid.*

The *Deutsch-Französischer Ministerrat* signed the Agreement on 4 February 2010. After ratification by the *Deutschen Bundestag* (15 March 2012)[7] and the French National Assembly (17 January 2013), resulting in the exchange of instruments of ratification, and following publication in the Bundesgesetzblatt/[8] Journal Officiel,[9] the Convention came into force on 1 May 2013.

While in the past, a major role was attributed to the circulation of models in Europe, efforts have now shifted towards looking for practicable solutions in the process of harmonization. It is hoped that the legal scheme of a joint matrimonial property regime will present a valid option for spouses and give a decisive impetus to this process. Initial favourable opinions already consider it a step full of symbolic power and a "little legal sensation" ("*kleine juristische Sensation*"), because of the "domestic" character typically attributed to family law. The real "sensation", however, lies in the availability of the conventional model not only to French-German "mixed" couples, but also to those formed by two German or French spouses, regardless of their residence, and its openness to other EU countries which may want to join the agreement.

The optional matrimonial property regime between spouses has been identified as the first stage of a common codification effort in specific areas of family law. Its aim is to provide for an additional optional regime without requiring countries to waive any legislative autonomy. In German law, the default statutory matrimonial property regime is the *Zugewinngemeinschaft*. Under this regime assets remain separate and at the dissolution of the regime an adjustment is made to account for increases in the assets of both spouses. In France, the legal regime is the *communauté légale* (*communauté réduite aux acquêts*). The assets acquired during the marriage become common property. The regime of the *participation aux acquêts*, based on the German model, exists in the French legal system as an alternative statutory regime. Spouses are able to opt for this regime by notarial deed. The two regimes – the *Zugewinngemeinschaft* in Germany and the *participation aux acquêts* in France – are not identical. Their practical differences are not easy to recognize because their effects are often not clear in either state. Hence the decision to offer a new optional regime that is oriented towards the German *Zugewinngemeinschaft*, but also incorporates the peculiarities of the French *régime de la participation aux acquêts*. The claimed advantage is to offer a joint instrument that does not require the parties to give up their other domestic laws.

---

7 See the German Ratification Act of 15 March 2012, *Bundesgesetzblatt (BGBl.)* 2012, Teil II, p. 178.

8 *Bekanntmachung über das Inkrafttreten* on 22 April 2013 (*BGBl.* 2013, II, p. 431).

9 See the French Ratifications Act, *Loi n. 2013-98 du 28 janvier 2013 autorisant la ratification de l'accord entre la République francaise et la République fédérale d'Allemaigne instituant un régime matrimonial optionnel de la participation aux acquêts, JORF n° 0024 du 29 janvier 2013*, p. 1721.

II. THE TRENDS TOWARDS HARMONIZATION IN EUROPE

Issues arising from the increasingly frequent movement of people across borders have long since revealed difficulties in defining the applicable law according to current private international law systems, even in the field of property relationships in family law. At the European level, the first step was the Green Paper on conflict of laws concerning matrimonial property regimes, as part of the completion of mutual recognition of decisions in civil and commercial matters,[10] going back to the Plan of Vienna of 1998. The objective has been to unify the rules of jurisdiction and the harmonization of conflict law, including the mutual recognition of decisions. This will be followed by a European regulation called Rome IV.[11]

Studies have revealed the complexity in this area, due to the relationship between the matrimonial property regimes (the primary regime and the chosen matrimonial property regime) and the dissolution of the marriage, and to the different approach to civil unions other than marriage.[12] It is necessary to distinguish the primary regime, like the general rights and duties of the spouse, from the matrimonial property regime. The matrimonial property regimes are also divided into two groups: the community of property, which is well established in almost all European countries, and the separation of assets, accompanied by a subsequent participation of accrued gains.

Even with the correctives made to the initial draft, more extensively there is no doubt that the harmonization of conflict law should be the first step. Matrimonial property regimes, as for other areas of common substantive family law, such as the relationship between parents and children or the duty of maintenance, have been identified as essential to the harmonization of family law.[13]

The idea of principles for European matrimonial property regimes is one that has been on the agenda of the Commission on European Family Law (CEFL) for some time. The aim of the CEFL is to assist in the harmonization of family law in Europe by the publication of EU principles in various areas.[14] The CEFL published its Principles of European Family Law Regarding Property Relations between Spouses

---

10 Doc. COM (2006) 400 Def.: see WAGNER, *Zeitschrift für das gesamte Familienrecht* 2009, 269.

11 Doc. COM (2011) 126/2 Def.: see WAGNER, *Neue Juristische Wochenschrift* 2013, 1654.

12 BOELE-WOELKI/MILES/SCHERPE (eds.), *The Future of Family Property in Europe*, 2011.

13 See VERBERKE/SCHERPE/DECLERCK/HELMS/SENAEVE (eds.), *Confronting the Frontiers of Family and Succession Law, Liber amicorum Walter Pintens*, 2012.

14 Further information is available on the CEFL's website <http://ceflonline.net>.

in 2013.[15] At the core of these principles are: general rights and the duty of contribution; protection of the family home; representation between spouses; and private autonomy to enter into marital property agreements. The remaining principles concern the development of two systems of matrimonial property regimes based on the participation in acquisitions and the community of acquisitions.

Typical examples of these different matrimonial property regimes are to be found in Germany, Switzerland, Italy and the Netherlands.

III. DEVELOPMENTS IN GERMANY, SWITZERLAND, ITALY AND THE NETHERLANDS

A) GERMANY

Meanwhile, in Germany the default statutory regime of the *Zugewinngemeinschaft* (community of accrued gains) (§§1363 et seq. BGB) was reformed.[16] The issues, which constituted the basis of the German law reform, were largely similar to those related to the Franco-German Agreement. Some proposals for modifying the *Zugewinngemeinschaft* were not realized in Germany, but were included in the common draft between Germany and France, due to their closeness to the French matrimonial property regime of the *participation aux acquêts*.

The German law reform was designed not to modify the fundamental rules of the *Zugewinngemeinschaft* – as in changing profiles more closely related to the personal assets of the spouses or in reducing the final share of the patrimonial increase – but to modify the criteria and procedures for determining the final assets and the value of the equalizing debt on the accrued gains (§§1373 et seq. BGB). In this regard, rather than a reform of the regime of the *Zugewinngemeinschaft* (or community of accrued gains) it can more accurately be termed a reform of the *Zugewinnausgleich* (or the settlement claim of accrued gains).

The reform has not changed the basic framework – which remains the separation of the property of both spouses and the independent administration of his or her property – but a number of aspects of the final settlement claim, such as the valuation of the initial and final assets, the duties of information and the date of the calculation of the debt on the accrued gains, due to adhere to fairness and good faith in their application in practice.

15 Boele-Woelki/Ferrand/Beilfuss/Jaenterae-Jareborg/Lowe/Martiny/Pintens (eds.), *Principles of European Family Law Regarding Property Relations Between Spouses*, 2013.

16 *Gesetz zur Änderung des Zugewinnausgleichs- und Vormundschaftsrecht* of 6 July 2009, *BGBl.* 2009, I, p. 1696.

B) SWITZERLAND

Swiss law also includes the separation of the property of the spouses during the marriage and a mutual claim to participation in gains at the termination of the property regime similar to the German *Zugewinngemeinschaft*. However, there are substantial differences.

In the event of marriage the statutory patrimonial regime of *Errungenschaftsbeteiligung* (or participation in acquisitions: Arts. 196–220 ZGB) applies if the spouses have not agreed on another regime through a matrimonial agreement, or if the regime of separation of property is ordered or applies on special grounds (Arts. 118, 137, 176, 2 no. 3185 et seq. ZGB).[17]

The regime of participation in acquisitions is similar at its core to the German *Zugewinngemeinschaft*. The assets of the spouses during the regime remain separate. At the termination of the matrimonial property regime there is a participation in accrued gains. The regime distinguishes between the assets of both spouses: personal and acquired property. Each spouse, therefore, owns two sets of assets and so there are four categories of assets overall: the separate property of each spouse (*Eigengut*) and the acquisitions of each spouse (*Errungenschaft*). The personal property of a spouse comprises those items that are for their exclusive personal use (such as clothes, jewellery, hobby items, etc.), the assets brought into the marriage, satisfaction of claims, as well as gifts, inheritances, and bequests acquired during the regime (see Arts. 198 et seq. ZGB). If assets are substituted, the assets, or a replacement for them, will be regarded as personal separate property. However, incomes from separate property fall into the acquisitions of that spouse, in particular acquisitions of work by each spouse and acquisitions of personal and social welfare institutions (AHV, IV, UV, ALV, pension, etc.) belong to the acquisitions, as does income from personal property and replacement for acquisitions (Arts. 197, 200 3, ZGB). Each spouse is the owner of his or her own property (*Eigenvermögen*) and acquisitions (*Errungenschaft*). They may use and administer these assets independently. Assets are presumed to be owned jointly by both spouses unless proven otherwise. If assets are co-owned they can only be disposed with the consent of both spouses. Debts incurred by one spouse are his or her personal debts (Art. 202 ZGB), for which he or she is liable with all their assets (Art. 202 ZGB). With the death of a spouse, divorce, annulment of marriage, legal separation, or a change to a community of acquisitions or separation of property regime, the matrimonial property regime is terminated. Upon the dissolution of the matrimonial property regime, each asset is assigned first to one of the four

17 Aebi-Müller, Schweiz, in: Bergman/Ferid/Henrich (eds.), *Internationales Ehe- und Kindschaftsrecht*, 2013.

categories of property. The financial contributions to the marital assets will be settled in the matrimonial property dispute. A spouse may claim half of the net amount of the acquisition of the other spouse. The pecuniary claims between the spouses are set off against each other (Art. 251 ZGB). On the dissolution of the matrimonial property regime of participation in acquisitions several steps have to be taken. First, the asset recovery handover follows and mutual debts are compensated. Then substitute grants are to be settled between the individual property and the acquisitions of each spouse (e.g. if items were to be acquired for exclusive personal use using employment income). What remains from the total value of acquisitions (after the replacement subsidies have been taken into account and the debt deducted) forms the *Vorschlag*. Each spouse shall have half of the surplus of the other. A negative amount is not considered. No compensation of the separate property takes place.

C) ITALY

In Italy a community of acquisition regime applies,[18] and as in most countries it is similar to the French Civil Code.[19] A distinction is made between personal and community property. The assets acquired before the marriage remain personal property. This also applies for gifts, inheritances and bequests acquired during the regime, assets personal in nature, as well as assets exclusively acquired for a spouse's profession. An immediate community of other assets bought after the entry into force of the regime is created. Debts which one spouse enters into alone or which relate only to him or her are personal debts. The liability for community debts is incurred generally by both spouses. The community property is shared upon dissolution of the regime.

The main "imperfections" of this model have been identified as including: (a) the limited flexibility in administering of the community property; (b) the function of guarantee which has common property for the debts entered into by only one spouse before the marriage; (c) the presumption accepted in most legal systems that fruits gained from personal property are included in the community property; and (d) the inclusion of items needed in employment in the personal property without obligation to compensation if they are acquired by means of common property. By way of further illustration of problem (c), for example, in the French matrimonial property regime of *communauté légale*, each spouse may

18 Henrich, Italien, in: Bergman/Ferid/Henrich (eds.), *Internationales Ehe- und Kindschaftsrecht*, 2009; see also Cubeddu/Wiedemann, Italien, in: Süss/Ring (eds.), *Eherecht in Europa*, 2012, pp. 607–261.

19 Chaussade-Klein/Henrich/Schönberger, Frankreich, in: Bergman/Ferid/Henrich (eds.), *Internationales Ehe- und Kindschaftsrecht*, 2009; see also Döbereiner, Frankreich, in: Süss/Ring (eds.), *Eherecht in Europa*, 2012, pp. 485–527.

independently dispose of his or her income, but what is acquired falls under the community property. The spouse who acquired assets with his or her own individual income obtains a claim to compensation at the dissolution of the regime. In Germany, in the case of the conventional community of property regime, the assets of both spouses are community property except for assets acquired by donations and inheritance. The remuneration received by way of a salary belongs to the community property even if the salary is credited to an account belonging to one of the spouses.

Among the solutions for the creation of a European model based on the community of acquisitions, as in Italian law, it has been suggested that each spouse's personal property be expanded and the powers of administration be extended (i.e. powers of management, enjoyment and disposition) with regard to the community property. Proposals are made to limit the common property on assets that are the result of an effective contribution of both spouses. In accordance with these considerations, the regime of the community of acquisitions in force in Italy can be defined as a compromise, to be used as a model for the community of acquisitions regime and to offer an alternative model like the optional community of property regime applicable in Germany or as amended by other default statutory regimes (see France and Switzerland).[20]

The Italian model is praised for its limits to the liability from debts. In principle, the creditors of each spouse can enforce against personal property. If this is not sufficient, enforcement will also extend to community property, but only up to the portion of community property (equivalent to half of net accruing) belonging to the debtor spouse.[21]

In addition, the *comunione de residuo* (community of the residue assets, Art. 177 Codice civile) permits an effective settlement of gains of personal assets and thereby realizes a function of solidarity between the spouses. This is especially so under the doctrine that not only the part of the income set aside without being invested falls into the *comunione de residuo*, but also the part used for acquisitions of personal property, such as assets of a personal nature or exclusively acquired for a spouse's profession. In so far as such assets count as patrimonial increases, the income of an employee could not be considered consumed and its value would fall under the community property at the dissolution of the regime.

---

20 Henrich, Zur Zukunft des Güterrechts in Europa, *Zeitschrift für das gesamte Familienrecht* 2002, p. 1521.

21 Patti, Eheliche Gemeinschaft, Partnerschaft und Vermögen in Italien, in: Henrich/Schwab (eds.), *Eheliche Gemeinschaft, Partnerschaft und Vermögen im europäischen Vergleich*, 1999, pp. 125–142; see also, Cubeddu/Patti, *Introduzione al diritto della famiglia in Europa*, 2008.

D) THE NETHERLANDS

Developments in the Netherlands are interesting not only because its property law has recently been reformed, but especially because the structure of its property law remained the same. Two new provisions deserve particular mention: the introduction of a general information obligation on the spouses and the premature equalization.

The Dutch matrimonial property regime was reformed in 2012 (Arts. 93 et seq. B.W.).[22] The spouses are free to choose their matrimonial property regime. The default statutory regime is the universal community of property. The assets of the spouses are common property. The community of property includes all assets of the spouses, both those existing at the beginning of the regime and those acquired throughout the matrimonial property regime. All debts incurred before or during marriage by one or both spouses are considered to be community debts, except for debts closely related to one spouse (debt contracted in relation to a personal asset and debt relating to an inheritance acquired under an exclusion clause), which are expressly excluded (s. Art. 126 (1) (2, a, b) Book 4). In the event of a dispute between the spouses about whom an asset belongs to, with neither of them able to prove ownership, the asset is considered community property. The spouses may derogate from this rule, e.g. exclude certain assets from the community property.

Under this regime personal property is: (a) assets expressly assigned by inheritance, gift or bequest to one of the spouses by the deceased or the donor; (b) pension rights to which the law of settlement claim upon divorce applies, and other claims related to these pension rights or survivor's benefits; (c) usufruct on the marital home and household goods (as provided in the Book 4 of B.W. (Succession));[23] and (d) assets closely connected to one spouse. Fruits of personal property are community property. Personal property are also assets, which one spouse acquires as a compensation for the depreciation of a personal asset.

There is an information obligation imposed on the spouses. On request the spouses must provide each other with information on their administration of the property, as well as on assets and duties (Art. 83 n.F. B.W.). Up until the recent

---

22 As adaptation of the community of property regime (*Wet aanpassing wettelijke gemeenschap van goederen dead wijziging van de titels 6, 7 en 8 BW*), which came into force on 1 January 2012. See Boele-Woelki/Braat, Marital Agreements and Partyautonomy in Dutch Law, in: Scherpe (ed.), *Marital Agreements and Private Autonomy in a Comparative Perspective*, 2012, pp. 231–255; see also Vlaardingerbroek, Niederlande, in: Süss/Ring (eds.), *Eherecht in Europa*, 2012, pp. 787–836.

23 As set out in Articles 29 and 30 or Articles 34 and following of Book 4 (Reusing of the marital home and the inventory).

law reform this information obligation came from Art. 98 B.W. This provision was repealed as of 1 January 2012 and transferred from title 7 (Default Statutory Matrimonial Property Regime) to title 6 (Rights and Duties of the Spouses) of Book 1 almost unaltered.

The community of property ends (under the new version of Art. 99 (1b) B.W.) at the date of petition for divorce ("premature equalization") and not – as before – only at the point that divorce is given legal effect. In principle, all existing assets at this point in time are subject to the matrimonial property liquidation.

IV. THE FRANCO-GERMAN AGREEMENT

As anticipated, on 1 May 2013 the Franco-German Agreement entered into force in both States.

In France the *régime de participation aux acquêts* – as part of the already applicable community of accrued gains – is not especially popular and so this new model could replace the existing one, which is why the German model was favoured in this process. When the project was presented for the first time at the *Tagung der Wissenschaftlichen Vereinigung für das Familienrecht* in Potsdam, Germany, in June 2008, numerous issues were open for consideration, including those concerning the matrimonial agreement's form, the parties of the matrimonial agreement (married couples only or registered partnerships too) and the consequences of disposals of patrimonial assets. The common optional matrimonial property regimes in force through a bilateral agreement shall be draw a "normative identity" to accompany an "identity of results", which proves to be neutral for the international private law.

The major differences between the matrimonial property regimes – *participation aux acquêts* and *Zugewinngemeinschaft* – which emerged in the preparatory work, were focused on: (a) the consequences of acts of disposals in the absence of consent of both spouses – ineffectiveness or annulment; (b) the application of the matrimonial property regime (married couples and civil unions); (c) the mandatory rule of the statutory primary matrimonial property regime; (d) the ownership of assets during the matrimonial property regime (separation of assets or common property); and (e) the provisions about the division/liquidation of the assets.

The optional regime of the Franco-German Agreement corresponds in substance to the model of participations in acquisitions, a regime existing as a default statutory matrimonial property regime in Germany (*Zugewinngemeinschaft*) and as optional regime in France (*participation aux acquêts*). The assets remain separate. At the termination of the regime the assets of both spouses are adjusted to take account of increases during the marriage. Despite the German origin of the new optional regime there are a series of provisions of French derivation, including, for example, the irrelevance of compensation, due for non-pecuniary damage or "accidental" increases (not resulting from own activities) of real estate assets, in the determination of the final assets of each spouse.

The specific provisions of the Agreement can be better understood by comparison with their respective domestic regulations.

A) LIMITATIONS ON ACTS OF DISPOSAL

One of the provisions that characterizes the new optional regime of community of accrued gains is contained in Article 5. Any acts of disposal pertaining to household items or rights which guarantee the family home can not be validly made by one of the spouses individually, but require the consent of both spouses. Any act of disposal contravening this rule shall be ineffective. The spouse who has not consented can approve the act later. The rule, which is mandatory in nature, is evocative of §§1365, 1369 BGB and Article 215 (3) Code civil. Compared to §1365 (and §1369) BGB, it is extensive. As well as what is regulated in the domestic German law, Article 5 includes not only acts of disposal concerning the entire assets, but all the "rights" to guarantee the family home. On the other hand, the rule has restricted contents, which finds its basis in the French law of *régime primaire.* Article 215 (3) Code civil concerns only domestic assets and the family home, not the whole property, as it does in German law.

B) JOINT LIABILITY

Article 6 of the Franco-German Agreement, which provides for contracts concluded by one spouse alone pertaining to the administration of the household to be jointly binding, has a counterpart in §1357 BGB. Compared to the German provision where joint liability for acts of disposal is regulated, which builds adequate coverage for the needs of the family life ("*angemessene Deckung des Lebensbedarfs der Familie*") (for example holidays or luxury goods if they conform to the lifestyle and assets of the spouses), Article 6 reduces the freedom of contract of each spouse as it relates to the management of the household. The liability of the spouses is therefore aggravated. However, the needs of the children in their entirety are protected even in extraordinary cases. In this regard this article is based upon the corresponding French provision, Article 220 Code civil.

C) DAMAGES FOR PAIN AND SUFFERING

Article 8 of the Franco-German Agreement has its counterparts in §1374 BGB and Article 1569 Code civil. Included in the initial assets, and deducted from the final debt of accrued gains, are the amounts obtained by either spouse by way of compensation for non-pecuniary damage. Interpretative problems arise as there are different definitions of non-pecuniary damage: in Germany it refers to the concept of *Schmerzensgeld* in §847 BGB; while the French law currently excludes all compensations for physical damage (*damage corporel*) or mental damage (*damage moral*) from the final valuation of accrued gains.

D) ASSETS TRANSFERRED AS A GIFT

The interpretation of Article 8 (3) requires it to be read together with Article 10 (2) (1, b). Both articles exclude assets which belong to the initial assets of one of the spouses and are gifted to lineal relatives during the matrimonial property regime from the valuation of the initial and final assets – in contrast to all other gifts. This provision is of French origin (see Article 1573 Code civil). In the French system, however, the exclusion of gifts from the initial asset applies independent of the relation to the recipient.

A corrective to protect the spouse is added in Article 10 (2) (1, b). If such gifts to lineal relatives have increased in value through improvements by means of resources "independent" from the initial assets of the donor, a claim for equalization is available. "Independently" refers to all assets acquired by the same during the marriage through means such as employment income and capital income.

These provisions have no equivalent in French or German law. They originate from German notaries' practice of executing matrimonial agreements (*Eheverträge*) that exclude some assets from the debt of community of accrued gains.

E) REAL ESTATE AND IMMOVABLE PROPERTY

Article 9 concerns the increase in the value of real estate and immovable property. In the German system real estate included in the initial assets (already existing or acquired by the same as a result of a donation or succession), shall be valued at the termination of the regime at their worth at this point in time. For example, this means that if the asset has increased its value from 10 to 100, it will be valued at 100, an increase of 90. This approach does not apply in the Franco-

German Agreement. Here the increase of value is of no importance. This means that if the asset had a value of 100 at the time of the determination of the final assets, the same value would be ascribed to the initial assets (even if the value is 10 times more than at the beginning of the regime) and the non-owner spouse could not claim regarding it at settlement. This is a corrective to the German domestic law, which has its origin in Article 1571 Code civil.

F) THE SETTLEMENT OF THE ACCRUED GAINS

The settlement of the accrued gains is regulated by Article 14 of the Agreement. As a result of the law reform in Germany in September 2009, the settlement of the accrued gains of one spouse cannot exceed the total value of the final assets (i.e. if the final assets equal 100, the debt shall be limited to 100). In the Franco-German Agreement, the debt on the accrued gains is further reduced and can only amount to half of the final available assets of the debtor spouse, after deduction of liabilities, at the point in time determinative for ascertaining the amount of the debt on the accrued gains (i.e. where final assets equal 100, the debt on the accrued gains shall be limited to a maximum of 50).

V. PERSPECTIVE ON THE FUTURE

The direction taken in the Franco-German Agreement on the optional matrimonial property regime of the community of accrued gains may help concentrate efforts towards matrimonial property regimes of the third millennium. Firstly, the creation of a unified law was significant. Secondly, it could ideally serve as a flagship-model for other countries. To complement such international endeavours, the creation of an additional optional matrimonial property regime of community of acquisitions in the near future would be a positive step.

Numerous other results may be desirable, i.e. the inclusion of the matrimonial property regime in the family property law; the reinforcement of the private autonomy; and the convergent evolution of matrimonial property law under the principles of equality and self-determination.[24]

These factors, typical of the regime of community of accrued gains, argue in favour of its circulation as an optional alternative model. In terms of application we will need to look to the development of practice to assess the effectiveness of the optional model created. Currently this model can not only be applied in

24 Scherpe (ed.), *Marital Agreements and Private Autonomy in a Comparative Perspective*, 2012.

relations between France and Germany, but also in all cases in which, according to international private law of other Member States, French or German law is applicable (e.g. by *renvoi* or choice of applicable law). This situation may change when the new European regulations on jurisdiction, applicable law and the recognition and enforcement of decisions in matters of matrimonial property regimes come into force. It is expected that the *renvoi* will be deleted. On the other hand, the choice of the law applicable to the property relations between spouses will be extended. This means that, within the scope of the new EU regulation, spouses shall be allowed to opt for the new matrimonial property regime, following the criteria of private international law, and regardless of the Franco-German Agreement being transformed in law of national membership.[25] Obviously the choice of optional regimes will be allowed on the basis of conflict of laws rules and then it shall normally be available in accordance with habitual residence or citizenship criteria. The Agreement expressly provides for the applicability of the optional matrimonial property regime by express matrimonial contract, even if couples are "only" French or German, rather than bi-national. In other countries, at present, and in the absence of French or German reference elements, the diffusion of the new optional regime depends on the explicit inclusion of the regime in a matrimonial agreement, where this is permitted by the domestic law.

[25] Henrich, Auf dem Weg zu einem europäischen internationalen Ehegüterrecht, in *Festschrift Brüdermüller*, 2014, pp. 311–322.

PART II

THE LAW AND COMMENTARY

ABKOMMEN ZWISCHEN DER BUNDESREPUBLIK DEUTSCHLAND UND DER FRANZÖSISCHEN REPUBLIK ÜBER DEN GÜTERSTAND DER WAHL-ZUGEWINNGEMEINSCHAFT*

ACCORD ENTRE LA RÉPUBLIQUE FÉDÉRALE D'ALLEMAGNE ET LA RÉPUBLIQUE FRANÇAISE INSTITUANT UN RÉGIME MATRIMONIAL OPTIONNEL DE LA PARTICIPATION AUX ACQUÊTS*

AGREEMENT BETWEEN THE FEDERAL REPUBLIC OF GERMANY AND THE FRENCH REPUBLIC ON THE OPTIONAL MATRIMONIAL PROPERTY REGIME OF THE COMMUNITY OF ACCRUED GAINS*

ACCORDO FRA LA REPUBBLICA FEDERALE TEDESCA E LA REPUBBLICA FRANCESE SUL REGIME DEI BENI OPZIONALE DELLA PARTECIPAZIONE AGLI INCREMENTI*

ACUERDO ENTRE LA REPÚBLICA FEDERAL DE ALEMANIA Y LA REPÚBLICA FRANCESA SOBRE EL RÉGIMEN MATRIMONIAL OPCIONAL DE PARTICIPACIÓN EN LAS GANANCIAS*

---

* Agreement of 4 February 2010 (Bundesgesetzblatt, 2012, II, p. 180–186); publication of the entry into force of 22 April 2013 (Bundesgesetzblatt, 2013, II, p. 431); entry into force on 1 May 2013. An unofficial English translation is also available at www.bmj.de/SharedDocs/Downloads/DE/pdfs/Uebersetzung_Abkommen_Wahlgueterstand.pdf?__blob=publicationFile. The official German and French versions of this Agreement are reproduced under the Creative Commons Licence 3.0 (Germany). The English, Italian and Spanish versions are unofficial translations. Commentary by Maria Giovanna Cubeddu Wiedemann.

KAPITEL I

Anwendungsbereich und Definition

Artikel 1
Anwendungsbereich

Der Güterstand der Wahl-Zugewinngemeinschaft steht Ehegatten zur Verfügung, deren Güterstand dem Sachrecht eines Vertragsstaates unterliegt. Der Inhalt dieses gemeinsamen Wahlgüterstandes ist in den Artikeln 2 bis 18 geregelt.

CHAPITRE I

Champ d'application et définition

Article 1
Champ d'application

Le régime matrimonial optionnel de la participation aux acquêts peut être choisi par des époux dont la loi applicable au régime matrimonial est celle d'un Etat contractant. Le contenu de ce régime matrimonial commun est régi par les articles 2 à 18.

Commentary

Art. 1
Art. 15(1), Art. 1(1, 2) EGBGB; Art. 4(1) Hague Convention 1978; §1519 BGB; §7 LPartG; Art. 17b(3) EGBGB; CEFL Principle 4:1.

Art. 1: I. A new joint matrimonial property regime of the community of accrued gains identical in both contracting states shall be established. This is the first attempt to unify substantive matrimonial property in Europe (Boele-Woelki/Ferrand/Beilfuss/Jänterä-Jareborg/Lowe/Martiny/Pintens (eds.), *Principles of European Family Law Regarding Property Relations Between Spouses* 2013, 23). The optional matrimonial property regime of the community of accrued gains shall be available to spouses whose property regime is subject to the property law of one of the contracting states (*Expl. Report, Art. 1(1)).* The Agreement does not regulate conflict of laws. The Agreement draws on the general regulations of the international private law. especially of the respective contracting states. The basic requirement is that under international private law either German or French law shall apply to the property regime of the spouses (Mayer, *FamRZ* 2010, 612, 614): **(a)** According to German IPR this is the case when at the time of marriage both spouses held German or French citizenship or had their joint habitual residence in Germany or in France (Art. 15(1), Art. 1(1, 2) EGBGB). Additionally Art. 15(2) EGBGB provides spouses with the option of submitting the effects of their matrimonial property regime to the legal system to which one of them belongs or where one of them has their habitual residence (Dethloff, *RabelsZ* 76 (2012), 509, 514); **(b)** In France the matrimonial property regime of the state where the spouses established their first joint habitual residence after the marriage is principally applied (Art. 4(1) Hague Convention 1978) (Martiny, *Festschrift Kropholler*, 2008, 373, 387 ff.). The spouses may, under French law, choose to submit their matrimonial property regime to the legal system to which one of them belongs or where one of them has their habitual residence; **(c)** According to both laws a choice of law is possible even if the choice of a property regime takes place before marriage. Lastly, for real property the law corresponding to its location is applied. In both states the applicable law for real property may be chosen according to its location (Art. 15(2)(3) EGBGB; Art. 3 Hague Convention 1978). – **II.** The optional matrimonial property regime offers a neutral provision. A direct international element is not required, so spouses living in the Federal Republic of Germany without any connection to the French Republic or spouses who consider the optional matrimonial property

CHAPTER I

Scope of Application and Definition

CAPITOLO I

Ambito di applicazione e definizione

CAPÍTULO I

Ámbito de aplicación y definición

Article 1
Scope of Application

The optional matrimonial property regime of the community of accrued gains shall be available to spouses whose property regime is subject to the property law of one of the contracting States. The contents of this joint optional matrimonial property regime shall be governed by Articles 2 to 18.

Articolo 1
Ambito di applicazione

Il regime dei beni opzionale della partecipazione agli incrementi può essere scelto dai coniugi il cui regime dei beni soggiace alla legge applicabile di uno Stato contraente. Il contenuto di questo regime opzionale comune è regolato dagli articoli da 2 a 18.

Artículo 1
Ámbito de aplicación

El régimen opcional de participación en las ganancias puede ser elegido por los cónyuges cuyo régimen económico matrimonial se rija por el Derecho de un Estado contratante. El contenido de este régimen matrimonial opcional común estará regulado por los artículos 2 a 18.

---

regime more attractive than other matrimonial property schemes can choose this optional regime by way of contract (Becker, *FF* 2012, 199). As long as the conflict law of a third state allows for such a choice of law, couples without any ties to either contracting state may agree upon the optional matrimonial property regime (Dethloff, *RabelsZ* 76 (2012), 509, 514). The choice of this property regime does not mean that the couple chooses the substantive law of a contracting state. Art. 1 only requires that the matrimonial property regime be subject to the law of a contracting state. In principle, a choice of law is not required. However, to avoid any doubt, in some cases it is advisable for the spouses to designate the law applicable to their matrimonial property regime in their matrimonial agreement, if permitted by private international law. In particular, it is advisable if the application of the substantive law of a contracting state is established only through the choice of law (Stürner, *JZ* 2011, 545, 548) or if there are widely differing national laws, e.g. for the enforcement of the nullity of an act of disposal of the matrimonial assets by one the spouses (Braun, *MittBayNot* 2012, 90). In summary, the choice of the optional property regime is possible for French spouses residing in Germany, German spouses residing in France, French-German couples residing in either Member State, spouses who are citizens of either Member State, spouses without citizenship of either Member State, but who have their habitual residence in either one, spouses without any ties to either Member State (neither citizenship nor habitual residence), when the applicable law allows for it (*Expl. Report, Art. 1(1)*). – **III.** Notwithstanding the Agreement expressly referring to spouses, its application to civil unions of same-sex couples depends on the applicable law. In Germany this may happen by virtue of §7 LPartG, which declares the default statutory matrimonial property regime applicable to same-sex couples. That is either the community of accrued gains or a different matrimonial property regime (Martiny, *ZEuP* 19 (2011), 577, 587) chosen according to §§1409–1563 BGB. Therefore the optional matrimonial property regime is available to partners registered under German law as well as same-sex couples, to which German law is applicable because of their registration in Germany according to Art. 17b(3) EGBGB (Klippstein, *DNotZ* 2010, 510; Becker, *Era Forum* 2011, 103, 116; contra Schaal, *ZNotP* 2010, 162, 162). – **V.** The word "optional" expresses the freedom of choice of the regime and, thus, may be understood as a synonym of the term "conventional" better known in other juridical traditions (e.g. Italian law). – **IV.** According to CEFL Principle 4:1 "the principles on general rights and duties of the spouses" contained in Chapter I "apply irrespective of the matrimonial property regime".

Artikel 2
Definition

Im Güterstand der Wahl-Zugewinngemeinschaft bleibt das Vermögen der Ehegatten getrennt. Zugewinn ist der Betrag, um den das Endvermögen eines Ehegatten sein Anfangsvermögen übersteigt. Bei Beendigung des Güterstandes ergibt sich die Zugewinnausgleichsforderung aus dem Vergleich der erzielten Zugewinne der Ehegatten.

Article 2
Définition

Dans le régime optionnel de la participation aux acquêts, le patrimoine des époux reste séparé. Les acquêts sont constitués du montant de la différence entre le patrimoine final d'un époux et son patrimoine originaire. A la dissolution du régime matrimonial, la créance de participation résulte de la comparaison des acquêts de chacun des époux.

Commentary

Art. 2
§§1373, 1378 BGB; Arts. 1569–1581 fr. CC; s. also §§1363 et seq. BGB; §§1409–1563 BGB; and CEFL Principles 4:17(1)(3), 4:21.

Art. 2: I. The optional matrimonial property regime is a form of the community of accrued gains. It favours the provisions of the default statutory matrimonial property regime in Germany: the *Zugewinngemeinschaft*. A variant of this property regime, called the *participation aux acquêts*, also exists in French law. It is not the default statutory matrimonial regime, but rather a statutory regime available to be chosen in a matrimonial agreement. The provisions of the Agreement are to a large extent consistent with the German provisions, but also integrate elements of the French *régime matrimonial primaire* and the *participation aux acquêts* (*Expl. Report, Art. 2(1)*). A form of the community of accrued gains regime also exists in Greece and a form of participation in acquisitions in Catalonia, the Netherlands and Switzerland (s. Boele-Woelki/Ferrand/Beilfuss/Jänterä-Jareborg/Lowe/Martiny/Pintens (eds.), *Principles of European Family Law Regarding Property Relations Between Spouses* 2013, 139 ff.). – **II.** Community of accrued gains means that during the property regime there is a separation of property. The adoption of this property regime does not affect the ownership and liabilities of the spouses. Unlike under the regime of community of property, there is no third set of assets shared by both spouses. The separation of property of the

Article 2
Definition

In the optional matrimonial property regime of the community of accrued gains the assets of the spouses shall remain separate. Accrued gains shall constitute the amount by which the final assets of a spouse exceed his or her initial assets. Upon termination of the matrimonial property regime, any debt on the accrued gains shall be determined by comparison of the accrued gains of the spouses.

Articolo 2
Definizione

Nel regime dei beni opzionale della partecipazione agli incrementi, il patrimonio dei coniugi resta separato. L'incremento patrimoniale è l'importo per il quale il patrimonio finale di un coniuge supera il suo patrimonio iniziale. Alla cessazione del regime dei beni, il credito di conguaglio risulta dal confronto fra gli incrementi patrimoniali conseguiti dai coniugi.

Artículo 2
Definición

En el régimen opcional de participación en las ganancias, el patrimonio de los cónyuges se mantiene separado. La ganancia es la cuantia en que el patrimonio final de un cónyuge excede el patrimonio inicial. A la disolución de este régimen matrimonial, el crédito de participación resulta de la comparación de las ganancias de cada uno de los cónyuges.

---

spouses has two consequences. First, the spouses retain the management, use and disposal of their own personal assets. In addition, each spouse is liable only for his or her own debts, incurred before or during the marriage (*Expl. Report, Art. 2(1)*). – **III.** The French text of the Agreement refers to the optional regime without further specification, while the German text qualifies the optional regime as a matrimonial property regime. Art. 2 defines the accrued gain as that amount by which the final assets of a spouse exceed their original assets. The spouse who produced the least gains can claim the settlement of a debt on the accrued gains from the other spouse amounting to half of the difference between the assets gained by each spouse. There shall be no settlement of the losses, but only of the gains (*Expl. Report, Art. 2(2)*). – **IV.** In principle, accrued gains shall be settled only upon termination of the matrimonial property regime. – **V.** In the French version the term "*acquêts*" is used in accordance with the traditional qualification of the optional regime *participation aux acquêts* (Arts. 1569–1581 fr. CC), which is inspired by the German model of *Zugewinngemeinschaft*. The optional community of accrued gains differs from the model of *Zugewinngemeinschaft* because of the differing valuation dates and the provisions on taking into account certain objects in the valuation of initial and final assets. – **VI.** According to CEFL Principle 4:17(1) "participation in acquisition is a matrimonial property regime during which property is owned separately by the spouses" and the CEFL Principle 4:17(3) "upon dissolution of the regime each spouse participates in the acquisition made by the other during the regime".

KAPITEL II

Begründung des Güterstandes

Artikel 3
Begründung des Güterstandes

(1) Die Ehegatten können durch Ehevertrag vereinbaren, dass die Wahl-Zugewinngemeinschaft ihr Güterstand ist.

CHAPITRE II

Adoption du régime matrimonial

Article 3
Adoption du régime matrimonial

(1) Les époux peuvent convenir par contrat de mariage que le régime optionnel de la participation aux acquêts constitue leur régime matrimonial.

Commentary

Art. 3
§1363 BGB; §§1408, 1410 BGB; Arts. 1394, 1395, 1397 fr. CC; Art. 11 EGBGB; Arts. 12, 13 Hague Convention 1978; (CE) Recommendation (89); Arts. 2(b), 20(2); 35(2) Rome IV-R-P; CEFL Principles 4:9, 4:10, 4:11, 4:12, 4:14, 4:15, 4:29.

Art. 3(1): I. An optional community of accrued gains is agreed upon by means of a matrimonial agreement. This may take place before or after the marriage. – **II.** The Agreement does not contain specific directives regarding the form of such an agreement. This shall be governed by the law designated under the relevant private international law, i.e. by the law in force in the place where the contract is concluded or by the internal law applicable to property regimes (Braun, *MittBayNot* 2012, 90). – **III.** According to German and French private international law the form of the contract must either be subject to the applicable law of the location of its conclusion or to the applicable law of the matrimonial property regime (Art. 11 EGBGB; Art. 12 Hague Convention 1978): **(a)** In

CHAPTER II
Creation of the Matrimonial Property Regime

Article 3
Creation of the Matrimonial Property Regime

(1) By marriage contract the spouses can optionally agree that their matrimonial property regime shall consist in the community of accrued gains.

CAPITOLO II
Costituzione del regime dei beni

Articolo 3
Costituzione del regime dei beni

(1) I coniugi possono convenire mediante contratto matrimoniale che il loro regime dei beni sia il regime opzionale della partecipazione agli incrementi.

CAPÍTULO II
Establecimiento del régimen matrimonial

Artículo 3
Establecimiento del régimen matrimonial

(1) Los cónyuges podrán convenir en capitulaciones matrimoniales que el régimen opcional de participación en las ganancias constituirá su régimen matrimonial.

Germany, the marriage agreement or the contract of a civil union must be concluded in the presence of both parties and in a notarial deed (§1410 BGB); **(b)** In France the marriage agreement, in principle, has to be drawn up by a notary as well (Art. 1394 fr. CC). However, according to prevailing private international law, in France the marriage contract may be drafted, dated and jointly signed by the spouses (Art. 12(3) Hague Convention 1978); **(c)** Art. 20(2) Rome IV-R-P also provides a document dated and signed by both spouses as minimum requirement. – **IV.** Through the agreement the default statutory matrimonial regime is replaced with the optional community of accrued gains. It is a matter of a substantive choice of law (Stürner, *JZ* 2011, 545, 549). – **V.** According to CEFL Principle 4:9 "spouses should be free to enter into agreements determining their marital property relationship". As a form requirement "matrimonial property agreements should be draw up by a notary or other legal professional with comparable functions, be dated and should be signed by both spouses" (CEFL Principle 4:11); "Spouses are free to agree on the participation in acquisition" (CEFL Principle 4:29).

(2) Der Vertrag kann vor Eingehung oder während des Bestandes der Ehe geschlossen werden. Der Güterstand wird mit Abschluss des Vertrages wirksam, wobei die Vorschriften über die Änderung eines bis dahin bestehenden Güterstandes unberührt bleiben. Er wird frühestens mit dem Tag der Eheschließung wirksam.

(3) Der Vertrag kann von Kapitel V abweichen.

(2) Le contrat peut être conclu avant ou pendant le mariage. Le régime matrimonial prend effet au moment de la conclusion du contrat, sans préjudice des dispositions applicables au changement de régime matrimonial. Il prend effet au plus tôt à la date de la célébration du mariage.

(3) Le contrat peut déroger aux règles du chapitre V

cont'd

Art. 3(2): I. As well as at the time of the conclusion of a matrimonial agreement, agreements on the matrimonial property regime may be reached before the marriage (according to §1408 BGB and Art. 1395 fr. CC). – **(a)** In the case of a marriage under French law, the possibility of concluding a contract before the marriage may, for example, prevent the initial entry into force of the community of property, which should then be liquidated before the adoption of a new property regime (*Expl. Report, Art. 3(1))*. – **(b)** Under German law, the spouses can change their property regime at any time by way of marriage contract. – **II.** The optional matrimonial property regime only takes effect if the marriage has actually been concluded. The agreement is not valid if it provides for a date preceding the marriage. As a general rule the matrimonial agreement cannot produce any effects before the marriage is celebrated: **(a)** Under German law the marital agreement produces its effects after the conclusion of the contract. From that moment, the spouses are subject to the rules of the new property regime; **(b)** Spouses under French property law can agree in the interests of the family to change their property regime after an application period of two years (Art. 1397 fr. CC) (*Expl. Report, Art. 3(1))*. Such change becomes effective on the date of execution of the notarial act providing for the change, if the spouses have no minor children and if the adult children or the creditors do not oppose the change. If there are minors or if a creditor dissents, the change of matrimonial property regime becomes effective on the date of the decision validating such change (Art. 139(4)(5) fr. CC). In these cases it is advisable to choose an applicable law – for example German law – pursuant to which the optional community of accrued gains shall then be agreed upon; a judicial fiat is not required (Jäger, *DNotZ* 2010, 804, 807; Braun, *MittBayNot* 2012, 89, 90;

(2) The contract can be concluded prior to entering into marriage or while the spouses are married. The matrimonial property regime shall become effective upon conclusion of the contract, and any provisions governing the amendment of a matrimonial property regime that existed up until that point shall remain unaffected. The matrimonial property regime shall become effective at the earliest on the date of marriage.

(3) The contract can deviate from Chapter V.

(2) Il contratto può essere concluso prima della celebrazione del matrimonio o in costanza di matrimonio. Il regime dei beni produce effetti con la conclusione del contratto. Le norme sulla modifica di un regime dei beni, fino a quel momento esistente, rimangono impregiudicate. Il regime dei beni acquista efficacia non prima del giorno della celebrazione del matrimonio.

(3) Il contratto può derogare alle disposizioni del Capitolo V.

(2) Las capitulaciones podrán otorgarse antes o después de la celebración del matrimonio. El régimen matrimonial es eficaz con el otorgamiento de las captulaciones, sin perjuicio de las disposiciones aplicables al cambio del régimen matrimonial. Su eficacia no se produce con anterioridad a la fecha de la celebración del matrimonio.

(3) En capitulaciones se puede pactar en sentido distinto a lo previso en el Capítulo V.

Dethloff, *RabelsZ* 76 (2012), 509, 515). – **III.** According to CEFL Principle 4:10(1) "in a marital property agreement made before the marriage the future spouses may choose their matrimonial property regime; during the marriage they may modify their matrimonial property regime or change it for another regime" (CEFL Principle 4:10(2)).

Art. 3(3): I. The provisions of the Franco-German Agreement are for the most part dispositive nature and may be replaced with matrimonial agreements. Art. 3(3) explicitly allows for a deviation from Chapter V. Arts. 8–12 (participation in acquisition) and Arts. 13–18 (enforcement and security) are considered to be of dispositive nature. Arts. 4–6 (asset management, usage and domain), as well as Art. 7 (causes for the termination of the matrimonial property regime), are considered mandatory. – **II.** An explicit rule on exceptional hardship as a ground for invalidating the agreement is not included. The validity and efficacy of such a clause contained in the contract, however, would be subject to the applicable law. – **III.** According to CEFL Principle 4:12 "when entering into a marital property agreement the spouses should be under a mutual duty to disclose their assets and debts". "The notary or other legal professional with comparable functions should give impartial advice to each spouse separately, ensure that each spouse understands the legal consequences of the matrimonial property agreement, ensure that both spouses freely consent to the agreement" (CEFL Principle 4:13). "Having regard to the circumstances when the agreement was concluded or those subsequently arising, the competent authority may, in cases of exceptional hardship, set aside or adjust a marital property agreement" (CEFL Principle 4:15).

KAPITEL III

Vermögensverwaltung, -nutzung und -verfügung

Artikel 4

Allgemeine Bestimmungen zur Vermögensverwaltung, -nutzung und verfügung

Jeder Ehegatte verwaltet und nutzt sein Vermögen allein; er verfügt allein über sein Vermögen. Das Recht, frei über das Vermögen zu verfügen, ist gleichwohl durch Artikel 5 beschränkt.

CHAPITRE III

Administration, jouissance et disposition du patrimoine

Article 4

Dispositions générales en matière d'administration, de jouissance et de disposition du patrimoine

Chaque époux a la gestion et la jouissance exclusive de son patrimoine; il en dispose seul. Néanmoins, le droit de disposer librement de l'article 5.

Commentary

Art. 4
§§1364–1365 BGB; Art. 1569 fr. CC; s. also Art. 1412 sp. CC; Art. 1397 gr. ZGB; CEFL Principles 4:4, 4:21, 4:23.

Art. 4: I. The aim of the optional matrimonial property regime of the Franco-German Agreement is to guarantee the complete independence of the spouses with reference to their own assets. In principle, each spouse shall be allowed to manage, use and dispose of his or her assets alone, without the consent of the other spouse (Braun, *MittBayNot* 2012, 89, 91). In return, each spouse is liable for debts incurred by him or her before or during the marriage. This principle of the separation of property is dealt with in the German *Zugewinngemeinschaft* regime (§1364 BGB) and in the French *participation aux acquêts* regime (Art. 1569 fr. CC). The independent management of assets also includes the right to acquire assets: for example, one of the spouses does not need the consent of the other to start a profession or to create, or enter into, a company (*Expl. Report, Art. 4(1))*. – **II.** However, the right to dispose is limited by the provisions in Art. 5, based on the French "*régime primaire*" (Arts. 215(3), 220; Art. 1571 fr. CC). Because of Art. 4(2) the provisions in Art. 4 are to be considered conclusive (Braun, *MittBayNot* 2012, 89, 91). These

CHAPTER III

Management, Use and Disposal of Assets

Article 4
General Provisions on the Management, Use and Disposal of Assets

Each spouse shall manage and use his or her assets alone; he or she alone shall dispose of his or her assets. Notwithstanding this, the right to dispose of these assets freely is restricted by Article 5.

CAPITOLO III

Amministrazione, godimento e disposizione del patrimonio

Articolo 4
Norme generali su amministrazione, godimento e disposizione del patrimonio

Ciascun coniuge ha l'amministrazione e il godimento disgiunto del proprio patrimonio; egli ne dispone in maniera autonoma. Il diritto di disporre liberamente del patrimonio è tuttavia limitato dall'articolo 5.

CAPÍTULO III

Administración, goce y disposición del patrimonio

Artículo 4
Disposiciones generales en materia de administración, goce y disposición del patrimonio

Cada cónyuge goza del derecho de gestión y disfrute exclusivo de su patrimonio. Sin embargo, el derecho a disponer libremente sobre el patrimonio está limitado por el artículo 5.

---

rules replace the corresponding provisions of the *régime primaire*, without prejudice to the other rules of this regime, which are applicable under the territorial principle (*Expl. Report, Art. 4(1))*. – **III.** The separation of property is not absolute, insofar as the spouses cannot derogate from the application of specific mandatory provisions: the consent of both spouses shall be required for all transactions involving the disposal of household items or the rights which guarantee the family home (Art. 5); expenditure incurred by one of the spouses in the interests of the household shall lead to automatic joint and several liability of the other spouse (Art. 6). The aim of both provisions is to secure the livelihood of the family when applying the optional matrimonial property regime (Dethloff, *RabelsZ* 76 (2012), 509, 516). – **IV.** According to CEFL Principle 4:21 "debts incurred by one spouse are his or her personal debts", but "each spouse should contribute to the needs of the family according to his or her ability. The contribution to the needs of the family encompasses contribution to the running of the household, the personal needs of the spouses and the maintenance, upbringing and education of the children" (CEFL Principle 4:4(1)(2)). "Subject to Principles 4:6 [Protection of the leased family home] and 4:7 [Representation], each spouse is entitled to administer his or her property independently" (CEFL Principle 4:23).

Artikel 5
Verfügungsbeschränkungen

(1) Rechtsgeschäfte eines Ehegatten über Haushaltsgegenstände oder über Rechte, durch die die Familienwohnung sichergestellt wird, sind ohne Zustimmung des anderen Ehegatten unwirksam. Sie können jedoch vom anderen Ehegatten genehmigt werden.

Article 5
Restrictions aux règles de disposition

(1) Les actes de disposition d'objets du ménage ou de droits par lesquels est assuré le logement de la famille passés par un époux sans le consentement de l'autre sont nuls. Toutefois, ils peuvent être ratifiés par l'autre époux.

Commentary

Art. 5
§1369 BGB; Arts. 215(3), 217, 220; Art. 1571 fr. CC; §1519 BGB; s. also Art. 1320(1)(1,2) sp. CC; Art. 231-9 Cat. CC; §§1365, 1366, 1368, 1454 BGB; (CE) Recommendation (81) 15; CEFL Principles 4:5, 4:6, 4:14.

Art. 5(1): I. With regard to the marital home and household items Art. 5 provides for a general prohibition of acts of disposal by one spouse unilaterally and a requirement of consensus from both spouses. The aim of this provision is the best possible protection of the family home (Mayer, *FamRZ* 2010, 612, 614; critical Steer, *Notar* 2010, 119, 121). – **II.** Art. 5(1) is based on the mandatory rules of the French *régime primaire* (Arts. 215(3), 220; Art. 1571 fr. CC). §1369 BGB provides for comparable limitations only in regards to household items. In German law there are no restrictions specifically regarding the family home or the general effects of the marriage. The family home is only protected if the spouses live under the statutory matrimonial property regime, the home is property of the disposing spouse or both spouses and the contracting party has notice of the home representing the entirety of the assets of the disposing party (*Expl. Report, Art. 5(1))*. A provision comparable to §1365 BGB is not included in the Franco-German Agreement such that even acts of disposal regarding almost the entirety of assets are valid, if the requirements of Art. 5 are not fulfilled (Braun, *MittBayNot* 2012, 89, 91). – **III.** This provision reflects the common European core regarding property relations between spouses (Dethloff, *RabelsZ* 76 (2012), 509, 517). Restrictions of legal capacity mostly affect transactions concerning the family home and household items, as these represent a basic foundation of family life – independent of matrimonial property regime and

Article 5
Restrictions on Disposal

(1) Any legal transactions of a spouse pertaining to household items or rights which guarantee the family home shall be ineffective without the consent of the other spouse. They can however be approved by the other spouse.

Articolo 5
Limiti di disposizione

(1) Gli atti giuridici posti in essere da un coniuge su beni dell'attività domestica o sui diritti che garantiscono la casa familiare sono inefficaci senza il consenso dell'altro coniuge. Tuttavia, gli atti possono essere ratificati dall'altro coniuge.

Artículo 5
Limitaciones a la disposición

(1) Los negocios jurídicos sobre el ajuar o sobre derechos por medio de los cuales se asegura la residencia de la familia que fueran contraídos por uno de los cónyuges sin el consentimiento del otro son ineficaces. Sin embargo, estos negocios podrán ser ratificados por el otro cónyuge.

---

ownership (cf. (CE) Rec (81) 15E). – **IV.** The family home includes all the areas which the spouses use as a home, where they lived together or which, in some circumstances, were designated as the family home even if, in the end, this did not actually happen. The family home may also include ancillary rooms (as per Braun, *MittBayNot* 2012, 91) even if they do not serve living purposes. The protection also extends to furniture and other objects jointly used by the family. Whether it includes multiple family homes has to be determined by national courts (Dethloff, *RabelsZ* 76 (2012), 509, 517). The provisions of Art. 5 are mandatory. A contractual exclusion of the restraint of disposal is impermissible (Art. 3(3)). Not only are disposition or mortgaging (*Belastungen*) of a family home subject to approval, but also the disposition or revocation of rental agreements (regarding further interpretation of limits of disposal, see also Jäger, *DNotZ* 2010, 804, 808). – **V.** This means that the spouse who owns the house used as the family home cannot sell the house without the consent of the other spouse. Similarly, the spouse who is tenant of the flat where the family lives cannot terminate the rental agreement on his or her own. The family home is thereby protected independently of its substantive value and the value of the other assets of the disposing spouse (Mecke, *AcP* 211 (2011), 886, 903). The protection of the family home is very extensive and may also affect third party interests. The ineffectiveness of the termination of a rental agreement may be objected to by the landlord of the flat used as family home, even if he or she was unaware of the property regime of the spouses and, as a result, of the restrictions on disposal by the tenant spouse (*Expl. Report, Art. 5(1))*. – **V.** According to CEFL Principle 4:5(1) "any act of disposal of rights to the family home or household goods requires the consent of both spouses". "Any act of disposal by one spouse without consent of the other is valid if the latter ratifies it" (CEFL Principle 4:5(2)).

(2) Ein Ehegatte kann gerichtlich ermächtigt werden, ein Rechtsgeschäft allein vorzunehmen, zu der die Zustimmung des anderen notwendig wäre, falls dieser zur Zustimmung außerstande ist oder sie verweigert, ohne dass Belange der Familie dies rechtfertigten.

(2) Un époux peut être autorisé par justice à passer seul un acte pour lequel le consentement de son conjoint serait nécessaire, si celui-ci est hors d'état de manifester sa volonté ou si son refus n'est pas justifié par l'intérêt de la famille.

cont'd

Art. 5(2): I. If the spouse is not in a position to provide such consent, for example if prevented by sickness, or if his or her refusal is not justified by the interests of the family, the court can authorize the other spouse alone to enter into any act mentioned in Art. 5(1). This solution, aimed above all at preventing a spouse from arbitrarily refusing consent to adversely affect the other spouse, was adopted from the French *régime primaire* (Art. 217(1) fr. CC) (*Expl. Report, Art. 5(2)*). – **II.** The authorization of the court in the case of the inability of a spouse to provide his or her consent for health reasons is similar to the right of management in the case of urgency provided for in §1454 BGB, but corresponds to a simplified procedure for the appointment of a guardian with the task of authorising a specific act. There is not necessarily a risk of deferral connected to this, as it is required for the replacement of an agreement according to §1365(2) BGB or the emergency-administrative law according to §1454 BGB. – **II.** The legal consequences of missing consent, as well as the modalities of the ascertainment, are not regulated in the Agreement. In Germany, the legal transaction is deemed provisionally invalid until the consent is definitely withheld (§1366(4) BGB).

(2) A spouse can be authorised by a court to enter alone into a legal transaction to which the other spouse would otherwise be required to consent, in a case where the latter is not in a position to, or refuses to, provide such consent and this refusal of consent is not justified by the interests of the family.

(2) Un coniuge può essere autorizzato dal giudice a compiere da solo un atto giuridico per il quale sarebbe necessario il consenso dell'altro coniuge, qualora quest'ultimo non sia in grado di manifestare la sua volontà o se il suo rifiuto non trovi giustificazione nell'interesse della famiglia.

(2) Un cónyuge puede ser autorizado judicialmente para otorgar un negocio jurídico para el cual sería necesario el consentimiento del otro cónyuge si este no pudiera manifestar su voluntad o si su denegación no estuviera justificada en el interés familiar.

The other spouse can also claim the nullity in respect of third parties (§1368 BGB). In France the nullity can only be claimed within a year of recognition by means of action for annulment (Art. 215(3) fr. CC). – **III.** The interdiction to dispose is definite. Since in France the provisions of the optional matrimonial property regime are not considered conclusive (Jäger, *DNotZ* 2010, 804, 808) and the territorial application of statute of the *régime primaire* is mandatory (Art. 215 fr. CC), an acquisition of legal estate in France in good faith would be pre-empted (Dethloff, *RabelsZ* 76 (2012), 509, 519). In Germany the implementation law provides in §1519(3) BGB that §1412 BGB, which allows for an acquisition in good faith without registration in the index of the matrimonial property regime, is not to be applied. – **IV.** According to CEFL Principle 4:5(3) "if a spouse refuses or is unable to give consent, the other spouse may request authorisation by the competent authority". "Any act of disposal in breach of the preceding paragraphs" (CEFL Principle 4:5(1)(2)(3), "may be annulled by the competent authority upon the application of the non-consenting spouse" (CEFL Principle 4:5(4)).

Artikel 6
Geschäfte zur Führung des Haushalts

(1) Jeder Ehegatte kann Verträge zur Führung des Haushalts und für den Bedarf der Kinder allein schließen. Diese Verträge verpflichten den anderen Ehegatten gesamtschuldnerisch.

Article 6
Actes relevant de l'entretien du ménage

(1) Chacun des époux a pouvoir pour passer seul les contrats qui ont pour objet l'entretien du ménage et l'éducation des enfants. Ces contrats obligent solidairement l'autre époux.

Commentary

Art. 6
§1357 BGB; Arts. 215–220 fr. CC; CEFL Principles 4:4, 4:21.

Art. 6(1): I. The mandatory nature of Arts. 5 and 6 is inspired by the rules in Arts. 215 and 220 fr. CC. In France the spouses will also be subject to the other rules of the French primary regime of territorial application (e.g. the provisions on the power of attorney under Art. 219 fr. CC). A comparable provision can be found in §1357 BGB (*Expl. Report, Art. 6(1)*). Notwithstanding differences, the transactions covered by Art. 6 should correspond in both legal systems (Dethloff, *RabelsZ* 76 (2012), 509, 519). – **II.** In accordance with the general principle of the separation of assets, each spouse alone may conclude transactions for the management of the household (e.g. acquiring household items). However, in derogation from the principle of the separation of assets, such transactions cause the other spouse, who was not originally a party to the contract and had not given consent to the contract, to be bound by the contract and to be jointly and severally liable for any resulting liabilities (provision of sustenance, clothing, housing, telephone connection, insurance coverage or medical attendance) (*Expl. Report, Art. 6(1)*). Art. 6 covers credit agreements if the procurement of the item through finance is necessary for the supplying the needs of the family; investment transactions, on the other hand, are not covered (Dethloff, *RabelsZ* 76 (2012), 509, 520). This also applies to contracts that affect the needs of the children. Therefore, both spouses shall be jointly and severally liable, for example, for liabilities resulting from a contract concluded by one spouse with a private tutor (*Expl. Report, Art. 6(1)*). – **III.** The contracts under Art. 6(1) bind the other spouse jointly and severally. This provision is grounded in Art. 220 fr. CC. The joint liability occurs independently from a respective consent of the acting spouses. It also does not require any

Article 6
Transactions pertaining to the Management of the Household

(1) Each spouse alone can conclude contracts pertaining to the management of the household and for the needs of the children. These contracts shall bind the other spouse jointly and severally.

Articolo 6
Atti di gestione dell'attività domestica

(1) Ciascun coniuge può concludere da solo contratti per la gestione dell'attività domestica e per i bisogni della prole. Questi contratti obbligano in solido l'altro coniuge.

Artículo 6
Negocios referentes al mantenimiento del hogar familiar

(1) Cada uno de los cónyuges puede celebrar por sí solo contratos que tengan por objeto el mantenimiento del hogar familiar y las necesidades de los hijos. Estos contratos obligarán solidariamente al otro cónyuge.

---

activity on the part of the other spouse (Dethloff, *RabelsZ* 76 (2012), 509, 521). In contrast to German law joint liability does not create joint ownership (Mecke, *AcP* 211 (2011) 887, 904). Joint liability is by act of law accessory and subsidiary. – **IV.** As Art. 6 is mandatory, the joint liability cannot be waived. A provision on restriction or termination of joint liability is also not contained in Art. 6. Thus, the joint liability shall, in contrast to §1357 (1) BGB, exist also in the event of separation of the spouses and pending divorce proceedings (Mecke, *AcP* 211 (2011) 887, 905). The grounds may differ in regards to both legal systems: **(a)** Because this provision is a modernized version of Art. 220 fr. CC spouses residing in France who chose the joint property regime shall be subject to Art. 6; **(b)** The adopted provision does not conflict with German law. It does go beyond §1357 BGB, as this applies to all matrimonial property – default or other statutory – regimes of the BGB; the spouses, however, must accept it since they chose the optional matrimonial property regime of the community of accrued gains by way of contract. They thereby voluntarily adopt the provisions of Art. 6, too (critical Braun, *MittBayNot* 2012, 89, 91). – **V.** In case of misuse of legal ability national law protect the non-acting spouse. Thus, German law would allow a spouse to restrict or revoke the joint liability of the other spouse by formless declaration, which is valid against a third party only in the case of registration in the matrimonial property regime listing or knowledge. On the other hand, according to Art. 220 fr. CC, in France only the court can revoke a spouse's ability if it is endangering the interests of the family. But this solution would impair the harmonizing effect of Art. 6 (Dethloff, *RabelsZ* 76 (2012), 509, 522). – **VI.** According to CEFL Principle 4:4 "each spouse should contribute to the needs of the family according to his or her ability. The contribution to the needs of the family encompasses contribution to the running of the household, the personal needs of the spouses and the maintenance, upbringing and education of the children".

(2) Wenn ein Ehegatte Zahlungsverpflichtungen eingeht, die insbesondere nach der Lebensführung der Ehegatten offensichtlich unangemessen sind, und dem Vertragspartner dies bekannt war oder er es erkennen musste, wird der andere Ehegatte abweichend von Absatz 1 nicht verpflichtet.

(2) Lorsque l'un des époux contracte des dettes dont le caractère manifestement excessif, notamment eu égard au train de vie des époux, est connu de l'autre partie au contrat ou aurait dû l'être, ces dettes n'engagent pas l'autre époux, par dérogationau paragraphe 1.

cont'd

Art. 6(2): I. Art. 6(2) provides that the aforementioned joint and several liability is excluded if the following conditions are met: the expenditure was disproportionate, and the contracting third party knew or should have known that the expenditure was disproportionate. This limitation is required to protect the other spouse, who cannot be held liable for such excessive expenditure (*Expl. Report, Art. 6(2)).* The evaluation of the whether expenditure is excessive is based on the lifestyle of the spouses (SCHAAL, *ZNotP* 2010, 162, 168). Thus, if the spouses earn a modest income, the acquisition of an expensive antique piece of furniture may be manifestly excessive expenditure. In such a case, the other spouse is not liable for such contract if the party to the contract was aware, or should have been aware, that the expenditure was disproportionate (*Expl. Report,*

(2) Notwithstanding paragraph (1), if a spouse enters into payment obligations which are manifestly unreasonable in particular having regard to the lifestyle of the spouses, and the party to the contract was aware of this or ought to have realised this, the other spouse shall not be bound by these obligations.

(2) Qualora un coniuge assuma obbligazioni di pagamento, il cui carattere manifestamente eccessivo, con particolare riferimento al tenore di vita dei coniugi, è noto alla controparte o avrebbe dovuto esserlo, queste obbligazioni, in deroga al comma 1, non vincolano l'altro coniuge.

(2) Cuando uno de los cónyuges contrajera deudas manifiestamente excesivas, especialmente respecto del nivel de vida de los cónyuges, y ello fuera conocido o debiera ser conocido por la otra parte contratante, en excepción al apartado 1, el otro cónyuge no quedará obligado.

Art. 6(2)). – **II.** The onus of proof about the disproportion of the expenditure lies with the spouse who is being called upon paying according to the joint guarantee. The measure for this is the obviousness of the disproportion of the expenditure. In this way creditor protection goes further than in German law, where only the outwardly discernible circumstances of individual families are taken into account and the average consumption habits of families in comparable social situations are only considered to some extent (Dethloff, *RabelsZ* 76 (2012), 509, 520 N. 55). – **III.** This provision is a modernized version of Art. 220 fr. CC, under which the living conditions of the spouses represent the basis of valuation and the benefit of the act, as well as good and bad faith, have to be taken into account.

KAPITEL IV

Beendigung des Güterstandes

Artikel 7
Gründe für die Beendigung des Güterstandes

Der Güterstand endet

1. durch Tod oder Todeserklärung eines Ehegatten,
2. durch Wechsel des Güterstandes oder
3. mit Rechtskraft der Ehescheidung oder jeder anderen gerichtlichen Entscheidung, die den Güterstand beendet.

CHAPITRE IV

Dissolution du régime matrimonial

Article 7
Causes de dissolution du régime

Le régime matrimonial est dissous

1. par le décès ou la déclaration d'absence de l'un des époux,
2. par le changement de régime matrimonial ou
3. par le jugement de divorce ou toute autre décision judiciaire emportant dissolution du régime matrimonial.

Commentary

Art. 7
Arts. 88 and 112 fr. CC; CEFL Principles 4:24, 4:25.

Art. 7: I. According to Art. 7, in combination with Art. 10, the regime is terminated when a decisive event takes place, or when any other ground for the termination of the regime occurs. Under Art. 7, the optional matrimonial property regime ends through death or the presumed death of a spouse, through a change of matrimonial property regime, or through the legal effect of a divorce or any other court decision terminating the matrimonial property regime. – **II.** The date of dissolution of the regime is essential. As a matter of fact, the determination of the debt on the accrued gains occurs pursuant to the composition and value of the assets of the spouses on that date (*Expl. Report, Art. 7(1)*).
Art. 7(1): The first provision makes it clear that a declaration of death shall terminate the property regime even when such declaration is incorrect.
Art. 7(2): I. The second provision makes it clear that a change of property regime shall also terminate the optional matrimonial property regime of the community of accrued gains. – **II.** In Germany, the property regime can be replaced by way of matrimonial agreement. Similarly, spouses under a French property regime can agree to change their property regime in the interests of the family two years after its adoption (*Expl. Report, Art. 7(1)(2)*).

CHAPTER IV

Termination of the Matrimonial Property Regime

Article 7
Grounds for Termination of the Matrimonial Property Regime

The matrimonial property regime shall end

1. with the death of, or declaration of death of, one of the spouses,
2. with a change of matrimonial property regime, or
3. when a divorce or another court decision which terminates the matrimonial property regime becomes final and binding.

CAPITOLO IV

Cessazione del regime dei beni

Articolo 7
Cause di estinzione del regime dei beni

Il regime dei beni cessa

1. con la morte o con la dichiarazione di morte di uno dei coniugi,
2. con il mutamento del regime dei beni, o
3. con la sentenza di divorzio o con ogni altra decisione giudiziale che pone fine al regime dei beni.

CAPÍTULO IV

Disolución del régimen matrimonial

Artículo 7
Causas de disolución del régimen matrimonial

El régimen económico matrimonial finaliza:

1. con la muerte o la declaración de fallecimiento de uno de los cónyuges;
2. con el cambio del régimen matrimonial;
3. con la firmeza de la sentencia de divorcio o cualquier otra disposición judicial que conlleve la disolución del régimen matrimonial.

Art. 7(3): I. The third provision relates to other grounds for the end of the marriage: a judgement of divorce or any other court decision which terminates the property regime (such as the separation or the early settlement of the debt on the accrued gains). – **II.** In France, these grounds include the separation of the spouses, the annulment of the marriage in good faith of the spouses and the early settlement of the debt on the accrued gains. In Germany, these grounds include decisions pertaining to the early settlement of the debt on the accrued gains and on the termination of a marriage declared null (*Expl. Report, Art. 7(1)(3)).* – **III.** According to CEFL Principle 4:24 "the regime on the participation in acquisitions is dissolved by the death of a spouse; the annulment of the marriage, divorce or legal separation; the change of the matrimonial property regime by agreement between the spouses or the decision of the competent authority based upon serious grounds". "The dissolution of the regime on the participation in acquisitions takes effect at the date of the death of a spouse; in the case of an annulment of the marriage, divorce or legal separation, at the date of the application; in the case of an agreement to change to another matrimonial property regime, at the date of the change; and in the case of a decision by the competent authority, at the date of the application" (CEFL Principle 4:25).

KAPITEL V

Festsetzung der Zugewinnausgleichsforderung bei der Beendigung des Güterstandes

ABSCHNITT 1
Anfangsvermögen

Artikel 8
Zusammensetzung des Anfangsvermögens

(1) Anfangsvermögen ist das Vermögen jedes Ehegatten am Tag des Eintritts des Güterstandes. Verbindlichkeiten werden im Anfangsvermögen berücksichtigt, auch wenn sie das Aktivvermögen übersteigen.

CHAPITRE V

Détermination de la créance de participation à la dissolution du régime

SECTION 1
Patrimoine originaire

Article 8
Composition du patrimoine originaire

(1) Le patrimoine originaire est le patrimoine de chacun des époux à la date à laquelle le régime matrimonial prend effet. Les dettes sont prises en compte dans le patrimoine originaire, même lorsqu'elles excèdent le montant de l'actif.

Commentary

Art. 8
§§1374, 1377 BGB; Arts. 1570–1571 fr. CC; CEFL Principles 4:18, 4:19, 4:26.

Art. 8(1): I. Art. 8 defines the initial assets as the assets of each spouse at the time of the matrimonial property regime's entry into force. Debts shall be included in the initial assets even when they exceed the existing assets. The calculation of the debt of accrued gains represents the "centrepiece" of the new optional regime. The spouse whose accrued gain exceeds the accrued gains of the other is obliged to pay an equalization of debts. Special provisions on the composition and valuation of initial and final assets, the claim to settlement of the accrued gains, its fulfilment and deferral, as well as the limitation of the accrued gains, are included. – **II.** The parties are free to agree by way of marriage contract (see Art. 3(3)) that other gains than those

CHAPTER V
Establishing the Debt on the Accrued Gains upon Termination of the Matrimonial Property Regime

CAPITOLO V
Determinazione del credito di conguaglio dell'incremento patrimoniale al momento della cessazione del regime dei beni

CAPÍTULO V
Determinación del crédito de participación en el momento de la disolución del régimen matrimonial

PART 1
Initial Assets

SEZIONE 1
Patrimonio iniziale

SECCIÓN 1
Patrimonio inicial

Article 8
Composition of the Initial Assets

(1) The initial assets shall consist in the assets of each spouse on the date on which the matrimonial property regime became effective. Liabilities shall be included in the initial assets also when they exceed the existing assets.

Articolo 8
Composizione del patrimonio iniziale

(1) Il patrimonio iniziale è il patrimonio di ciascun coniuge alla data di entrata in vigore del regime dei beni. I debiti sono compresi nel patrimonio iniziale anche quando questi eccedono il patrimonio attivo.

Artículo 8
Composición del patrimonio inicial

(1) El patrimonio inicial es el patrimonio de cada uno de los cónyuges en la fecha en que el régimen matrimonial entra en vigor. Las deudas se tienen en cuenta en el patrimonio inicial aunque su superen al activo.

---

referred to in Art. 8(1) will be included in the initial assets. – **III.** The initial assets, relevant for the calculation of the gain, are taken into account as far as they exceed the actives. Therefore, initial debts are in fact treated as they are under the matrimonial property regime of the community of acquisition, which is based on material contribution. This rule is in conformity with the fundamental idea of the community of accrued gains. The liquidation of debts during the marriage rests upon the joint performance of the partners, such that it is to be regarded as an economically significant gain (Dethloff, *RabelsZ* 76 (2012), 509, 523). – **IV.** According to CEFL Principle 4:18(1) "the acquisitions comprise the assets acquired during the regime, other than the reserved property. In particular, the acquisitions include each spouse's income and gains either derived from earnings or property; assets acquired by means of either spouse's income or gains".

(2) Vermögen, das ein Ehegatte später durch Erbschaft, Schenkung oder als Schmerzensgeld erwirbt, wird dem Anfangsvermögen hinzugerechnet. Die Verbindlichkeiten, die dieses Vermögen betreffen, werden beim Anfangsvermögen selbst dann berücksichtigt, wenn sie das Aktivvermögen überschreiten.

(3) Dem Anfangsvermögen werden nicht zugerechnet:

1. dessen Früchte, und

2. die Gegenstände des Anfangsvermögens, die ein Ehegatte während des Güterstands Verwandten in gerader Linie geschenkt hat.

(2) Les biens reçus ultérieurement par l'un des époux par succession ou donation ou les indemnités perçues en réparation d'un dommage corporel ou moral sont ajoutés au patrimoine originaire. Les dettes afférentes à ces biens sont prises en compte dans le patrimoine originaire, même lorsqu'elles excèdent le montant de l'actif.

(3) Le patrimoine originaire ne comprend pas :

1. Les fruits des biens qui le composent ; et

2. Les biens du patrimoine originaire donnés par un époux à des parents en ligne directe au cours du régime matrimonial.

cont'd

Art. 8(2): I. Certain gains occur totally independent of the cooperation or activity of the other spouse, and should therefore not be settled. In order not to discourage donations of initial assets to any lineal relative, Arts. 8 and 10 guarantee the neutrality of such donations: these assets shall not be taken into account in any of the assets of the spouses. In the legal systems of both states, gains resulting from a gift or inheritance shall be included in the initial assets (§1374(2) BGB; Art. 1570 fr. CC) (*Expl. Report, Art. 8(2)*). – **II.** Compensation for pain and suffering is not included in the equalization of gains: **(a)** French law includes compensation for pain and suffering in the initial assets, thus not considering it as gain; **(b)** This is not the case in the German default statutory matrimonial property regime of the community of accrued gains, but is regularly the object of debate, given the personal nature of such claim (Mayer, *FamRZ* 2010, 612, 618). Even though an analogue expansion of the privileged assets of a spouse to other assets is prohibited under §1374(2) BGB, the parties are free to agree on such inclusion in the initial assets. (Braun, *MittBayNot* 2012, 89, 92). – **III.** The initial assets shall consist of the assets of a spouse less his or her liabilities at the reference date. Initial assets do not correspond to a specific set of assets, but are rather one of the two parameters to establish the accrued gains. The deduction of the liabilities may also exceed the existing assets. This means that the initial assets may even be negative. Similar provisions can be found in French law (Arts. 1570, 1571 fr. CC) and in German law (§1374(3) BGB – Reform of 1 September 2009). – **IV.** According to CEFL Principle 4:19 "reserved property comprises assets acquired before the commencement of the regime; gifts, inheritance and bequests acquired during the regime; assets substituting reserved property;

(2) Any assets that a spouse acquires at a later date by means of inheritance, transfer as a gift, or damages for pain and suffering shall be included in the initial assets. Any liabilities that affect these assets shall be included in the initial assets also when they exceed the existing assets.

(2) Il patrimonio che un coniuge acquista successivamente per effetto di successione, donazione o come risarcimento danni non patrimoniali viene computato al patrimonio iniziale. Dei vincoli obbligatori inerenti questo patrimonio, si tiene conto nel patrimonio iniziale anche quando superino l'ammontare dell'attivo.

(2) Se añaden al patrimonio inicial los bienes recibidos posteriormente por uno de los cónyuges a título de herencia, donación o indemnización por daños materiales o morales. Las deudas correspondientes a este patrimonio se imputan al patrimonio inicial, aunque su importe exceda del activo.

(3) The following shall not be included in the initial assets:

1. the fruits thereof, and
2. any items of the initial assets that a spouse has transferred as a gift to lineal relatives throughout the duration of the matrimonial property regime.

(3) Non si inputano al patrimonio iniziale:

1. i suoi frutti, e
2. i beni del patrimonio iniziale che un coniuge ha donato ai parenti in linea retta in costanza di regime dei beni.

(3) Bienes excluidos del patrimonio inicial:

1. sus frutos, y
2. los bienes del patrimonio inicial donados por un cónyuge a parientes en línea recta durante la vigencia del régimen matrimonial.

---

assets that are personal in nature; assets exclusively acquired for a spouse's profession; increases in value of the property included in (a) to (e)".

Art. 8(3)(1): I. The fruits of the initial assets realized by a spouse shall not be included in the initial assets. These fruits shall constitute accrued gains. This idea is also found in the legal systems of both states (§1374(2) BGB; Art. 1570 fr. CC) (*Expl. Report, Art. 8(3)(1)*). – **II.** According to CEFL Principle 4:18(1) "the acquisitions comprise the assets acquired during the regime, other than the reserved property. In particular, the acquisitions include each spouse's income and gains either derived from earnings or property; assets acquired by means of either spouse's income or gains".

Art. 8(3)(2): I. Any items of the initial assets that a spouse has transferred as a gift to lineal relatives throughout the duration of the matrimonial property regime shall be completely excluded from the calculation of the accrued gains. For this reason, such items shall be included neither in the final assets nor in the initial assets. This provision is based on French law. Any increase in value of one of such items by means independent of the initial assets shall be included in the final assets (see Art. 10 on the composition of the final assets). This provision is a compromise between the German law, which includes the items donated in such a way in the initial assets, and the French law, which allows the donation of items of the initial assets (Art. 1570(1)(2) fr. CC), which should not be included in the accrued gains, with the exception of the increase in value of such items (more detailed Mayer, *FamRZ* 2010, 612, 619). In this way the accrued gains to be compensated is not diminished at the expense of the partner through gratuitous alienation of any property from the initial assets (Dethloff, *RabelsZ* 76 (2012), 509, 524).

(4) Die Ehegatten erstellen bei Abschluss des Ehevertrages ein Verzeichnis über ihr Anfangsvermögen. Es wird vermutet, dass dieses Verzeichnis richtig ist, wenn es von beiden Ehegatten unterzeichnet wurde.

(4) Lors de la conclusion du contrat de mariage, les époux établissent un inventaire de leur patrimoine originaire respectif. Cet inventaire est présumé exact lorsque les deux époux l'ont signé.

(5) Ist kein Verzeichnis erstellt worden, so wird vermutet, dass kein Anfangsvermögen vorhanden ist.

(5) Si aucun inventaire n'a été établi, le patrimoine originaire est présumé nul.

cont'd

Art. 8(4): I. In order to avoid disputes on the value of the initial assets upon termination of the property regime, it is advisable to have a notary compile an inventory of the initial assets at the conclusion of the marriage contract. The spouses may also compile a private inventory in writing. Such inventory is presumed to be correct if both spouses sign it. The notarial form is not compulsory. The presumption of correctness can be refuted if any incorrectness is proved. It can also be advisable to include the value of the items of the initial assets in the inventory. In this case, the presumption of correctness shall also apply to this value, insofar as these items shall be valued on the date on which the property regime becomes effective under the first point of Art. 9(1) (or on

(4) Upon conclusion of the marriage contract, the spouses shall compile an inventory of their initial assets. It shall be assumed that this inventory is correct if it is signed by both spouses.

(4) I coniugi, alla conclusione del contratto matrimoniale, redigono un inventario del loro patrimonio iniziale. Si presume che questo inventario sia corretto qualora sia sottoscritto da entrambi i coniugi.

(4) En el momento de otorgar las capitulaciones matrimoniales, los cónyuges formarán un inventario de su patrimonio inicial respectivo. El inventario firmado por ambos cónyuges se presumirá exacto.

(5) If no inventory has been compiled, it shall be assumed that there are no initial assets.

(5) Se non è stato redatto alcun inventario, si presume che non esista alcun patrimonio iniziale.

(5) En defecto de formación de inventario, se presumirá que no existe el patrimonio inicial.

---

the date of acquisition in the case of the assets referred to in Art. 8(2) (*Expl. Report, Art. 8)*. – **II.** The legal systems of both states provide for such inventories and a presumption of correctness (§1377 BGB; Art. 1570 fr. CC). – **III.** If such an inventory does not exist the refutable assumption is made that no initial assets were in place (Braun, *MittBayNot* 2012, 89, 92).

Art. 8(5): I. This presumption can be refuted too. – **II.** The provision has to be understood as meaning the initial property has to be equal to zero in terms of accounting. – **III.** According to CEFL Principle 4:20 "assets are presumed to be owned jointly by both spouses unless otherwise proved".

Artikel 9
Bewertung des Anfangsvermögens

(1) Das Anfangsvermögen wird wie folgt bewertet:

1. Am Tag des Eintritts des Güterstandes vorhandene Gegenstände werden mit dem Wert angesetzt, den sie zu diesem Zeitpunkt hatten.

2. Nach dem Tag des Eintritts des Güterstandes erworbene Gegenstände, die nach Artikel 8 Absatz 2 dem Anfangsvermögen zuzurechnen sind, werden mit dem Wert angesetzt, den sie am Tag des Erwerbs hatten.

Article 9
Evaluation du patrimoine originaire

(1) Le patrimoine originaire est évalué comme suit :

1. Les biens existant à la date de prise d'effet du régime matrimonial sont évalués à cette date.

2. Les biens acquis après la date de prise d'effet du régime matrimonial et qui, en vertu du paragraphe 2 de l'article 8, font partie du patrimoine originaire, sont évalués à la date de leur acquisition.

Commentary

Art. 9
Art. 1571 (1)(1) fr. CC; CEFL Principle 4:26.

Art. 9(1): I. Art. 9 deals with the valuation of the initial assets. Different methods may apply to conduct the valuation of the items that make up the initial assets of the spouses. Art. 9 provides that the items belonging to a spouse on the date on which the property regime becomes effective shall be valued (Art. 9(1)(1). The items acquired after that date (such as the assets acquired by inheritance) shall be valued at their value on the date of their acquisition (Art. 9(1)(2) (*Expl. Report, Art. 9)).* Insofar as such items are valued on a date prior to the termination of the property regime, their value is indexed to the date of their valuation. An important exemption applies for real property and other real estate rights. They are valuated on the day of termination of the matrimonial property regime (Art. 9(2)(1)). However, appreciation during the matrimonial property regime is disregarded for the initial assets (Art. 9(2)(3)). – **II.** The provisions of Art. 9 are connected with Art. 11. As a result, a valuation method oriented by both legal systems would have been developed (Mayer, *FamRZ* 2010, 612, 621).

Article 9
Valuation of the Initial Assets

(1) The initial assets shall be valued as follows:

1. All items in existence on the date on which the matrimonial property regime became effective shall be valued pursuant to their worth at this point in time.

2. Items acquired after the date on which the matrimonial property regime became effective, being items which, pursuant to Article 8 paragraph (2) must be included in the initial assets, shall be valued pursuant to their worth on the date of their acquisition.

Articolo 9
Valutazione del patrimonio iniziale

(1) Il patrimonio iniziale è valutato come segue:

1. I beni esistenti alla data di entrata in vigore del regime dei beni vengono valutati con il valore che hanno in quel momento.

2. I beni acquisiti dopo la data di entrata in vigore del regime dei beni che, ai sensi dell'articolo 8 comma 2 sono da imputare al patrimonio iniziale, vengono valutati con il valore che avevano il giorno dell'acquisto.

Artículo 9
Valoración del patrimonio inicial

(1) El patrimonio inicial se valorará como sigue:

1. Los bienes existentes en la fecha de inicio del régimen matrimonial se valoran conforme al valor que tienen en esta fecha.

2. Los bienes adquiridos con posterioridad a la fecha de inicio del régimen matrimonial y que de acuerdo con el artículo 8, apartado 2, forman parte del patrimonio inicial, se valorarán según el valor que tenían en la fecha de la adquisición.

Art. 9(1)(1): I. Art. 9(1)(1) is based on the German valuation model. The French *participation aux acquêts* reaches further than the optional matrimonial property regime and sets the valuation of the initial assets entirely on the date of the termination of the matrimonial property regime (Art. 1571(1)(1) fr. CC) (*Expl. Report, Art. 9*). – **II.** Under the joint regime the spouse who is not the owner of those items participates in any increase in value of those items, even if they occurred without his or her activity (with the exception of the changes in value due to currency fluctuations). The initial assets of a spouse include, for example, a painting whose worth increased throughout the duration of the marriage because the artist had become increasingly famous; this increase constitutes accrued gains (*Expl. Report, Art. 9*).
Art. 9(1)(2): For a spouse's privileged assets (gifts, inheritances or damages for pain and suffering), which have been acquired at a later date but belong to the initial assets in accordance with Art. 8(2), the date of valuation is the date of acquisition of those assets, in accordance with Art. 9(1)(2).

(2) Alle Grundstücke und grundstücksgleichen Rechte des Anfangsvermögens mit Ausnahme des Nießbrauchs und des Wohnrechts werden jedoch mit dem Wert angesetzt, den sie am Tag der Beendigung des Güterstandes haben. Wurden diese Gegenstände während der Ehe veräußert oder ersetzt, so ist der Wert am Tag der Veräußerung oder Ersetzung zugrunde zu legen. Änderungen ihres Zustandes, die während der Ehe vorgenommen worden sind, werden bei der Bewertung des Anfangsvermögens nicht berücksichtigt.

(2) Toutefois, les immeubles et droits réels immobiliers du patrimoine originaire, autres que l'usufruit et le droit d'usage et d'habitation, sont évalués à la date de la dissolution du régime. Si ces biens ont été cédés ou remplacés au cours du mariage, est retenue leur valeur à la date de la cession ou du remplacement. Les modifications de leur état entreprises au cours du mariage ne sont pas prises en compte dans l'évaluation du patrimoine originaire.

cont'd

Art. 9(2): I. Art. 9(2) is based on the French valuation model. It provides that all plots of land and equivalent rights included in the initial assets, with the exception of usufruct and dwelling entitlements, shall be valued on the date of termination of the property regime. The valuation model described in Art. 9(2) shall therefore apply to the main less-than-lifetime property rights. Such assets shall be valued at their worth on the date of termination of the property regime or on the date of calculation in special cases in accordance with Art. 13 (*Expl. Report, Art. 9*). – **II.** The objective of this provision is to exclude from the accrued gains the increases in value of immovables of the initial assets that occurred without the activity of one of the spouses. Immovables usually constitute a significant fraction of the assets and can be subject to value fluctuations, which are generally not due to the activity of the spouses. This is the case, for example, if the family home increased in value based solely on the appreciation of its location. For example, the worth of an immovable can increase considerably because an airport nearby was closed, thus stopping the noise nuisance. In such a case, it is in the interests of the parties not to share such improvements with the other spouse (*Expl. Report, Art. 9*). However, the risk of depreciation lies solely on the spouse whose original assets the property belonged to (Dethloff, *RabelsZ* 76 (2012), 509, 526). – **III.** To avoid

(2) All plots of land and equivalent rights included in the initial assets, with the exception of usufruct and dwelling entitlements, shall be valued pursuant to their worth on the date of termination of the matrimonial property regime. If these items are alienated or substituted during the marriage, they shall be valued pursuant to their worth on the date of alienation or substitution. Changes to the condition of these items that are made during the marriage shall not be taken into consideration in the valuation of the initial assets.

(2) Tuttavia, gli immobili e i diritti reali immobiliari del patrimonio iniziale, ad eccezione dell'usufrutto e del diritto di abitazione, vengono valutati con il valore che hanno il giorno della cessazione del regime dei beni. Se questi beni sono stati alienati o sostituiti durante il matrimonio, si valutano alla data dell'alienazione o della sostituzione. Le modifiche del loro stato, intervenute durante il matrimonio, non sono contemplate dalla valutazione del patrimonio iniziale.

(2) No obstante, todos los inmuebles y derechos reales inmobiliarios del patrimonio inicial, excepto los derechos de usufructo, uso y habitación, se valorarán en la fecha de la disolución del régimen. Si estos bienes se han enajenado o sustituido durante el matrimonio, se valorarán en la fecha de su enajenación o sustitución. Las modificaciones de estos bienes efectuados durante el matrimonio no se tendrán en cuenta para la valoración del patrimonio inicial.

---

potential conflict during the valuation an individual contractual agreement regarding concrete auction sale measures and usage compensation is advised (Steer, *Notar* 2010, 119, 122; Braun, *MittBayNot* 2012, 89, 93). By contrast, an immovables' increase in value due to the cooperation of the spouse constitutes accrued gains. Thus, it shall not increase the worth of the initial assets. – **IV.** Exempt from special regulation remain other assets such as stock and company shares (critical Martiny, *ZEuP* 2011, 599; Mecke, *AcP* 211 (2011), 886, 907). – **V.** Not considered in the valuation of the initial assets are changes in the condition of the property or immovables made during the marriage. Therefore, renovations of real estate by the spouses, which led to an increase in value, are taken into account for the accrued gains to be compensated (so-called real appreciation). This is justified as a result of regarding the effectuated appreciation as a product of joint creation of value by the spouses (see Dethloff, *RabelsZ* 76 (2012), 509, 526). In particular, the provisions on the valuation of real property are depicted as one of the more attractive compromises, as an equalization for real appreciation, not based on currency devaluation, frequently clashes with the sense of justice of the spouses (Braeuer, *FF* 2010, 113, 115; Becker, *Era Forum* 12, 1 (2011) 103, 112).

(3) Werden die Gegenstände zu einem Zeitpunkt vor der Beendigung des Güterstandes bewertet, so ist ihr nach den Absätzen 1 und 2 bestimmter Wert von diesem Zeitpunkt an um den Betrag anzupassen, der sich aus den gemittelten Preisänderungsraten für allgemeine Verbraucherpreise der Vertragsstaaten ergibt.

(4) Die Absätze 1 und 3 gelten auch für die Bewertung von Verbindlichkeiten.

(3) Lorsque les biens sont évalués à une date antérieure à la dissolution du régime matrimonial, leur valeur déterminée en application des paragraphes 1 et 2 est indexée sur la variation moyenne de l'indice général des prix à la consommation des Etats contractants.

(4) Les paragraphes 1 et 3 s'appliquent aussi à l'évaluation des dettes.

cont'd

Art. 9(3): Depending on individual cases, a marriage can last many years. However, under Art. 9(1), the initial assets shall be valued pursuant to their specific monetary value on the date on which the property regime became effective (or on the date of acquisition of the assets under Art. 8(2). Nevertheless, such monetary value can decrease over the years due to inflation. Mere increases in value occurring solely due to inflation shall not constitute accrued gains. Hence, Art. 9(3) provides that the value of the initial assets shall be adjusted for inflation (*Expl. Report, Art. 9).*
Art. 9(4): Insofar as such items are valued at a date prior to the termination of the property regime, their value is indexed to the date of their valuation. The value of liabilities is also indexed. This

(3) If the items are valued at a point in time prior to termination of the matrimonial property regime, their value as determined at this point in time pursuant to paragraphs (1) and (2) shall be adjusted by an amount determined by the average price-change rates for overall consumer prices in the contracting States.

(4) Paragraphs (1) and (3) shall also apply to the valuation of liabilities.

(3) Se i beni vengono valutati in un momento precedente alla cessazione del regime dei beni, il loro valore, determinato secondo i commi 1 e 2, è da adeguare con un importo corrispondente alla variazione media dell'indice generale dei prezzi al consumo degli Stati contraenti.

(4) I commi 1 e 3 si applicano anche alla valutazione dei vincoli obbligatori.

(3) Cuando los bienes se valoren en una fecha anterior a la disolución del régimen matrimonial, su valor, determinado en este momento, según los apartados anteriores 1 y 2, deberá ajustarse a la variación media del índice general de precios de consumo de los Estados contratantes.

(4) Los apartados 1 y 3 se aplican también para la valoración de las deudas.

---

system inspired by the valuation rules in Germany (indexation) and in France (debt of value for immovables), guarantees a modernized method of valuation of the items that make up the initial assets. Apparent accrued gains, occurring solely because of depreciation of money, should not be equalized. It should be noted that the index used is the average price-change rates for overall consumer prices in the contracting states (*Expl. Report, Art. 9)*. If additional states were to join the convention, averaged price-change rates in all Member States would be taken into account (more detailed Jäger, *DNotZ* 2010, 804, 813).

ABSCHNITT 2 **Endvermögen**	SECTION 2 **Patrimoine final**
Artikel 10 **Zusammensetzung des Endvermögens**	**Article 10** **Composition du patrimoine final**
(1) Das Endvermögen ist das Vermögen jedes Ehegatten am Tag der Beendigung des Güterstandes. Verbindlichkeiten werden im Endvermögen berücksichtigt, auch wenn sie das Aktivvermögen übersteigen.	(1) Le patrimoine final est constitué des biens appartenant à l'époux à la date de la dissolution du régime. Les dettes sont prises en compte, même lorsqu'elles excèdent le montant de l'actif.
(2) Dem Endvermögen wird der Wert der Gegenstände hinzugerechnet, die ein Ehegatte:	(2) Est ajouté au patrimoine final la valeur des biens qu'un époux:
1. verschenkt hat, es sei denn,	1. a donnés, sauf:
a) die Schenkung ist nach der Lebensführung der Ehegatten angemessen oder	a) si la donation n'est pas excessive eu égard au train de vie des époux ou

Commentary

Art. 10
§1375 BGB; Arts. 1572, 1574 fr. CC; CEFL Principles 4:26, 4:27.

Art. 10(1): I. Art. 10(1) defines the final assets as the assets owned by each spouse on the date of termination of the property regime or on the reference date under Art. 13, after the deduction of liabilities, even if they exceed the existing assets. As with initial assets, the final assets can also be negative. Final assets do not correspond to a specific set of assets, but are rather a parameter to establish the accrued gains (*Expl. Report, Art. 10*). – **II.** The legal systems of both states contain a similar provision in their property regimes of the community of accrued gains (§1375 BGB; Arts. 1572, 1574 fr. CC).

Art. 10(2)(1): I. Under specific conditions, certain assets shall be included in the final assets. This is to prevent one of the spouses from decreasing his or her accrued gains by way of disposal of certain assets, thus putting the other spouse at a disadvantage. – **II.** The legal systems of both states provide for the inclusion in the final assets of asset reductions due to gifts without the consent of the other spouse and alienations with the intention to disadvantage (§1375(2) BGB; Art. 1573 fr. CC). The initial asset reduction due to squandering is only provided for in German law, §1375(2)(2) BGB. In

PART 2
Final Assets

Article 10
Composition of the Final Assets

(1) The final assets shall consist in the assets of each spouse on the date of termination of the matrimonial property regime. Liabilities shall be included in the final assets also if they exceed the existing assets.

(2) The final assets shall include the value of any items that a spouse

1. has transferred as a gift, unless

   a) the gift is reasonable having regard to the lifestyle of the spouses, or

SEZIONE 2
Patrimonio finale

Articolo 10
Composizione del patrimonio finale

(1) Il patrimonio finale è il patrimonio di ciascun coniuge alla data della cessazione del regime dei beni. Dei vincoli obbligatori si tiene conto nel patrimonio finale anche quando eccedono l'ammontare dell'attivo.

(2) Nel patrimonio finale viene incluso il valore dei beni che un coniuge:

1. ha donato, tranne nel caso in cui,

   a) la donazione sia congrua al tenore di vita dei coniugi o

SECCIÓN 2
Patrimonio final

Artículo 10
Composición del patrimonio final

(1) El patrimonio final es el patrimonio de cada cónyuge en la fecha de disolución del régimen de participación. Las deudas se tendrán en cuenta aunque excedan del activo.

(2) Debe añadirse al patrimonio final el valor de los bienes que un cónyuge:

1. ha donado, salvo que

   a) la donación sea adecuada al nivel de vida del matrimonio o

---

order to protect the other spouse, this provision is included in the optional matrimonial property regime of the community of accrued gains (*Expl. Report, Art. 10*). – **III.** In combination with this, Art. 18 allows for a premature settlement of debt on accrued gains if one of the spouses manages their assets in such a way that he or she adversely affects the rights of the other in the calculation of the debt on the accrued gains. – **IV.** In principle, gifts shall be included in the final assets. However, this shall not apply, if the gift is "reasonable" having regard to the lifestyle of the spouses. This is the case if the gift does not significantly exceed the budget of the spouses for daily expenses (*Expl. Report, Art. 10*). The interpretation of the term "reasonable" has to be extended. However, the provision pertains to transmissions with intention to disadvantage and not, unlike German law, generally to "actions" performed by a spouse (§1375(2)(1, 3) BGB). – **V.** Gifts shall also not be included if they are part of the initial assets gifted to one of that spouse's lineal relatives (Art. 8(3)(2)). However, any increase in value of such items that has occurred throughout the duration of the property regime by means independent of the initial assets shall be included in the final assets. Where there is a dispute it will be necessary to determine appreciation during the marriage. – **VI.** In addition, the value of the gift shall not be notionally included in the final assets if the other spouse had given consent or if the item was donated more than ten years prior to the termination of the property regime.

b) es wurde einem Verwandten in gerader Linie ein Gegenstand aus dem Anfangsvermögen geschenkt. Der Wertzuwachs durch Verbesserungen an einem solchen Gegenstand, der während der Dauer des Güterstands durch vom Anfangsvermögen unabhängige Mittel erzielt wurde, ist dem Endvermögen gleichwohl zuzurechnen,

2. in der Absicht, den anderen zu benachteiligen, veräußert hat, oder

3. verschwendet hat.

Dies gilt nicht, wenn die Schenkung, Veräußerung in Benachteiligungsabsicht oder Verschwendung mehr als zehn Jahre vor der Beendigung des Güterstandes erfolgt ist oder der andere Ehegatte damit einverstanden gewesen ist.

b) la donation porte sur un bien du patrimoine originaire donné à des parents en ligne directe. Toutefois, la plusvalue apportée par les améliorations réalisées sur ce bien, pendant la durée du régime matrimonial, avec des deniers ne dépendant pas du patrimoine originaire, est ajoutée au patrimoine final,

2. a cédés dans le but de léser l'autre époux ou

3. a dissipés.

Ces dispositions ne s'appliquent pas si la donation, l'aliénation frauduleuse ou la dissipation est intervenue plus de dix ans avant la dissolution du régime matrimonial ou si l'autre époux y a consenti.

cont'd

Art. 10(2)(2): I. This relates to legal transactions entered into with the aim of reducing the other spouse's accrued gains or depriving the other spouse of the accrued gains. Such intention to disadvantage must have been the principal motive. This relates, for example, to a valuable item which was sold significantly under price, if the aim was to affect the accrued gains. – **II.** The gain resulting from such alienation shall not be notionally included in the final assets if the other spouse had given consent or if the item was alienated more than ten years prior to the termination of the property regime (*Expl. Report, Art. 10)*.

Art. 10(2)(3): I. This point covers expenditures that are unnecessary and excessive having regard to the assets. This would include, for example, a luxury cruise taken by one of the spouses, if the spouses earn a modest income. This also includes the destruction of an item by a spouse, whether or not the intent was to cause damage. – **II.** The burden of proof for an unnecessary and excessive reduction in assets lies with the presuming party (Mecke, *AcP* 211 (2011) 887, 912).

b) an item included in the initial assets has been transferred as a gift to a lineal relative. Any increase in value through improvements to such items that is achieved throughout the duration of the matrimonial property regime using resources that are independent of the initial assets shall however be included in the final assets.

2. has alienated with the intention to disadvantage the other, or

3. has squandered.

This shall not apply if the transfer as a gift, alienation with the intention to disadvantage, or squandering took place more than ten years prior to termination of the matrimonial property regime or if the other spouse had agreed thereto.

b) sia stato donato un bene del patrimonio iniziale ad un parente in linea retta. L'incremento di valore apportato da miglioramenti realizzati su questo bene durante la vigenza del regime di beni, con risorse indipendenti dal patrimonio iniziale, è incluso nel patrimonio finale.

2. ha alienato nell'intento di pregiudicare l'altro, o

3. ha sperperato.

Ciò non vale se la donazione, l'alienazione con intento di pregiudicare o lo sperpero si è verificato oltre dieci anni prima della cessazione del regime dei beni o l'altro coniuge vi abbia acconsentito.

b) la donación se refiera a un bien del patrimonio inicial donado a un pariente en línea recta. La plusvalía procedente de mejoras realizadas sobre este bien durante la vigencia del régimen matrimonial con fondos no procedentes del patrimonio inicial debe añadirse al patrimonio final.

2. ha enajenado con el objeto de perjudicar al otro cónyuge, o

3. ha dilapidado.

Estas disposiciones no se aplican si la donación, la enajenación con finalidad de perjudicar o la dilapidación de bienes se ha producido en una fecha que exceda los diez años anteriores a la disolución del régimen matrimonial o si el otro cónyuge los ha consentido.

Art. 10(2)(3): I. The value of the squandered item shall not be notionally included in the final assets if the other spouse had given consent or if the item was squandered more than ten years prior to the termination of the property regime. – **II.** The limit of ten years is provided for in the German community of accrued gains (§1375(3) BGB). The reason behind such a limit is that, after a certain time, it is no longer assumed that such action was aimed at putting the other spouse at a disadvantage or it is assumed that the other spouse accepted it. Moreover, this provision provides for legal certainty. For these reasons, the limit of ten years has also been adopted in the optional matrimonial property regime of the community of accrued gains (*Expl. Report, Art. 10*). – **III.** According to CEFL Principle 4:27 "in calculating the acquisitions of each spouse account should be taken of excessive gifts; dissipation of assets; other acts that have intentionally diminished the value of the acquisitions to the detriment of the other spouse".

Artikel 11
Bewertung des Endvermögens

(1) Dem Endvermögen wird sowohl hinsichtlich Aktivvermögen als auch Verbindlichkeiten der Wert zugrunde gelegt, den das Vermögen bei Beendigung des Güterstandes hatte.

(2) Die Gegenstände nach Artikel 10 Absatz 2 werden nach ihrem Wert zum Zeitpunkt der Schenkung, Veräußerung in Benachteiligungsabsicht oder Verschwendung bewertet. Die Wertverbesserung nach Artikel 10 Absatz 2 Nummer 1 Buchstabe b wird zum Zeitpunkt der Schenkung des Gegenstands bewertet.

(3) Die Werte nach Absatz 2 sind um den Betrag anzupassen, der sich aus den gemittelten Preisänderungsraten für allgemeine Verbraucherpreise der Vertragsstaaten ergibt.

Article 11
Evaluation du patrimoine final

(1) Le patrimoine final est évalué, tant en ce qui concerne l'actif que le passif, à la date de la dissolution du régime matrimonial.

(2) La valeur des biens visés au paragraphe 2 de l'article 10 est fixée à la date de la donation, de l'aliénation frauduleuse ou de la dissipation. La plus-value visée au paragraphe 2. 1b de l'article 10, est évaluée à la date de la donation du bien.

(3) Les valeurs indiquées au paragraphe 2 sont indexées sur la variation moyenne de l'indice général des prix à la consommation des Etats contractants.

Commentary

Art. 11
Art. 1574 fr. CC; CEFL Principle 4:26.

Art. 11(1): I. Final assets shall be valued pursuant to their worth on the date of termination of the regime or on the date of calculation in special cases in accordance with Art. 13. In particular, Art. 13 prescribes that in the case of a divorce or termination of the optional matrimonial property regime through other court decision the time of filing the petition at the court supersedes the time of termination of the matrimonial property regime. – **II.** In France, subject to the special valuation rules in the case of divorce, separation or early settlement of the debt on the accrued gains, the value of the items that constitute the final assets shall be determined pursuant to their condition on the date of termination of the regime and to their value on the date of liquidation of the regime. The latter can occur many years after the former (Art. 1574 fr. CC). In Germany, the accrued gains and, thus the initial and final assets of the spouses, are calculated on the date of termination of the regime. They can be calculated on an earlier date, such as the date of submission of the petition for the early settlement of the debt on the accrued gains or when the petition of divorce becomes pending (*Expl. Report, Art. 11*). – **III.** According to CEFL Principle 4:26 "the acquisitions of each spouse should be determined at the date of the dissolution of the regime, as specified by principle 4:25. The acquisition should be valued at the date of the liquidation of the regime".

Article 11
Valuation of the Final Assets

(1) With regard to both existing assets and liabilities the final assets shall be valued pursuant to their worth upon termination of the matrimonial property regime.

(2) The items pursuant to Article 10 paragraph (2) shall be valued pursuant to their worth at the time of the transfer as a gift, alienation with the intention to disadvantage, or squandering. Any improvement in value pursuant to Article 10 paragraph (2) number 1 letter b shall be determined as that applicable at the point in time when the item was transferred as a donation.

(3) The values pursuant to paragraph (2) shall be adjusted by the amount determined by the average price-change rates for overall consumer princes in the contracting States.

Articolo 11
Valutazione del patrimonio finale

(1) Il patrimonio finale viene valutato, sia in relazione all'attivo che ai vincoli obbligatori, in base al valore che il patrimonio aveva alla cessazione del regime dei beni.

(2) I beni di cui all'articolo 10, comma 2, vengono valutati secondo il loro valore al momento della donazione, dell'alienazione fraudolenta o dello sperpero. L'incremento di valore, di cui all'articolo 10, comma 2, numero 1, lettera b, viene valutato al momento della donazione del bene.

(3) I valori di cui al comma 2 sono adeguati alla variazione media dell'indice generale dei prezzi al consumo degli Stati contraenti.

Artículo 11
Valoración del patrimonio final

(1) El patrimonio final deberá valorarse, en relación con el activo y el pasivo, conforme al valor del patrimonio en la fecha de disolución del régimen matrimonial.

(2) El valor de los bienes indicados en el apartado 2 del artículo 10 corresponde al valor de los mismos en la fecha de su donación, de su enajenación con finalidad de perjuicio o de su dilapidación. La plusvalía referente a los bienes indicados en el número 1, letra b, del apartado 2 del artículo 10, deberá valorarse en la fecha de la donación.

(3) El valor de los bienes indicados en el apartado 2 deberá ajustarse a la variación media del índice general de precios de consumo de los Estados contratantes.

Art. 11(2): I. The value of the items under Art. 10(2) (gifts, alienation with intention to disadvantage and squander) shall be calculated on the date of the gift, alienation with the intention to disadvantage or squandering. The increase in value of items gifted from the initial assets, that has occurred throughout the duration of the regime by means independent of the initial assets, are calculated on the date of the gift. – **II.** Deviating from the French text provides that in case of disloyal reductions of assets during the matrimonial property regime the hypothetical value of the alienated object at the date of termination of the matrimonial property regime is decisive even though it is a question of the condition of the object at the date of alienation (Art. 1574(1)(1) fr. CC).
Art. 11(3): I. From the date of calculation, the values pursuant to Art. 11(2) shall be adjusted by the average price-change rates for overall consumer prices in the Member States. – **II.** The question of which valuable assets are to be included in the calculation of final assets may create difficulties though. Problems may arise regarding household items, life insurance, labour gratuities or company shares, as these are subject to partially or completely differing mechanisms of equalization in the national laws (Dethloff, *RabelsZ* 76 (2012), 509, 525).

ABSCHNITT 3
Zugewinnausgleichsforderung

Artikel 12
Anspruch auf Zugewinnausgleich

(1) Übersteigt bei Beendigung des Güterstandes der Zugewinn des einen Ehegatten den Zugewinn des anderen, so kann der andere Ehegatte die Hälfte des Überschusses als Zugewinnausgleichsforderung verlangen.

(2) Die Zugewinnausgleichsforderung ist ein Geldanspruch. Das Gericht kann jedoch auf Antrag eines der Ehegatten anordnen, dass Gegenstände des Schuldners dem Gläubiger zum Zweck des Ausgleichs übertragen werden, wenn das der Billigkeit entspricht.

SECTION 3
Créance de participation

Article 12
Droit à créance de participation

(1) Si à la dissolution du régime matrimonial, les acquêts d'un époux excèdent les acquêts de l'autre époux, ce dernier peut faire valoir à l'encontre de son conjoint une créance de participation égale à la moitié de la différence.

(2) La créance de participation donne lieu à un paiement en argent. Toutefois, le tribunal peut, à la demande de l'un ou l'autre des époux, ordonner, à l'effet de ce paiement, le transfert de biens du débiteur au créancier, si cela répond au principe de l'équité.

Commentary

Art. 12
§1378 BGB; Art. 1575 fr. CC; see also §§1371, 1372, 1376, 1383 BGB and Art. 1569 fr. CC; CEFL Principle 4:31.

Art. 12(1): I. The spouse who achieved the lower accrued gains throughout the duration of the regime can claim from the other spouse the settlement of a debt on the accrued gains amounting to half of the difference between the assets gained by each spouse during the marriage upon termination of the regime. – **II.** The principle of halving is applicable Europe-wide to matrimonial property regimes of the community of accrued gains and the participation in acquisitions (Dethloff, *RabelsZ* 76 (2012), 509, 527). – **III.** The initial and final assets of each spouse are compared to establish whether and to what extent each spouse achieved any gains during the marriage. The provisions on the composition and valuation of the initial and final assets, which are not identical, are contained in Arts. 8–11. If the final assets exceed the initial assets, the difference shall constitute the accrued gains of that spouse. There is no settlement of the losses, but only of the accrued gains. If the accrued gains of one spouse exceed the accrued gains of the other, he or she owes half of the difference to the other spouse. – **IV.** Deviations from the principle of halving may be contractually agreed upon by the spouses according to Art. 3. However, the optional matrimonial property regime does not include a hardship clause. That is to

PART 3
Debt on the Accrued Gains

SEZIONE 3
Credito di conguaglio dell'incremento patrimoniale

SECCIÓN 3
Crédito de participación

Article 12
Claim to Settlement of the Debt on the Accrued Gains

(1) If the accrued gains of one spouse exceed on the termination of the matrimonial property regime the accrued gains of the other spouse, the other spouse can claim half of the surplus as debt on the accrued gains.

(2) The debt on the accrued gains shall be a pecuniary claim. However, upon petition of one of the spouses, the court can order items of the debtor to be transferred to the creditor for the purposes of settling the debt if this is equitable.

Articolo 12
Pretesa al conguaglio dell'incremento patrimoniale

(1) Se alla cessazione del regime dei beni l'incremento patrimoniale di un coniuge eccede l'incremento patrimoniale dell' altro, quest'ultimo può pretendere la metà di tale eccedenza quale credito di conguaglio.

(2) Il credito di conguaglio dell'incremento patrimoniale è una pretesa pecuniaria. Tuttavia il giudice, su istanza di uno dei coniugi, può disporre che, ai fini della compensazione, vengano ceduti beni del debitore al creditore, qualora ciò corrisponda ad equità.

Artículo 12
Pretensión a la participación

(1) Si, en el momento de la disolución del régimen matrimonial, las ganancias de un cónyuge exceden las ganancias del otro, este último podrá reclamar la mitad del exceso como crédito de participación.

(2) El crédito de participación es una pretensión dineraria, pero, a petición de uno u otro cónyuge y si ello responde a equidad, el tribunal podrá acordar que el pago se realice mediante la adjudicación de bienes del deudor al acreedor.

---

say that the equalization of accrued gains can not be refused because of gross inequity or hardness (critical Dethloff, *RabelsZ* 76 (2012), 509, 528). The claim to settlement of the debt on accrued gains subsists in all cases of the termination of the matrimonial property regime.

Art. 12(2): I. In principle it is a pecuniary debt. Nevertheless the court may order the transmission of specific assets as settlement. – **II.** For the most part the regulation corresponds with German and French law. While the claim as pecuniary debt is explicitly governed in France in Art. 1576 fr. CC, in Germany there is no special provision. However, the pecuniary nature of the claim of settlement of the debt on the accrued gains results from the provisions of §1372 BGB. The legal systems of both states provide for the settlement in kind only in special cases (Art. 1576 fr. CC; §1383 BGB only on request of the debtor or because of gross inequity). – **III.** It was made clear that in this way the family home may be devolved as well, taking it into account for the claim to settlement and in this manner establishing a protected real estate. In general, this allows for consideration of fulfilment difficulties or interests in items or real estate (material assets) (Dethloff, *RabelsZ* 76 (2012), 509, 529). – **IV.** According to CEFL Principle 4:31(4) "the claim of participation is a monetary one, unless the spouses agree otherwise". "The competent authority may, in the interest of the family and subject to payment of compensation, allocate the family home and household goods to one of the spouse" (CEFL Principle 4:30).

(3) Die Zugewinnausgleichsforderung ist nach Beendigung des Güterstandes vererblich und übertragbar.

(3) Après la dissolution du régime matrimonial, la créance de participation est transmissible à cause de mort et cessible entre vifs.

cont'd

Art. 12(3): I. Both in France and Germany, the debt on the accrued gains is transferable as long as the property regime is not terminated. This applies regardless of whether the transfer was made free of charge or not. By contrast, the claim is transferable after the termination of the property regime and inheritable in the case of death (§1378(3) BGB; Art. 1569 fr. CC). A similar provision has thus been included in the optional matrimonial property regime of the community of accrued gains (*Expl. Report, Art. 12*). – **II.** The death of a spouse creates matrimonial property right claims for the

(3) After termination of the matrimonial property regime, the debt on the accrued gains shall be inheritable and transferable.

(3) Dopo la cessazione del regime dei beni, il credito di conguaglio dell'incremento patrimoniale è trasmissibile per causa di morte o per atto tra vivi.

(3) Después de la disolución del régimen matrimonial, el crédito de participación es transmisible por causa de muerte y por actos inter vivos.

spouse who is entitled to equalization. A claim to settlement of accrued gains as a hereditary right, based on the model of §1371(1) BGB, is not provided for (critical Dethloff, *RabelsZ* 76 (2012), 509, 528). This means that, even in the case of death, the concretely calculated debt of accrued gains is always owed and therefore affects the legal shares of the spouses and all others entitled to legal shares (on possible special agreement, Braun, *MittBayNot* 2012, 89, 93). – **III.** After the death of the spouse entitled to equalization, the debt on the accrued gains shall be inheritable.

Artikel 13
Berechnungszeitpunkte in Sonderfällen

Wird die Ehe geschieden oder der Güterstand durch eine andere gerichtliche Entscheidung aufgelöst, bestimmt sich die Zugewinnausgleichsforderung nach Zusammensetzung und Wert des Vermögens der Ehegatten zum Zeitpunkt der Einreichung des Antrags bei Gericht.

Article 13
Date d'effet dans des cas particuliers

Si le mariage est dissous par divorce ou si le régime matrimonial est dissous par une autre décision judiciaire, la créance de participation est déterminée en fonction de la composition et de la valeur du patrimoine des époux à la date d'introduction de la demande en justice

Commentary

Art. 13
§1384 BGB; Art. 1572 fr. CC; CEFL Principle 4:31.

Art. 13: I. To calculate the composition and value of the assets of the spouses, if the marriage is dissolved or the matrimonial property regime terminated by other court decision the joint property regime provides that the date of termination of the property regime shall be substituted with the date of submission of the petition (and not the *assignation en divorce* as in France). In addition, when the judge does not decide on the divorce and the settlement of the debt during the same proceedings, this provision enables the reduction of the time period during which the debtor

Article 13
Date of Calculation in Special Cases

If the marriage is dissolved or the matrimonial property regime terminated by other court decision, the debt on the accrued gains shall be determined pursuant to the composition and value of the assets of the spouses at the time the petition was filed in court.

Articolo 13
Momento del calcolo in casi particolari

Se il matrimonio viene sciolto per divorzio o il regime dei benî è sciolto per effetto di un altro provvedimento giudiziale, il credito di conguaglio dell'incremento patrimoniale si determina in base alla composizione e al valore del patrimonio dei coniugi al momento della presentazione della domanda in giudizio.

Artículo 13
Fecha de cálculo en casos especiales

En el supuesto de disolución del régimen matrimonial por causa de divorcio o por otra decisión judicial, el crédito de participación será determinado en función de la composición y el valor del patrimonio de los cónyuges a la fecha de interposición de la demanda ante el juzgado.

---

spouse can reduce his or her assets, thus also reducing the debt on the accrued gains for the other spouse. – **II.** German law provides for such mechanism (§1384 BGB). French law provides that the property regime shall be considered terminated on the date of submission of a petition aimed solely at establishing the composition of the assets (Art. 1572 fr. CC). – **III.** This mechanism is not only effective in case of divorce. It applies equally when the regime is terminated otherwise by court order. This includes, for example, a decision on the early settlement of the debt on the accrued gains under Art. 18. Also by divorce, it is advisable to calculate the accrued gains already during the proceedings for the early settlement of the debt on the accrued gains. In this case, the date of calculation shall be the date of submission of the petition to the court (*Expl. Report, Art. 13).*

Artikel 14
Begrenzung der Zugewinnausgleichsforderung

Die Zugewinnausgleichsforderung wird auf den halben Wert des Vermögens des Ausgleichspflichtigen begrenzt, das nach Abzug der Verbindlichkeiten zu dem Zeitpunkt, der für die Feststellung der Höhe der Zugewinnausgleichsforderung maßgebend ist, vorhanden ist. Die Begrenzung der Zugewinnausgleichsforderung erhöht sich in den Fällen des Artikel 10 Absatz 2 mit Ausnahme von Nummer 1 Buchstabe b um die Hälfte des dem Endvermögen hinzuzurechnenden Betrages.

Article 14
Limitation de la créance de participation

La créance de participation est limitée à la moitié de la valeur du patrimoine de l'époux débiteur tel qu'il existe, après déduction des dettes, à la date retenue pour la détermination du montant de cette créance. La limite de la créance de participation est relevée de la moitié du montant ajouté au patrimoine final en application des dispositions du paragraphe 2 de l'article 10, à l'exception du cas visé à l'alinéa 1. b du dit article.

Commentary

Art. 14
§1378 BGB; CEFL Principles 4:15, 4:31.

Art. 14: I. According to Art. 14, the debt on the accrued gains shall be limited to half the value of the available assets of the debtor spouse. This provision guarantees that, even taking into account negative initial assets, no spouse shall give the other spouse more than 50% of the assets actually available on the reference date (date of calculation under Art. 13 or actual termination of the regime) (*Expl. Report, Art. 13)*. – **II.** This restriction on the amount of the debt on the accrued gains corresponds to the basic principle of the property regime of the community of accrued gains, under which both spouses shall fairly participate in half of the assets acquired during the marriage. In contrast to this §1378(2)(1) BGB provides for a restriction on the entire assets of the person obliged to compensate. A planned revision of §1378 BGB was not carried out due to substantial criticism as the redemption of debts during a marriage represents an economic gain (Dethloff, *RabelsZ* 76 (2012), 509, 530). – **III.** Art. 14 also guarantees that a debt on the accrued gains, apart from the case of the notional inclusion under Art. 10(2) (with the exception of point 1(b)), shall only exist if there are positive assets on the date of calculation of the accrued gains. If, for example, during the regime both spouses only repaid their debts or if one spouse accrued no gains and the other repaid the debts, then no debt exists. This limitation only pertains to the debt on the accrued gains and not to other possible claims and liabilities between the spouses. However, the aim of the provision, to enable the debtor spouse to at least keep half of his or her assets, is not justified if he or she decreased

Article 14
Limitation of the Debt on the Accrued Gains

The debt on the accrued gains shall be limited to half the value of the assets of the debtor spouse that are available, after deduction of the liabilities, at the point in time determinative for ascertaining the amount of the debt on the accrued gains. The limitation of the debt on the accrued gains shall increase in the cases stipulated in Article 10 paragraph (2), with the exception of number 1 letter b, by half of the amount to be included in the final assets.

Articolo 14
Limitazione del credito di conguaglio dell'incremento patrimoniale

Il credito di conguaglio dell'incremento patrimoniale è limitato alla metà del valore del patrimonio del coniuge obbligato al conguaglio, esistente, al netto dei vincoli obbligatori, nel momento stabilito per l'accertamento dell'ammontare del credito di conguaglio. Il limite del credito di conguaglio dell'incremento patrimoniale è aumentato, nei casi dell'articolo 10, comma 2 con eccezione del numero 1 lettera b, della metà dell'importo da computare al patrimonio finale.

Artículo 14
Limitación del crédito de participación

El crédito de participación está limitado a la mitad del valor del patrimonio del cónyuge obligado a la compensación en su estado final, después de la deducción de las deudas, en el momento en que se haya determinado el importe de este crédito. La limitación del crédito de participación se incrementará con la mitad de la cuantía añadida al patrimonio final en aplicación de las disposiciones indicadas en el artículo 10 apartado 2, con la excepción del número 1, letra b.

---

his or her assets disloyally (Art. 10(2) with the exception of point 1(b)). – **IV.** To avoid limiting the amount of the debt if a spouse engaged in disloyal actions, resulting in a notional inclusion in the final assets, Art. 14 provides that the limitation of the debt on the accrued gains shall amount to half of the amount to be included in the final assets in accordance with Art. 10(2), with the exception of gifts at point 1(b). In case of gifts, it is not assumed that the spouse wanted to decrease his or her assets disloyally. The dishonest spouse can be forced to use all of his or her assets, and even to incur into debts, to settle the debt on the accrued gains after a notional inclusion (*Expl. Report, Art. 14)*. – **V.** Under Art. 3(3), the spouses can derogate from the application of this provision by way of contract. A specific contractual clause for the exclusion of determinate assets from the settlement on the accrued gains, for the limitation of the amount of the debt on the accrued gains or for a change in quota payments would be possible (Dethloff, *RabelsZ* 76 (2012), 509, 530). – **VI.** In principle the settlement of accrued gains can be ruled out by agreement clause in the case of divorce. The validity and efficacy of such a clause, however, would be subject to the applicable national law. Regarding German law, concrete exam of the contents of matrimonial agreement is necessary. A eventual nullity of a renunciation of maintenance or of an exclusion of *Versorgungsausgleich* (pension splitting) may lead to the invalidity or nullity of the entire marital agreement, thereby voiding or annulling the exclusion of the settlement of accrued gains as well (so Dethloff, *RabelsZ* 76 (2012), 509, 530). With regard to French law in the event of divorce the *prestation compensatoire* would have to be taken into consideration (Dethloff, *RabelsZ* 76 (2012), 509, 530).

KAPITEL VI	CHAPITRE VI

KAPITEL VI

Sonstiges

Artikel 15
Verjährung

Der Anspruch auf Zugewinnausgleich verjährt in drei Jahren; die Frist beginnt mit dem Zeitpunkt, in dem der Ehegatte von der Beendigung des Güterstandes erfährt, spätestens jedoch zehn Jahre nach der Beendigung des Güterstandes.

CHAPITRE VI

Dispositions diverses

Article 15
Prescription

Le droit à la créance de participation se prescrit par trois ans à compter de la date à laquelle l'époux a connaissance de la dissolution du régime matrimonial, et au plus tard dix ans après la dissolution du régime.

Commentary

Art. 15
§1378 (4) BGB; Art. 1578 fr. CC.

Art. 15: I. The claim to settlement of the debt on the accrued gains shall become statute-barred three years after the termination of the matrimonial property regime. This three-year limitation is also found in the legal systems of both states (§1378(4) BGB; Art. 1578 fr. CC). – **II.** However, the beginning of the limitation period differs in the two states. While in Germany the emphasis is on the knowledge

CHAPTER VI

Miscellaneous

Article 15
Limitation

The claim to settlement of the debt on the accrued gains shall become statute-barred after three years; this period shall commence on the date on which the spouse learns of the termination of the matrimonial property regime, but at the latest ten years after termination of the matrimonial property regime.

CAPITOLO VI

Altre disposizioni

Articolo 15
Prescrizione

La preseta conguaglio dell'incremento patrimoniale si prescrive in tre anni e il termine decorre dal momento in cui il coniuge ha notizia della cessazione del regime dei beni, in ogni caso in dieci anni dalla cessazione del regime dei beni.

CAPÍTULO VI

Otras disposiciones

Artículo 15
Prescripción

La pretensión al crédito de participación prescribirá a los tres años de la fecha en que el cónyuge tenga conocimiento de la disolución del régimen matrimonial y como muy tarde a los diez años de la disolución del régimen.

---

of the termination of the regime, in France the limitation period begins with the termination itself. To protect the creditor spouse, the joint regime has adopted the German period of time. However, under certain circumstances, if the limitation period depends on the knowledge of the spouses, it may even commence many years after the termination of the regime. To provide legal certainty from a certain date to the debtor spouse, Art. 15 also provides for a limitation period of ten years from the termination of the regime, independent of the knowledge of the spouses (*Expl. Report, Art. 15)*. – **III.** Therefore, the ten years refers to the prescription (Jäger, *DNotZ* 2010, 804, 817; Braun, *MittBayNot* 2012, 89, 94).

Artikel 16
Auskunftspflicht, Verzeichnis

(1) Nach Beendigung des Güterstandes ist jeder Ehegatte verpflichtet, dem anderen Ehegatten über den Bestand seines Anfangs- und Endvermögens Auskunft zu erteilen. Auf Verlangen sind Belege vorzulegen. Jeder Ehegatte kann die Vorlage eines vollständigen und richtigen Verzeichnisses verlangen. Bei dessen Erstellung ist er auf sein Verlangen hinzuzuziehen. Er kann außerdem verlangen, dass das Verzeichnis auf seine Kosten durch einen Notar aufgenommen wird.

(2) Absatz 1 gilt auch, sobald ein Ehegatte die Auflösung der Ehe oder den vorzeitigen Ausgleich des Zugewinns beantragt hat.

Article 16
Obligation d'information, inventaire

(1) Après la dissolution du régime matrimonial, chacun des époux a l'obligation de fournir à l'autre époux toutes informations sur la composition de ses patrimoines originaire et final. Sur demande, il doit présenter des justificatifs. Chacun des époux peut exiger la présentation d'un inventaire sincère et véritable. A sa demande, il doit être appelé à cet inventaire. Il peut en outre exiger que l'inventaire soit établi par un notaire à ses frais.

(2) Le paragraphe 1 ci-dessus s'applique également dès lors que l'un des époux a demandé la dissolution du mariage ou la liquidation anticipée de la créance de participation.

Commentary

Art. 16
§1379 BGB; Art. 1572(2) fr. CC; see also §170 (1) ch. ZGB; (CE) Resolution (78) 37; CEFL Principle 4:8.

Art. 16: I. A spouse has to know the value of the initial and final assets of the other spouse. Therefore, the spouses are entitled to information and to the submission of an inventory. The right to present supporting documents shall be granted. That spouse can thereby better verify the information submitted by the other spouse and better defend his or her own interests. Moreover, litigation may be avoided if convincing evidence is presented. Each spouse has the right to an inventory to be compiled by a notary at his or her expense (similar in §1379 BGB). In the French law the entitlement to information is not explicitly provided for, but is recognized (Art. 1572 fr. CC) (*Expl. Report, Art. 16*). – **II.** In addition, it is emphasized that Art. 16 (in contrast to §1379 BGB) does not directly regulate a claim to assessment of value. This may be agreed upon in a matrimonial

Article 16
Duty of Information, Inventory

(1) After termination of the matrimonial property regime, each spouse shall have a duty to inform the other spouse of the inventory of his or her final assets. Supporting documents must be submitted on request. Each spouse can demand that a full and correct inventory be submitted. Upon his or her request, he or she shall be consulted in the compilation thereof. He or she can also demand that an inventory be taken by a notary at his or her expense.

(2) Paragraph (1) shall also apply as soon as a spouse has petitioned for dissolution of the marriage or early settlement of debt on the accrued gains.

Articolo 16
Obbligo di informazione, inventario

(1) Dopo la cessazione del regime dei beni, ciascun coniuge è obbligato a fornire all'altro informazioni sulla consistenza del proprio patrimonio iniziale e finale. Su richiesta sono da esibire i documenti giustificativi. Ciascun coniuge può pretendere la presentazione di un inventario corretto e completo. A sua richiesta, egli deve essere coinvolto nella redazione di questo inventario. Egli può pretendere inoltre che l'inventario sia predisposto a sue spese da un notaio.

(2) Il comma 1 trova applicazione anche quando un coniuge ha chiesto lo scioglimento del matrimonio o il conguaglio anticipato dell'incremento patrimoniale.

Artículo 16
Obligación de informar, inventario

(1) Después de la disolución del régimen matrimonial, cada uno de los cónyuges estará obligado a facilitar al otro cónyuge toda la información necesaria sobre la composición de su patrimonio inicial y final, y a petición de uno de ellos deberá aportar los correspondientes justificantes. Cada cónyuge podrá solicitar la formación de un inventario completo y fiel. Si así lo solicita, deberá ser convocado a la formación del inventario. Además podrá solicitar que, a sus expensas, el inventario sea practicado por un notario.

(2) El apartado 1 se aplicará también cuando uno de los cónyuges haya solicitado la disolución del matrimonio o la liquidación anticipada de su crédito de participación.

---

agreement, though (Braun, *MittBayNot* 2012, 89, 94). – **III.** The right to information and to the compilation of an inventory provided for here enables the creditor spouse to pursue the claim to settlement of the debt on the accrued gains. – **IV.** According to CEFL Principle 4:8 "each spouse has the duty to inform the other about his or her assets and debts and about significant acts of administration in so far as it is necessary to enable the other to exercise his or her rights".

Art. 16(2): I. Art. 16(1) also applies as soon as a spouse has petitioned for dissolution of the marriage or early settlement of debt on the accrued gains. That the obligation to disclosure does not exist at the point of time of separation, as is the case under German law, such that no sufficient protection against potential disloyal reduction of assets is provided, has been criticized (Mecke, *AcP* 211 (2011) 887, 912; see also Dethloff, *RabelsZ* 76 (2012), 509, 530). In addition, it is emphasized that Art. 16 (in contrast to §1379 BGB) does not directly include a claim to assessment of value. This may however be agreed upon by the parties in the marital agreements (Braun, *MittBayNot* 2012, 89, 94).

Artikel 17
Stundung

(1) Das Gericht kann auf Antrag dem Schuldner die Zugewinnausgleichsforderung stunden, wenn die sofortige Zahlung für den Schuldner eine unbillige Härte wäre, insbesondere wenn sie ihn zur Aufgabe eines Gegenstandes zwingen würde, der seine wirtschaftliche Lebensgrundlage bildet.

(2) Eine gestundete Forderung ist zu verzinsen.

(3) Das Gericht kann auf Antrag des Gläubigers anordnen, dass der Schuldner für eine gestundete Forderung Sicherheit leistet; über Art und Umfang der Sicherheitsleistung entscheidet das Gericht nach billigem Ermessen.

Article 17
Délais de paiement

(1) Si le règlement immédiat de la créance de participation pénalise de manière inéquitable le débiteur, notamment en l'obligeant à céder un bien constituant son moyen de subsistance, le tribunal peut, à sa demande, lui accorder des délais pour le règlement de la créance.

(2) La créance dont le paiement est différé porte intérêts.

(3) Le tribunal peut, à la demande du créancier, imposer au débiteur la fourniture de sûretés dont il détermine la nature et le montant en équité.

Commentary

Art. 17
§1382 BGB; Art. 1576 fr. CC; CEFL Principle 4:31.

Art. 17(1): I. German law and French law provide for the possibility of granting additional time for the settlement of the debt on the accrued gains under specific conditions and of claiming the provision of securities. – **II.** Art. 17(1) governs the conditions under which the deferral can be granted. The deferral shall be granted in the interests of the creditor spouse and only in exceptional

Article 17
Deferral

(1) Upon petition the court can grant additional time for the debtor to settle the debt on the accrued gains if immediate payment would constitute an inequitable hardship for the debtor, in particular if it would compel him or her to surrender an item constituting the means of his or her subsistence.

(2) Interest must be paid on a deferred debt.

(3) Upon petition of the creditor the court can order the debtor to provide security for a deferred debt; the court shall decide at its equitable discretion on the nature and scope of the security provided.

Articolo 17
Dilazione

(1) Su istanza il giudice può dilazionare il credito di conguaglio dell'incremento patrimoniale, qualora il pagamento immediato risulti eccessivamente oneroso per il debitore, in particolare qualora ciò lo costringa alla cessione di un bene che rappresenta il suo sostentamento economico.

(2) Il credito dilazionato produce interessi.

(3) Il giudice può ordinare, su istanza del creditore, che il debitore fornisca garanzia per un credito dilazionato; sulla natura e sull'ammontare della prestazione di garanzia decide il giudice secondo equo apprezzamento.

Artículo 17
Aplazamiento

(1) El tribunal, a petición del deudor, podrá acordar un aplazamiento para el pago de la deuda, en el supuesto de que el pago inmediato del crédito de participación grave al deudor de forma contraria a la equidad, en especial cuando le obligue a ceder un bien que constituya su medio de subsistencia.

(2) Este aplazamiento devengará intereses.

(3) A petición del cónyuge acreedor, el tribunal podrá imponer al cónyuge deudor la aportación de garantías cuya naturaleza e importe se fijarán con criterios de equidad.

---

cases. The court shall decide in each case whether there is an undue hardship (*Expl. Report, Art. 17*). – **III.** According to CEFL Principle 4:31(5) "upon request of the debtor spouse the competent authority may, where there are serious grounds for doing so, authorize payments to be deferred or payable instalments".
Art. 17(2): Interest must be paid on a deferred debt.
Art. 17(3): Art. 17(3) provides that the court can order the debtor to provide security for a deferred debt. The court shall decide in its equitable discretion on the nature and scope of the security provided.

Artikel 18
Vorzeitiger Zugewinnausgleich

(1) Wenn ein Ehegatte sein Vermögen so verwaltet, dass er dadurch die Rechte des anderen bei der Berechnung der Zugewinnausgleichsforderung beeinträchtigt, kann der andere Ehegatte vorzeitigen Ausgleich des Zugewinns verlangen. Dies gilt insbesondere in den Fällen, die zu der fiktiven Hinzurechnung nach Artikel 10 Absatz 2 führen.

(2) Mit Rechtskraft der Entscheidung, durch die dem Antrag stattgegeben wird, gilt für die Ehegatten Gütertrennung.

Article 18
Liquidation anticipée de la créance de participation

(1) Si la gestion de son patrimoine par l'un des époux est de nature à compromettre les droits de l'autre au titre du calcul de la créance de participation, ce dernier peut demander la liquidation anticipée de la créance de participation. Il en est notamment ainsi dans les cas qui conduisent à la réunion fictive visée au paragraphe 2 de l'article 10.

(2) A compter de la décision définitive faisant droit à la demande, les époux sont placés sous le régime de la séparation de biens.

Commentary

Art. 18
§1386 BGB, §1388 BGB; Art. 1580 fr. CC; See also §1385(1)(1); Art. 1400(2) gr. ZGB; Arts. 232-16(2)(a) kt. CC; Art. 176(1)(3) ch. ZGB; and §916 ZPO; Art. 220-1 fr. CC.

Art. 18(1): I. The early settlement of the debt on the accrued gains can be sought in the event that the management of assets by one spouse is such that it compromises the interests of the other spouse in the calculation of the debt. This shall apply, in particular, when one spouse commits any actions which, under Art. 10(2) (with the exception of point 1(b)), can lead to a notional inclusion in the final assets (*Expl. Report, Art. 18).* In this case, the mere apprehension of a financial loss or separate living do not

Article 18
Premature Settlement of Debt on the Accrued Gains

(1) If a spouse manages his or her assets in such a way that he or she adversely affects the rights of the other in the calculation of the debt on the accrued gains, the other spouse can demand premature settlement of the debt on the accrued gains. This shall apply in particular in cases that result in notional inclusion pursuant to Article 10 paragraph (2).

(2) When the decision through which the petition is granted becomes final and binding, the separation of matrimonial property shall apply for the spouses.

Articolo 18
Conguaglio anticipato degli incrementi patrimoniali

(1) Se un coniuge amministra il suo patrimonio in modo da pregiudicare i diritti dell'altro nel computare il credito di calcolo del incrementi patrimoniali, l'altro coniuge può pretendere il conguaglio anticipato dell'incremento patrimoniale. Questo vale in particolare nei casi che conducono alla riunione fittizia secondo l'articolo 10, comma 2.

(2) Con il passaggio in giudicato della decisione che accoglie la domanda, vige fra i coniugi il regime di separazione dei beni.

Artículo 18
Liquidación anticipada del crédito de participación

(1) Podrá solicitarse la liquidación anticipada del crédito de participación cuando la gestión del patrimonio propio de uno de los cónyuges comprometa los derechos del otro en el cómputo del crédito de participación. Ello rige especialmente en los casos que llevan a la adición ficticia conforme al artículo 10 apartado 2.

(2) En el momento en que sea firme la decisión judicial, los cónyuges quedarán sometidos al régimen matrimonial de separación de bienes.

---

suffice (Dethloff, *RabelsZ* 76 (2012), 509, 530, resulting lower protection than in German law). – **II.** In contrast to Art. 1580 fr. CC, Art. 18 also enables the debtor spouse to claim early settlement if the actions of the other spouse, under Art. 18(1), adversely affect the amount of the debt on the accrued gains at his or her expense. If the debt is compromised, it may be useful to obtain provisional measures in court for the protection of the claim. – **III.** The provisional measures are not governed in the optional matrimonial property regime of the community of accrued gains. As such, the provisions of the state where the claim is submitted shall apply. In France the application of the measures of Art. 220-1 fr. CC can be requested. In Germany, the debt on the accrued gains can be secured by way of provisional measures through a preventive seizure under §916 ZPO (*Expl. Report, Art. 18).*

KAPITEL VII

Schlussbestimmungen

Artikel 19
Zeitliche Anwendung

Dieses Abkommen findet auf die Eheverträge Anwendung, die die Ehegatten nach seinem Inkrafttreten geschlossen haben.

CHAPITRE VII

Dispositions finales

Article 19
Application dans le temps

Le présent accord s'appliquera pour les contrats conclus par les époux après son entrée en vigueur.

Commentary

Art. 19: The Agreement shall apply to marriage contracts that the spouses have concluded after its entry into force.

CHAPTER VII

Final Provisions

Article 19
Temporal Application

The present Agreement shall apply to marriage contracts that the spouses have concluded after the entry into force thereof.

CAPITOLO VII

Disposizioni finali

Articolo 19
Applicazione temporale

Il presente accordo si applica ai contratti matrimoniali stipulati dai coniugi dopo la sua entrata in vigore.

CAPÍTULO VII

Disposiciones finales

Artículo 19
Aplicación temporal

El presente Acuerdo se aplicará a las capitulaciones matrimoniales otorgadas por los cónyuges después de su entrada en vigor.

Artikel 20
Ratifikation und Inkrafttreten

(1) Dieses Abkommen bedarf der Ratifikation.

(2) Dieses Abkommen tritt am ersten Tag des Monats in Kraft, der dem Austausch der Ratifikationsurkunden folgt.

(3) Dieses Abkommen gilt zunächst zehn Jahre. Nach Ablauf dieser zehn Jahre wird es stillschweigend auf unbestimmte Zeit verlängert.

(4) Dieses Abkommen kann frühestens zehn Jahre nach seinem Inkrafttreten durch einen Vertragsstaat gekündigt werden. Das Abkommen tritt am ersten Tag des dreizehnten Monats außer Kraft, der dem Tag des Eingangs der Notifikation beim anderen Vertragsstaat folgt.

Article 20
Ratification et entrée en vigueur

(1) Le présent accord est soumis à ratification.

(2) Le présent accord entrera en vigueur le premier jour du mois suivant l'échange des instruments de ratification.

(3) Le présent accord est conclu pour une période initiale de dix ans. A l'issue de cette période initiale de dix ans, il est renouvelable par tacite reconduction pour une durée indéterminée.

(4) Le présent accord peut être dénoncé par un des Etats contractants au plus tôt à l'expiration de la dixième année après son entrée en vigueur. Le présent accord cessera de produire ses effets le premier jour du treizième mois suivant la date de la réception de la notification par l'autre Etat contractant.

Commentary

Art. 20
§1519 BGB.

Art. 20(1): I. This Agreement shall be subject to ratification in accordance with the applicable provisions of international law. – **II.** The *Deutsch-Französischer Ministerrat* signed the Agreement on 4 February 2010. After ratification by the *Deutscher Bundestag* (see the German Ratification Act of 15 March 2012, *BGBl.* 2012, II, p. 178 and the announcement of the entry into force on 22 April 2013, *BGBl.* 2013, II, p. 431)) and the National Assembly (see the French Ratifications Act, *Loi no. 2013-98 du 28 janvier 2013 autorisant la ratification de l'accord entre la République francaise et la République fédérale d'Allemaigne instituant un régime matrimonial optionnel de la partecipation aux acquets, JORF no. 0024 du 29 janvier 2013*, p. 1721), resulting in the exchange of instruments of ratification, and following publication in their official collections.
Art. 20(2): I. The Agreement entered into force on 1 May 2013. – **II.** In Germany the Ratification Act of 15 March 2012 introduced the §1519 BGB (Agreement by way of marriage contract): "If the

Article 20
Ratification and Entry into Force

(1) The present Agreement shall be subject to ratification.

(2) The present Agreement shall enter into force on the first day of the month following the exchange of the ratification instruments.

(3) The present Agreement shall initially remain in force for ten years. After these ten years it shall be renewed tacitly for an indefinite period of time.

(4) The present Agreement can be denounced by a contracting State at the earliest ten years following its entry into force. The present Agreement shall cease to have effect on the first day of the thirteenth month following the date of receipt of notification by the other contracting State.

Articolo 20
Ratifica ed entrata in vigore

(1) Il presente accordo è soggetto a ratifica.

(2) Il presente accordo entrerà in vigore il primo giorno del mese successivo allo scambio degli strumenti di ratifica.

(3) Il presente accordo vige per un periodo iniziale di dieci anni. Al termine di questo periodo di dieci anni l'accordo è rinnovato automaticamente per un periodo indeterminato.

(4) L'accordo può essere disdetto da uno Stato contraente a partire dalla scadenza del decimo anno dalla sua entrata in vigore. L'accordo cesserà di avere effetto il primo giorno del tredicesimo mese successivo alla data di ricevimento della notifica all'altro Stato contraente.

Artículo 20
Ratificación y entrada en vigor

(1) El presente Acuerdo está sujeto a ratificación.

(2) El presente Acuerdo entrará en vigor el primer día del mes siguiente al intercambio de los instrumentos de ratificación.

(3) El presente Acuerdo se concluye por un plazo inicial de diez años renovables tácitamente de forma indefinida.

(4) El presente Acuerdo podrá ser denunciado por uno de los Estados contratantes a partir des transcurso de diez años desde su entrada en vigor. El presente Acuerdo quedará sin vigencia el primer día del decimotercer mes siguiente a la fecha de la recepción de la notificación por el otro Estado contratante.

---

spouses agree by way of marriage contract on the optional matrimonial property regime of the community of accrued gains, the provisions of the Agreement of 4 February 2010 between the Federal Republic of Germany and the French Republic on the optional matrimonial property regime of the community of accrued gains shall apply. §1368 shall apply accordingly. §1412 shall not apply."
Art. 20(3): The Agreement shall initially remain in force for ten years. After these ten years it shall be tacitly renewed for an indefinite period of time. However, the Agreement can be terminated by any party to the Agreement.
Art. 20(4): I. The question arises as to how the remittal would understood if the Agreement – potentially as a result of termination – was not valid anymore. The government assumes that if the Agreement were terminated on the part of France it would remain valid in the form of German law (Braun, *MittBayNot* 2012, 89, 90). – **II.** In case of the Agreement's expiry through termination the creation of transitional provisions is expected (Stürner, *JZ* 2011, 545, 549).

Artikel 21
Beitritt

(1) Nach Inkrafttreten dieses Abkommens kann jeder Mitgliedstaat der Europäischen Union diesem Abkommen beitreten. Im Fall des Beitritts eines oder mehrerer Staaten handelt die Regierung der Bundesrepublik Deutschland als Verwahrer des Übereinkommens. Die Beitrittsurkunden sind beim Verwahrer zu hinterlegen.

(2) Das Übereinkommen tritt für den beitretenden Staat am ersten Tag des Monats in Kraft, der auf die Hinterlegung der Beitrittsurkunde folgt. Der Verwahrer notifiziert den Vertragsstaaten jeden neuen Beitritt, sowie den Zeitpunkt des Inkrafttretens des Übereinkommens für die beitretenden Staaten.

(3) Ab dem Zeitpunkt des Beitritts eines oder mehrerer Staaten ist eine Kündigung dem Verwahrer zu notifizieren. Jeder Vertragsstaat kann dieses Übereinkommen frühestens zehn Jahre, nachdem es für ihn in Kraft getreten ist, kündigen. Die Kündigung wird am ersten Tag des dreizehnten Monats wirksam, der dem Tag des Eingangs der Notifikation beim Verwahrer folgt. Der Verwahrer notifiziert den Vertragsstaaten jede Kündigung und das Datum, an dem diese Kündigung wirksam wird.

Article 21
Adhésion

(1) Après l'entrée en vigueur du présent accord, tout Etat membre de l'Union européenne peut adhérer à celui-ci. En cas d'adhésion d'un ou de plusieurs Etats, le Gouvernement de la République fédérale d'Allemagne agira comme dépositaire de l´accord. Les instruments d'adhésion seront déposés auprès du dépositaire.

(2) Le présent accord entrera en vigueur pour l'Etat adhérent le premier jour du mois suivant le dépôt de son instrument d'adhésion. Le dépositaire notifie toute nouvelle adhésion aux Etats contractants, ainsi que la date d'entrée en vigueur de l'accord pour les Etats adhérents.

(3) Après l'adhésion d'un ou de plusieurs Etats contractants, la dénonciation du présent accord doit être notifiée au dépositaire. Chaque Etat contractant peut dénoncer le présent accord au plus tôt dix ans après son entrée en vigueur pour lui. Cette dénonciation entre en vigueur pour l'Etat qui l'a notifiée le premier jour du treizième mois suivant la date de la réception de la notification. Le dépositaire notifie toute dénonciation aux Etats contractants, ainsi que la date d'entrée en vigueur de la dénonciation.

Commentary

Art. 21(1): I. Due to the increasing mobility of married couples in the European Union, it is preferable to also allow the other Member States to accede to the Agreement at a later date. – **II.** In the case of accession of one or more states, Germany shall act as depositary for the Agreement.

Article 21
Accession

(1) Following the entry into force of the present Agreement, any Member State of the European Union can accede to the present Agreement. In the case of accession of one or of more States, the Government of the Federal Republic of Germany shall act as depositary for the Agreement. The instruments of accession shall be deposited with the depositary.

(2) The Agreement shall enter into force for the acceding State on the first day of the month following deposit of the instruments of accession. The depositary shall notify the contracting States of every new accession and of the date of entry into force of the Agreement for the acceding States.

(3) As of the date of accession of one or of more States, any denunciation shall be notified to the depositary. Any contracting State can denounce the present Agreement at the earliest ten years following its entry into force for that State. The denunciation shall take effect on the first day of the thirteenth month following the day of receipt of the notification by the depositary. The depositary shall notify the contracting States of every denunciation and of the date upon which this denunciation takes effect.

Articolo 21
Adesione

(1) Dopo l'entrata in vigore del presente accordo, qualsiasi Stato membro dell'Unione europea può aderire ad esso. In caso di adesione di uno o più Stati, il Governo della Repubblica Federale di Germania fungerà da depositario dell'accordo. Gli strumenti di adesione devono essere depositati presso il depositario.

(2) L'accordo entrerà in vigore per lo Stato aderente il primo giorno del mese successivo al deposito del suo strumento di adesione. Il depositario notifica ogni nuova adesione agli Stati contraenti, nonché la data di entrata in vigore dell'accordo per i paesi aderenti.

(3) Dopo l'adesione di uno o più Stati contraenti, la disdetta del presente accordo deve essere notificata al depositario. Ogni Stato contraente può disdire il presente accordo non prima che siano trascorsi dieci anni dalla sua entrata in vigore in quello Stato. La disdetta produrrà effetto per lo Stato che l'ha notificata dal primo giorno del tredicesimo mese successivo alla data di ricevimento della notifica. Il depositario notifica agli Stati contraenti ogni disdetta nonché la data di efficacia della medesima.

Artículo 21
Adhesión

(1) Después de la entrada en vigor del presente Acuerdo, todos los Estados miembros de la Unión Europea podrán adherirse al mismo. En caso de la adhesión de uno o más Estados, el Gobierno de la República Federal de Alemania actuará como depositario del Acuerdo. Los instrumentos de adhesión deberán ser depositados ante el depositario.

(2) Para el Estado que se adhiera, el Acuerdo entrará en vigor el primer día del mes siguiente al depósito del instrumento de adhesión. El depositario notificará a los Estados contratantes cada nueva adhesión, así como la fecha de entrada en vigor del Acuerdo para los Estados que se adhieren.

(3) A partir de la fecha de la adhesión de uno o más Estados, la denuncia del presente Acuerdo deberá ser notificada al depositario. Cada Estado contratante podrá denunciar el presente Acuerdo una vez transcurridos diez años a partir de su entrada en vigor para este Estado. La denuncia será eficaz el primer día del decimotercer mes siguiente a la fecha de la recepción de la notificación por parte del depositario. El depositario notificará a todos los Estados contratantes cada denuncia y la fecha de eficacia de esta denuncia.

Artikel 22
Sprachen des Übereinkommens

Beim Beitritt eines Staates entscheiden die Vertragsstaaten über die Festlegung einer weiteren verbindlichen Sprachfassung.

Article 22
Régime linguistique de l'accord

Les Etats contractants décident, lors de l'adhésion d'un autre Etat, s'il y a lieu ou non d'établir une version linguistique supplémentaire faisant foi.

Commentary

Art. 22: In the case of accession, a further binding version of the Agreement can be produced in the official language of the acceding State.

Article 22
Languages of the Agreement

Upon accession of a State the contracting States shall decide upon the stipulation of a further binding version in another language.

Articolo 22
Regime linguistico dell'accordo

Gli Stati contraenti decidono, nel momento dell'adesione da parte di un altro Stato, sulla determinazione di un'ulteriore versione linguistica vincolante.

Artículo 22
Régimen lingüístico del Acuerdo

A la adhesión de un Estado, los Estados contratantes decidirán sobre el establecimiento de una versión lingüística adicional auténtica.

Artikel 23
Registrierung

Die Registrierung dieses Abkommens beim Sekretariat der Vereinten Nationen nach Artikel 102 der Charta der Vereinten Nationen wird unverzüglich nach seinem Inkrafttreten durch die Regierung der Bundesrepublik Deutschland veranlasst.

Geschehen zu Paris am 4. Februar 2010 in zwei Urschriften, jede in deutscher und in französischer Sprache, wobei jeder Wortlaut gleichermaßen verbindlich ist.

Article 23
Enregistrement

Le présent accord sera enregistré sans délai, dès son entrée en vigueur, par le Gouvernement de la République fédérale d'Allemagne auprès du Secrétariat des Nations Unies conformément à l'article 102 de la Charte des Nations Unies.

Fait à Paris, le 4 février 2010 en deux originaux, chacun en langues allemande et française, les deux textes faisant également foi.

Commentary

Art. 23: The present agreement has been submitted by the Government of the Federal Republic of Germany for registration with the Secretariat of the United Nations pursuant to Art. 102 of the Charter of the United Nations.

Article 23
Registration

The present Agreement shall be submitted by the Government of the Federal Republic of Germany for registration with the Secretariat of the United Nations pursuant to Article 102 of the Charter of the United Nations immediately following its entry into force.

Done at Paris on February 4, 2010 in duplicate in the German and French languages, both texts being equally authentic.

Articolo 23
Registrazione

La registrazione del presente accordo sarà disposta immediatamente, dopo la sua entrata in vigore, dal Governo della Repubblica Federale di Germania presso il Segretariato delle Nazioni Unite, a norma dell'articolo 102 della Carta delle Nazioni Unite.

Redatto a Parigi, il 4 febbraio 2010 in due originali, entrambi nelle lingua tedesca e francese, ove entrambi i testi sono vincolanti.

Artículo 23
Registro

Inmediatamente después de su entrada en vigor, el Gobierno de la República Federal de Alemania se encargará del registro de este Acuerdo en el Secretariado de las Naciones Unidas conforme al artículo 102 de la Carta de las Naciones Unidas.

Hecho en París, el 4 de febrero de 2010, en dos originales, cada uno en los idiomas alemán y francés, siendo cada texto igualmente auténtico.

PART III
EXPLANATIONS

GERMAN

CONTENTS

DENKSCHRIFT*

I. ALLGEMEINES

1. AUSGANGSSITUATION

Ehen mit Auslandsberührung sind weit verbreitet. Im Jahr 2009 hatten bei 13 Prozent der in Deutschland lebenden Ehepaare entweder beide Ehegatten eine ausländische oder ein Ehegatte eine deutsche, der andere Ehegatte eine ausländische Staatsangehörigkeit. Hinzu kommen deutsche Ehepaare, die im Ausland leben, sowie ausländische Ehepaare, die in der Bundesrepublik Deutschland leben. Da sich die rechtlichen Folgen der Ehe unter anderem nach der Staatsangehörigkeit richten, können Ehen mit Auslandsbezug zu rechtlichen Schwierigkeiten, insbesondere im Hinblick auf güterrechtliche Fragen führen. Gesetzlicher Güterstand in der Bundesrepublik Deutschland ist die Zugewinngemeinschaft. Die Vermögen der Ehegatten bleiben getrennt, nur am Ende des Güterstandes – etwa wegen Scheidung – wird der in der Ehe erwirtschaftete Zugewinn ausgeglichen. Gesetzlicher Güterstand in der Französischen Republik ist die Errungenschaftsgemeinschaft. Errungenschaften während der Ehe werden zum gemeinsamen Vermögen. Lebt zum Beispiel ein Paar in der Errungenschaftsgemeinschaft nach französischem Recht in der Bundesrepublik Deutschland, so zeigen sich Probleme, wenn die Ehegatten in diesem Güterstand ein Grundstück in der Bundesrepublik Deutschland erwerben. Da der französische Güterstand in der Regel in der Bundesrepublik Deutschland nicht bekannt ist, führt zum Beispiel die präzise Einschätzung der Tragweite der den einzelnen Eheleuten zustehenden Rechte bei Eintragung eines Eigentumsrechts in das Grundbuch zu erheblichen Unsicherheiten. Für ein deutsches Kreditinstitut ist insbesondere fraglich, welche Auswirkungen Verbindlichkeiten eines Ehegatten oder seine Insolvenz auf das in der Errungenschaftsgemeinschaft gebundene Vermögen haben. Die praktisch häufig anzutreffende Lösung, dass für in der Bundesrepublik Deutschland belegenes Vermögen gemäß Artikel 15 Absatz 2 EGBGB deutsches Güterrecht gewählt wird, beantwortet zwar diese Frage, mutet den Ehegatten aber einen gespaltenen Güterstand zu, der bei einem güterrechtlichen Ausgleich zu Abrechnungsschwierigkeiten führen kann. Ähnliche Probleme werden deutsche Paare in der

* Bundesrat Drucksache 67/11, of 4 February 2011, pp. 18–19. This text is reproduced under the Creative Commons Licence 3.0 (Germany).

Französischen Republik angesichts der gänzlich anderen Traditionen vorfinden. Auch in den anderen Ländern der Europäischen Union ist das Eherecht national sehr unterschiedlich ausgestaltet.

Angesichts dieser Situation besteht ein Bedürfnis, international möglichst vergleichbare oder identische Regelungen zu schaffen, die den Betroffenen Rechtsklarheit und Rechtssicherheit bieten. Auf europäischer Ebene wird daher nach gemeinsamen Antworten auf die Fragen gesucht, welches nationale Recht bei Ehen mit Auslandsberührung Anwendung findet und welche Gerichte zuständig sind. Hingegen steht eine inhaltliche Angleichung des Familienrechts in den Mitgliedstaaten aufgrund von unterschiedlichen, häufig in Jahrhunderten gewachsenen und tief in der Bevölkerung verwurzelten Rechtstraditionen derzeit nicht auf der europäischen Agenda. Deshalb verspricht der in diesem Abkommen verfolgte Ansatz, zunächst bilateral und für einen überschaubaren Rechtsbereich zu handeln, um möglichst schnell Lösungen für die betroffenen Eheleute anzubieten, ein effizienter Weg zu sein. Dazu gibt es für die Französische Republik und die Bundesrepublik Deutschland auch einen politischen Auftrag. Aus der gemeinsamen Erklärung zum 40. Jahrestag des Elysée-Vertrages 2003 stammt der Wunsch, das deutsche und französische Familienrecht einander anzugleichen.

2. GRUNDZÜGE DES GELTENDEN INTERNATIONALEN PRIVATRECHTS

Die güterrechtlichen Kollisionsvorschriften der Bundesrepublik Deutschland und der Französischen Republik sind relativ ähnlich. Dies gilt insbesondere für die Möglichkeiten der Rechtswahl gemäß Artikel 15 Absatz 2 EGBGB. Danach können Ehegatten deutsches Recht wählen, wenn mindestens ein Ehegatte die deutsche Staatsanghörigkeit besitzt oder seinen gewöhnlichen Aufenthalt in der Bundesrepublik Deutschland hat. Für unbewegliches Vermögen, das in der Bundesrepublik Deutschland belegen ist, kann ebenfalls deutsches Recht gewählt werden.

In der Französischen Republik kann das französische Recht für die güterrechtlichen Wirkungen der Ehe nach dem Haager Übereinkommen vom 14. März 1978 über das auf eheliche Güterstände anwendbare Recht gewählt werden. Dieses Abkommen enthält neben den im deutschen Recht bekannten Voraussetzungen einen weiteren Tatbestand: Die Eheleute können französisches. Recht wählen, wenn einer der Ehegatten seinen ersten gewöhnlichen Aufenthalt nach der Eheschließung in der Französischen Republik begründet.

3. WESENTLICHER INHALT DES ABKOMMENS

Am 4. Februar 2010 haben aus Anlass des deutsch-französischen Ministerrates in Paris die Justizministerinnen beider Länder das Abkommen über den Güterstand der Wahl-Zugewinngemeinschaft unterzeichnet, mit dem erstmals einheitliches materielles Recht auf dem Gebiet des Familienrechts für die Bundesrepublik Deutschland und die Französische Republik geschaffen werden soll und in dem ein in der Bundesrepublik Deutschland und der Französischen Republik identischer Wahlgüterstand normiert wird. Dieser Güterstand entspricht in seiner Grundstruktur dem deutschen Zugewinnausgleich, weist aber auch Modifikationen auf, die der französischen Rechtstradition Rechnung tragen. Ehegatten in beiden Ländern können diesen Güterstand anstelle des gesetzlichen Güterstandes neben den anderen nationalen Wahlgüterständen wählen. Damit soll Ehegatten ein Wahlgüterstand zur Verfügung gestellt werden, der sowohl in der Französischen Republik als auch in der Bundesrepublik Deutschland identisch ist und dadurch in beiden Staaten rechtliche Schwierigkeiten beseitigt, die im Hinblick auf unbekannte ausländische Güterstandsregelungen entstehen können.

II. BESONDERES

Hinsichtlich der Entstehungsgeschichte des Abkommens und des Inhalts der einzelnen Vorschriften wird auf den Erläuternden Bericht Bezug genommen. Dieser Bericht ist dieser Denkschrift in deutscher und französischer Sprachfassung als Anlage beigefügt.

Zu Artikel 1

Der Güterstand der Wahl-Zugewinngemeinschaft steht gemäß Artikel 1 Ehegatten zur Verfügung, deren Güterstand dem Sachrecht eines Vertragsstaates unterliegt. Er ist daher wählbar, sofern entweder deutsches oder französisches Recht auf den Güterstand der Ehegatten Anwendung findet. Eines direkten internationalen Bezuges bedarf es nicht, sondern auch ein in der Bundesrepublik Deutschland lebendes Ehepaar ohne Verbindung zur Französischen Republik kann diesen Güterstand vertraglich vereinbaren.

Zu Artikel 2

Inhaltlich legt Artikel 2 fest, dass das Vermögen der Ehegatten in der Wahl-Zugewinngemeinschaft getrennt bleibt und „Zugewinn“ der Betrag ist, um den das Endvermögen das Anfangsvermögen eines Ehegatten übersteigt. Ausgeglichen wird der Zugewinn grundsätzlich erst bei Beendigung des Güterstandes.

Zu Artikel 3

Die Vereinbarung des Güterstandes erfolgt gemäß Artikel 3 Absatz 1 durch Ehevertrag. Artikel 3 Absatz 2 legt fest, dass der Vertrag vor und während des Bestandes der Ehe geschlossen werden kann; wirksam wird er jedoch frühestens mit dem Tag der Eheschließung.

Zu den Artikeln 4 bis 6

Artikel 4 bestimmt, dass jeder Ehegatte grundsätzlich allein über sein Vermögen verfügen kann. Artikel 5 Absatz 1 nimmt von diesem Grundsatz jedoch die Verfügungen eines Ehegatten über Haushaltsgegenstände und Rechte, durch die die Familienwohnung sichergestellt wird, aus und unterstellt sie dem Genehmigungsvorbehalt des anderen Ehegatten. Ferner werden gemäß Artikel 6 Absatz 1 Ehegatten aus Verträgen zur Führung des Haushalts und für den Bedarf der Kinder gesamtschuldnerisch verpflichtet, es sei denn, ein Ehegatte geht den Vermögensverhältnissen unangemessene Zahlungsverpflichtungen ein, was dem Vertragspartner bekannt ist oder hätte bekannt sein müssen (Artikel 6 Absatz 2).

Zu den Artikeln 7 bis 14

Gemäß Artikel 7 endet der Güterstand mit dem Tod oder der Todeserklärung eines Ehegatten, dem Wechsel des Güterstandes oder mit Rechtskraft der Ehescheidung oder jeder anderen gerichtlichen Entscheidung, die den Güterstand beendet. Um die Zugewinnausgleichsforderung zu ermitteln, bedarf es des Vergleichs zwischen den jeweiligen Anfangs- und Endvermögen der Ehegatten. Dabei enthalten die Artikel 8 und 9 die zur Festsetzung des Anfangsvermögens relevanten Bestimmungen; das Endvermögen wird anhand der Artikel 10 und 11 ermittelt. Das Anfangsvermögen ist das Vermögen jedes. Ehegatten am Tag des Eintritts in den Güterstand, das Endvermögen das beim Ende des Güterstandes, wobei auch die Verbindlichkeiten des Ehegatten jeweils zu berücksichtigen sind, selbst wenn sie das Aktivvermögen übersteigen. Gemäß Artikel 12 kann der Ehegatte, dessen Zugewinn geringer ist, von dem anderen Ehegatten die Hälfte des Überschusses als Zugewinnausgleichsforderung verlangen. Gemäß Artikel 14 ist die Zugewinnausgleichsforderung jedoch auf den halben Wert des Endvermögens des Ausgleichspflichtigen begrenzt.

Zu den Artikeln 15 bis 18

Die Artikel 15 bis 18 enthalten Vorschriften über die Verjährung, die gegenseitige Auskunftspflicht der Ehegatten zur Ermittlung der Zugewinnausgleichs forderung, zur Stundung und zum vorzeitigen Zugewinnausgleich. Letzterer ist insbesondere im Falle böswilliger Verfügungen eines Ehegatten zuungunsten der Zugewinnausgleichsforderung des anderen denkbar.

Zu den Artikeln 19 bis 23

Artikel 19 bestimmt, dass das Abkommen nur für Eheverträge Anwendung findet, die nach seinem Inkrafttreten geschlossen werden. Gemäß Artikel 20 Absatz 1 bedarf es der Ratifikation beider Staaten und tritt gemäß Artikel 20 Absatz 2 am ersten Tag nach dem Austausch der Ratifikationsurkunden in Kraft. Die Ratifikationsurkunden sind bei der Regierung der Bundesrepublik Deutschland zu hinterlegen. Gemäß Artikel 21 steht es auch allen anderen Mitgliedstaaten der Europäischen Union zum Beitritt offen. Artikel 22 enthält eine Bestimmung über die Sprachen des Abkommens und Artikel 23 die Regelung, dass die Bundesrepublik Deutschland das Abkommen nach Inkrafttreten unmittelbar bei den Vereinten Nationen anmelden wird.

ANLAGE ZUR DENKSCHRIFT*

ERLÄUTERNDER BERICHT

A. ALLGEMEINER TEIL

1. AUSGANGSLAGE

Ehen zwischen Angehörigen verschiedener Staaten sind heute keine Seltenheit mehr. Bei ca. 13% der Eheschließungen (im Jahr 2006) und Ehescheidungen (im Jahr 2005) in Deutschland hatten die Ehegatten unterschiedliche Staatsangehörigkeiten.

Im Jahr 2006 lag in Frankreich der Prozentsatz der Eheschließungen binationaler Paare bei 14,59%. Außerdem beliefen sich die deutsch-französischen Ehen im Jahr 2003 in Frankreich auf 2% aller binationalen Eheschließungen.

Das eheliche Güterrecht regelt die rechtlichen Auswirkungen einer Eheschließung auf das Vermögen der Ehegatten, die vermögensrechtlichen Beziehungen der Ehegatten zueinander und die vermögensrechtlichen Beziehungen der Ehegatten zu Dritten. Die Bestimmung des Güterstandes ist nicht nur von Bedeutung für die Frage, wie die vermögensrechtlichen Bindungen der Eheleute mit Beendigung des Güterstandes wieder aufgelöst werden. Der Güterstand hat auch Auswirkungen während bestehender Ehe, z. B. auf die Vermögensverwaltung und den Vermögenserwerb, aber eben auch für die Haftung des einen Ehegatten für die vor und während der Ehe eingegangenen Verbindlichkeiten des anderen Ehegatten.

Das internationale Privatrecht der Staaten räumt den Ehegatten in bestimmten Fällen die Wahl des auf den Güterstand anzuwendenden Rechts ein.

Die Ehegatten haben die Wahl, ihren ehelichen Güterstand nach bestimmten Kriterien dem französischen oder dem deutschen Recht zu unterstellen.

So räumt das deutsche internationale Privatrecht (Artikel 15 Absatz 2 EGBGB) den Ehegatten die Möglichkeit ein, die güterrechtlichen Wirkungen ihrer Ehe dem deutschen Recht zu unterstellen, wenn:

- einer von ihnen die deutsche Staatsangehörigkeit besitzt;
- einer von ihnen seinen gewöhnlichen Aufenthalt in Deutschland hat;

* Bundesrat Drucksache 67/11, of 4 February 2011, pp. 20–40. This text is reproduced under the Creative Commons Licence 3.0 (Germany).

– unbewegliches Vermögen der Ehegatten in Deutschland belegen ist, für dieses Vermögen.

Haben die Ehegatten das anzuwendende Recht nicht gewählt, kommen die objektiven Anknüpfungen in Artikel 15 Absatz 1 in Verbindung mit Artikel 14 EGBGB zum Tragen. Deutsches Güterrecht ist danach beispielsweise anzuwenden, wenn beide Ehegatten Deutsche sind oder wenn sie ihren gewöhnlichen Aufenthalt während der Ehe in Deutschland haben.

Nach französischem Recht gestattet das Haager Übereinkommen über das auf eheliche Güterstände anwendbare Recht vom 14. März 1978 den Ehegatten, die güterrechtlichen Wirkungen ihrer Ehe dem französischen Recht zu unterwerfen, wenn:

– einer von ihnen die französische Staatsangehörigkeit besitzt;
– einer von ihnen seinen gewöhnlichen Aufenthalt in Frankreich hat;
– einer von ihnen seinen ersten gewöhnlichen Aufenthalt nach der Eheschließung in Frankreich begründet.

Außerdem können Ehegatten für die in Frankreich belegenen unbeweglichen Sachen französisches Recht wählen (Artikel 3 des genannten Haager Übereinkommens).

Wenn die Ehegatten keine Rechtswahl getroffen haben, findet auf ihren Güterstand das Recht des Staates Anwendung, in dem sie nach der Eheschließung ihren ersten gewöhnlichen Aufenthalt begründet haben.

Wenn deutsches oder französisches Sachrecht zur Anwendung kommt, ergeben sich für die Ehegatten folgende Wahlmöglichkeiten von deutschen oder französischen Güterständen:

a) Deutsches Güterrecht
   Das deutsche Güterrecht kennt drei Güterstände:
   - Zugewinngemeinschaft;
   - Gütertrennung;
   - Gütergemeinschaft.

   Die Zugewinngemeinschaft ist der gesetzliche Güterstand. Die anderen Güterstände kommen erst zur Anwendung, wenn die Eheleute dies in einem Ehevertrag vereinbart haben.
b) Französisches Güterrecht
   Das französische Güterrecht kennt ebenfalls drei Arten von Güterständen:
   - Gütergemeinschaft (Fahrnis- und Errungenschaftsgemeinschaft, allgemeine Gütergemeinschaft);
   - Zugewinngemeinschaft;
   - Gütertrennung.

In Frankreich ist die Errungenschaftsgemeinschaft der gesetzliche Güterstand. Die anderen Güterstände kommen erst zur Anwendung, wenn die Eheleute dies in einem Ehevertrag vereinbart haben.

Die Unterschiede schon zwischen den beiden gesetzlichen Güterständen sind erheblich:

Zugewinngemeinschaft nach deutschem Recht bedeutet Gütertrennung während des Bestehens des Güterstandes mit einem Ausgleich des Zugewinns nach Beendigung des Güterstandes, §1363 Absatz 2 des Bürgerlichen Gesetzbuchs (BGB). Der Güterstand führt damit nicht von selbst zu einem gemeinschaftlichen Eigentum der Ehegatten. Vielmehr behält jeder Ehegatte sein vor und während der Ehe erworbenes Vermögen als sein Eigentum und haftet im Gegenzug auch nur für seine Schulden mit seinem Vermögen. Das gilt letztlich auch für einen Gegenstand, der beiden Ehegatten zu bestimmten Teilen gehört (sog. Bruchteilsgemeinschaft). So kann z. B. bei einem Haus, das beiden Ehegatten jeweils zur Hälfte gehört, jeder Ehegatte grundsätzlich über seine Hälfte verfügen.

Die Errungenschaftsgemeinschaft französischen Rechts dagegen kennt drei verschiedene Gütermassen: das Eigengut der Ehefrau, das Eigengut des Ehemannes und das Gemeingut (Gesamtgut).

Das Gemeingut setzt sich nach Artikel 1401 des Code Civil (CC) aus den Errungenschaften zusammen, die die Eheleute entweder allein oder gemeinsam während der Ehe erworben haben. Dazu gehört auch all das, was aufgrund eigener Arbeit erworben wurde oder was als Früchte oder Ertrag aus den eigenen Gütern erwirtschaftet wurde. Zwar darf jeder Ehegatte grundsätzlich das Gemeingut allein und selbständig verwalten und darüber verfügen. Allerdings dürfen bestimmte Handlungen nur von den Ehegatten gemeinsam vorgenommen werden. So darf er Schenkungen unter Lebenden aus dem Gemeingut nur mit Zustimmung des anderen vornehmen. Ferner kann in Frankreich einigen unabhängig vom ehelichen Güterstand geltenden Regeln des „régime primaire" zufolge insbesondere die Befugnis der Ehegatten eingeschränkt werden, allein über das Gemeingut zu verfügen.

So kann ein Ehegatte weder allein über die Rechte, durch die die Familienwohnung sichergestellt wird, noch über die Haushaltsgegenstände verfügen (Auflösung des Mietvertrages oder Veräußerung der Familienwohnung). Diese Einschränkung würde sogar gelten, wenn die Ehewohnung ein Eigengut des Ehegatten ist.

2. ZWECKMÄSSIGKEIT DER SCHAFFUNG EINES GEMEINSAMEN GÜTERSTANDES

Die Schaffung eines gemeinsamen Güterstandes, der nach identischen Vorschriften in den Vertragsstaaten zusammengesetzt, praktisch gestaltet und aufgelöst wird, stellt für Paare, Dritte und Rechtsanwender einen erheblichen rechtlichen Fortschritt dar. Mit dieser Güterstandsregelung wird im Ergebnis in den Vertragsstaaten ein gemeinsames materielles Recht geschaffen.

Wählt das Paar diese Form der Gemeinschaft, führt dies nicht zu den Schwierigkeiten, die gegenwärtig aus der Begründung der Errungenschaftsgemeinschaft nach französischem Recht entstehen, wenn die Ehegatten während der Ehe ein Grundstück in Deutschland erwerben. Da dieser gesetzliche französische Güterstand in Deutschland nicht bekannt ist, gestattet es die Eintragung eines Eigentumsrechts in das Grundbuch Dritten nicht, die präzise Tragweite der den einzelnen Ehegatten zustehenden Rechte einzuschätzen. Die praktisch häufig anzutreffende Variante, dass für in Deutschland belegenes Vermögen deutsches Güterrecht gewählt wird (Artikel 15 Absatz 2 Nummer 3 EGBGB) löst zwar dieses Problem, mutet den Ehegatten aber einen gespaltenen Güterstand zu, der bei einem güterrechtlichen Ausgleich zu Abrechnungsschwierigkeiten führen kann.

Bei dieser Ausgangslage und weil es die Zugewinngemeinschaft im französischen wie deutschen Recht gibt (gesetzlicher Güterstand in Deutschland, optionaler Güterstand in Frankreich) bietet es sich an, durch ein bilaterales Abkommen einen zusätzlichen neuen Wahlgüterstand zu schaffen, der an die in beiden Staaten bereits bestehende Zugewinngemeinschaft stark angelehnt wird und nach einfachen und modernisierten Normen ausgestaltet ist, die in Frankreich und Deutschland identisch sind.

Um anderen Staaten der Europäischen Union zu ermöglichen, dem Abkommen später beizutreten, sieht dieses vor, dass nach seinem Inkrafttreten jeder Mitgliedstaat der Europäischen Union dem Abkommen beitreten kann (Artikel 21).

B. DARSTELLUNG DES GÜTERSTANDES

KAPITEL I. ANWENDUNGSBEREICH UND DEFINITION

Artikel 1. Anwendungsbereich

Der Güterstand der Wahl-Zugewinngemeinschaft soll allen Eheleuten offen stehen, für die das Güterrecht eines Vertragsstaates anwendbar ist, ohne dass die Ehe einen internationalen Bezug aufweisen müsste. Somit kann dieser optionale Güterstand von Ehegatten gewählt werden, deren ehelicher Güterstand nach dem anwendbaren internationalen Privatrecht, auch dem eines Drittstaates, dem französischen oder dem deutschen Recht unterliegt.

Das gilt beispielsweise in Anwendung des französischen oder deutschen Internationalen Privatrechts für Ehegatten,

- von denen einer französischer oder deutscher Staatsangehöriger ist;
- von denen einer seinen gewöhnlichen Aufenthalt in Frankreich oder Deutschland hat;
- von denen einer seinen ersten gewöhnlichen Aufenthalt in Frankreich begründet;
- von denen einer unbewegliches Vermögen in Frankreich oder Deutschland hat, für dieses Vermögen.

Danach kann der Güterstand der Wahl-Zugewinngemeinschaft beispielsweise zur Anwendung kommen bei zwei Deutschen, die in Frankreich leben, bei zwei Franzosen, die in Deutschland leben, aber auch bei zwei Deutschen, die in Deutschland leben und bei zwei Franzosen, die in Frankreich leben.

Die Wahl dieses Güterstandes erfordert nicht, dass die Eheleute das Recht eines Vertragsstaates wählen. Erforderlich ist nach Artikel 1 nur, dass der Güterstand dem Sachrecht eines Vertragsstaates unterliegt. Dennoch ist es in einigen Fällen zur Vermeidung von Zweifelsfragen für die Eheleute ratsam, in ihrem Ehevertrag das für ihr Güterrecht anwendbare Recht zu benennen, sofern dies nach dem internationalen Privatrecht zulässig ist.

Artikel 2. Definition

Zugewinngemeinschaft bedeutet, dass während des Bestehens des Güterstandes Gütertrennung besteht. Die Begründung des Güterstandes lässt die Eigentumsverhältnisse und Verbindlichkeiten der Ehegatten unberührt. Eine den beiden Ehegatten gemeinsame dritte Vermögensmasse wie bei Gütergemeinschaften gibt es damit nicht.

Erst mit Beendigung des Güterstandes wird dann der während des Güterstandes erwirtschaftete Vermögenszuwachs bei den beiden Vermögensmassen zwischen den Ehegatten ausgeglichen.

KAPITEL II. BEGRÜNDUNG DES GÜTERSTANDES

Artikel 3. Begründung des Güterstandes

Zu Absatz 1:
Die Eheleute können durch Ehevertrag den Güterstand der Wahl-Zugewinngemeinschaft wählen. Für die Form dieses Vertrages gilt das nach dem jeweiligen internationalen Privatrecht berufene Recht. Dabei handelt es sich um das am Ort des Vertragsschlusses anwendbare Recht oder das auf den Güterstand anwendbare innerstaatliche Recht.

Zu Absatz 2:
Die Ehegatten können vor oder während der Ehe den Güterstand der Wahl-Zugewinngemeinschaft vertraglich vereinbaren. Die Möglichkeit, einen Vertrag vor der Eheschließung zu schließen, kann z. B. bei einer Eheschließung nach französischem Recht verhindern, dass zunächst eine Errungenschaftsgemeinschaft entsteht, die dann wieder abgewickelt werden müsste, bevor ein neuer Güterstand begründet wird.

Der Eintritt des Wahlgüterstandes knüpft daran an, dass eine Ehe eingegangen wird. Aus diesem Grund kann der Güterstand der Wahl-Zugewinngemeinschaft seine Wirkungen erst entfalten, wenn die Ehe auch geschlossen wird. In Deutschland ist dies nicht ausdrücklich geregelt, sondern ergibt sich aus §1408 BGB, nach dem die Vertragsparteien Ehegatten sein müssen. In Frankreich ergibt sich das ausdrücklich aus Artikel 1395 CC.

Der gemeinsame Güterstand kann auch während der Ehe vereinbart werden.

Nach deutschem Recht können die Ehegatten jederzeit den Güterstand durch Ehevertrag ändern, um damit auch auf den gesetzlichen Güterstand der Zugewinngemeinschaft zu verzichten. Der Ehevertrag entfaltet seine Wirkung mit Vertragsschluss. Ab diesem Zeitpunkt kommen zwischen den Ehegatten die Regeln des neuen Güterstandes zur Anwendung.

Die einem französischen Güterstand unterliegenden Ehegatten können im Interesse der Familie vereinbaren, den ehelichen Güterstand nach einer Anwendungsdauer von zwei Jahren zu ändern (Artikel 1397 CC). Diese Änderung wird am Tage der Ausstellung der notariellen Urkunde wirksam, die den Wechsel vorsieht, wenn die Ehegatten keine minderjährigen Kinder haben und die volljährigen Kinder oder die Gläubiger sich dem Wechsel nicht widersetzen. Dagegen wird der Güterstandswechsel in den beiden vorgenannten Fällen zum Zeitpunkt des Urteils wirksam, in dem er festgestellt wird.

Zu Absatz 3:
Der Grundsatz der Vertragsfreiheit nach Artikel 3 Absatz 3 ermöglicht den Ehegatten, durch Vertrag von den Vorschriften zur Festsetzung der Zugewinnausgleichsforderung abzuweichen. Beispielsweise können sie die Zusammensetzung der Vermögen, die Bewertungsregeln für die Vermögensgegenstände, die Höhe der Beteiligung am jeweiligen Vermögenszuwachs und die Verteilung des Zugewinns anders regeln. Durch die Änderungsmöglichkeit kann den nationalen Besonderheiten oder den besonderen Bedürfnissen der Ehegatten Rechnung getragen werden.

Soweit der Text bestimmt, dass die Ehegatten von den Regeln des Kapitels V abweichen können, können sie nicht von den in Artikel 5 und 6 aufgeführten Regeln abweichen, in denen die wichtigsten Bestimmungen des französischen „régime primaire" aufgeführt sind. Durch die nicht mögliche Abweichung wird eine identische Anwendung des gemeinsamen Güterstandes in Frankreich und Deutschland gewährleistet.

KAPITEL III. VERMÖGENSVERWALTUNG, -NUTZUNG UND -VERFÜGUNG

Der gemeinsame Güterstand ist so gestaltet, dass für die Ehegatten der Güterstand der Gütertrennung gilt. Die Trennung des Vermögens hat zwei Auswirkungen.

Zunächst behalten die Ehegatten die Verwaltung, Nutzung und Verfügung über ihre persönlichen Vermögensgegenstände. Im Übrigen haftet jeder Ehegatte für die durch ihn vor oder während der Ehe entstandenen Schulden.

Gleichwohl ist die Trennung des Vermögens der Ehegatten insoweit nicht vollständig, als sie nicht von der Anwendung bestimmter zwingender Vorschriften abweichen können.

Soweit die Vorschriften, die die Wirkungen der Vermögenstrennung der Ehegatten in Frankreich und Deutschland begrenzen, nicht identisch sind, übernimmt der gemeinsame Güterstand die wesentlichen Bestimmungen des französischen „régime primaire“, damit das Güterrechtsregime in Frankreich und Deutschland in gleicher Weise funktionieren kann (Artikel 5 und 6).

Artikel 4. Allgemeine Bestimmungen zur Vermögensverwaltung, -nutzung und -verfügung

Ziel des Güterstandes der Zugewinngemeinschaft ist die Sicherung einer völligen Unabhängigkeit der Ehegatten in Bezug auf ihr Vermögen. Daher soll jeder Ehegatte sein Vermögen grundsätzlich allein und ohne Zustimmung des anderen Ehegatten verwalten, nutzen und auch darüber verfügen dürfen. Im Gegenzug haftet jeder Ehegatte allein für die durch ihn vor oder während der Ehe entstandenen Schulden.

Dieser Grundsatz der Trennung des Ehegattenvermögens ist in den deutschen (§1364 BGB) und französischen (Artikel 1569 CC) Zugewinnregelungen aufgeführt. Zur selbständigen Vermögensverwaltung gehört auch das Recht, Vermögen zu erwerben: Kein Ehegatte braucht z. B. für die Aufnahme einer Erwerbstätigkeit, die Gründung oder den Eintritt in eine Gesellschaft die Zustimmung des anderen.

Diese Trennung des Ehegattenvermögens enthält jedoch einige Beschränkungen, die in Artikel 5 und 6 der Güterstandsregelung aufgeführt sind.

Diese Beschränkungen gehen auf die zwingenden Regeln des französischen „régime primaire“ (Artikel 215 und 220 CC) zurück. Diese Regeln treten an die Stelle des „régime primaire“, unbeschadet der anderen Regelungen dieses Regimes; diese sind nach Maßgabe des Territorialprinzips anwendbar.

Artikel 5. Verfügungsbeschränkungen

Allgemeines:
In den Rechtsordnungen beider Länder ist die Vermögensverwaltung in Ausnahmefällen zum Schutze des anderen Ehegatten beschränkt.

In Deutschland ist für den gesetzlichen Güterstand der Zugewinngemeinschaft in §§1365, 1369 BGB ein Verfügungsverbot über das Vermögen als Ganzes und über Haushaltsgegenstände vorgesehen. Ein Verstoß gegen dieses Verfügungsverbot führt zur Unwirksamkeit des Rechtsgeschäfts, wenn es der andere Ehegatte nicht genehmigt. Die Unwirksamkeit tritt automatisch ein und wirkt gegenüber jedermann.

Frankreich kennt ebenfalls eine Verfügungsbeschränkung bei Rechten, die die Ehewohnung und den Hausrat gewährleisten. Das bedeutet z. B., dass ein Ehegatte den Mietvertrag bezüglich der Hauptwohnung ohne die Zustimmung des anderen Ehegatten nicht kündigen darf. Eine Verfügung ohne Zustimmung des anderen Ehegatten ist allerdings nicht automatisch unwirksam wie in Deutschland. Vielmehr muss der Ehegatte eine Nichtigkeitsklage erheben.

Die Kündigung kann allerdings durch den Ehegatten, der seine Zustimmung nicht erteilt hatte, genehmigt werden.

In Frankreich ist diese Verfügungsbeschränkung, die die Ehewohnung und die Einrichtung samt Hausrat sicherstellt, in Artikel 215 CC aufgeführt.

Um zu vermeiden, dass in beiden Ländern bei Vereinbarung des Güterstandes der Wahl-Zugewinngemeinschaft unterschiedliche Verfügungsbeschränkungen hinsichtlich des Rechts auf freie Verfügung über die Ehewohnung und die Haushaltsgegenstände gelten, erweitert Artikel 5 des gemeinsamen Güterstandes, der den im französischen Recht bekannten Schutz der Ehewohnung vorsieht, den Schutz auf die Haushaltsgegenstände, auf die im deutschen Recht Bezug genommen wird.

Die französische Regelung über den Hausrat (Artikel 215 CC) schützt den Ehegatten nicht so stark wie das deutsche Recht der Haushaltsgegenstände. Der gemeinsame Güterstand übernimmt daher die deutsche Schutzregel, die z. B. auch auf das für die Bedürfnisse der Familie gebrauchte Fahrzeug Anwendung findet.

Eine zusätzliche Schutzvorschrift gegen Verfügungen über das Vermögen als Ganzes ähnlich §1365 BGB erschien nicht notwendig. In vielen Fällen dürfte die Ehewohnung bereits einen Großteil des Vermögens ausmachen. Darf ein Ehegatte über sein Eigentum oder Miteigentum an der als Ehewohnung genutzten Immobilie nicht ohne Zustimmung des anderen Ehegatten verfügen, so ist dessen Schutz noch besser gewährleistet als im deutschen Recht, da es nicht darauf ankommt, ob dieses Eigentum das ganze Vermögen oder nur einen großen Teil (das sind nach der deutschen Rechtsprechung 85% bei kleineren Vermögen oder weniger als 90% bei größeren Vermögen) davon ausmacht.

Zu Absatz 1:
In Absatz 1 ist die Verfügungsbeschränkung über Rechte an einer Ehewohnung und den Haushaltsgegenständen geregelt.

Zur Ehewohnung gehören alle Räume, die die Ehegatten als Wohnung nutzen, gemeinsam bewohnt haben oder die nach den Umständen dazu bestimmt waren, Ehewohnung zu werden, auch wenn dies nicht zur Ausführung gekommen ist. Zur Ehewohnung können damit auch Nebenräume gehören (z. B. Keller, Dachboden, Garage, Sport- und Fitnessräume).

Ziel der Regelung des Artikels 5 ist es, den Schutz der Familie bezogen auf die Ehewohnung umfassend sicherzustellen.

Wird über Eigentum oder über Mietverhältnisse an der Ehewohnung verfügt, so ist eine solche Verfügung ohne Zustimmung des anderen Ehegatten grundsätzlich unwirksam. Das bedeutet, dass der Ehegatte, der Eigentümer eines Hauses ist, das als Ehewohnung genutzt wird, das Haus nicht ohne Zustimmung des anderen Ehegatten wirksam verkaufen kann. Auch der Ehegatte, der Mieter einer Wohnung ist, in der die Familie lebt, kann den Mietvertrag nicht allein wirksam kündigen. Der Ehegatte, der einem solchen Verhalten nicht zugestimmt hat, kann diese Kündigung jedoch genehmigen.

Der Schutz der Ehewohnung ist damit sehr weitgehend und kann auch Drittinteressen betreffen. Dem Vermieter einer Wohnung, die Ehewohnung ist, kann die Unwirksamkeit der Kündigung eines Mietvertrags entgegengehalten werden, auch wenn er vom Güterstand der Ehegatten und damit von der Verfügungsbeschränkung des mietenden Ehegatten keine Kenntnis hatte.

Auch über Haushaltsgegenstände – egal ob sie sich in der Wohnung befinden oder schon aus ihr entfernt sind – kann der Eigentümer nicht allein verfügen. Der andere Ehegatte kann allerdings das Rechtsgeschäft über die Ehewohnung oder die Haushaltsgegenstände genehmigen.

Wie sich diese Unwirksamkeit auswirkt, ist den Rechtsordnungen beider Länder überlassen.

In Frankreich muss die Unwirksamkeit mittels einer Nichtigkeitsklage geltend gemacht werden. Dies ergibt sich aus Artikel 215 Absatz 3 CC, der von einer Regel des französischen „régime primaire" ausgeht, die nicht in den gemeinsamen Güterstand übernommen wurde, jedoch weiterhin auf alle in Frankreich wohnhaften Ehegatten Anwendung findet, unabhängig von ihrem ehelichen Güterstand.

In Deutschland dagegen führt eine entsprechende Verfügung automatisch zur Unwirksamkeit gegenüber jedermann, wenn die Zustimmung des anderen Ehegatten fehlt. Der Erhebung einer Klage zur Geltendmachung der Unwirksamkeit bedarf es im Gegensatz zum französischen Recht nicht. Im Streitfall kann direkt auf Herausgabe geklagt werden.

Verfahren, die zur Geltendmachung der Rechtsfolgen führen, die mit der Verletzung der durch diesen Artikel eingeführten Regel im Zusammenhang stehen, unterliegen der jeweiligen nationalen Rechtsordnung. In Frankreich findet daher Artikel 215 Absatz 3 CC auf die Nichtigkeitsklage Anwendung.

Zu Absatz 2:
Ein Ehegatte kann nicht ohne den anderen über die Rechte verfügen, welche die Ehewohnung oder Haushaltsgegenstände sichern. Ist der Ehegatte aber außerstande, eine solche Willenserklärung abzugeben, weil er z. B. gesundheitlich dazu nicht in der Lage ist, oder verweigert er seine Zustimmung, ohne dass Belange der Familie seine Weigerung rechtfertigen würden, so kann das Gericht den Ehegatten ermächtigen, die in Absatz 1 genannten Rechtshandlungen allein vorzunehmen.

Die Ermächtigung durch das Gericht bei krankheitsbedingter Unfähigkeit des Ehegatten zur Zustimmung hat Ähnlichkeit mit dem Notverwaltungsrecht des §1454 BGB, entspricht aber der Sache nach einer vereinfachten Betreuerbestellung mit dem Aufgabenkreis „Einwilligung in ein bestimmtes Rechtsgeschäft".

Diese Lösung, mit der vor allem verhindert werden soll, dass ein Ehegatte seine Zustimmung willkürlich verweigert, nur um dem anderen Ehegatten zu schaden, ist aus dem französischen „régime primaire" übernommen worden (Artikel 217 Absatz 1 CC).

Artikel 6. Geschäfte zur Führung des Haushalts

Zu Absatz 1:
In Absatz 1 ist geregelt, welche Geschäfte mit Wirkung auch für den anderen Ehegatten abgeschlossen werden können.

So kann jeder Ehegatte gemäß dem allgemeinen Grundsatz der Vermögenstrennung allein Verträge zur Führung des Haushalts abschließen (er kann z. B. Haushaltsgegenstände erwerben). Abweichend vom Grundsatz der Vermögenstrennung bewirken diese Verträge jedoch, dass der Ehegatte, der ursprünglich nicht Vertragspartei ist, und auch nicht dem Vertragsschluss zugestimmt hat, trotzdem durch den Vertrag gebunden ist und für daraus entstehende Verbindlichkeiten gesamtschuldnerisch haftet.

Dies gilt auch für Verträge, die den Bedarf der Kinder betreffen. So haftet der andere Ehegatte auch gesamtschuldnerisch für Verbindlichkeiten aus einem Vertrag seines Ehegatten mit einem Nachhilfelehrer.

Zu Absatz 2:
Absatz 2 sieht vor, dass die vorgenannte gemeinsame Verpflichtung ausgeschlossen ist, wenn zwei Voraussetzungen kumulativ vorliegen:

- es handelt sich um unangemessene Ausgaben und
- der vertragschließende Dritte wusste von den unangemessenen Ausgaben oder hätte es wissen müssen.

Diese Beschränkung der gemeinsamen Verpflichtung ist erforderlich, um den anderen Ehegatten zu schützen, der nicht für unangemessene Ausgaben seines Ehegatten haftbar gemacht werden darf. Die Bewertung des übermäßigen Charakters orientiert sich an den Lebensverhältnissen beider Ehegatten. So kann der Erwerb eines teuren antiken Möbelstücks dann eine offensichtlich unangemessene Ausgabe sein, wenn beide Eheleute nur über ein geringes Einkommen verfügen. In einem solchen Fall kann der andere Ehegatte nicht aus diesem Vertrag in Anspruch genommen werden, wenn der Vertragspartner davon wusste oder davon hätte wissen müssen.

Diese Bestimmung ist eine modernisierte Übernahme des Artikels 220 CC. Die in Frankreich wohnhaften Ehegatten, die den gemeinsamen Güterstand vereinbart haben, unterliegen Artikel 6.

Die übernommene Regel steht nicht im Widerspruch zum deutschen Recht. Zwar geht sie über §1357 BGB hinaus: die Eheleute müssen sie aber hinnehmen, wenn sie den Güterstand der Wahl-Zugewinngemeinschaft durch Vertrag selbst gewählt haben. Damit haben sie auch die Regelung des Artikels 6 freiwillig übernommen.

KAPITEL IV. BEENDIGUNG DES GÜTERSTANDES

Artikel 7. Gründe für die Beendigung des Güterstandes

Der Zeitpunkt der Güterstandsbeendigung ist hier maßgeblich. Zu diesem Zeitpunkt erfolgt nämlich die Festsetzung der Zugewinnausgleichsforderung je nach Zusammensetzung und Wert des Ehegattenvermögens.
Artikel 7 sieht vor, dass der eheliche Güterstand endet:

- durch Tod oder Todeserklärung eines Ehegatten;
- durch Wechsel des ehelichen Güterstandes;
- mit Rechtskraft des Scheidungsurteils oder jeder anderen gerichtlichen Entscheidung, die den Güterstand beendet.

Mit der ersten Regelung wird klargestellt, dass eine Todeserklärung den Güterstand auch dann beendet, wenn diese Erklärung unrichtig ist.

Mit der zweiten Regelung wird klargestellt, dass auch der Wechsel des Güterstandes den Güterstand der Wahl Zugewinngemeinschaft beendet. In Deutschland kann der Güterstand nämlich durch ehevertragliche Vereinbarung eines anderen Güterstandes gewechselt werden. Ebenso können die Ehegatten, die in einem französischen Güterstand leben, im Interesse der Familie vereinbaren, den Güterstand zwei Jahre nach seiner Anwendung zu wechseln.

Der dritte Fall erfasst andere Gründe für die Auflösung der Ehe.

In Frankreich entspricht dies der Trennung ohne Auflösung des Ehebandes, der Ungültigerklärung der Ehe bei gutgläubigen Ehegatten und der vorzeitigen Begleichung der Ausgleichsforderung.

In Deutschland sind darunter Entscheidungen über den vorzeitigen Zugewinnausgleich und über die Aufhebung einer Ehe infolge ihrer Nichtigkeit zu verstehen.

KAPITEL V. FESTSETZUNG DER ZUGEWINNAUSGLEICHS-FORDERUNG BEI DER BEENDIGUNG DES GÜTERSTANDES

ABSCHNITT 1. ANFANGSVERMÖGEN

Artikel 8. Zusammensetzung des Anfangsvermögens

Zu Absatz 1 und 2:
In Absatz 1 und 2 sind die Vermögensgegenstände beschrieben, die Teil des Anfangsvermögens sind.

Das Anfangsvermögen enthält drei Arten von Vermögensgegenständen:

a) Die Gegenstände, die einem Ehegatten zu dem Zeitpunkt gehören, an dem der eheliche Güterstand wirksam wird.
Vielfach werden die Ehepaare einen Ehevertrag vor der Eheschließung vereinbaren. Da nach Artikel 3 der früheste Termin für das Wirksamwerden des Ehevertrags die Eheschließung ist, ist der früheste Termin für den Eintritt des Güterstandes der Tag der Eheschließung.
b) Die Gegenstände, die ein Ehegatte später durch Erbschaft oder Schenkung erwirbt.
Vermögenszuwächse aufgrund Schenkung oder Erbrecht sind in den Rechtsordnungen beider Länder dem Anfangsvermögen hinzuzurechnen (Deutschland: §1374 Absatz 2 BGB; Frankreich: Artikel 1570 CC).
c) Das von einem Ehegatten später als Schmerzensgeld erworbene Vermögen.

Im französischen Recht zählt das Schmerzensgeld zum Anfangsvermögen. In Deutschland ist dies im gesetzlichen Güterstand der Zugewinngemeinschaft nicht der Fall, wird aber durchaus mit dem Hinweis auf die Höchstpersönlichkeit dieser Forderung immer wieder diskutiert. Auch wenn eine Erweiterung des privilegierten Vermögens um weitere Tatbestände in §1374 Absatz 2 BGB abgelehnt wird, so steht es den Parteien frei, eine solche Zurechnung zum Anfangsvermögen zu vereinbaren.

Der Zugewinn soll den von beiden Ehegatten während der Wirksamkeit des Güterstandes erwirtschafteten Vermögenszuwachs ausgleichen. Es gibt aber Vermögenszuwächse, die von der Mitwirkung oder Leistung der Ehegatten völlig unabhängig erworben wurden und deshalb nicht ausgeglichen werden sollen. Das gilt vor allem für Vermögenswerte, die vorstehend unter b) und c) genannt werden und die ein Ehegatte durch Erbschaft, Schenkung oder als Ausgleich für erlittene Schmerzen (Schmerzensgeld) erworben hat. Deshalb sind diese Vermögenswerte nach Absatz 2 auch dem Anfangsvermögen zuzurechnen und so dem Zugewinnausgleich zu entziehen.

Die Parteien sind in ihrer Privatautonomie frei zu vereinbaren, dass auch noch andere Vermögenszuwächse als die in Absatz 1 genannten dem Anfangsvermögen zugerechnet werden. Die Ehegatten können eine entsprechende Vereinbarung im Ehevertrag treffen (vgl. Artikel 3 Absatz 3 der Güterstandsregelung).

Anfangsvermögen ist das Vermögen, das einem Ehegatten abzüglich der Verbindlichkeiten am entscheidenden Stichtag gehört. Das Anfangsvermögen ist keine besondere Vermögensmasse, sondern eine der beiden Rechnungsgrößen zur Ermittlung des Zugewinns.

Die Verbindlichkeiten können auch über die Höhe des Aktivvermögens hinaus abgezogen werden. Das bedeutet, dass das Anfangsvermögen auch negativ sein kann.

Entsprechende Regelungen finden sich im französischen Recht (Artikel 1570, 1571 CC) und im deutschen Recht (§1374 BGB). Zwar sah die geltende deutsche Regelung zum Anfangsvermögen vor, dass dieses, im Gegensatz zur französischen Regelung, nicht negativ sein konnte und ließ Abzüge von Verbindlichkeiten nur bis zur Höhe des Vermögens zu. Allerdings wurde diese Regelung schon seit langem kritisiert. Mit der Reform des Zugewinnausgleichsrechts vom 1. September 2009 ist das negative Anfangsvermögen künftig zugelassen worden.

Zu Absatz 3:
Dem Anfangsvermögen nicht zugerechnet werden:

a) Die Früchte dieses Vermögens.
   Mit dieser Regelung wird klargestellt, dass die Früchte, die aus dem Anfangsvermögen gezogen werden, z. B. Mieteinnahmen aus einer Eigentumswohnung, nicht zum Anfangsvermögen zu rechnen sind. Dabei handelt es sich auch um Zugewinn.
   Dieser Grundgedanke findet sich auch in den Rechtsordnungen beider Länder (Deutschland: §1374 Absatz 2 BGB; Frankreich: Artikel 1570 CC).
b) Die Gegenstände des Anfangsvermögens, die Verwandten in gerader Linie während des ehelichen Güterstandes von einem Ehegatten geschenkt werden.
   Hat ein Ehegatte während des Güterstandes Gegenstände des Anfangsvermögens an Verwandte in gerader Linie verschenkt, so sollen diese nach Absatz 3 Nummer 2 bei der Berechnung des Zugewinns völlig ausgenommen

werden. Aus diesem Grund werden sie weder beim Anfangsvermögen, noch beim Endvermögen berücksichtigt. Diese Bestimmung lehnt sich an das französische Recht an.

Die eventuellen Wertverbesserungen, die an einem solchen Gut vorgenommen werden und nicht aus dem Anfangsvermögen stammen, werden im Endvermögen berücksichtigt (vgl. Artikel 10 über die Zusammensetzung des Endvermögens).

Diese Regelung stellt einen Kompromiss dar zwischen dem deutschen Recht, das Gegenstände, die auf diese Weise geschenkt worden sind, beim Anfangsvermögen berücksichtigt, und dem französischen Recht, welches Geschenke aus dem Anfangsvermögen zulässt, ohne dass diese beim Zugewinn berücksichtigt werden, mit Ausnahme der Wertzuwächse, die das verschenkte Vermögen erfahren hat.

Zu Absatz 4:
Um bei Beendigung des Güterstandes Streitigkeiten über die Höhe des Anfangsvermögens zu vermeiden, bietet es sich an, bereits bei Abschluss des Ehevertrags ein Verzeichnis über das Anfangsvermögen durch den Notar aufnehmen zu lassen. Die Ehegatten können aber auch ein privatschriftliches Verzeichnis erstellen.

Ein solches Verzeichnis über das Anfangsvermögen gilt als richtig, wenn es von beiden Ehegatten unterzeichnet wurde. Die notarielle Form ist nicht vorgeschrieben. Die Vermutung der Richtigkeit kann widerlegt werden, indem die Unrichtigkeit nachgewiesen wird. Es kann sich auch anbieten, bei Erstellung des Verzeichnisses bereits den Wert der Gegenstände aus dem Anfangsvermögen aufzunehmen. In diesem Fall gilt die Vermutung der Richtigkeit auch für diesen Wert, soweit diese Vermögensgegenstände gemäß Artikel 9 Absatz 1 Nummer 1 am Tag des Eintritts des Güterstandes bewertet werden (oder am Tag ihres Erwerbs in Bezug auf die Vermögensgegenstände nach Artikel 8 Absatz 2).

Die Rechtsordnungen beider Länder kennen solche Verzeichnisse, deren Richtigkeit vermutet wird (Deutschland: §1377 BGB; Frankreich: Artikel 1570 CC).

Zu Absatz 5:
Haben die Ehegatten kein Vermögensverzeichnis erstellt, wird vermutet, dass kein Anfangsvermögen vorhanden war. Auch diese Vermutung kann widerlegt werden.

Artikel 9. Bewertung des Anfangsvermögens

Allgemeines:
So ähnlich die Regelungen beider Länder zum jeweiligen Güterstand der Zugewinngemeinschaft grundsätzlich sind, so unterschiedlich sind sie in einem sehr wesentlichen Punkt: der Bewertung des Anfangsvermögens.

Frankreich legt der Bewertung der Vermögensgegenstände aus dem Anfangsvermögen grundsätzlich den Wert zugrunde, den diese Vermögensgegenstände bei Beendigung des Güterstandes haben (Artikel 1571 CC).

Deutschland stellt dagegen auf den Wert ab, den das Vermögen bei Eintritt des Güterstandes hatte (§1376 Absatz 1 BGB). Werterhöhungen, die auf der normalen Geldentwertung beruhen, stellen jedoch nach der Rechtsprechung keinen Zugewinn dar und bleiben daher unberücksichtigt.

Diese unterschiedlichen Bewertungszeitpunkte können z. B. folgende nachhaltige Auswirkungen haben:

- So tragen nach der französischen Regelung im Gegensatz zur deutschen Regelung die Ehegatten die Gefahr der Wertminderung von Vermögensgegenständen aus dem Anfangsvermögen.
  Beispiel Deutschland:
  Ein Ehegatte bringt als einzigen Vermögenswert ein Aktiendepot mit in den Güterstand, das bei Beginn des Güterstandes 100 000 € wert ist. Bei Beendigung des Güterstandes ist das Aktiendepot nur noch 20 000 € wert. Das Endvermögen des Ehegatten beträgt insgesamt 100 000 € (inklusive des Aktiendepots). Damit hat der Ehegatte keinen Zugewinn erzielt, an dem der andere Ehegatte zu beteiligen wäre.
  Beispiel Frankreich:
  Ausgangslage wie bei Beispiel oben. Das Anfangsvermögen des Ehegatten wird mit 20 000 € angesetzt. Das Endvermögen mit 100 000 € (20 000 und 80 000). Damit hat der Ehegatte einen Zugewinn von 80 000 € erzielt, an dem der andere Ehegatte mit einer Zugewinnausgleichsforderung von 40 000 € zu beteiligen ist (wenn der andere Ehegatte keinen Zugewinn erzielt hat).

- Nach deutschem Recht partizipiert im Gegensatz zur französischen Regelung der Ehegatte an Wertsteigerungen des Anfangsvermögens (ausgenommen Wertveränderungen, die auf Währungsschwankungen beruhen, die keine Berücksichtigung finden), die ohne sein Zutun eintreten. So entsteht ein Zugewinn, wenn z. B. ein Grundstück unverändert bleibt, aber aufgrund seiner Lage über den Lauf der Zeit an Wert gewinnt. Nach französischem Recht dagegen führt dies nicht zu einem Zugewinn.
  Beispiel Deutschland:
  Ein Ehegatte bringt ein Grundstück mit in den Güterstand, das zu Beginn des Güterstandes einen Wert von 100 000 € hat. Bei Beendigung des Güterstandes hat das Grundstück einen Wert von 200 000 €, weil es zu Bauland erklärt worden ist. Der Zugewinn, an dem der andere Ehegatte zu beteiligen ist, beträgt damit 100 000 €. Der ausgleichsberechtigte Ehegatte erhält damit 50 000 € (wenn er selbst keinen Zugewinn erzielt hat).

Beispiel Frankreich:
Ausgangslage wie bei Beispiel oben. Das Grundstück wird im Anfangs- wie im Endvermögen mit 200 000 € angesetzt. Ein Zugewinn, an dem der andere Ehegatte zu beteiligen wäre, ist hier nicht entstanden.
Um sowohl den nationalen Regelungen Deutschlands als auch Frankreichs Rechnung zu tragen, wurde ein Bewertungsmodell in Artikel 11 konzipiert, das sich an beiden Rechtsordnungen orientiert:

Zu Absatz 1:
In Absatz 1 Nummer 1 wird an das deutsche Bewertungsmodell angeknüpft. Die Vermögensgegenstände, die am Tag des Eintritts des Güterstandes vorhanden waren, werden mit dem Wert angesetzt, den sie an diesem Tag hatten.

Das bedeutet, dass der Ehegatte, dem der Gegenstand nicht gehört, an den Wertsteigerungen dieser Vermögenswerte partizipiert, auch wenn sie ohne sein Zutun eintreten (mit Ausnahme von Wertveränderungen, die auf Währungsschwankungen beruhen). Gehört zum Anfangsvermögen eines Ehegatten z. B. ein Bild, das im Laufe der Ehejahre an Wert gewinnt, weil der Künstler immer bekannter wird, so fließt diese Wertsteigerung in den Zugewinn ein.

Für privilegiertes Vermögen (Schenkungen, Erbschaft, Schmerzensgeld), das zwar später erworben wurde, aber nach Artikel 8 Absatz 2 zum Anfangsvermögen gehört, ist Bewertungszeitpunkt nach Absatz 1 Nummer 2 der Tag, an dem dieses Vermögen erworben wurde.

Zu Absatz 2:
Absatz 2 bestimmt, dass Grundstückeigentum und sonstige Grundstücksrechte am Anfangsvermögen mit Ausnahme des Nießbrauchs und des Wohnrechts am Tage der Beendigung des Güterstandes bewertet werden. Die in Absatz 2 beschriebene Bewertungsmethode findet somit Anwendung auf die wesentlichen dinglichen, nicht auf Lebenszeit (Leibrente) angelegten Rechte. Diese Vermögensbestandteile werden mit dem Wert zum Zeitpunkt der Beendigung des Güterstandes oder zum Berechnungsstichtag in Sonderfällen nach Artikel 13 angesetzt.

Sinn und Zweck der Regelung ist es, Wertsteigerungen an Immobilien des Anfangsvermögens, die ohne Zutun eines der Ehegatten eingetreten sind, aus dem Zugewinn herauszunehmen. Immobilien stellen regelmäßig einen wesentlichen Teil des Vermögens dar und können Wertschwankungen unterworfen sein, die in der Regel nicht auf der Leistung der Ehegatten beruhen. Das ist z. B. der Fall, wenn eine Wertsteigerung einer Ehewohnung des Anfangsvermögens eingetreten ist, die lediglich auf der Wertsteigerung der Lage beruht. So können Immobilien z. B. erheblich an Wert gewinnen, weil ein nahe gelegener Flughafen geschlossen wird und damit die Lärmbelästigung wegfällt. Hier ist es durchaus interessengerecht, den anderen Ehegatten an solchen Wertsteigungen nicht partizipieren zu lassen.

Die Wertsteigerungen von Immobilien, die auf der gemeinsamen Leistung der Ehegatten beruhen, stellen dagegen einen Zugewinn dar. Sie erhöhen daher nicht den Wert des Anfangsvermögens.

Beispiel:

Ein Ehegatte hat ein Grundstück (Wert zu Beginn des Güterstandes z. B. 50 000 €) mit in den Güterstand gebracht, das während des Güterstandes mit einem Haus bebaut wird. Bei Beendigung des Güterstandes hat das bloße Grundstück ohne Haus einen Wert von 100 000 €, da die Lage des Grundstücks im Wert gestiegen ist. Das Grundstück mit Haus hat bei Beendigung des Güterstandes einen Wert von 200 000 €. Bei der Bewertung des Anfangsvermögens wird nur der Wert des bloßen Grundstücks mit dem Wert bei Beendigung des Güterstandes eingestellt: 100 000 €. (Die aufgrund der Lage erfolgte Wertsteigerung während der Ehe um 50 000 € führt nicht zu Zugewinn). Beim Endvermögen wird das Grundstück inklusive Haus bei dem Ehegatten berücksichtigt, dem es gehört: 200 000 €. Der Zugewinn beträgt damit 100 000 €. Ohne sonstige Zugewinne beträgt die Zugewinnausgleichsforderung des anderen Ehegatten 50 000 €.

Wurden Immobilien und wesentliche, nicht auf Lebenszeit angelegte dingliche Rechte während der Ehejahre veräußert oder ersetzt, so wird dieser Vermögenswert mit dem Wert am Tag der Veräußerung oder Ersetzung zugrunde gelegt.

Beispiel:

Ausgangslage wie oben (Grundstück wird in den Güterstand eingebracht und während des Bestehens des Güterstandes mit einem Haus bebaut). Das Grundstück inklusive Haus wird während der Ehe veräußert. Bei der Veräußerung hat das Grundstück einen Wert von 80 000 € und das Haus einen Wert von 100 000 €. Beim Anfangsvermögen wird nur der Wert des Grundstücks in Höhe von 80 000 € eingestellt, dessen Wert nach Absatz 3 anzupassen ist. Beim Endvermögen kommt es darauf an, was der Ehegatte an Vermögen insgesamt noch hat. Der Verkaufserlös findet sich beim Endvermögen nur dann wieder, wenn davon noch etwas vorhanden ist. Hat der Ehegatte z. B. bei Beendigung des Güterstandes nicht mehr als 80 000 €, dann hat er keinen Zugewinn gemacht, den er ausgleichen muss.

Nießbrauch und Wohnrecht sind von dieser Regel ausgenommen, da die Ehegatten den Wert dieser Rechte durch Nutzung vermindert haben.

Zu Absatz 3:

Eine Ehe kann je nach Einzelfall viele Jahre dauern. Das Anfangsvermögen wird aber nach Absatz 1 mit einem bestimmten Geldwert zum Zeitpunkt des Eintritts des Güterstandes bilanziert (oder zum Zeitpunkt des Erwerbs der in Artikel 8 Absatz 2 genannten Vermögensgegenstände). Dieser Geldwert kann über die Jahre aufgrund der Inflation aber geringer werden. Bloße Wertsteigerungen, die allein aufgrund der Inflation eintreten, sollen aber keinen Zugewinn bilden. Deshalb wird mit Absatz 3 eine Regelung geschaffen, wonach der Geldwert des Anfangsvermögensum die Inflation zu bereinigen ist.

Beispiel:

(fiktiv und ohne konkret gemittelte Preisveränderungsraten, da der Güterstand der Wahl-Zugewinngemeinschaft erst ab dem Tag der Ratifizierung des Abkommens angewandt werden kann):

Bei Beginn des Güterstandes hat ein Ehegatte ein Vermögen von 100 000 €. Die Ehe dauert zehn Jahre. Bei Beendigung des Güterstandes hat der Ehegatte ein Endvermögen von 200 000 €. Es wird nun fiktiv davon ausgegangen, dass die 100 000 € zu Beginn des Güterstandes zehn Jahre vorher einem Geldwert von 150 000 € bei Beendigung des Güterstandes entsprechen. Das hat zur Folge, dass das Anfangsvermögen mit 150 000 € anzusetzen ist und das Endvermögen mit 200 000 €. Der Zugewinn beträgt daher 50 000 €, die Zugewinnausgleichsforderung beträgt 25 000 €, wenn der andere Ehegatte keinen Zugewinn gemacht hat.

Frankreich erlaubt keine Indexierungen, die auf dem allgemeinen Preisniveau oder dem Preis von Gütern, Produkten oder Dienstleistungen beruhen und keine unmittelbare Verbindung zu dem Gegenstand des Abkommens oder der Tätigkeit einer der Parteien aufweisen (Artikel L. 112-2 Absatz 1 des französischen Währungs- und Finanzgesetzbuches). Soweit jedoch Artikel 55 der französischen Verfassung den Grundsatz des Vorrangs zwischenstaatlicher Übereinkommen vor Gesetzen vorsieht, kann der gewählte Indexierungsmechanismus rechtsgültig im Rahmen des gemeinsamen Güterstandes Anwendung finden.

Treten weitere Staaten dem Abkommen bei, so berechnet sich die gemittelte Preisänderungsrate aus den Preisänderungsraten sämtlicher Vertragsstaaten.

Zu Absatz 4:

Die in Absatz 1 und 3 vorgesehenen Bewertungsregelungen gelten auch für die Bewertung von Verbindlichkeiten.

Beispiel:

(fiktives Beispiel ohne konkrete gemittelte Preisveränderungsraten, da der Güterstand der Wahl-Zugewinngemeinschaft noch nicht in Kraft ist):

Bei Beginn des Güterstandes hat der Ehegatte nur Schulden in Höhe von 10 000 €. Die Ehe dauert zehn Jahre. Bei Beendigung des Güterstandes hat der Ehegatte ein Endvermögen von 200 000 €. Es wird nun fiktiv davon ausgegangen, dass die 10 000 € Schulden zu Beginn des Güterstandes zehn Jahre vorher einem Geldwert von 14 000 € bei Beendigung des Güterstandes entsprechen. Das hat zur Folge, dass das Anfangsvermögen mit Schulden und daher einem Minus von 14 000 € anzusetzen ist und das Endvermögen mit 200 000 €. Der Zugewinn beträgt daher 214 000 €.

ABSCHNITT 2. ENDVERMÖGEN

Artikel 10. Zusammensetzung des Endvermögens

Zu Absatz 1:
Absatz 1 regelt, was Endvermögen ist: das Vermögen, das einem Ehegatten abzüglich der Verbindlichkeiten bei Beendigung des Güterstandes bzw. an dem Stichtag nach Artikel 13 gehört, auch wenn sie das Aktivvermögen übersteigen. Das Endvermögen kann wie das Anfangsvermögen auch negativ sein. Es ist keine besondere Vermögensmasse, sondern eine der Rechnungsgrößen zur Ermittlung des Zugewinns.

Die Rechtsordnungen beider Länder kennen für ihren jeweiligen Güterstand der Zugewinngemeinschaft eine entsprechende Regelung (Deutschland: §1375 BGB; Frankreich: Artikel 1572 und 1574 CC).

Zu Absatz 2:
Dem Endvermögen sind unter bestimmten Voraussetzungen Vermögenswerte hinzuzurechnen. Damit soll verhindert werden, dass ein Ehegatte durch bestimmte Vermögensverfügungen seinen Zugewinn schmälert und den anderen Ehegatten benachteiligt.

Vermögensminderungen durch Schenkungen ohne Zustimmung des Ehegatten oder in Benachteiligungsabsicht, die dem Endvermögen zuzurechnen sind, sind den Rechtsordnungen beider Länder bekannt (Deutschland: §1375 Absatz 2 BGB; Frankreich: Artikel 1573 CC). Die missbilligte Vermögensminderung aufgrund von Verschwendung findet sich nur in Deutschland, §1375 Absatz 2 Nr. 2 BGB. Zum Schutz des anderen Ehegatten wird diese Bestimmung auch in den Güterstand der Wahl-Zugewinngemeinschaft aufgenommen.

Zu Nummer 1:
Schenkungen sind grundsätzlich dem Endvermögen zuzurechnen.

Das gilt jedoch nicht, wenn:

a) die Schenkung nach der Lebensführung der Ehegatten angemessen ist (das ist der Fall, wenn sie nicht erheblich den geldlichen Rahmen übersteigt, den die Eheleute zum täglichen Leben haben),
b) die Schenkung mit Mitteln aus dem Anfangsvermögen eines Ehegatten an einen Verwandten in gerader Linie bewirkt wird (Artikel 8 Absatz 3 Nummer 2). Wertverbesserungen an diesen verschenkten Gegenständen, die während der Dauer des Güterstandes mit Mitteln vorgenommen worden sind, die nicht zum Anfangsvermögen gehören, werden gleichwohl beim Endvermögen berücksichtigt.

Darüber hinaus soll der Wert der Schenkung dem Endvermögen nicht fiktiv hinzugerechnet werden, wenn der andere Ehegatte der Schenkung zugestimmt hat oder wenn die Schenkung mehr als zehn Jahre vor der Beendigung des Güterstandes erfolgt ist.

Zu Nummer 2:
Hierzu gehören Rechtsgeschäfte mit dem Ziel, den Zugewinn des anderen Ehegatten zu schmälern oder ihm den Zugewinn zu entziehen. Die Benachteiligungsabsicht muss das leitende Motiv gewesen sein. Dazu kann z. B. der Verkauf eines wertvollen Gegenstandes erheblich unter Wert gehören, wenn das beabsichtigte Ziel ist, den Zugewinn zu beeinflussen.

Der Wertgewinn aus solchen Veräußerungen soll dem Endvermögen nicht fiktiv hinzugerechnet werden, wenn die Veräußerung mit Zustimmung des anderen Ehegatten oder mehr als zehn Jahre vor der Beendigung des Güterstandes erfolgt ist.

Zu Nummer 3:
Unter Nummer 3 fallen Ausgaben, die unnütz und im Verhältnis zum Vermögen übermäßig sind. Dazu würde z. B. eine Luxuskreuzfahrt durch einen Ehegatten zählen, wenn die Eheleute lediglich ein geringes Einkommen haben. Hierunter fällt auch die Zerstörung eines Gegenstandes durch einen Ehegatten unabhängig von einer Schädigungsabsicht.

Der Wert der verschwendeten Gegenstände soll dem Endvermögen nicht fiktiv hinzugerechnet werden, wenn der andere Ehegatte der Verschwendung zugestimmt hat oder wenn sie mehr als zehn Jahre vor der Beendigung des Güterstandes erfolgt ist.

Die Regelungen über den deutschen Zugewinnausgleich sehen eine Ausschlussfrist von zehn Jahren vor (§1375 Absatz 3 BGB). Hintergrund ist, dass nach Ablauf einer bestimmten Zeit nicht mehr davon ausgegangen wird, dass die vermögensmindernde Handlung mit dem Ziel der Benachteiligung des anderen Ehegatten erfolgt oder von dem anderen Ehegatten letztlich akzeptiert worden ist. Zudem dient diese Regelung der Rechtssicherheit.

Aus diesen Gründen wird die zeitliche Grenze von zehn Jahren auch hier in den Güterstand der Wahl-Zugewinngemeinschaft aufgenommen.

Artikel 11. Bewertung des Endvermögens

Zu Absatz 1:
In Absatz 1 wird die Bewertung des Endvermögens geregelt: Dem Endvermögen ist der Wert zugrunde zu legen, den das Vermögen bei Beendigung des Güterstandes oder zum Berechnungszeitpunkt in Sonderfällen nach Artikel 13 hatte.

In Frankreich wird vorbehaltlich der besonderen Bewertungsregeln im Fall der Scheidung, der Trennung oder des vorzeitigen Zugewinnausgleichs der

Wert der vorhandenen Vermögensgegenstände, die das Endvermögen bilden, nach ihrem Zustand am Tag der Auflösung des Güterstandes und nach ihrem Wert am Tag der Abwicklung des Güterstandes ermittelt. Letzterer kann mehrere Jahre nach dem Zeitpunkt der Auflösung liegen (Artikel 1574 CC).

In Deutschland wird der Zugewinn und damit das Anfangs- und Endvermögen der Ehegatten zum Zeitpunkt der Beendigung des Güterstandes berechnet. Sie können zu einem früheren Zeitpunkt berechnet werden, nämlich zu dem der Antrag auf vorzeitigen Zugewinnausgleich gestellt worden oder an dem der Scheidungsantrag rechtshängig geworden ist (§§1378, 1384, 1387 BGB).

Zu Absatz 2:
Absatz 2 legt den Zeitpunkt fest, zu dem Vermögen bewertet wird, das nach Artikel 10 Absatz 2 dem Endvermögen fiktiv hinzugerechnet wird.

- Der Wert der Güter nach Artikel 10 Absatz 2 wird zum Zeitpunkt der Schenkung, Veräußerung in Benachteiligungsabsicht oder Verschwendung berechnet.
- Der Wert der Wertverbesserungen, die während der Dauer des Güterstandes an einem an Verwandte in direkter Linie verschenkten Gut des Anfangsvermögens mit Mitteln vorgenommen wurden, die nicht zum Anfangsvermögen gehören, wird zum Zeitpunkt der Schenkung berechnet.

Zu Absatz 3:
Die nach Absatz 2 hinzuzurechnenden Werte sind ab dem Berechnungszeitpunkt um den Betrag anzupassen, der sich aus den gemittelten Preisänderungsraten für allgemeine Verbraucherpreise der Vertragsstaaten ergibt.

ABSCHNITT 3. ZUGEWINNAUSGLEICHSFORDERUNG

Artikel 12. Anspruch auf Zugewinnausgleich

Zu Absatz 1:
In Absatz 1 ist geregelt, dass der Ehegatte, der den geringeren Zugewinn während des Güterstandes erzielt hat, bei dessen Beendigung von dem anderen Ehegatten den Ausgleich des Zugewinns in Höhe der Hälfte des Unterschieds zwischen den Vermögensbeträgen verlangen kann, die beide Ehegatten während der Ehe hinzugewonnen haben.

Das Anfangs- und das Endvermögen jedes Ehegatten werden einander gegenübergestellt, um festzusetzen, inwieweit jeder Ehegatte einen Vermögenszuwachs während der Ehe zu verzeichnen hat oder nicht. Die Regeln hinsichtlich der Zusammensetzung und Bewertung des Anfangs- und des Endvermögens, die nicht identisch sind, sind in den nachstehenden Artikeln des Güterstandes aufgeführt. Übersteigt das Endvermögen das Anfangsvermögen, so ist dieser Überschuss der Zugewinn des Ehegatten. Es gibt keinen Ausgleich des Vermögensverlustes (negativen Vermögenserwerbs), sondern nur einen Ausgleich des Zugewinns. Wenn der Zugewinn des einen Ehegatten den des anderen übersteigt, schuldet derjenige Ehegatte, der einen höheren Zugewinn erzielt hat, dem anderen Ehegatten die Hälfte des Unterschieds.

Zu Absatz 2:
Die Zugewinnausgleichsforderung ist im Prinzip ein Geldanspruch. Das ist in beiden Ländern, Deutschland und Frankreich, nach geltendem Recht gleich.

Während dies in Frankreich ausdrücklich in Artikel 1576 CC geregelt ist, gibt es in Deutschland keine besondere Vorschrift. Dass es sich beim Zugewinnausgleichsanspruch um einen Zahlungsanspruch handelt, ergibt sich aber aus den Voraussetzungen der §§1372 ff. BGB. Zur Klarstellung wurde die französische Regelung in den Güterstand der Wahl-Zugewinngemeinschaft aufgenommen.

Beide Rechtsordnungen kennen die Abgeltung in Natur nur als Sonderfall (Frankreich: Artikel 1576 CC; Deutschland: §1383 BGB). Aus diesem Grund sieht auch der Güterstand der Wahl- Zugewinngemeinschaft vor, dass das Gericht auf Antrag der einen oder anderen Partei zum Zwecke dieser Zahlung die Übertragung von Vermögensgegenständen an den Gläubiger anordnen kann, wenn dies der Billigkeit entspricht. Das Gericht hat unter Abwägung der Interessen beider Ehegatten zu entscheiden.

Zu Absatz 3:
Die Zugewinnausgleichsforderung ist in Frankreich wie in Deutschland nicht übertragbar, solange der eheliche Güterstand nicht beendet ist. Dies gilt unabhängig davon, ob die Übertragung entgeltlich oder unentgeltlich erfolgt. Dagegen ist der Anspruch nach Auflösung des Güterstandes übertragbar und im Todesfall vererblich (Deutschland: §1378 Absatz 3 BGB; Frankreich: Artikel 1569 CC). Eine entsprechende Regelung wurde daher auch für den Güterstand der Wahl-Zugewinngemeinschaft aufgenommen.

Artikel 13. Berechnungszeitpunkte in Sonderfällen

Grundsätzlich kann die Zusammensetzung und der Wert des Ehegattenvermögens erst berechnet werden, wenn der Güterstand beendet ist.

Wird allerdings ein Antrag auf Scheidung der Ehe gestellt, so ist es wenig zweckmäßig, erst über diesen Antrag und im Anschluss, also nach Rechtskraft des Scheidungsbeschlusses, über die Zugewinnausgleichsforderung zu entscheiden. Sinnvoller ist es, im Zusammenhang mit dem Verfahren auf Scheidung durch einen Richter auch über den Zugewinn zu entscheiden. Um die Zusammensetzung und den Wert des Ehegattenvermögens berechnen zu können, sieht der gemeinsame Güterstand vor, dass an die Stelle des Zeitpunkts der Beendigung des Güterstandes in diesen Fällen der Zeitpunkt der Einreichung des Antrags bei Gericht tritt (und nicht die „assignation en divorce" in Frankreich). Selbst wenn der Richter nicht gleichzeitig über den Ausgleich und die Scheidung entscheidet, gestattet es diese Regel, dass der Zeitraum verkürzt wird, in dem der zugewinnausgleichspflichtige Ehegatte sein Vermögen mindern und damit den Ausgleichsanspruch des anderen Ehegatten verkürzen kann.

Der gesetzliche Güterstand der Zugewinngemeinschaft nach deutschem Recht kennt diesen Mechanismus (§1384 BGB). Er weicht dagegen zum Teil von dem in Frankreich geltenden Mechanismus ab. Das französische Recht sieht vor, dass der Ehegüterstand an dem Tag als aufgelöst gilt, an dem der Antrag gestellt wird, der allein auf die Festsetzung der Vermögenszusammensetzung abzielt (Artikel 1572 CC).

Dieser Mechanismus ist nicht nur bei der Scheidung wirksam. Gleiches gilt, wenn der Güterstand auf andere Weise durch gerichtliche Entscheidung beendet wird. Dazu gehört z. B. die Entscheidung über den vorzeitigen Ausgleich des Zugewinns nach Artikel 18. Auch in diesen Fällen ist es sinnvoll, bereits während des Verfahrens über den vorzeitigen Ausgleich des Zugewinns diesen auch berechnen zu können. Hierbei ist Berechnungszeitpunkt die Einreichung des Antrags bei Gericht.

Artikel 14. Begrenzung der Zugewinnausgleichsforderung

Mit dieser Vorschrift soll sichergestellt werden, dass auch bei einer Berücksichtigung des negativen Anfangsvermögens niemand mehr als 50% von seinem am Berechnungsstichtag (Berechnungszeitpunkt in Artikel 13 oder tatsächliche Beendigung des Güterstandes) tatsächlich vorhandenen Endvermögen an seinen Ehepartner abgeben muss.

Diese Beschränkung der Höhe der Zugewinnausgleichsforderung entspricht dem Grundgedanken des Zugewinnausgleichsrechts, wonach beide Ehegatten an dem, was sie während der Ehe erworben haben, gerecht je zur Hälfte beteiligt werden.

Durch Artikel 14 wird auch sichergestellt, dass eine Ausgleichsforderung, von den Fällen der fiktiven Hinzurechnung nach Artikel 10 Absatz 2 (mit Ausnahme von Nummer 1 Buchstabe b) abgesehen, nur entsteht, wenn am Stichtag, zu dem der Zugewinn berechnet wird, auch ein positives Vermögen vorhanden ist. Haben z. B. beide Ehegatten während des Bestehens des Güterstandes nur Schulden abgetragen oder hat ein Ehegatte keinen Zugewinn erzielt und nur der andere Schulden abgetragen, so entsteht keine Zugewinnausgleichsforderung. Es gibt nämlich keinen Ausgleich des negativen Vermögenserwerbs.

Diese Begrenzung betrifft nur die Zugewinnausgleichsforderung und nicht die anderen möglicherweise zwischen den Ehegatten bestehenden Ansprüche und Verbindlichkeiten. Das Ziel der Regelung, dass der zugewinnausgleichspflichtige

Ehegatte zumindest die Hälfte seines Vermögens behalten darf, ist aber dann nicht gerechtfertigt, wenn der ausgleichspflichtige Ehegatte sein Vermögen illoyal verringert hat (Artikel 10 Absatz 2 mit Ausnahme von Nummer 1 Buchstabe b).

Um die Höhe der Ausgleichsforderung nicht zu begrenzen, wenn ein Ehegatte illoyale Handlungen begangen hat, die eine fiktive Hinzurechnung zum Endvermögen bewirken, sieht Artikel 14 vor, dass die Begrenzung der Zugewinnausgleichsforderung um die Hälfte des Betrages erhöht wird, der dem Endvermögen in Anwendung von Artikel 10 Absatz 2 hinzuzurechnen ist. Ausgenommen sind Schenkungen nach Artikel 10 Absatz 2 Nummer 1 Buchstabe b. In einem solchen Fall kann man nicht unterstellen, dass ein Ehegatte sein Vermögen illoyal mindern wollte.

Deshalb kann der unehrliche Ehegatte gezwungen sein, sein ganzes Vermögen einzusetzen und sich sogar zu verschulden, um die Zugewinnausgleichsforderung mit dem fiktiv hinzugerechneten Betrag zu erfüllen.

Nach Artikel 3 Absatz 3 können die Ehegatten durch Vertrag die Anwendung dieser Bestimmung abbedingen.

KAPITEL VI. SONSTIGES

Artikel 15. Verjährung

Die Zugewinnausgleichsforderung verjährt in drei Jahren ab Kenntnis des Ehegatten von der Beendigung des Güterstandes. Eine dreijährige Regelverjährung entspricht den Regelungen der nationalen Rechtsordnungen (Deutschland: §1378 Absatz 4 BGB; Frankreich: Artikel 1578 CC).

Allerdings ist der Fristbeginn in beiden Ländern unterschiedlich. Während in Deutschland auf die Kenntnis von der Beendigung des Güterstandes abgestellt wird, beginnt die Frist in Frankreich ab der Beendigung des Güterstandes. Zum Schutz des zugewinnausgleichsberechtigten Ehegatten wird der deutsche Fristbeginn übernommen. Allerdings kann u. U. Bei kenntnisabhängigem Fristbeginn eine Verjährung auch erst viele Jahre nach der Beendigung des Güterstandes erfolgen. Um auch dem zugewinnausgleichspflichtigen Ehegatten Rechtssicherheit ab einem bestimmten Zeitpunkt zu gewähren, sieht Artikel 15 auch eine kenntnisunabhängige Verjährungsfrist von zehn Jahren ab Beendigung des Güterstandes vor.

Artikel 16. Auskunftspflicht, Verzeichnis

Zu Absatz 1:
Will ein Ehegatte seine Zugewinnausgleichsforderung geltend machen, so muss er wissen, wie hoch das Anfangs- und das Endvermögen des anderen Ehegatten sind. Deshalb wird den Ehegatten ein Anspruch auf Auskunft und auf Vorlage eines

Verzeichnisses zugebilligt. Dem Auskunftsberechtigten wird im Rahmen seines Auskunftsanspruchs ein Recht auf die Vorlage von Belegen eingeräumt. Damit kann der Auskunftsberechtigte die Angaben des Auskunftsverpflichteten besser überprüfen und seine Interessen besser durchsetzen. Zusätzlich können aber auch Rechtsstreitigkeiten vermieden werden, wenn überzeugende Belege vorgelegt werden. Jeder Ehegatte kann verlangen, dass das Verzeichnis durch einen Notar auf Kosten des antragstellenden Ehegatten aufgenommen wird. Eine entsprechende Regelung findet sich im deutschen Recht in §1379 BGB. In den französischen Regelungen zum Güterstand der Zugewinngemeinschaft ist in Artikel 1572 CC auch ein Anspruch auf Vorlage eines Verzeichnisses für das Endvermögen geregelt; der Auskunftsanspruch ist zwar nicht ausdrücklich geregelt, aber anerkannt.

Um dem ausgleichsberechtigten Ehegatten die Realisierung seiner Zugewinnausgleichsforderung zu ermöglichen, wird hier ein Anspruch auf Auskunft und auf Vorlage eines Verzeichnisses vorgesehen.

Zu Absatz 2

Dieselbe Interessenslage ergibt sich, wenn ein Ehegatte die Auflösung der Ehe beantragt oder auf vorzeitigen Ausgleich des Zugewinns klagen will. Deshalb gilt der Auskunftsanspruch des Absatzes 1 auch in diesem Fall.

Artikel 17. Stundung

Sowohl das deutsche Recht (§1382 BGB) als auch das französische Recht (Artikel 1576 CC) kennen die Möglichkeit, einerseits die Zugewinnausgleichsforderung unter bestimmten Voraussetzungen zu stunden und andererseits die Leistung von Sicherheiten zu verlangen.

Zu Absatz 1:

Absatz 1 regelt die Voraussetzungen, unter denen eine Stundung angeordnet werden kann. Eine Stundung soll im Interesse des ausgleichsberechtigten Ehegatten nur in Ausnahmefällen angeordnet werden. Das Gericht hat zu entscheiden, ob im Einzelfall eine unbillige Härte vorliegt.

> *Beispiel:*
>
> Der ausgleichspflichtige Ehegatte muss an den anderen Ehegatten 50 000 € bezahlen. Der einzige Vermögenswert, den der ausgleichspflichtige Ehegatte aber besitzt, ist sein Haus, in dem er lebt und in dem er sein Geschäft, von dem er seinen Lebensunterhalt bestreitet, untergebracht hat. Hier wäre es unbillig, dem Ehegatten die Veräußerung seines Hauses zuzumuten. Eine Stundung käme in Betracht.

Zu Absatz 2:

Eine gestundete Ausgleichsforderung ist zu verzinsen.

Zu Absatz 3:
Absatz 3 regelt, dass das Gericht anordnen kann, dass der Schuldner für eine gestundete Forderung Sicherheit leistet. Über Art und Umfang der Sicherheitsleistung entscheidet das Gericht nach billigem Ermessen.

Artikel 18. Vorzeitiger Zugewinnausgleich

Die Rechtsordnungen beider Länder kennen die Möglichkeit, bei Gefährdung der Zugewinnausgleichsforderung unter bestimmten Voraussetzungen, diese Forderung bereits vorzeitig geltend zu machen (Deutschland: §§1385, 1386 BGB; Frankreich: Artikel 1580 CC).

Im deutschen Recht kann neben dem Gestaltungsantrag ein Leistungsantrag gestellt werden, der es ermöglicht, die Zugewinnausgleichsforderung in bestimmten Fällen vorzeitig und direkt verlangen zu können.

Im französischen Recht kann ein Ehegatte vorzeitigen Zugewinnausgleich verlangen, wenn aufgrund der Unordnung des anderen Ehegatten in seinen Angelegenheiten, seiner schlechten Vermögensverwaltung oder seines ungebührlichen Lebenswandels zu befürchten ist, dass die Fortsetzung des Güterstandes die Rechte des anderen Ehegatten beeinträchtigt. Im Fall eines solchen Antrags kommen die Bestimmungen über die Gütertrennung zur Anwendung. Wenn das Gericht dem Antrag stattgegeben hat, tritt für die Ehegatten Gütertrennung ein.

Diese Möglichkeit, vorzeitigen Zugewinnausgleich verlangen zu können, wird auch für den Güterstand der Wahl Zugewinngemeinschaft vorgeschlagen. Ein vorzeitiger Ausgleich des Zugewinns kann nach Artikel 18 geltend gemacht werden, wenn ein Ehegatte sein Vermögen nicht ordnungsgemäß verwaltet und dadurch die Rechte des anderen bei der Berechnung der Zugewinnausgleichsforderung beeinträchtigt. Das gilt besonders, wenn ein Ehegatte Handlungen begeht, die in Anwendung von Artikel 10 Absatz 2 (mit Ausnahme von Artikel 10 Absatz 2 Nummer 1 Buchstabe b) dazu führen, dass dem Endvermögen etwas fiktiv hinzugerechnet werden muss.

Im Unterschied zu Artikel 1580 CC erlaubt Artikel 18 auch dem ausgleichspflichtigen Ehegatten, vorzeitigen Zugewinnausgleich zu verlangen, wenn Handlungen seines Ehegatten im Sinne des Artikels 18 Absatz 1 die Höhe der Zugewinnausgleichsforderung zu seinen Lasten beeinträchtigen.

Ist die Zugewinnausgleichsforderung gefährdet, so wird es in vielen Fällen sinnvoll sein, bei Gericht vorläufige Maßnahmen zur Sicherung des Anspruchs zu erwirken. Die prozessualen Maßnahmen sind im Rahmen des Güterstandes der Wahl Zugewinngemeinschaft nicht eigenständig geregelt. Hier sind die Regelungen des Landes anzuwenden, in dem die Maßnahme geltend gemacht wird.

In Frankreich können hier die Maßnahmen nach Artikel 220-1 CC beantragt werden. In Deutschland kommt die Sicherung der Zugewinnausgleichsforderung im Wege des vorläufigen Rechtsschutzes durch Arrest nach §916 der Zivilprozessordung (ZPO) in Betracht.

KAPITEL VII. SCHLUSSBESTIMMUNGEN

Artikel 19. Zeitliche Anwendung

Das Abkommen soll nur auf Eheverträge Anwendung finden, die die Ehegatten nach seinem Inkrafttreten geschlossen haben.

Artikel 20. Ratifikation und Inkrafttreten

Dieses Abkommen bedarf der Ratifikation nach den gültigen völkerrechtlichen Regeln.

Es soll möglichst bald in Kraft treten.

Es ist kündbar.

Artikel 21. Beitritt

Wegen der zunehmenden Mobilität von Ehepaaren in der Europäischen Union ist es wünschenswert, auch anderen Mitgliedstaaten einen späteren Beitritt zu dem Abkommen zu ermöglichen.

Im Fall des Beitritts eines oder mehrerer Staaten wird Deutschland zum Depositar des Übereinkommens bestimmt.

Artikel 22. Sprachen des Übereinkommens

Für den Fall des Beitritts kann eine neue verbindliche Sprachfassung des Übereinkommens in der Amtssprache des Beitrittsstaates erstellt werden.

Artikel 23. Registrierung

Die Pflicht zur Registrierung des Abkommens beruht auf Artikel 102 der Charta der Vereinten Nationen.

GESETZENTWURF DER BUNDESREGIERUNG*

Entwurf eines Gesetzes zu dem Abkommen vom 4. Februar 2010 zwischen der Bundesrepublik Deutschland und der Französischen Republik über den Güterstand der Wahl-Zugewinngemeinschaft

A. Problem und Ziel

Bei binationalen Ehen können Probleme hinsichtlich des Vermögens der Ehegatten entstehen, da die gesetzlichen Güterstände in den verschiedenen Ländern unterschiedlich und im jeweils anderen Land in der Regel nicht bekannt sind. Diese Probleme sind auch praktisch bedeutsam, weil im Jahr 2009 bei ca. 13 Prozent der Ehen in Deutschland mindestens ein Ehegatte eine ausländische Staatsangehörigkeit besaß. Probleme treten nicht nur bei Auflösung der Ehe auf, sondern auch während ihres Bestandes, z. B. bei der Finanzierung von Immobilienkrediten. Vor diesem Hintergrund soll eine staatsvertragliche Regelung mit der notwendigen Ergänzung im nationalen Recht mehr Rechtssicherheit und Rechtsklarheit schaffen.

B. Lösung

Die Bundesrepublik Deutschland und die Französische Republik haben sich entschlossen, einen gemeinsamen, in beiden Staaten identischen Wahlgüterstand zu schaffen, der in modifizierter Form dem deutschen Zugewinnausgleich entspricht. Dieser Güterstand kann von den Ehegatten in beiden Ländern statt des jeweiligen gesetzlichen Güterstandes und neben den jeweiligen anderen nationalen Wahlgüterständen gewählt werden. Die Möglichkeit, dem Abkommen deutsch-französischen Ursprungs beizutreten, steht auch anderen Mitgliedstaaten der Europäischen Union offen.

Mit dem vorliegenden Vertragsgesetz werden die innerstaatlichen Voraussetzungen nach Artikel 59 Absatz 2 Satz 1 des Grundgesetzes für die Ratifikation geschaffen.

Gleichzeitig regelt das Gesetz die innerstaatliche Umsetzung des Abkommens.

---

* Bundesrat Drucksache 67/11, of 4 February 2011, pp. 1–2. This text is reproduced under the Creative Commons Licence 3.0 (Germany).

C. Alternativen
Keine.

D. Finanzielle Auswirkungen
Bund, Länder und Gemeinden werden nicht mit Kosten belastet.

E. Sonstige Kosten
Für die Wirtschaft, insbesondere für kleine und mittlere Unternehmen, entstehen keine Mehrkosten. Auswirkungen des Gesetzes auf Einzelpreise und auf das allgemeine Preisniveau, insbesondere auf das Verbraucherpreisniveau, sind nicht zu erwarten.

F. Bürokratiekosten
Es werden keine Informationspflichten für die Wirtschaft, die Bürgerinnen und Bürger und die Verwaltung eingeführt, geändert oder aufgehoben.

BEGRÜNDUNG ZUM VERTRAGSGESETZ*

A. ALLGEMEINER TEIL

1. TATSÄCHLICHE UND RECHTLICHE AUSGANGSSITUATION

Ehen mit Auslandsberührung sind weit verbreitet. Im Jahr 2009 hatten bei 13 Prozent der in Deutschland lebenden Ehepaare entweder beide Ehegatten eine ausländische oder ein Ehegatte die deutsche, der andere Ehegatte eine ausländische Staatsangehörigkeit. Darunter waren mindestens 34 000 deutsch-französische Ehepaare, nach deutsch-polnischen, deutsch-italienischen und deutschösterreichischen Ehepaaren die viertstärkste Gruppe (Hammes u. a., WiSta 2010 S. 904/911 f). Hinzu kommen deutsche Ehepaare, die im Ausland leben, sowie ausländische Ehepaare, die in Deutschland leben. Da sich die rechtlichen Folgen der Ehe unter anderem nach der Staatsangehörigkeit richten, können Ehen mit Auslandsbezug zu rechtlichen Schwierigkeiten, insbesondere im Hinblick auf güterrechtliche Fragen, führen. Gesetzlicher Güterstand in Deutschland ist die Zugewinngemeinschaft. Die Vermögen der Ehegatten bleiben getrennt, nur bei Beendigung des Güterstandes – etwa wegen Scheidung – wird der in der Ehe erwirtschaftete Zugewinn ausgeglichen. Gesetzlicher Güterstand in Frankreich ist die Errungenschaftsgemeinschaft. Errungenschaften während der Ehe werden zum gemeinsamen Vermögen. Lebt zum Beispiel ein Paar in der Errungenschaftsgemeinschaft nach französischem Recht in Deutschland, so zeigen sich Probleme, wenn die Ehegatten in diesem Güterstand ein Grundstück in Deutschland erwerben. Da der französische Güterstand in Deutschland in der Regel nicht bekannt ist, führt z. B. die präzise Einschätzung der Tragweite der den einzelnen Eheleuten zustehenden Rechte bei Eintragung eines Eigentumsrechts in das Grundbuch zu erheblichen Unsicherheiten (zur Errungenschaftsgemeinschaft nach spanischem Recht vgl. z. B. OLG Düsseldorf, FamRZ 2010, 1564 f.). Für ein deutsches Kreditinstitut ist insbesondere fraglich, welche Auswirkungen Verbindlichkeiten eines Ehegatten oder seine Insolvenz auf das in der Errungenschaftsgemeinschaft gebundene Vermögen haben. Die praktisch häufig anzutreffende Lösung, dass die Ehegatten für in Deutschland belegenes Vermögen gemäß Artikel 15 Absatz 2 des Einführungsgesetzes zum Bürgerlichen Gesetzbuche

* Bundesrat Drucksache 67/11, of 4 February 2011, pp. 7–10. This text is reproduced under the Creative Commons Licence 3.0 (Germany).

(EGBGB) deutsches Güterrecht wählen, beantwortet zwar diese Frage, mutet ihnen aber einen gespaltenen Güterstand zu, der bei einem güterrechtlichen Ausgleich zu Abrechnungsschwierigkeiten führen kann. Ähnliche Probleme werden deutsche Paare in Frankreich angesichts der gänzlich anderen Traditionen vorfinden.

Die Wahl einer bilateralen staatsvertraglichen Lösung bietet den Vorteil, möglichst zeitnah Lösungen für die betroffenen Ehegatten anbieten zu können, weil eine inhaltliche Angleichung des Familienrechts in allen Mitgliedstaaten der Europäischen Union aufgrund von unterschiedlichen, häufig in Jahrhunderten gewachsenen und tief in der Bevölkerung verwurzelten Rechtstraditionen notwendigerweise nur sehr viel langsamer vorankommen kann. Dazu gibt es für die Französische Republik und die Bundesrepublik Deutschland auch einen politischen Auftrag. Aus der gemeinsamen Erklärung zum 40. Jahrestag des Elysée-Vertrages 2003 stammt der Wunsch, das deutsche und französische Familienrecht einander anzugleichen.

Die Möglichkeit, dem Abkommen vom 4. Februar 2010 zwischen der Bundes republik Deutschland und der Französischen Republik über den Güterstand der Wahl-Zugewinngemeinschaft (im Folgenden: Abkommen) beizutreten, steht weiteren Mitgliedstaaten der Europäischen Union offen. Auch in diesen Staaten ist das Eherecht, insbesondere das Ehegüterrecht, national sehr unterschiedlich ausgestaltet und führt zu ähnlichen Problemen wie in Deutschland und Frankreich.

2. ZIEL DER ÄNDERUNGSVORSCHLÄGE

Angesichts der rechtlichen Unsicherheiten bei Ehen mit Auslandsbezug soll mit dem Abkommen ein (zunächst) binationaler Wahlgüterstand geschaffen werden, der für beide Rechtsordnungen identische Regelungen enthält und den Betroffenen damit Rechtsklarheit und Rechtssicherheit bieten kann. Um dem neuen Güterstand der Wahl-Zugewinngemeinschaft sowohl in Frankreich als auch in Deutschland Akzeptanz zu verleihen, berücksichtigt er aus beiden Rechtsordnungen stammende güterrechtliche Besonderheiten. In ihrer Grundstruktur entspricht die Wahl-Zugewinngemeinschaft der deutschen Zugewinngemeinschaft, weist aber auch Modifikationen auf, die der französischen Rechtstradition Rechnung tragen. Ehegatten in beiden Ländern können diesen Güterstand anstelle des gesetzlichen Güterstandes neben den anderen nationalen Wahlgüterständen wählen, wenn ihr Güterstand dem Sachrecht eines der Vertragsstaaten unterliegt. Vorschriften des internationalen Privatrechts in beiden Staaten werden nicht berührt. Eines direkten internationalen Bezuges bedarf es nicht, doch wird der Güterstand der Wahl-Zugewinngemeinschaft vor allem bei Ehen mit internationalem Bezug Vorteile für die Ehegatten bieten.

Mit der vorgeschlagenen Änderung des Bürgerlichen Gesetzbuchs (BGB) wird der Wahlgüterstand in das deutsche Familienrecht eingefügt. Die erbschaft- und schenkungsteuerlichen Regelungen entsprechen den Vorschriften über die Zugewinngemeinschaft nach deutschem Recht und sollen sicherstellen, dass Eheleute nicht aus steuerlichen Gründen von der Wahl des neuen Güterstandes Abstand nehmen.

3. GESETZGEBUNGSZUSTÄNDIGKEIT

Die Gesetzgebungszuständigkeit des Bundes folgt aus Artikel 73 Absatz 1 Nummer 1 (Auswärtige Angelegenheiten), Artikel 74 Absatz 1 Nummer 1 (Bürgerliches Recht) und Artikel 105 Absatz 2 zweite Alternative in Verbindung mit Artikel 72 Absatz 2 des Grundgesetzes (Steuerrecht).

Ein Bundesgesetz ist nach Artikel 72 Absatz 2 des Grundgesetzes zur Wahrung der Rechtseinheit im gesamtstaatlichen Interesse erforderlich. Um eine Vereinheitlichung des Rechts in Frankreich und Deutschland zu erreichen, ist zwingende Voraussetzung, dass in der Bundesrepublik Deutschland ein einheitliches Recht gilt. Das kann nur durch eine bundesgesetzliche Regelung erfolgen. So würden unterschiedliche Regelungen bei der Erbschaftsteuer Rechtsunsicherheit im Erbfall erzeugen und aufgrund der Streubreite der im einzelnen Erbfall begünstigten Personen zu einer Rechtszersplitterung mit problematischen Folgen führen, die im Interesse sowohl des Bundes als auch der Länder nicht hingenommen werden kann.

Die Zustimmung des Bundesrates ist nach Artikel 105 Absatz 3 des Grundgesetzes erforderlich, da das Aufkommen der Erbschaft- und Schenkungsteuer nach Artikel 106 Absatz 2 Nummer 2 des Grundgesetzes den Ländern zusteht.

B. BESONDERER TEIL

Zu Artikel 1 (Zustimmung)

Da sich das Abkommen auf Gegenstände der Bundesgesetzgebung bezieht, ist Artikel 59 Absatz 2 Satz 1 des Grundgesetzes anzuwenden.

Zu Artikel 2 (Änderung des Bürgerlichen Gesetzbuchs)

Zu Nummer 1 (Änderung der Inhaltsübersicht)

Da ein neues Kapitel 4 in das Buch 4 – Familienrecht – des Bürgerlichen Gesetzbuchs eingefügt werden soll, ist auch die Inhaltsübersicht zu ergänzen.

Zu Nummer 2

a) Allgemeines

Mit der Einführung des neuen Kapitels 4 „Wahl-Zugewinngemeinschaft" soll deutlich gemacht werden, dass der Güterstand der Wahl-Zugewinngemeinschaft nach dem Abkommen ein weiterer, durch Ehevertrag wählbarer Güterstand ist, der gleichberechtigt neben die in den Kapiteln 2 und 3 genannten Wahlgüterstände der Gütertrennung und der Gütergemeinschaft tritt.

b) §1519 BGB – neu –

aa) Grundsatz

§1519 BGB – neu – trägt der Beschränkung der Vertragsfreiheit in §1409 BGB Rechnung. Nach den §§1408 f. BGB können die Ehegatten statt des gesetzlichen Güterstandes der Zugewinngemeinschaft vertraglich die Gütertrennung oder die Gütergemeinschaft wählen. Mit dem neuen §1519 BGB tritt der Güterstand der Wahl-Zugewinngemeinschaft nach dem Abkommen zwischen der Bundesrepublik Deutschland und der Französischen Republik über den Güterstand der Wahl-Zugewinngemeinschaft als weiterer, durch Ehevertrag wählbarer Güterstand hinzu. Die einzelnen in Deutschland und Frankreich identischen Regelungen finden sich in den Artikeln 1 bis 19 des Abkommens. Zur Begründung wird auf die Denkschrift verwiesen, die den Erläuternden Bericht zu dem Abkommen, den Frankreich und Deutschland abgestimmt haben, in sich aufnimmt.

bb) Anwendung der §§1368 und 1412 BGB

Artikel 5 des Abkommens regelt die Unwirksamkeit von Verfügungen über Haushaltsgegenstände und die Ehewohnung. Die Durchsetzung eines unwirksamen Rechtsgeschäfts gegenüber einem dadurch begünstigten Dritten regelt die Vorschrift nicht. Mit der Bezugnahme auf §1368 BGB im Vertragsgesetz soll deshalb auch der Ehegatte, der bei einer unberechtigten Veräußerung durch Artikel 5 des Abkommens geschützt wird, die Möglichkeit erhalten, die sich aus der Unwirksamkeit der Verfügung über Haushaltsgegenstände oder die Familienwohnung ergebenden Rechte gegen einen Dritten geltend zu machen.

Die Anwendung von §1412 BGB hingegen wird ausgeschlossen. Die Unwirksamkeit einer Verfügung gegenüber einem Dritten soll nicht davon abhängen, dass der die Wahl-Zugewinngemeinschaft begründende Ehevertrag in das Güterrechtsregister eingetragen ist oder dem Dritten bekannt war. Die Eintragung in das Güterrechtsregister wäre angesichts seiner geringen praktischen Bedeutung eine überflüssige Förmlichkeit, die für den Verkehrsschutz keinen Mehrwert brächte. Insbesondere bei Verfügungen über Immobilien werden beurkundende Notare in Zukunft die Möglichkeit eines Verfügungsverbots in Betracht zu ziehen haben.

c) Abgrenzung zum sonstigen Güterrecht im weiteren Sinne

Der neue Güterstand verdrängt in seinem Anwendungsbereich das eheliche Güterrecht.

aa) §1357 BGB

Neben der speziellen Regelung in Artikel 6 des Abkommens, der die gesamtschuldnerische Haftung der Eheleute für Geschäfte eines Ehegatten zur Führung des Haushaltes regelt, besteht für eine Anwendung des §1357 BGB kein Raum mehr.

bb) §1365 BGB

Artikel 5 Absatz 1 des Abkommens, der abschließenden Charakter hat, verhindert, dass daneben auch noch §1365 BGB Anwendung finden kann. Eine solche Schutzvorschrift wurde bewusst nicht in das Abkommen übernommen (siehe den Erläuternden Bericht zu Artikel 5 Absatz 1 des Abkommens).

cc) §1382 BGB

Artikel 17 Absatz 2 des Abkommens enthält keine spezielle Regelung über die Höhe des Zinssatzes bei einer Stundung. Gleichwohl wird eine Verweisung auf §1382 Absatz 4 BGB nicht vorgesehen. Deshalb gilt insoweit §246 BGB. Der Zinssatz beträgt daher 4 Prozent. Ist der Ausgleichsschuldner in Verzug, beträgt der Zinssatz 5 Prozentpunkte über dem Basiszinssatz (§288 Absatz 1 Satz 2, §247 BGB). Auch ein besonderes Bedürfnis, die verfahrensrechtliche Spezialnorm des §1382 Absatz 5 BGB zu übernehmen, nach der ein Stundungsantrag nur in einem anhängigen Rechtsstreit über den Zugewinnausgleich gestellt werden kann, besteht nicht.

dd) §1384 BGB

Bei Auflösung der Ehe durch gerichtliche Entscheidung ist nach Artikel 13 des Abkommens für die Ermittlung des Zugewinns der Zeitpunkt der Einreichung des Antrages beim Gericht maßgeblich. Damit wird nicht – wie in §1384 BGB – auf die Rechtshängigkeit durch Zustellung des Antrags an den Antragsgegner abgestellt. Maßgeblich ist der Zeitpunkt, zu dem der Antrag bei Gericht eingeht.

ee) Versorgungsausgleich

Ein güterrechtlicher Ausgleich für die dem Versorgungsausgleich unterliegenden Anrechte zur Altersversorgung findet nicht statt, §1587 BGB in Verbindung mit §2 Absatz 4 des Versorgungsausgleichsgesetzes. Dies gilt auch bei der Wahl-Zugewinngemeinschaft. Die Ehegatten können die in Deutschland und Frankreich unterschiedliche Zuordnung des Altersvorsorgevermögens durch Abschluss eines Ehevertrages regeln. Eine Lösung der unterschiedlichen Zuordnung des Altersvorsorgevermögens hätte angesichts der Besonderheiten des deutschen Versorgungsausgleichs den neuen Wahlgüterstand überfrachtet.

d) Erbrechtliche Abwicklung des Güterstandes
Im Gegensatz zum Bürgerlichen Gesetzbuch, das für die Abwicklung des gesetzlichen Güterstandes beim Tod eines Ehegatten die spezielle Bestimmung des §1371 BGB enthält, trifft das Abkommen für diesen Fall keine gesonderte Regelung.
§1371 Absatz 1 BGB erhöht den gesetzlichen Erbteil des überlebenden Ehegatten (§1931 Absatz 1 BGB) um ein Viertel, um den Zugewinn pauschal auszugleichen. Die Verbindung von Güterrecht und Erbrecht, die auch im deutschen Recht immer wieder kritisiert wird, ist dem Abkommen fremd. Durch eine Anwendung von §1371 Absatz 1 BGB stünde dem überlebenden Ehegatten, für den deutsches Recht gilt, trotz des vereinbarten Güterstandes der Wahl-Zugewinngemeinschaft materiellrechtlich ein anderer Zugewinnausgleich zu als dem überlebenden Ehegatten, für den französisches Recht gilt. Dies widerspräche dem Zweck des Abkommens, einen einheitlichen Güterstand zu schaffen, der sich in den beteiligten Ländern weitestgehend gleicht. Beim Tod eines Ehegatten ist daher zunächst der Zugewinn auszugleichen.
e) Einbeziehung des Lebenspartnerschaftsrechts
Der neue Güterstand der Wahl-Zugewinngemeinschaft soll auch Lebenspartnern im Sinne des Lebenspartnerschaftsgesetzes (LPartG) offenstehen. Nach den §§6 und 7 LPartG gelten für Lebenspartner bereits die güterrechtlichen Regelungen, die auch für Ehegatten zur Anwendung kommen. Eine vollständige Gleichstellung mit der Ehe ist damit erreicht. Für den Güterstand der Wahl-Zugewinngemeinschaft soll hiervon keine Ausnahme gemacht werden. §6 LPartG lässt die Wahl eines anderen als des gesetzlichen Güterstandes der Zugewinngemeinschaft im Lebenspartnerschaftsvertrag zu. §7 Satz 2 LPartG erklärt insoweit die §§1409 bis 1563 BGB für entsprechend anwendbar. Der neue §1519 BGB ist damit von dieser Verweisung bereits erfasst.
f) Rechtslage bei Kündigung des Abkommens
Sollte Deutschland das Abkommen kündigen, wären die Konsequenzen in einem Begleitgesetz zu regeln: Entweder wird der materielle Gehalt des Abkommens aufrechterhalten oder es werden Abwicklungsregelungen z. B. nach dem Vorbild des Einigungsvertrages (Artikel 234 §4 des Einführungsgesetzes zum Bürger lichen Gesetzbuche) geschaffen.
Sollte Frankreich das Abkommen kündigen, bleibt der Güterstand wegen der statischen Verweisung auf die Vorschriften des Abkommens als ein dann nur noch deutscher Güterstand erhalten.

Zu Artikel 3 (Änderung des Rechtspflegergesetzes)

Gemäß Artikel 12 Absatz 2 Satz 2 des Abkommens kann das Gericht auf Antrag eines der Ehegatten anordnen, dass Gegenstände des Schuldners dem Gläubiger zum Zwecke des Ausgleichs übertragen werden, wenn das der Billigkeit entspricht. Ferner kann das Gericht gemäß Artikel 17 des Abkommens auf

Antrag dem Schuldner die Zugewinnausgleichsforderung stunden und die Leistung einer Sicherheit anordnen. Diese Geschäfte des Gerichts sind mit denjenigen vergleichbar, die das nationale Recht bereits in den §§1382, 1383 BGB dem Rechtspfleger übertragen hat, soweit nicht über die Ausgleichsforderung ein Rechtsstreit anhängig ist (§1382 Absatz 5 BGB). Der Grund für die Übertragung dieser Aufgaben war, dass in diesen Fällen im Allgemeinen keine rechtlichen Schwierigkeiten auftreten, sondern tatsächliche Fragen zu klären und wirtschaftliche Belange abzuwägen sind. Diese Erwägungen treffen – nicht zuletzt wegen der gleichen Grundstruktur der vertraglich vereinbarten Wahl-Zugewinngemeinschaft und der gesetzlich geregelten Zugewinngemeinschaft – auch auf die in Artikel 12 Absatz 2 Satz 2 und Artikel 17 des Abkommens geregelten Fälle zu.

Zu Artikel 4 (Änderung des Gesetzes über das Verfahren in Familiensachen und in den Angelegenheiten der freiwilligen Gerichtsbarkeit)

Zu Nummer 1
In der Inhaltsübersicht ist die neu gefasste Überschrift zum §264 des Gesetzes über das Verfahren in Familiensachen und in den Angelegenheiten der freiwilligen Gerichtsbarkeit (FamFG) anzupassen.

Zu Nummer 2
Die sich aus dem Abkommen ergebenden Ansprüche aus dem Güterstand der Wahl-Zugewinngemeinschaft sind Güterrechtssachen nach §261 Absatz 1 FamFG. Die nach Artikel 5 Absatz 2, Artikel 12 Absatz 2 Satz 2 und Artikel 17 des Abkommens vorgesehenen Verfahren sind denen des §1369 Absatz 2 und der §§1382, 1383 BGB vergleichbar. Durch Aufnahme in §!261 Absatz 2 FamFG werden diese Verfahrensgegenstände auch zu Güterrechtssachen erklärt.

Zu Nummer 3
§264 Absatz 1 Satz 1 FamFG regelt für Verfahren nach den §§1382 und 1383 BGB als Ausnahme zu §40 Absatz 2 FamFG, dass eine Entscheidung des Gerichts erst mit Rechtskraft wirksam wird. Wie §1383 BGB beim Güterstand der Zugewinngemeinschaft sieht Artikel 12 Absatz 2 Satz 2 des Abkommens beim Güterstand der Wahl-Zugewinngemeinschaft eine Abgeltung der Ausgleichsforderung in Natur als Sonderfall auf Antrag eines Beteiligten vor, wenn das der Billigkeit entspricht. Artikel 17 des Abkommens sieht die Möglichkeit einer gerichtlichen Stundung der Ausgleichsforderung vor, für die gegebenenfalls auch Sicherheit zu leisten ist, und trifft damit für den Güterstand der Wahl-Zugewinngemeinschaft eine §1382 BGB vergleichbare Regelung. Die Regelungen der Artikel 12 Absatz 2 Satz 2 und Artikel 17 des Abkommens sind denen der §§1382 und 1383 BGB ähnlich und sollen im güterrechtlichen Verfahren entsprechend gleich behandelt werden. Aus diesem Grund soll auch in Verfahren

nach Artikel 12 Absatz 2 Satz 2 und Artikel 17 des Abkommens die Entscheidung des Gerichts erst mit Rechtskraft wirksam werden.

Zu Nummer 4
§269 Absatz 1 FamFG regelt, welche Verfahren Lebenspartnerschaftssachen sind. Dazu zählen nach §269 Absatz 1 Nummer 11 FamFG auch Entscheidungen nach §6 LPartG in Verbindung mit §1365 Absatz 2, §1369 Absatz 2, §§1382 und 1383 BGB und nach §269 Absatz 1 Nummer 12 FamFG Entscheidungen nach §7 LPartG in Verbindung mit §§1426, 1430 und 1452 BGB. Um die bereits unter Artikel 2 Nummer 2 Buchstabe e des Vertragsgesetzes beschriebene Gleichstellung der Lebenspartnerschaft mit der Ehe auch im güterrechtlichen Verfahrensrecht umzusetzen, soll die Regelung in §269 Absatz 1 Nummer 12 FamFG klarstellen, dass Entscheidungen in diesem Sinne auch solche aufgrund von §1519 BGB in Verbindung mit Artikel 5 Absatz 2, Artikel 12 Absatz 2 Satz 2 und Artikel 17 des Abkommenssind.

Zu Artikel 5 (Änderung des Erbschaftsteuer- und Schenkungsteuer gesetzes)

Die erbschaft- und schenkungsteuerrechtlichen Folgen einer Beendigung des Güterstandes der Wahl-Zugewinngemeinschaft sollen denjenigen bei Beendigung des gesetzlichen Güterstandes des Bürgerlichen Gesetzbuchs angeglichen werden. Eine steuerrechtliche Ungleichbehandlung gegenüber dem gesetzlichen Güterstand der Zugewinngemeinschaft würde den neuen Güterstand andernfalls in der Praxis zu einer eher zweitrangigen Alternative machen. Entsprechend §5 Absatz 2 des Erbschaftsteuerund Schenkungsteuergesetzes (ErbStG) soll die Zugewinnausgleichsforderung nach Artikel 12 des Abkommens keinen Erwerb im Sinne der §§3 und 7 ErbStG darstellen. Das soll unabhängig davon gelten, ob der Güterstand der Wahl-Zugewinngemeinschaft durch den Tod eines Ehegatten oder bereits zu Lebzeiten der Ehegatten beendet wurde. Damit unterliegt die Zugewinnausgleichsforderung, sofern sie konkret errechnet wurde und Grundlage eines Vermögenstransfers ist, nicht der Besteuerung nach dem ErbStG.

Einer Befreiung entsprechend §5 Absatz 1 ErbStG bedarf es nicht. Im Fall der erbrechtlichen Abwicklung des Zugewinnausgleichs (§1371 Absatz 1 BGB) wird der überlebende Ehegatte durch die Vorschrift für einen Erwerb im Sinne der §§3 und 7 ErbStG in Höhe der fiktiven Ausgleichsforderung von der Erbschaftsteuer befreit, die dieser unter den Voraussetzungen der §§1373 bis 1383, 1390 BGB hätte geltend machen können. Da im Güterstand der Wahl-Zugewinngemeinschaft der Zugewinnausgleich bei Beendigung des Güterstandes nur durch Ermittlung der tatsächlichen Zugewinnausgleichsforderung geltend gemacht werden kann, fehlt für §5 Absatz 1 ErbStG der Anwendungsbereich.

Ferner bedarf es keiner entsprechenden Anwendung von §29 Absatz 1 Nummer 2 ErbStG. Nach §29 Absatz 1 Nummer 2 ErbStG erlischt die Steuer mit Wirkung für die Vergangenheit, soweit in den Fällen des §5 Absatz 2 ErbStG unentgeltliche Zuwendungen, die steuerpflichtig waren, gemäß §1380 Absatz 1 BGB auf die Ausgleichsforderung angerechnet worden sind. Da das Abkommen eine derartige Anrechnung nicht regelt, fehlt für §29 Absatz 1 Nummer 2 ErbStG der Anknüpfungspunkt.

Zu Artikel 6 (Inkrafttreten)

Die Absätze 1 und 2 regeln das Inkrafttreten des Gesetzes. Die Bestimmungen entsprechen dem Erfordernis des Artikels 82 Absatz 2 Satz 1 des Grundge setzes. Nach Absatz 2 Satz 2 ist der Zeitpunkt, zu dem das Abkommen nach seinem Artikel 20 in Kraft tritt, im Bundesgesetzblatt bekannt zu geben.

Schlussbemerkungen

Mit dem Abkommen zwischen der Bundesrepublik Deutschland und der Französischen Republik über den Güterstand der Wahl-Zugewinngemeinschaft haben die beteiligten Staaten ein neues Modell für die Integration der Zivilrechtsordnungen in Europa entwickelt. Das Abkommen steht grundsätzlich jedem Mitgliedstaat der Europäischen Union zum Beitritt offen und erweitert damit unter dem Regime der Privatautonomie die Handlungsoptionen der Bürgerinnen und Bürger, indem es ein neues Sachrecht schafft. Der hiermit vorgelegte Entwurf eines Ratifikations- und Umsetzungsgesetzes macht denen, für die deutsches Güterrecht gilt, diese neue Option nach Inkrafttreten des Abkommens zugänglich.

Für die öffentlichen Haushalte und für die Wirtschaft, insbesondere für kleinere und mittlere Unternehmen, entstehen keine Mehrkosten. Auswirkungen des Gesetzes auf Einzelpreise und das allgemeine Preisniveau, insbesondere auf das Verbraucherpreisniveau, sind nicht zu erwarten.

Der Gesetzentwurf steht im Einklang mit den Leitgedanken der Bundesregierung zur nachhaltigen Entwicklung im Sinne der nationalen Nachhaltigkeitsstrategie. Die beabsichtigten Regelungen sollen zu mehr Rechtsklarheit bei Ehen mit Auslandsbezug beitragen.

Es werden keine Informationspflichten für die Wirtschaft, die Bürgerinnen und Bürger und Verwaltung eingeführt, geändert oder aufgehoben.

Der Gesetzentwurf ist mit dem Recht der Europäischen Union und völkerrechtlichen Verträgen, die die Bundesrepublik Deutschland abgeschlossen hat, vereinbar.

Auswirkungen von gleichstellungspolitischer Bedeutung sind nicht zu erwarten.

RATIFIZIERUNGSGESETZ*

Gesetz zu dem Abkommen vom 4. Februar 2010 zwischen der Bundesrepublik Deutschland und der Französischen Republik über den Güterstand der Wahl-Zugewinngemeinschaft vom 15 März 2012
Der Bundestag hat mit Zustimmung des Bundesrates das folgende Gesetz beschlossen:

Artikel 1. Zustimmung

Dem in Paris am 4. Februar 2010 unterzeichneten Abkommen zwischen der Bundesrepublik Deutschland und der Französischen Republik über den Güterstand der Wahl-Zugewinngemeinschaft wird zugestimmt. Das Abkommen wird nachstehend veröffentlicht.

Artikel 2. Änderung des Bürgerlichen Gesetzbuchs

Das Bürgerliche Gesetzbuch in der Fassung der Bekanntmachung vom 2. Januar 2002 (BGBl. I S. 42, 2909; 2003 I S. 738), das zuletzt durch Artikel 1 des Gesetzes vom 17. Januar 2011 (BGBl. I S. 1600) geändert worden ist, wird wie folgt geändert:

1. In der Inhaltsübersicht wird nach der Angabe zum Buch 4 Abschnitt 1 Titel 6 Untertitel 2 Kapitel 3 folgende Angabe eingefügt:
   „Kapitel 4
   Wahl-Zugewinngemeinschaft".

2. Nach §1518 wird folgendes Kapitel 4 eingefügt:
   „Kapitel 4
   Wahl-Zugewinngemeinschaft
   §1519
   Vereinbarung durch Ehevertrag
   Vereinbaren die Ehegatten durch Ehevertrag den Güterstand der Wahl-Zugewinngemeinschaft, so gelten die Vorschriften des Abkommens vom 4. Februar 2010 zwischen der Bundesrepublik Deutschland und der Französischen Republik über den Güterstand der Wahl-Zugewinngemeinschaft. §1368 gilt entsprechend. §1412 ist nicht anzuwenden."

* Bundesgesetzblatt, 2012, II, p. 178–179. This text is reproduced under the Creative Commons Licence 3.0 (Germany).

Artikel 3. Änderung des Rechtspflegergesetzes

§25 Nummer 3 des Rechtspflegergesetzes vom 5. November 1969 (BGBl. I S. 2065), das zuletzt durch Artikel 5 des Gesetzes vom 7. Dezember 2011 (BGBl. I S. 2582) geändert worden ist, wird wie folgt geändert:

1. In Buchstabe b wird der Punkt am Ende durch ein Komma ersetzt.

2. Folgender Buchstabe c wird angefügt:
   „c) die Entscheidung über die Stundung einer Ausgleichsforderung und Übertragung von ermögensgegenständen nach §1519 des Bürgerlichen Gesetzbuchs in Verbindung mit Artikel 12 Absatz 2 Satz 2 und Artikel 17 des Abkommens vom 4. Februar 2010 zwischen der Bundesrepublik Deutschland und der Französischen Republik über den Güterstand der Wahl-Zugewinngemeinschaft, jeweils auch in Verbindung mit §7 des Lebenspartnerschaftsgesetzes, soweit nicht über die Ausgleichsforderung ein Rechtsstreit anhängig wird."

Artikel 4. Änderung des Gesetzes über das Verfahren in Familiensachen und in den Angelegenheiten der freiwilligen Gerichtsbarkeit

Das Gesetz über das Verfahren in Familiensachen und in den Angelegenheiten der freiwilligen Gerichtsbarkeit vom 17. Dezember 2008 (BGBl. I S. 2586, 2587), das zuletzt durch Artikel 2 Absatzes 32 des Gesetzes vom 22. Dezember 2011 (BGBl. I S. 3044) geändert worden ist, wird wie folgt geändert:

1. In der Inhaltsübersicht wird die Angabe zu §264 wie folgt gefasst:
   „§264 Verfahren auf Stundung und auf Übertragung von Vermögensgegenständen".

2. §261 Absatz 2 wird wie folgt gefasst:
   „(2) Güterrechtssachen sind auch Verfahren nach §1365 Absatz 2, §1369 Absatz 2, den §§1382, 1383, 1426, 1430 und 1452 des Bürgerlichen Gesetzbuchs sowie nach §1519 des Bürgerlichen Gesetzbuchs in Verbindung mit Artikel 5 Absatz 2, Artikel 12 Absatz 2 Satz 2 und Artikel 17 des Abkommens vom 4. Februar 2010 zwischen der Bundesrepublik Deutschland und der Französischen Republik über den Güterstand der Wahl-Zugewinngemeinschaft."

3. §264 wird wie folgt geändert:
   a) Die Überschrift wird wie folgt gefasst:
      „§264
      Verfahren auf Stundung und auf Übertragung von Vermögensgegenständen".

   b) Absatz 1 Satz 1 wird wie folgt gefasst:
      „In den Verfahren nach den §§1382 und 1383 des Bürgerlichen Gesetzbuchs sowie nach §1519 des Bürgerlichen Gesetzbuchs in Verbindung mit Artikel 12 Absatz 2 Satz 2 und Artikel 17 des Abkommens vom 4. Februar 2010 zwischen

der Bundesrepublik Deutschland und der Französischen Republik über den Güterstand der Wahl-Zugewinngemeinschaft wird die Entscheidung des Gerichts erst mit Rechtskraft wirksam."

4. §269 Absatz 1 Nummer 12 wird wie folgt gefasst:
„12. Entscheidungen nach §7 des Lebenspartnerschaftsgesetzes in Verbindung mit den §§1426, 1430, 1452 des Bürgerlichen Gesetzbuchs oder mit §1519 des Bürgerlichen Gesetzbuchs und Artikel 5 Absatz 2, Artikel 12 Absatz 2 Satz 2 oder Artikel 17 des Abkommens vom 4. Februar 2010 zwischen der Bundesrepublik Deutschland und der Französischen Republik über den Güterstand der Wahl-Zugewinngemeinschaft".

Artikel 5. Änderung des Erbschaftsteuer- und Schenkungsteuergesetzes

Dem §5 des Erbschaftsteuer- und Schenkungsteuergesetzes in der Fassung der Bekanntmachung vom 27. Februar 1997 (BGBl. I S. 378), das zuletzt durch Artikel 11 des Gesetzes vom 7. Dezember 2011 (BGBl. I S. 2592) geändert worden ist, wird folgender Absatz 3 angefügt:

„(3) Wird der Güterstand der Wahl-Zugewinngemeinschaft (§1519 des Bürgerlichen Gesetzbuchs) beendet und der Zugewinn ausgeglichen, so gehört die Ausgleichsforderung (Artikel 12 Absatz 1 des Abkommens vom 4. Februar 2010 zwischen der Bundesrepublik Deutschland und der Französischen Republik über den Güterstand der Wahl-Zugewinngemeinschaft) nicht zum Erwerb im Sinne der §§3 und 7."

Artikel 6. Inkrafttreten

(1) Die Artikel 2 bis 5 treten an dem Tag in Kraft, an dem das Abkommen vom 4. Februar 2010 zwischen der Bundesrepublik Deutschland und der Französischen Republik über den Güterstand der Wahl-Zugewinngemeinschaft nach seinem Artikel 20 Absatz 2 in Kraft tritt. Der Tag des Inkrafttretens ist im undesgesetzblatt bekannt zu geben.

(2) Im Übrigen tritt dieses Gesetz am Tag nach der Verkündung in Kraft.
Das vorstehende Gesetz wird hiermit ausgefertigt.
Es ist im Bundesgesetzblatt zu verkünden.
Berlin, den 15. März 2012

Für den Bundespräsidenten
Der Präsident des Bundesrates
Horst Seehofer
Die Bundeskanzlerin
Dr. Angela Merkel
Die Bundesministerin der Justiz
S. Leutheusser-Schnarrenberger
Der Bundesminister des Auswärtigen
Guido Westerwelle

FRENCH

CONTENTS

ACCORD ENTRE LA FRANCE ET L'ALLEMAGNE PORTANT CREATION D'UN REGIME MATRIMONIAL COMMUN*

La création, par accord bilatéral entre la France et l'Allemagne, d'un régime matrimonial commun constitue le principal projet de coopération entre les ministères de la justice français et allemand en matière civile.

Ce régime matrimonial nouveau, inspiré des régimes de participation aux acquêts existant dans chacun des deux pays, fonctionnera selon des règles simples et modernisées, identiques en France et en Allemagne.

Outre une importante dimension politique, ce projet, qui crée un droit matériel commun à nos deux pays, constituera une avancée juridique majeure, encore jamais réalisée, correspondant parfaitement aux objectifs définis dans le cadre de la feuille de route franco-allemande.

Il convient de préciser par ailleurs que d'autres Etats de l'Union européenne pourront adopter le régime matrimonial commun.

I. CHAMP D'APPLICATION DE L'ACCORD

Il a été décidé de prévoir un large champ d'application à l'accord. Le régime matrimonial commun pourra être choisi par l'ensemble des couples dont le régime matrimonial est soumis à la loi d'un Etat contractant. Il ne s'agira donc pas que des couples franco-allemands.

II. NATURE DU RÉGIME

Le régime commun est un régime optionnel de participation aux acquêts, qui ne peut être choisi que par contrat de mariage. Il fonctionne comme un régime séparatiste pendant le mariage, mais à son issue, les époux se répartissent l'écart existant entre leurs enrichissements respectifs. A la dissolution du régime, le patrimoine originaire et le patrimoine final de chaque époux sont comparés

* Available at www.presse.justice.gouv.fr.

pour déterminer dans quelle mesure chacun s'est enrichi ou non pendant le mariage. L'époux qui a réalisé le moins d'acquêts peut alors faire valoir à l'encontre de l'autre une créance de participation égale à la moitié de la différence entre les acquêts de chaque époux. Il n'y a pas de participation au déficit, seulement une participation aux acquêts.

III. FONCTIONNEMENT DU RÉGIME

Le régime commun fonctionne comme si les époux étaient mariés sous le régime de la séparation de biens.

La séparation du patrimoine des époux entraîne deux conséquences.

Tout d'abord, les époux conservent l'administration, la jouissance et la libre disposition de leurs biens personnels. Par ailleurs, chacun d'eux reste seul tenu des dettes nées de son chef, avant ou pendant le mariage.

La séparation du patrimoine des époux n'est cependant pas entière, dans la mesure où ils ne peuvent déroger à l'application de certaines règles impératives :

- le consentement des deux époux est nécessaire pour les actes de disposition qui concernent les objets du ménage ou les droits par lesquels est assuré le logement de la famille (article 5)
- les dépenses engagées par l'un des époux dans l'intérêt du ménage entraînent la solidarité automatique de l'autre (article 6).

Ces règles impératives sont inspirées des règles prévues aux articles 215 et 220 du code civil.

Il convient de préciser qu'en France, les époux seront en outre soumis aux autres règles du régime primaire français, d'application territoriale (par exemple les règles du mandat fixées à l'article 219 du code civil).

IV. LIQUIDATION DU RÉGIME

1. LA DISSOLUTION DU RÉGIME

La date de la dissolution du régime est essentielle. En effet, la détermination de la créance de participation s'effectue en fonction de la composition et de la valeur du patrimoine des époux à cette date.

L'article 7 prévoit que le régime matrimonial est dissous par le décès ou la déclaration de décès de l'un des époux, par le changement de régime matrimonial et par le jugement de divorce ou toute autre décision judiciaire emportant dissolution du régime matrimonial (telle que la séparation de corps ou la liquidation anticipée de la créance de participation). Ces causes de dissolution du régime sont identiques à celles qui existent en France. Par exception, l'article 13 précise que cette date est avancée à la date d'introduction de la demande devant le tribunal lorsque le mariage est dissous par divorce ou par tout autre décision judiciaire.

Ce système diffère en partie de celui qui existe en France. En effet, le code civil prévoit que la détermination du montant de la créance de participation s'effectue en fonction, d'une part, de la composition du patrimoine des époux à la date de la dissolution et, d'autre part, de la valeur du patrimoine au jour de la liquidation du régime.

Outre une simplification des règles de droit applicables, la détermination de la valeur du patrimoine des époux à la date de la dissolution du régime semble opportune dans la mesure où elle permet d'éviter des manœuvres dans le but de rallonger artificiellement les procédures, fondés notamment sur des motivations spéculatrices.

Par ailleurs, la détermination de la valeur du patrimoine des époux à la date de la dissolution du régime ne porte pas préjudice à l'application de la règle selon laquelle le patrimoine doit être valorisé au plus près de la date du partage. En effet, la liquidation du régime de la participation aux acquêts n'entraîne aucun partage.

2. LA DÉTERMINATION DU MONTANT DE LA CRÉANCE DE PARTICIPATION

A titre liminaire, il convient de préciser que l'article 3 précise que les époux peuvent, dans le contrat de mariage, déroger aux règles du chapitre V, c'est-à-dire aux règles qui concourent à la détermination du montant de la créance de participation (notamment les règles qui concernent la composition et l'évaluation du patrimoine).

A la dissolution du régime, l'époux qui a réalisé le moins d'acquêts pendant le régime peut faire valoir à l'encontre de son conjoint une créance de participation, égale à la moitié de la différence entre les acquêts de chacun des époux.

Sauf cas particuliers, cette créance est toutefois limitée à la moitié de la valeur du patrimoine de l'époux débiteur tel qu'il existe, après déduction des dettes, à la date de la dissolution du régime (ou à la date d'introduction de la demande au tribunal, lorsque le régime est dissous par divorce ou par une autre décision judiciaire).

La comparaison du patrimoine originaire et du patrimoine final de chaque époux permet de déterminer dans quelle mesure chaque époux s'est enrichi ou non pendant le mariage.

– LE PATRIMOINE ORIGINAIRE

a. Composition

Le patrimoine originaire comprend, d'une part, les biens qui appartiennent à l'époux à la date à laquelle le régime matrimonial entre en vigueur et, d'autre part, les biens qu'il a reçus ultérieurement par succession ou donation ou les indemnités perçues en réparation d'un dommage corporel ou moral.

Les fruits de ces biens ne font pas partie de ce patrimoine. Ils seront donc considérés comme des acquêts s'ils ne sont pas dépensés.

En outre, pour ne pas décourager les donations de biens originaires consenties au profit de parents en ligne directe, les articles 8 et 10 assurent la neutralité de ces libéralités pour le calcul de la créance de participation. En effet, ces biens ne sont pris en compte dans aucun des patrimoines des époux.

Enfin, l'article 8 prévoit que les dettes sont inscrites dans le patrimoine originaire, et ce même lorsqu'elles dépassent le montant de l'actif. La prise en compte du patrimoine originaire négatif, qui existe également en France, assure une certaine justice entre les époux pour le calcul du montant de la créance de participation.

La preuve du patrimoine originaire est en principe rapportée par un inventaire, qui est présumé exact lorsque les deux époux l'ont signé. Toutefois, lorsqu'un tel descriptif du patrimoine n'a pas été établi, chaque époux est libre de rapporter la preuve de la consistance de son patrimoine originaire. Si aucun inventaire patrimonial n'a été établi, le patrimoine originaire est présumé nul.

b. Estimation

Différentes méthodes ont vocation à s'appliquer pour procéder à l'évaluation des biens qui composent le patrimoine originaire des époux.

Tout d'abord, l'article 9 prévoit d'une part, que les biens qui appartiennent à l'époux à la date à laquelle le régime matrimonial entre en vigueur sont évalués à la valeur qu'ils ont à cette date et, d'autre part, que les biens qui sont acquis après la date de prise d'effet du régime matrimonial (tels que les biens reçus par succession) sont évalués à la valeur qu'ils ont lors de l'acquisition.

Dans la mesure où ces biens sont évalués à une date antérieure à la dissolution du régime matrimonial, leur valeur est indexée, à compter de leur date d'évaluation.

Par ailleurs, l'article 9 précise que les immeubles et droits réels immobiliers du patrimoine originaire, autres que l'usufruit et le droit d'usage et d'habitation, sont évalués à la date de la dissolution du régime. Ces biens sont estimés d'après leur état au jour de l'entrée en vigueur du régime, ou de l'acquisition, et d'après leur valeur au jour où le régime matrimonial est dissous. Si les biens ont été aliénés, on retient leur valeur au jour de l'aliénation, en fonction de leur état au jour du mariage. Dans la mesure où ces derniers sont évalués à une date antérieure à la dissolution du régime matrimonial, leur valeur est indexée, à compter de l'aliénation.

En ce qui concerne les dettes, leur valeur est également indexée.

Ce système, inspiré des règles d'évaluation qui existent en Allemagne (indexation) et en France (dette de valeur pour les biens immeubles), assure une méthode de valorisation modernisée des biens qui composent le patrimoine originaire. Il convient de préciser que l'indice retenu est la variation moyenne de l'indice général des prix à la consommation des Etats contractants.

– LE PATRIMOINE FINAL

a. Composition

Le patrimoine final regroupe l'ensemble des biens qui appartiennent à l'époux au jour de la dissolution du régime matrimonial.

Certains actifs sont fictivement réunis au patrimoine final. Il s'agit de la valeur des biens qu'un époux :

- a donnés, sauf :
  a) si la donation n'est pas excessive eu égard au train de vie des époux ou
  b) si la donation porte sur un bien du patrimoine originaire donné à des parents en ligne directe. Toutefois, la plus-value apportée par les améliorations réalisées sur ce bien, pendant la durée du régime matrimonial, avec des deniers ne dépendant pas du patrimoine originaire, est ajoutée au patrimoine final ;
- a cédés dans le but de léser l'autre époux ;
- a dissipés.

Toutefois, la valeur de ces biens n'est pas fictivement réunie au patrimoine final lorsque la donation, l'aliénation frauduleuse ou la dissipation est intervenue plus de dix ans avant la dissolution du régime ou si l'autre époux y a consenti.

Enfin, l'article 10 prévoit que les dettes sont déduites du patrimoine final, et ce même lorsqu'elles dépassent le montant de l'actif.

Chacun des époux peut exiger la présentation d'un inventaire établi par un notaire pour établir la preuve de la consistance du patrimoine final.

b. Estimation

Les actifs qui appartiennent à l'époux au jour de la dissolution du régime matrimonial sont évalués à la date de la dissolution du régime.

La valeur des biens qui sont réunis fictivement au patrimoine final se détermine à la date de la donation, de l'aliénation aux fins de nuire ou de la dissipation (la plus-value précédemment visée se détermine à la date de la donation du bien). La valeur est indexée à compter de cette date sur la variation moyenne de l'indice général des prix à la consommation français et allemand.

3. LE RÈGLEMENT DE LA CRÉANCE DE PARTICIPATION

- Prescription de l'action en liquidation de la créance
  L'action en liquidation de la créance de participation se prescrit par trois ans à compter de la connaissance par l'époux de la dissolution du régime. Cette action est en tout état de cause prescrite au plus tard dix ans après la dissolution du régime (article 15).
- Exigibilité de la créance
  En principe, la créance de participation est exigible dès l'achèvement des opérations de liquidation.
  Toutefois, le tribunal peut, si le règlement immédiat de la créance de participation pénalise de manière inéquitable le débiteur, accorder des délais pour le règlement de la créance.
- Paiement de la créance de participation
  En principe, la créance de participation donne lieu à un paiement en argent.
  Toutefois, le tribunal peut, à la demande de l'un ou l'autre des époux, ordonner le règlement en nature de la créance de participation, lorsque celui-ci répond au principe d'équité. Il ordonne alors, à l'effet de ce paiement, le transfert de biens du débiteur au créancier.

RAPPORT EXPLICATIF*

A. PRÉSENTATION GÉNÉRALE

1. SITUATION ACTUELLE

Les mariages entre nationaux de pays différents ne sont plus chose rare aujourd'hui. Près de 13 % des mariages célébrés (en 2006) et des divorces prononcés (en 2005) en Allemagne concernaient des époux de nationalités différentes.

En France, 14,59 % des mariages célébrés en 2006 concernaient des couples mixtes. En outre, en France, les mariages franco-allemands ont représenté en 2003 2 % des mariages binationaux célébrés.

Le droit des régimes matrimoniaux régit les conséquences juridiques d'un mariage sur le patrimoine des époux, les rapports patrimoniaux entre les époux et les relations patrimoniales entre les époux et les tiers. La détermination du régime n'est pas seulement importante pour savoir comment s'éteignent les obligations patrimoniales des époux à la dissolution du régime matrimonial. Le régime produit aussi des effets pendant la durée du mariage, notamment en matière de gestion du patrimoine et d'acquisition de biens, mais aussi en matière de responsabilité d'un époux pour les dettes engagées par l'autre époux avant et pendant le mariage.

Le droit international privé des États permet aux époux de choisir dans des cas déterminés le droit applicable au régime matrimonial.

Les époux peuvent choisir de soumettre leur régime matrimonial à la loi française ou à la loi allemande en fonction de plusieurs critères.

Ainsi, le droit international privé allemand (art. 15 par. 2 EGBGB) permet aux époux de soumettre leur régime matrimonial à la loi allemande dès lors que:

- l'un des époux a la nationalité allemande;
- l'un des époux réside habituellement en Allemagne;
- des biens immobiliers des époux sont situés en Allemagne, pour ces biens.

Si les époux n'ont pas choisi le droit applicable, les rattachements objectifs prévus à l'article 15 par. 1 en relation avec l'article 14 EGBGB s'appliquent. Le droit

* Bundesrat Drucksache 67/11, of 4 February 2011, pp. 20–40.

allemand des régimes matrimoniaux doit ainsi être appliqué lorsque les deux époux sont de nationalité allemande ou si, pendant le mariage, ils résident habituellement en Allemagne.

En ce qui concerne le droit français, la convention de La Haye sur la loi applicable aux régimes matrimoniaux du 14 mars 1978 permet aux époux de soumettre leur régime matrimonial à la loi française dès lors que :

- l'un des époux a la nationalité française ;
- l'un des époux réside habituellement en France ;
- l'un des époux établira sa première résidence habituelle en France après le mariage.

En outre, les époux pourront choisir la loi française pour les biens immobiliers situés en France (art. 3 de la Convention de La Haye précitée).

Enfin si les époux n'ont pas fait de choix, la loi applicable à leur régime matrimonial est la loi de l'Etat sur le territoire duquel ils établissent leur première résidence habituelle après le mariage.

Si la loi allemande ou la loi française est applicable au régime matrimonial, les époux ont alors la possibilité de choisir l'un des régimes existants en Allemagne ou en France :

a) Le droit des régimes matrimoniaux allemand
   Le droit allemand connaît trois régimes matrimoniaux :
   - La participation aux acquêts ;
   - La séparation de biens ;
   - La communauté.

   Le régime de la participation aux acquêts est le régime légal. Les autres régimes ne s'appliquent que lorsque les époux en sont convenus par un contrat de mariage.
b) Le droit des régimes matrimoniaux français
   Le droit français connaît également trois types de régimes matrimoniaux :
   - La communauté (réduite aux acquêts, de meubles et acquêts, universelle) ;
   - La participation aux acquêts ;
   - La séparation de biens.

   Dans le cas de la France, c'est la communauté réduite aux acquêts qui constitue le régime légal. Les autres régimes ne s'appliquent que si les époux en sont convenus par un contrat de mariage.

Les différences, notamment entre les deux régimes légaux, sont considérables :

La participation aux acquêts allemande équivaut à une séparation de biens pendant l'existence du régime, assortie d'une participation aux acquêts à la dissolution du régime, (art. 1363, par. 2 du code civil allemand (BGB)). Ce régime matrimonial ne conduit donc pas à créer une communauté de biens ou de dettes entre les époux. Ainsi, chaque époux conserve l'administration, la jouissance et la libre disposition de ses biens personnels, acquis avant ou pendant le mariage. Réciproquement, chaque époux est seul responsable de ses dettes, nées avant ou pendant le mariage. Cela vaut également pour un objet qui est la propriété indivise des époux. Ainsi, lorsque les époux acquièrent une maison en indivision, chacun d'eux ne peut disposer que de la part indivise qui lui appartient.

Le régime français de la communauté réduite aux acquêts connaît trois masses patrimoniales distinctes : les biens propres de chacun des époux forment deux masses distinctes, et les biens communs en forment une troisième.

Selon l'article 1401 du code civil français (CC), la communauté se compose des acquêts faits par les époux ensemble ou séparément durant le mariage et provenant tant de leur industrie personnelle que des économies faites sur les fruits et revenus de leurs biens propres. En principe, chaque époux a le pouvoir d'administrer seul les biens communs et d'en disposer. Par exception, la réalisation de certains actes requiert une gestion conjointe des époux. Par exemple, les époux ne peuvent l'un sans l'autre consentir des donations entre vifs portant sur les biens de la communauté. En outre, en France, certaines règles du régime primaire, qui s'appliquent quel que soit le régime matrimonial des époux, peuvent notamment restreindre le pouvoir des époux de disposer seul des biens communs.

Ainsi, un époux ne pourra disposer seul des droits par lesquels est assuré le logement de la famille, ni des meubles meublants dont il est garni (résiliation du bail ou vente du logement familial). Cette restriction s'appliquera même si le logement de la famille est un bien propre de l'époux.

2. OPPORTUNITÉ DE CRÉER UN RÉGIME MATRIMONIAL COMMUN

La création d'un régime matrimonial commun, qui se compose, fonctionne et se liquide selon des règles identiques dans les États contractants, constitue une avancée juridique majeure pour les couples, les tiers et les praticiens. En effet, ce régime crée un droit matériel commun aux États contractants.

Dès lors, le choix de ce régime par les couples n'entraînera pas les difficultés qui résultent actuellement de l'adoption du régime de la communauté réduite aux acquêts de droit français lorsque les époux acquièrent, pendant leur mariage, un bien immobilier en Allemagne. En effet dans la mesure où le régime légal français n'est pas connu en Allemagne, l'inscription au registre foncier du droit de propriété au nom des époux en communauté de biens ne permet pas aux tiers de mesurer la portée exacte des droits de chacun des époux. La solution souvent retenue en pratique et qui consiste à choisir, pour un patrimoine sis en Allemagne, un régime matrimonial allemand (art. 15, par. 2, al. 3 EGBGB) résout certes ce problème, mais oblige les époux à un régime matrimonial divisé qui peut entraîner des difficultés de calcul de la créance de participation.

Dans la mesure où le droit français et le droit allemand connaissent le régime de la participation aux acquêts (régime légal en Allemagne, régime optionnel en France), il est apparu ainsi opportun de créer, par le biais d'un accord bilatéral, un régime optionnel supplémentaire, inspiré des régimes de la participation aux acquêts existants dans chacun des deux pays, qui fonctionne selon des règles simples et modernisées, identiques en France et en Allemagne.

Afin de permettre à d'autres États de l'Union européenne d'adhérer ultérieurement à l'Accord, celui-ci prévoit qu'après son entrée en vigueur, tout Etat membre de l'Union européenne pourra y adhérer (art. 21 du régime).

B. PRÉSENTATION DU RÉGIME

CHAPITRE I. CHAMP D'APPLICATION ET DÉFINITION

Article 1. Champ d'application

Le régime matrimonial de la participation aux acquêts est ouvert à tous les époux qui peuvent choisir le régime matrimonial d'un Etat contractant, même en l'absence d'élément d'extranéité. Ainsi, ce régime optionnel peut être choisi par des époux dont le régime matrimonial relève de la loi française ou de la loi allemande en application des règles de droit international privé, même de celles d'un Etat tiers.

Cela est par exemple le cas, en application des règles de droit international privé française ou allemande, pour des époux :

- dont l'un ou l'autre a la nationalité française ou allemande ;
- dont l'un ou l'autre réside habituellement en France ou en Allemagne ;
- dont l'un ou l'autre établira sa première résidence habituelle en France ;
- dont l'un ou l'autre possède des biens immobiliers en France ou en Allemagne, pour ces biens immobiliers.

Ainsi le régime matrimonial optionnel de la participation aux acquêts peut être choisi par deux Allemands qui vivent en France ou par deux Français qui vivent en Allemagne, mais aussi par deux Allemands qui vivent en Allemagne et par deux Français qui vivent en France.

Le choix de ce régime n'implique pas pour les époux de choisir la loi d'un Etat contractant. L'article 1er requiert seulement que le régime matrimonial soit régi par la loi d'un État contractant. Toutefois, dans certains cas, afin d'éviter toute ambiguïté, il pourra être conseillé aux époux de désigner dans leur contrat de mariage la loi applicable à leur régime matrimonial, dans la mesure où le droit international privé le leur permet.

Article 2. Définition

La participation aux acquêts signifie que pendant la durée du régime les patrimoines des époux demeurent séparés. Le régime n'affecte ni les biens, ni les dettes des époux. Il n'existe donc pas une troisième masse patrimoniale commune aux deux époux comme dans les régimes de communauté.

Ce n'est qu'à la dissolution du régime qu'on compare les acquêts réalisés par chacun des époux pendant la durée du régime, en vue de déterminer la créance de participation due par l'un des époux à l'autre.

CHAPITRE II. ADOPTION DU RÉGIME MATRIMONIAL

Article 3. Adoption du régime matrimonial

Au paragraphe 1 :
Les époux peuvent choisir par contrat de mariage le régime optionnel de la participation aux acquêts. Conformément aux règles de droit international privé allemand et français, la forme du contrat doit respecter, soit le droit interne en vigueur au lieu où il est conclu, soit la loi interne applicable au régime matrimonial.

Au paragraphe 2 :
Les époux peuvent choisir par contrat, avant ou pendant le mariage, le régime optionnel de la participation aux acquêts. La possibilité de conclure un contrat avant la célébration du mariage permet, par exemple, d'éviter, lorsque le mariage est célébré en France, que prenne effet une communauté réduite aux acquêts, qu'il faudrait par la suite liquider pour adopter un autre régime.

L'application du régime est évidemment liée à la célébration du mariage. C'est la raison pour laquelle le régime optionnel de la participation aux acquêts ne peut produire ses effets que lorsque le mariage a été effectivement célébré. En Allemagne, ceci n'est pas réglé expressément, mais résulte de l'article 1408 BGB, qui dispose que les parties contractantes doivent être les époux. En France, cela résulte expressément de l'article 1395 CC.

Le régime commun peut également être choisi pendant le mariage.

En droit allemand, les époux peuvent à tout moment choisir de changer de régime matrimonial par contrat de mariage, y compris pour renoncer au régime légal de la participation aux acquêts. Le contrat de mariage prend alors effet au moment de sa conclusion. Ainsi, à compter de la prise d'effet du contrat de mariage, le nouveau régime convenu entre les époux s'applique.

Les époux mariés sous un régime français peuvent, dans l'intérêt de la famille, convenir de changer de régime matrimonial après deux années d'application du régime matrimonial (art. 1397 CC). Ce changement prend alors effet à la date de l'acte notarié qui le prévoit lorsque les époux n'ont pas d'enfants mineurs et lorsque les enfants majeurs ou les créanciers ne se sont pas opposés au changement. En revanche, dans les deux hypothèses précitées, le changement de régime prend effet à la date du jugement qui l'homologue.

Au paragraphe 3:
En vertu du principe de la liberté contractuelle, le paragraphe 3 de l'article 3 précise que les époux ont la faculté de déroger conventionnellement aux règles qui concourent à la détermination de la créance de participation. Par exemple, ils pourront ainsi modifier la composition des patrimoines, les règles d'évaluation des biens, ou encore la hauteur de la participation à leur enrichissement respectif et la répartition des acquêts. Cette faculté de dérogation permet de tenir compte des spécificités nationales et des spécificités du couple.

Dans la mesure où le texte précise que les époux peuvent déroger aux règles du chapitre V, ils ne pourront donc pas déroger à l'application des règles décrites aux articles 5 et 6, qui reprennent les dispositions les plus importantes du régime primaire français. Cette impossibilité de dérogation assure une application identique du régime commun en France et en Allemagne.

CHAPITRE III. ADMINISTRATION, JOUISSANCE ET DISPOSITION DU PATRIMOINE

Le régime commun fonctionne comme si les époux étaient mariés sous le régime de la séparation de biens. La séparation du patrimoine entraîne deux conséquences.

Tout d'abord, les époux conservent l'administration, la jouissance et la libre disposition de leurs biens personnels. Par ailleurs, chacun d'eux reste seul tenu des dettes nées de son chef, avant ou pendant le mariage.

Toutefois, la séparation du patrimoine des époux n'est pas entière dans la mesure où ils ne peuvent déroger à l'application de certaines règles impératives.

Dans la mesure où les règles qui limitent les effets de la séparation du patrimoine des époux ne sont pas les mêmes en France et en Allemagne, le régime commun reprend les dispositions essentielles du régime primaire français afin de permettre au régime de fonctionner de manière identique en France et en Allemagne (art. 5 et 6).

Article 4. Dispositions générales en matière d'administration, de jouissance et de disposition du patrimoine

Le but du régime de la participation aux acquêts est d'assurer une totale indépendance des époux sur leur patrimoine. Par conséquent, en principe, chaque époux doit pouvoir, seul et sans le consentement de l'autre époux, administrer son patrimoine, en user et en disposer. Réciproquement, chaque époux est seul responsable des dettes nées de son chef, avant ou pendant le mariage.

Ce principe de séparation du patrimoine des époux est inscrit dans les régimes allemand (art. 1364 BGB) et français (art. 1569 CC) de participation aux acquêts. La gestion autonome du patrimoine englobe aussi le droit d'acquérir des biens : ainsi, aucun des époux n'a besoin du consentement de l'autre, par exemple, pour entreprendre une activité professionnelle, créer une société ou s'y associer.

Cette séparation du patrimoine des époux comporte toutefois certaines limites, qui sont mentionnées aux articles 5 et 6 du régime.

Ces limites sont inspirées des règles du régime primaire impératif français (art. 215 et 220 CC). Ces règles se substituent aux dispositions correspondantes du régime primaire français, sans préjudice des autres règles de ce régime, lesquelles sont d'application territoriale.

Article 5. Restrictions aux règles de disposition

Généralités :

Dans les ordres juridiques des deux pays, le droit d'un époux de gérer seul son patrimoine peut être restreint, dans des cas exceptionnels, pour protéger l'autre époux.

En Allemagne, pour le régime légal de la participation aux acquêts, les articles 1365 et 1369 BGB prévoient une interdiction de disposer seul du patrimoine dans son intégralité ainsi que d'objets du ménage. Le non-respect de cette interdiction entraîne la nullité de l'acte juridique si l'autre époux ne le confirme pas. La nullité est automatique et opposable à tous.

La France connaît également une restriction du droit de disposer en ce qui concerne les droits par lesquels est assuré le logement de la famille et les meubles meublants dont il est garni. Cela signifie, par exemple, qu'un époux ne peut résilier le contrat de bail afférent au logement principal sans le consentement de son conjoint. Un acte de disposition réalisé sans le consentement de ce dernier n'est toutefois pas automatiquement annulé comme c'est le cas en Allemagne. Il incombe en effet à l'autre époux d'engager pour cela une action en annulation.

Cet acte peut être confirmé par l'époux qui n'a pas donné son consentement.

En France, la restriction à la libre disposition des droits qui assurent le logement familial et des meubles qui le garnissent est inscrite à l'article 215 CC.

Pour éviter que le choix du régime optionnel de la participation aux acquêts n'entraîne dans les deux pays des restrictions différentes en ce qui concerne le droit de disposer librement du logement familial et des objets du ménage, l'article 5 du régime commun, qui reprend la protection du logement familial connue en droit français, étend cette protection à l'ensemble des objets du ménage, qui sont visés en droit allemand.

En effet, la règle française sur les meubles meublants (art. 215 CC) ne protège pas autant l'époux que la règle allemande qui vise les objets du ménage. Le régime commun reprend donc la règle de protection allemande, qui s'applique également, par exemple, à la voiture utilisée pour les besoins de la famille.

En revanche, il n'a pas été nécessaire de prévoir de disposition supplémentaire restreignant les actes de disposition du patrimoine dans son intégralité, à l'instar de l'article 1365 BGB. Dans de nombreux cas, le logement familial constituera en effet vraisemblablement une part importante du patrimoine. Si un époux n'a pas le droit de disposer de sa propriété ou de sa part d'indivision d'un bien immobilier servant de logement familial sans le consentement de l'autre époux, la protection de ce dernier s'en trouve encore mieux assurée qu'en droit allemand, puisque la question ne se pose pas de savoir si la propriété constitue l'intégralité ou seulement une part importante du patrimoine (soit, selon la jurisprudence allemande, 85 % du tout pour les petits patrimoines ou moins de 90 % pour les fortunes plus importantes).

Au paragraphe 1 :
Le paragraphe 1 régit les restrictions aux actes de disposition sur les droits par lesquels est assuré le logement de la famille et les objets du ménage.

Le logement de la famille inclut toutes les pièces que les époux utilisent comme logement, dans lesquelles ils ont habité ensemble ou qui étaient destinées à devenir le logement de la famille, même si le projet n'a pas été mené à son terme. Peuvent ainsi faire partie du logement de la famille les pièces annexes (par exemple la cave, le grenier, le garage, la pièce consacrée au sport et à l'exercice physique).

L'objectif de l'article 5 est d'assurer la protection générale de la famille par rapport au logement familial.

Si un époux dispose de la propriété ou du bail du logement de la famille, cet acte de disposition est par principe nul lorsqu'il a été réalisé sans le consentement de l'autre époux. Cela signifie que l'époux qui est propriétaire d'une maison utilisée comme logement de la famille ne peut pas valablement vendre la maison sans le consentement de l'autre époux. De même, l'époux qui est locataire d'un logement dans lequel vit la famille ne peut pas valablement résilier seul son contrat de location. L'époux qui n'aura pas consenti à la réalisation de l'acte pourra toutefois le confirmer.

La protection du logement de la famille est donc très ample et peut toucher les intérêts des tiers. Le bailleur d'un appartement qui constitue le logement de la famille peut se voir opposer la nullité de la résiliation du bail, même s'il n'avait pas connaissance du régime matrimonial des époux, ni par conséquent, des restrictions opposables aux actes de dispositions de l'époux locataire.

De même, le propriétaire ne peut pas disposer seul des objets du ménage, qu'ils se trouvent dans le logement ou qu'ils en aient déjà été retirés. Toutefois, l'autre époux peut ratifier l'acte de disposition portant sur le logement de la famille ou sur les objets du ménage.

Les conséquences de la nullité des actes ainsi réalisés sont régies par les ordres juridiques des deux pays.

En France, la nullité doit être demandée en justice. Cela ressort de l'article 215 alinéa 3 CC, qui relève d'une règle du régime primaire français qui n'a pas été reprise dans le régime commun, mais qui continue de s'appliquer à tous les époux qui résident en France, quel que soit leur régime matrimonial.

En Allemagne, en revanche, si un tel acte de disposition n'a pas été réalisé avec le consentement de l'autre époux, il est alors automatiquement nul envers quiconque. Contrairement au droit français, il n'est pas nécessaire pour cela d'engager une action en annulation et, en cas de litige, il est possible d'engager directement une action en restitution.

Les procédures conduisant à faire valoir les conséquences juridiques qui s'attachent à la violation de la règle instituée par cet article relèvent de chaque ordre juridique national. En France, l'article 215 alinéa 3 CC s'appliquera donc à l'action en nullité.

Au paragraphe 2:

Les époux ne peuvent disposer l'un sans l'autre des droits par lesquels est assuré le logement de la famille ou des objets du ménage. Toutefois, si l'autre époux n'est pas en mesure de faire connaître un tel consentement, notamment parce que son état de santé ne le lui permet pas, ou s'il refuse de donner son consentement sans que la situation de la famille ne justifie son refus, le juge peut autoriser l'époux à passer seul les actes visés au paragraphe 1er.

L'autorisation par le juge, en cas d'incapacité de l'époux de donner son consentement pour raison médicale, est similaire aux règles d'administration d'urgence de l'article 1454 BGB, mais correspond sur le fond à une procédure simplifiée de désignation d'un assistant, chargé « d'autoriser un acte juridique particulier ».

Cette solution, qui vise notamment à éviter qu'un époux refuse arbitrairement son consentement aux seules fins de nuire à l'autre époux, est reprise du régime primaire français (art. 217 al. 1 CC).

Article 6. Actes relevant de l'entretien du ménage

Au paragraphe 1:

Le paragraphe 1 précise la nature des actes qui, bien que conclus par un seul des époux, entraîne des effets pour l'autre époux.

Conformément au principe général de la séparation des patrimoines, chaque époux peut conclure seul les contrats qui ont pour objet l'entretien du ménage (il peut, par exemple, acheter des objets ménagers). Toutefois, par exception au principe de la séparation des patrimoines, ces contrats ont pour effet d'engager solidairement l'époux qui n'y est pas partie, et ce même lorsqu'il n'y a pas consenti.

Cette règle s'applique aussi aux contrats destinés à pourvoir aux besoins des enfants. Ainsi, les dettes issues d'un contrat conclu par un époux avec un professeur particulier obligeront solidairement son conjoint.

Au paragraphe 2:
Le paragraphe 2 précise que la solidarité précitée est écartée lorsque deux conditions cumulatives sont réunies:

- dans le cas de dépenses manifestement excessives et
- lorsque le tiers contractant avait ou aurait dû avoir connaissance de ce caractère manifestement excessif.

Cette limitation au jeu de la solidarité est nécessaire pour protéger l'autre époux, qui ne saurait être tenu comptable des dépenses déraisonnables engagées par son conjoint. L'appréciation du caractère manifestement excessif de la dette dépend notamment du train de vie des époux. Ainsi, l'achat d'un meuble antique onéreux peut être considéré comme une dépense manifestement excessive si les deux époux ne disposent que d'un revenu modeste. Dans un tel cas, l'autre époux ne sera pas obligé solidairement à la dette si le tiers contractant avait connaissance ou aurait dû avoir connaissance de ce caractère manifestement excessif.

Cette règle est une reprise modernisée de l'article 220 CC existant en France, les époux résidant en France, qui auront choisi le régime commun, seront soumis à l'article 6.

La règle retenue n'est aucunement en contradiction avec le droit allemand. Certes, elle va plus loin que l'article 1357 BGB, mais les époux doivent l'accepter dès lors qu'ils choisissent eux-mêmes par contrat le régime optionnel de la participation aux acquêts. Ils ont ce-faisant accepté librement les dispositions de l'article 6.

CHAPITRE IV. DISSOLUTION DU RÉGIME MATRIMONIAL

Article 7. Causes de dissolution du régime

La date de la dissolution du régime est essentielle. En effet, la détermination de la créance de participation s'effectue en fonction de la composition et de la valeur du patrimoine des époux à cette date.

L'article 7 prévoit que le régime matrimonial est dissous par:

- le décès ou la déclaration d'absence de l'un des époux;
- le changement de régime matrimonial;
- le jugement de divorce ou toute autre décision judiciaire devenus définitifs, emportant dissolution du régime matrimonial.

Dans les dispositions du point n° 1, il est indiqué que la déclaration d'absence met fin au régime matrimonial, y compris dans les cas où elle est inexacte.

Au point n° 2, il est indiqué que le changement de régime matrimonial met également fin au régime optionnel de la participation aux acquêts. En Allemagne, il est en effet possible de changer de régime matrimonial par convention conclue entre les époux. De même, les époux mariés sous un régime français peuvent, dans l'intérêt de la famille, convenir de changer de régime matrimonial après deux années d'application du régime.

Le point n° 3 prévoit d'autres causes de dissolution du régime.

En France, cela correspond aux hypothèses de la séparation de corps, de l'annulation du mariage lorsque les époux sont de bonne foi et de la liquidation anticipée de la créance de participation.

En Allemagne, les décisions concernées sont celles relatives à la liquidation anticipée de la créance de participation et celles relatives à la dissolution du mariage pour cause de nullité.

CHAPITRE V. DÉTERMINATION DE LA CRÉANCE DE PARTICIPATION À LA DISSOLUTION DU RÉGIME

SECTION 1. PATRIMOINE ORIGINAIRE

Article 8. Composition du patrimoine originaire

Aux paragraphes 1 et 2:
Les paragraphes 1 et 2 décrivent les biens qui sont compris dans le patrimoine originaire.
Le patrimoine originaire comprend 3 types de biens:

(a) les biens d'un époux à la date à laquelle le régime matrimonial entre en vigueur.

Bien souvent, les époux concluent un contrat de mariage avant la date de la célébration. Puisque, en vertu de l'article 3, le contrat de mariage prend effet au plus tôt le jour de la célébration du mariage, le régime matrimonial prend effet au plus tôt le jour de la célébration du mariage.

(b) les biens d'un époux reçus ultérieurement par succession ou donation.

Les augmentations d'actif par libéralité ou succession sont comptabilisées au patrimoine originaire dans le droit des deux pays (Allemagne: art. 1374, par. 2 BGB; France: art. 1570 CC).

(c) les indemnités reçues ultérieurement par un époux en réparation d'un dommage corporel ou moral.

En droit français, les sommes reçues à titre d'indemnisation d'un dommage corporel ou moral font partie du patrimoine originaire. En Allemagne, ce n'est pas le cas dans le régime légal de la participation aux acquêts, mais cela fait régulièrement l'objet de débats eu égard au caractère éminemment personnel d'une telle créance. Même si l'article 1374 paragraphe 2 BGB ne permet pas d'élargir l'actif réservé à d'autres faits, les parties peuvent convenir librement de comptabiliser de tels éléments au patrimoine originaire.

La participation doit équilibrer l'enrichissement du patrimoine respectif des époux pendant la durée du régime. Mais il existe des augmentations d'actifs qui sont réalisées totalement indépendamment de la contribution de l'autre époux et qui ne doivent, par conséquent, pas être équilibrées. Cela vaut en particulier pour les actifs énumérés ci-dessus aux points b) et c) que l'époux a reçus par succession, donation ou au titre d'une indemnisation d'un dommage subi (pretium doloris). C'est la raison pour laquelle, conformément au paragraphe 2, ces éléments d'actif doivent également être compris dans le patrimoine originaire et partant être exclus de la participation aux acquêts.

En vertu de l'autonomie contractuelle, les parties sont libres de convenir que d'autres biens que ceux stipulés au paragraphe 1 seront compris dans le patrimoine originaire. Les époux peuvent prendre une disposition en ce sens dans le contrat de mariage (cf art 3. par. 3 du régime).

Le patrimoine originaire est le patrimoine appartenant à un époux diminué du passif à la date de référence. Le patrimoine originaire ne constitue donc pas une masse particulière mais un élément de calcul dans la détermination des acquêts.

Le passif peut donc être déduit même au-delà de la valeur de l'actif. Cela signifie que le patrimoine originaire peut également être négatif.

On trouve des règles correspondantes en France (art. 1570, 1571 CC) et en Allemagne (art. 1374 BGB). Certes, la règle allemande prévoyait, contrairement à la règle française, que le patrimoine originaire ne pouvait pas être négatif, et ne permettait la déduction du passif qu'à concurrence de l'actif. Toutefois, cette règle, qui faisait depuis longtemps l'objet de critiques, a été modifiée par la réforme du droit de la participation aux acquêts du 1er septembre 2009, laquelle permet désormais la prise en compte d'un patrimoine originaire négatif.

Au paragraphe 3:
Le patrimoine originaire ne comprend pas:

(a) les fruits des biens qui le composent.

Cette règle précise que les fruits tirés du patrimoine originaire, comme par exemple les loyers perçus sur un logement détenu en propre, ne sont pas comptabilisés au patrimoine originaire. Ils forment donc également des acquêts. Ce principe de base se retrouve également dans le droit des deux pays (Allemagne: art. 1374, par. 2 BGB; France: art. 1570 CC).

(b) les biens originaires donnés par un époux à des parents en ligne directe au cours du régime matrimonial.

Si l'époux a, pendant l'existence du régime, donné des biens dépendant du patrimoine originaire à des parents en ligne directe, ces biens devront, en vertu du paragraphe 3, point n° 2, être totalement exclus du calcul de la participation. C'est pour cette raison qu'ils ne seront pris en compte ni dans le patrimoine originaire, ni dans le patrimoine final. Cette disposition est inspirée du droit français.

Toutefois, sera prise en considération dans le patrimoine final l'éventuelle plus-value apportée sur un tel bien si elle n'a pas été financée par des deniers dépendant du patrimoine originaire (cf art. 10 sur la composition du patrimoine final).

Cette réglementation opère donc un compromis entre le droit allemand qui prévoit que les biens ainsi donnés sont pris en compte dans le patrimoine originaire et le droit français qui prévoit que les biens du patrimoine originaire peuvent être donnés à toute personne sans entraîner, sous réserve des plus-values réalisées sur ces biens, d'effets sur le calcul des acquêts.

Au paragraphe 4:
Pour éviter des litiges sur le montant du patrimoine originaire lors de la dissolution du régime matrimonial, il peut être opportun de faire établir par notaire un inventaire du patrimoine originaire dès la conclusion d'un contrat de mariage. Les époux peuvent également établir un inventaire sous seing privé.

Un tel inventaire du patrimoine originaire est réputé exact lorsqu'il est signé par les deux époux. La forme notariée n'est pas obligatoire. La présomption d'exactitude de l'inventaire peut être combattue par la preuve de son caractère inexact. Il peut être judicieux d'indiquer la valeur des biens lors de l'établissement de l'inventaire du patrimoine originaire. Dans ce cas, la présomption d'exactitude s'applique également à cette valeur, dans la mesure où, en application de l'article 9 paragraphe 1 n° 1, ces biens sont évalués au jour de l'entrée en vigueur du régime matrimonial (ou à la date de leur acquisition pour les biens visés à l'art. 8 par. 2).

Les ordres juridiques des deux pays connaissent de tels inventaires, qui sont présumés exacts (Allemagne: art. 1377 BGB; France: art. 1570 CC).

Au paragraphe 5:
Si les époux n'ont pas établi d'inventaire du patrimoine, le patrimoine originaire est présumé nul. Cette présomption peut, elle aussi, être combattue.

Article 9. Evaluation du patrimoine originaire

Généralités:
Si les règles encadrant dans les deux pays le régime de participation aux acquêts sont en principe très similaires, elles diffèrent cependant fortement sur un point tout à fait essentiel: l'évaluation du patrimoine originaire.

La France base l'évaluation des éléments qui composent le patrimoine originaire sur leur valeur à la liquidation du régime matrimonial (art. 1571 CC).

L'Allemagne, en revanche, s'appuie sur la valeur qu'avait le patrimoine lorsque le régime matrimonial est entré en vigueur (art. 1376, par. 1 BGB). Les augmentations de valeur basées sur la dévalorisation normale de l'argent ne constituent toutefois pas des acquêts pour la jurisprudence, et ne sont donc pas prises en compte.

Ces différences de date de référence pour l'évaluation peuvent avoir notamment les effets adverses suivants:

- Selon la loi française, au contraire de la loi allemande, les époux courent le risque d'une diminution de la valeur des éléments d'actif qui composent leur patrimoine originaire.
  Exemple en Allemagne:
  Un époux apporte au régime comme seule valeur d'actif un portefeuille d'actions d'une valeur de 100 000 € à l'origine du régime matrimonial. A la dissolution du régime, les actions ne valent plus que 20 000 €. Le patrimoine final de l'époux s'élève au total à 100 000 € (portefeuille d'actions compris). L'époux n'a ainsi pas réalisé d'acquêts auxquels il faudrait faire participer l'autre époux.
  Exemple en France:
  Même situation de départ que dans l'exemple ci-dessus. Le patrimoine originaire de l'époux est valorisé à 20 000 €. Le patrimoine final s'élève à 100 000 € (20 000 et 80 000). L'époux a donc réalisé des acquêts pour un montant de 80 000 €, qui appellent un règlement d'une créance de participation de 40 000 € au profit de l'autre époux (si l'autre époux n'a pas réalisé d'acquêts).

- En droit allemand, contrairement au droit français, l'époux participe aux augmentations de valeur du patrimoine originaire (exception faite des variations dues aux fluctuations monétaires, qui ne sont pas prises en compte) qui inter viennent sans sa contribution. Ainsi existe-t-il des acquêts lorsque l'état d'un bien foncier n'est pas modifié, mais prend de la valeur au fil du temps du fait de son emplacement. En droit français, en revanche, ce cas de figure n'est pas constitutif d' acquêts.

Exemple en Allemagne :
Un époux apporte dans son patrimoine un terrain d'une valeur de 100 000 € au début du régime matrimonial. A la dissolution du régime, le terrain a une valeur de 200 000 €, parce qu'il a été déclaré constructible. Les acquêts donnant lieu à participation se montent donc à 100 000 €. L'époux titulaire de la créance de participation recevra donc 50 000 € (s'il n'a pas lui-même réalisé d'acquêts).
Exemple en France :
Même situation de départ. Le terrain est valorisé à 200 000 €, tant dans le patrimoine originaire que dans le patrimoine final. Il n'y a donc pas création d'acquêts auxquels il faudrait faire participer l'autre époux.

Pour tenir compte à la fois des règles nationales françaises et allemandes, l'article 11 du régime crée un modèle de valorisation qui s'inspire des deux ordres juridiques :

Au paragraphe 1 :
Le point n° 1 du paragraphe 1 s'appuie sur le modèle allemand de valorisation. Les biens existants lors de l'entrée en vigueur du régime matrimonial sont évalués à la valeur qu'ils avaient à cette date.

Cela signifie que l'époux auquel n'appartient pas le bien participe aux augmentations de valeur de ces éléments de patrimoine, même si elles interviennent sans sa contribution (exception faite des variations de valeur dues aux fluctuations monétaires). Ainsi, si, par exemple, un tableau fait partie du patrimoine originaire d'un époux, et si ce tableau voit sa valeur augmenter au fil des ans, parce que l'artiste a gagné en notoriété, cette augmentation de valeur alimente les acquêts.

Pour le patrimoine réservé (donations, successions, sommes versées en indemnisation d'un préjudice subi) qui a été acquis plus tard, mais qui, en vertu de l'article 8, paragraphe 2 fait partie du patrimoine originaire, la date de valorisation est, en vertu du paragraphe 1, point n° 2, le jour auquel ce patrimoine a été acquis.

Au paragraphe 2 :
Le paragraphe 2 précise que les immeubles et droits réels immobiliers du patrimoine originaire, autres que l'usufruit et le droit d'usage et d'habitation sont évalués à la date de la dissolution du régime. La méthode d'évaluation décrite au paragraphe 2 s'applique aux droits réels principaux non viagers. Ces biens sont donc valorisés à la dissolution du régime, ou à la date d'effet retenue dans les cas particuliers mentionnés à l'article 13.

L'objectif de cette disposition est d'exclure des acquêts les augmentations de valeur des biens immobiliers compris dans le patrimoine originaire, lorsqu'elles sont réalisées sans la contribution de l'un ou l'autre des époux. Les biens immobiliers, qui constituent souvent une part essentielle du patrimoine, peuvent en effet subir des fluctuations de valeur qui ne sont en général pas le fait de la contribution des époux. C'est notamment le cas lorsque l'augmentation de valeur d'un logement familial est intervenue du simple fait de la hausse de la cote de son emplacement. Ainsi des biens immobiliers peuvent voir leur valeur augmenter considérablement parce qu'un aéroport situé à proximité ferme ses portes, faisant ainsi disparaître les nuisances sonores qu'il générait. Dans un tel cas, il est tout à fait logique de ne pas faire participer le conjoint à de telles augmentations de valeur.

Les augmentations de valeur des biens immobiliers qui sont dues à la contribution des époux sont, en revanche, constitutives d'acquêts. Elles n'augmentent donc pas la valeur du patrimoine originaire.

Exemple :

Un époux apporte lors de l'adoption du régime un terrain d'une valeur de 50 000 €. Une maison est construite sur ce terrain pendant la durée du régime. A la dissolution du régime, le terrain nu, sans la maison, a une valeur de 100 000 €, l'emplacement ayant pris de la valeur. Le terrain avec la maison a une valeur de 200 000 € à la dissolution du régime. Dans le calcul du patrimoine originaire, on ne retiendra alors que la valeur du terrain nu à la dissolution du régime, soit 100 000 € (l'augmentation de valeur de 50 000 € pendant le mariage qui est due à l'emplacement n'est pas constitutive d'acquêts). Dans le patrimoine final, on tiendra compte du terrain avec la maison, soit 200 000 €. Les acquêts s'élèveront donc à 100 000 €. En l'absence d'autres acquêts, la créance de participation sera donc de 50 000 €.

Si les immeubles et droits réels principaux non viagers ont été vendus ou remplacés pendant le mariage, ces éléments d'actif seront retenus pour leur valeur au jour de la cession ou de la substitution.

Exemple :

Même situation de départ (terrain apporté au jour de l'adoption du régime et sur lequel une maison a été construite pendant l'existence du régime). Ce terrain est vendu avec la maison pendant le mariage. Lors de la vente, le terrain a une valeur de 80 000 €, et la maison une valeur de 100 000 €. Dans le patrimoine originaire, on ne retiendra que la valeur du terrain à hauteur de 80 000 €, qu'il conviendra d'indexer conformément au paragraphe 3. Pour le patrimoine final, ce qui est déterminant, c'est la totalité des actifs encore détenus par l'époux. Le produit de la cession ne se retrouve dans le patrimoine final que s'il en subsiste quelque chose. Si, à la dissolution du régime, l'époux n'a plus par exemple qu'un patrimoine de 80 000 €, il n'a pas d'acquêts à soumettre à participation.

L'usufruit et le droit d'usage et d'habitation sont exclus de cette règle parce qu'en les consommant les deux époux en ont réduit la valeur.

Au paragraphe 3 :

Selon les cas, un mariage peut durer de nombreuses années. La valeur du patrimoine originaire est toutefois déterminée, en vertu du paragraphe 1, au jour de l'entrée en vigueur du régime matrimonial (ou à la date d'acquisition des biens visés à l'art. 8, par. 2). Mais cette valeur monétaire peut diminuer au fil des ans du fait de l'inflation. Les simples augmentations de valeur dues au seul fait de l'inflation ne sauraient pourtant constituer des acquêts. C'est pourquoi le paragraphe 3 établit une règle selon laquelle la valeur monétaire du patrimoine originaire doit être corrigée de l'inflation.

Exemple :

(fictif et sans taux d'inflation concret, puisque le régime conventionnel de la participation aux acquêts ne pourra être applicable qu'au jour de la ratification de l'accord bilatéral) :

A l'origine du régime matrimonial, l'époux a un patrimoine de 100 000 €. Le mariage dure 10 ans. A la dissolution du régime, l'époux a un patrimoine final de 200 000 €. On va considérer de manière fictive que les 100 000 € au début du régime correspondent à une valeur monétaire de 150 000 € à la dissolution du régime. Cela a pour conséquence qu'il faut fixer à 150 000 € la valeur du patrimoine originaire, et à 200 000 € la valeur du patrimoine final. Les acquêts s'élèvent donc à 50 000 €, et la créance de participation, dans la mesure où le conjoint n'a pas fait d' autres acquêts, à 25 000 €.

La France ne permet pas les indexations fondées sur le niveau général des prix ou sur les prix des biens, produits ou services n'ayant pas de relation directe avec l'objet de la convention ou avec l'activité de l'une des parties (art. L. 112-2 al. 1 du code monétaire et financier). Toutefois, dans la mesure où l'article 55 de la Constitution française pose le principe de la primauté des conventions internationales sur les lois, le mécanisme d'indexation retenu pourra donc valablement s'appliquer dans le cadre du régime commun.

Si d`autres Etats adhèrent à l'accord, les valeurs indiquées seront calculées sur la variation moyenne de l'indice général des prix à la consommation de tous les États contractants.

Au paragraphe 4 :

Les règles d'évaluation prévues aux paragraphes 1 et 3 s'appliquent également à l'évaluation des dettes.

Exemple :

(exemple fictif, sans taux d'inflation réel moyen, puisque le régime optionnel de la participation aux acquêts n'est pas encore en vigueur) :

A l'origine du régime, l'époux n'a que des dettes pour un total de 10 000 €. Le mariage dure 10 ans. A la dissolution du régime, l'époux a un patrimoine final de 200 000 €. On va considérer, de façon fictive, que les 10 000 € de dettes au début du régime représentent une valeur de 14 000 € à la dissolution du régime. Cela conduit à évaluer le patrimoine originaire avec son passif pour un montant négatif de 14 000 €, tandis que le patrimoine final s'élève à 200 000 €. Les acquêts se montent donc à 214 000 €.

SECTION 2. PATRIMOINE FINAL

Article 10. Composition du patrimoine final

Au paragraphe 1:
Le premier paragraphe définit ce qu'est le patrimoine final: l'ensemble des biens détenus par un époux à la dissolution du régime ou à la date d'effet prévue à l'article 13, sous déduction des dettes, y compris lorsque le solde est négatif. A l'instar du patrimoine originaire, le patrimoine final peut aussi être négatif. Il ne constitue pas une masse particulière mais un élément de calcul dans la détermination des acquêts.

Les ordres juridiques des deux pays connaissent dans leur régime respectif de participation aux acquêts une disposition en ce sens (Allemagne: art. 1375 BGB; France: art. 1572 et 1574 CC).

Au paragraphe 2:
Il convient dans certaines conditions d'ajouter certains éléments d'actif au patrimoine final. Il s'agit d'éviter qu'un époux cherche, par certains actes de disposition, à réduire ses acquêts, et lèse ainsi son conjoint.

L'ajout à la valeur du patrimoine final des diminutions d'actif qui résultent de donations faites sans le consentement du conjoint ou de cessions réalisées dans l'intention de léser l'autre époux est un fait connu dans les deux systèmes juridiques (Allemagne: art 1375, par. 2 BGB; France: art. 1573 CC). En revanche, la réunion fictive de la valeur des biens dissipés n'existe qu'en droit allemand, à l'article 1375, paragraphe 2, alinéa 2 BGB. Afin de protéger le conjoint, cette dernière disposition est intégrée dans le régime optionnel de la participation aux acquêts.

Au chiffre 1:
La valeur des donations doit en principe être ajoutée au patrimoine final.

Toutefois, elle n'est pas à réunir fictivement lorsque:

(a) elle n'est pas excessive eu égard au train de vie des époux (c'est-à-dire qu'elle ne dépasse pas considérablement le cadre financier correspondant au train de vie des époux);
(b) elle porte sur un bien du patrimoine originaire donné à des parents en ligne directe (cf art. 8 par. 3, point 2). Toutefois, il conviendra de réunir la valeur de la plus-value apportée par les améliorations réalisées pendant la durée du régime sur un tel bien avec des deniers ne dépendant pas du patrimoine originaire.

En outre, aucune valeur ne devra être fictivement réunie au patrimoine final lorsque la donation aura été approuvée par le conjoint ou lorsque la donation est intervenue plus de dix ans avant la dissolution du régime.

Au chiffre 2:
Sont inclus ici les actes juridiques ayant pour but de porter atteinte aux acquêts de l'autre époux ou de l'en priver. L'intention de nuire doit avoir été le motif dominant. Cela comprend, par exemple, la vente d'un objet de valeur pour un prix bien inférieur à sa valeur, si l'objectif était d'influer sur les acquêts.

La valeur de telles cessions ne devra pas être fictivement réunie au patrimoine final lorsque les cessions sont intervenues avec le consentement de l'autre époux ou plus de dix ans avant la dissolution du régime.

Au chiffre 3:
On trouve ici les dépenses inutiles et manifestement excessives par rapport au patrimoine. Cela comprendrait, par exemple, une croisière de luxe effectuée par l'un des époux, alors que les époux n'ont qu'un revenu modeste. Sont aussi pris en compte les biens détruits par l'un des époux, qu'il ait eu ou non pour but de léser l'autre.

La valeur des biens dissipés ne devra pas être fictivement réunie au patrimoine final lorsque la dissipation aura été approuvée par le conjoint ou lorsqu'elle est intervenue plus de dix ans avant la dissolution du régime.

La prescription extinctive décennale est prévue dans le régime allemand de la participation aux acquêts (§ 1375, par. 3 BGB). Cela s'explique par le fait qu'après l'écoulement d'un certain délai, on ne considère plus que l'acte d'aliénation d'actif a été commis dans le but de léser l'autre époux, ou on juge qu'il a finalement été accepté par l'autre époux. En outre, cette disposition apporte une mesure de sécurité juridique.

C'est la raison pour laquelle le délai de dix ans a également été repris dans le régime optionnel de la participation aux acquêts.

Article 11. Evaluation du patrimoine final

Au paragraphe 1:
Le premier paragraphe régit l'évaluation du patrimoine final: on retient comme valeur du patrimoine final la valeur des actifs à la date de dissolution du régime matrimonial ou à la date d'effet prévue dans des cas particuliers à l'article 13.

En France, sous réserve des règles d'évaluation particulières en cas de divorce, séparation de corps ou liquidation anticipée des acquêts, les biens existants qui composent le patrimoine final sont estimés d'après leur état au jour de la dissolution et d'après leur valeur au jour de la liquidation du régime, cette dernière pouvant intervenir plusieurs années après la date de dissolution (art. 1574 CC).

En Allemagne, la valeur des acquêts, et par suite celle du patrimoine originaire et celle du patrimoine final, sont en principe déterminées au moment de la dissolution du régime. Toutefois, elles peuvent être déterminées à un moment plus précoce lorsqu'une demande de liquidation anticipée de la créance de participation a été déposée ou lorsque la demande de divorce est pendante (art. 1378, 1384, 1387 BGB).

Au paragraphe 2:
Le paragraphe 2 concerne la date à laquelle il convient d'apprécier la valeur des biens qui est fictivement réintégrée au patrimoine final, en application de l'article 10 paragraphe 2.

- La valeur des biens visés à l'article 10 paragraphe 2 se détermine à la date de la donation, de la cession aux fins de nuire ou de la dissipation.
- La valeur de la plus-value apportée par les améliorations réalisées, pendant la durée du régime, sur un bien du patrimoine originaire donné à des parents en ligne directe avec des deniers qui ne proviennent pas du patrimoine originaire se détermine à la date de la donation du bien.

Au paragraphe 3:
A compter de cette date, les valeurs indiquées au paragraphe 2 sont indexées sur la variation moyenne de l'indice général des prix à la consommation des États contractants.

SECTION 3. CRÉANCE DE PARTICIPATION

Article 12. Droit à créance de participation

Au paragraphe 1:
Le paragraphe 1 précise qu'à la dissolution du régime, l'époux qui a réalisé le moins d'acquêts pendant le régime peut faire valoir à l'encontre de l'autre une créance de participation, égale à la moitié de la différence entre les acquêts de chacun.

Le patrimoine originaire et le patrimoine final de chaque époux sont comparés pour déterminer dans quelle mesure chacun s'est enrichi ou non pendant le mariage. Les règles de composition et d'évaluation du patrimoine originaire et du patrimoine final, qui ne sont pas identiques, sont précisées aux articles suivants du régime. Si le patrimoine final dépasse le patrimoine originaire, cet excédent constitue les acquêts de l'époux concerné. Il n'y a pas de participation aux déficits, seulement une participation aux acquêts. L'époux dont les acquêts excèdent ceux de l'autre est redevable d'une créance égale à la moitié de la différence.

Au paragraphe 2:
En principe, le règlement de la créance de participation s'effectue en argent. Il en va de même dans les deux pays, en Allemagne et en France, en vertu du droit applicable.

Tandis qu'en France, cela est stipulé expressément à l'article 1576 CC, il n'existe pas en Allemagne de disposition spécifique. Mais il ressort des dispositions des articles 1372 et suivants du BGB qu'il s'agit d'un règlement en argent. Par souci de clarification, la règle française a été reprise dans le régime optionnel de la participation aux acquêts.

Les deux ordres juridiques ne connaissent un règlement en nature que dans des cas particuliers (France : art. 1576 CC ; Allemagne : art. 1383 BGB). Ainsi, le régime commun précise que le tribunal peut, sur demande de l'une ou l'autre des parties, ordonner, à l'effet de ce paiement, le transfert de biens du débiteur au créancier, si cela correspond au principe d'équité. Le juge tiendra compte des intérêts des deux époux.

Au paragraphe 3 :
En France comme en Allemagne, la créance de participation est incessible entre vifs tant que le régime matrimonial n'est pas dissous. Peu importe que la cession soit effectuée à titre gratuit ou onéreux. En revanche, la créance est, après la dissolution du régime, cessible entre vifs et transmissible à cause de mort (Allemagne, art. 1378, par. 3 BGB ; France : art. 1569 CC). Une disposition similaire a donc été reprise pour le régime optionnel de la participation aux acquêts.

Article 13. Date d'effet dans des cas particuliers

En principe, la composition et la valeur du patrimoine des époux ne peuvent être déterminées avant la dissolution du régime matrimonial.

Si le régime est dissous par divorce, il est toutefois souhaitable de ne pas attendre que le jugement soit devenu définitif pour être en mesure de statuer sur le montant de la créance de participation. Il est en effet préférable que le juge puisse statuer sur le montant de la créance de participation et sur le divorce dans le cadre de la même procédure. Ainsi, le régime commun prévoit qu'il convient de substituer la date à laquelle la requête en divorce a été déposée (et non, en France, la date de l'assignation en divorce) à la date de la dissolution du régime pour apprécier la composition et la valeur du patrimoine des époux. Cette règle, qui s'applique même si le juge ne statue pas sur la participation en même temps que sur le divorce, permet de réduire le délai pendant lequel l'époux débiteur de la créance de participation peut diminuer son patrimoine, et ainsi réduire la créance de l'autre époux.

Le régime légal de la participation aux acquêts de droit allemand connaît ce mécanisme (art. 1384 BGB). En revanche, il diffère en partie de celui qui s'applique en France dans la mesure où le droit français prévoit que le régime matrimonial est réputé dissous au jour de la demande pour la seule détermination de la composition du patrimoine (art. 1572 CC).

Ce mécanisme ne joue pas seulement en cas de divorce. Le régime commun prévoit également son application lorsque le régime est dissous par une autre décision judiciaire, notamment en cas de liquidation anticipée de la créance de participation (art. 18 du régime). Il apparaît pertinent également dans ces cas de permettre le calcul du montant de la créance de participation au cours de la procédure tendant à sa liquidation anticipée. Dans ce cas, la date d'évaluation est fixée à la date de l'introduction de l'instance devant le tribunal.

Article 14. Limitation de la créance de participation

Cette disposition vise à assurer que même en tenant compte d'un patrimoine originaire négatif, personne ne soit contraint de céder à son conjoint plus de 50 % du patrimoine final effectivement disponible à la date de son évaluation (date de dissolution ou date d'effet particulière selon l'art. 13).

Cette limitation du montant de la créance de participation correspond à l'idée de base du droit de la participation aux acquêts, selon lequel les deux époux participent équitablement, chacun pour moitié, aux acquêts réalisés pendant le mariage.

L'article 14 garantit, en outre, qu'une créance de participation, hors les cas de réunion fictive mentionnés à l'article 10, paragraphe 2 (sauf le 1. b.), n'apparaît que si, à la date d'effet retenue pour le calcul des acquêts, il existe effectivement un patrimoine positif. Si, par exemple, les deux époux n'ont fait que rembourser des dettes pendant l'existence du régime, ou si l'un des époux n'a pas réalisé d'acquêts et seul l'autre époux a remboursé des dettes, il n'en résultera pas de créance de participation. En effet, il n'y a pas de participation aux déficits.

Cette limitation ne concerne que la créance de participation et non les autres créances et dettes éventuellement nées entre les époux. Cette règle, dont l'objectif vise à conserver à l'époux débiteur de la créance de participation au moins la moitié de son patrimoine, n'est toutefois plus justifiée si l'époux débiteur a diminué son patrimoine de façon déloyale (art. 10, par. 2, à l'exception de l'hypothèse visée au 1. b.).

Ainsi, afin de ne pas limiter le montant de la créance de participation au patrimoine disponible lorsque l'époux a réalisé des actes déloyaux entraînant réunion fictive, l'article 14 du régime prévoit que la limite de la créance de participation est relevée de la moitié du montant ajouté au patrimoine final en application des dispositions de l'article 10 paragraphe 2, à l'exception de l'hypothèse visée au 1. b. En effet, dans ce dernier cas, on ne peut pas considérer que l'époux a diminué ses acquêts de manière déloyale.

De ce fait, l'époux indélicat pourra être contraint de verser tout son patrimoine, et même du fait de la prise en compte de la valeur réunie fictivement, de s'endetter pour honorer la créance de participation.

Conformément à l'article 3 paragraphe 3, les époux peuvent déroger conventionnellement à l'application de cet article.

CHAPITRE VI. DISPOSITIONS DIVERSES

Article 15. Prescription

La créance de participation se prescrit par trois ans à partir de la connaissance par l'époux de la dissolution du régime matrimonial. La règle de prescription par trois ans correspond aux dispositions des ordres juridiques nationaux (Allemagne : art. 1378, par. 4 BGB ; France : art. 1578 CC).

Toutefois, l'ouverture du délai de prescription diffère dans les deux pays. Tandis qu'en Allemagne, le délai court à compter de la connaissance de la dissolution du régime, en France, il court à compter de la dissolution du régime elle-même. Pour protéger l'époux titulaire de la créance de participation, la règle allemande est adoptée pour l'ouverture du délai. Toutefois, dans certaines circonstances, dans la mesure où le délai de prescription court à partir de la connaissance des faits, il peut arriver que la prescription n'intervienne que de nombreuses années après la dissolution du régime. Pour garantir à l'époux débiteur de la participation la sécurité juridique à partir d'une certaine date, l'article 15 prévoit de surcroît une prescription indépendante de la connaissance des faits par 10 ans à compter de la dissolution du régime.

Article 16. Obligation d'information, inventaire

Au paragraphe 1 :
Pour que le montant de la créance de participation puisse être déterminé, chaque époux doit être en mesure de connaître la composition et la valeur du patrimoine originaire et du patrimoine final de son conjoint. C'est pourquoi on accorde aux époux un droit à l'information et à présentation d'un inventaire. L'époux qui sollicite les informations se voit accorder dans ce cadre un droit à présentation de justificatifs. Ainsi, l'époux demandeur de l'information est mieux à même de vérifier les informations transmises par son conjoint, et de faire respecter ses intérêts. En outre, cela permet aussi d'éviter des litiges, dans la mesure où les justificatifs produits sont convaincants. Chaque époux a le droit de demander un inventaire notarial à ses frais. Il existe une disposition correspondante en droit allemand, à l'article 1379 BGB. Dans les dispositions françaises du régime de participation aux acquêts, le droit à présentation d'un inventaire du patrimoine final est aussi défini à l'article 1572 CC, le droit à l'information n'est certes pas mentionné expressément mais il est implicite.

Ce droit à l'information et à la présentation de l'inventaire permettra ainsi à l'époux qui s'est le moins enrichi pendant le régime de faire valoir sa créance de participation.

Au paragraphe 2 :
La situation est la même lorsqu'un époux demande la dissolution du mariage ou la liquidation anticipée de la créance de participation. Le paragraphe 1 s'applique également dans ce cas.

Article 17. Délais de paiement

Le droit allemand (art. 1382 BGB) et le droit français (art. 1576 CC) connaissent la possibilité, d'une part, d'accorder des délais pour le paiement de la créance de participation aux acquêts dans certaines circonstances et, d'autre part, de demander que soient fournies des sûretés.

Au paragraphe 1 :
Le premier paragraphe établit les conditions dans lesquelles peut être accordé un délai de paiement. Dans l'intérêt de l'époux créancier, un tel délai ne saurait être accordé que dans des cas exceptionnels. Il incombe donc au juge de décider si la situation est contraire ou non à l'équité.

Exemple :
L'époux débiteur doit verser à son conjoint une participation de 50 000 €. Le seul élément d'actif que détient l'époux débiteur est une maison, dans laquelle il vit et dans laquelle il exerce son activité, qui lui fournit les revenus de son existence. Dans ce cas, il serait injuste d'imposer à l'époux de vendre sa maison. On peut envisager que soit accordé un délai de paiement.

Au paragraphe 2 :
La créance dont le paiement est différé porte intérêts.

Au paragraphe 3 :
Le paragraphe 3 précise que le juge peut ordonner que le débiteur fournisse des sûretés. La nature et le montant des sûretés sont laissés à l'appréciation équitable du tribunal.

Article 18. Liquidation anticipée de la créance de participation

Les ordres juridiques des deux pays connaissent la possibilité, en cas de mise en péril de la créance de participation et dans des circonstances particulières, de demander la liquidation de cette créance par anticipation (en Allemagne, art. 1385, 1386 BGB ; en France, art. 1580 CC).

En droit allemand une action en indemnisation, engagée parallèlement à l'action en dissolution du régime, permet dans certains cas de demander directement et par anticipation la liquidation de la créance de participation.

En droit français, un époux peut demander la liquidation anticipée de sa créance de participation lorsque le désordre des affaires de son conjoint, sa mauvaise administration ou son inconduite donnent lieu à craindre que la continuation du régime matrimonial ne compromette ses intérêts. Les règles de la séparation de biens judiciaire sont applicables à cette demande. Lorsque la demande est acceptée par le tribunal, les époux sont placés sous le régime de la séparation de biens.

Cette possibilité de demander la liquidation de la créance de participation par anticipation est également proposée pour le régime optionnel de la participation aux acquêts. En vertu de l'article 18, la liquidation anticipée de la créance de participation peut être demandée lorsque la gestion de son patrimoine par l'un des époux est de nature à compromettre les intérêts de l'autre au titre du calcul de cette créance. Il en est notamment ainsi lorsqu'un époux réalise des actes qui sont de nature à entraîner réunion fictive dans le patrimoine final, en application de l'article 10 paragraphe 2 (sauf le cas de l'art. 10 par. 2 point 1. b)

A la différence du système existant en droit français (art. 1580 CC), l'article 18 permet à l'époux qui s'est le plus enrichi de demander la liquidation anticipée de la créance de participation qu'il devra verser, lorsque la gestion de son conjoint au sens de l'article 18 paragraphe 1 est de nature à en aggraver le montant.

Si la créance de participation est mise en péril, il sera utile, dans de nombreux cas, de demander au tribunal des mesures provisoires visant à assurer cette créance. Les actions de procédure ne sont pas réglées dans le cadre du régime optionnel de la participation aux acquêts. En effet, il convient en la matière d'appliquer les règles du pays dans lequel l'action est intentée.

En France, l'application des mesures de l'article 220-1 CC pourra être demandée. En Allemagne, on envisagera d'assurer la créance par la voie d'une mesure provisoire de sauvegarde par saisie conservatoire, en vertu de l'article 916 du code allemand de procédure civile (ZPO).

CHAPITRE VII. DISPOSITIONS FINALES

Article 19. Application dans le temps

L'accord ne s'appliquera qu'aux contrats conclus par les époux après son entrée en vigueur.

Article 20. Ratification et entrée en vigueur

L'accord est soumis à ratification selon les règles classiques du droit international.

Il devra entrer en vigueur le plus tôt possible.

Il peut être dénoncé.

Article 21. Adhésion

Compte tenu de la mobilité croissante des couples au sein de l'Union européenne, il est souhaitable de permettre à d'autres États membres d'adhérer ultérieurement à l'accord bilatéral.

En cas d'adhésion d'un ou de plusieurs Etats, l'Allemagne sera nommée comme dépositaire de l'accord.

Article 22. Régime linguistique de l'accord

En cas d'adhésion une nouvelle version authentique de l'accord dans la langue officielle de l'Etat souhaitant adhérer peut être produite.

Article 23. Enregistrement

L'enregistrement de l'accord est soumis à l'article 102 de la Charte des Nations Unies.

PROJET DE LOI DU GOUVERNEMENT FÉDÉRAL*

Projet de loi relatif au traité du 4 février 2010 entre la République Fédérale d'Allemagne et la République Française sur le régime matrimonial optionnel de participation aux acquêts

A. Problématique et but

Dans les mariages binationaux, des problèmes peuvent naître relatifs au patrimoine des époux, car les régimes matrimoniaux légaux sont dissemblables dans les différents pays et ne sont en règle générale pas connus d'un pays à l'autre. Ces problèmes sont aussi pratiquement importants puisqu'en 2009 dans près de 13 % des mariages en Allemagne un époux au moins possédait une nationalité étrangère. Des problèmes n'existent pas seulement lors de la dissolution du mariage mais aussi pendant son existence, par exemple lors du financement de crédits immobiliers. Dans ce contexte, un règlement par un traité doit créer, avec le complément nécessaire dans le droit national, plus de sécurité et de clarté juridiques.

B. Solution

La République Fédérale d'Allemagne et la République Française ont décidé de créer un régime matrimonial commun et dans les deux Etats identique qui correspond à la compensation allemande des acquêts dans une forme modifiée. Ce régime matrimonial pourra être choisi par les époux dans les deux pays au lieu de leur régime légal respectif et à côté des autres régimes matrimoniaux optionnels nationaux. La possibilité d'adhérer au traité de source franco-allemand est ouverte aux autres Etats membres de l'Union Européenne.

Par cette présente loi de ratification seront créées les conditions nationales internes d'après l'art. 59 alinéa 2 phrase 1 de la loi fondamentale (GG) pour la ratification.

Dans le même temps, la loi règle la transposition interne du traité.

C. Alternatives

Aucune.

* Unofficial translation of Bundesrat Drucksache 67/11, of 4 February 2011, pp. 1–2, by Bernadette Chaussade-Klein.

D. Les conséquences financières

La fédération, les Länder et les communes n'auront pas de charges financières.

E. Autres frais

Pour l'économie, et particulièrement pour les petites et moyennes entreprises, il n'apparait pas de frais supplémentaires. On ne doit pas attendre des conséquences de la loi sur les prix au détail ou sur le niveau général des prix, particulièrement sur le niveau du prix au consommateur.

F. Coûts de bureaucratie

Pas d'introduction, ni de changement, ni de dissolution d'obligations d'information pour l'économie, les citoyennes et citoyens et l'administration.

MOTIF POUR LA LOI DE RATIFICATION DU TRAITÉ*

A. PARTIE GÉNÉRALE

1. SITUATION DE BASE CONCRÈTE ET JURIDIQUE

Les mariages avec un élément d'extraneité sont fréquents. En 2009, des 13 % de couples mariés vivant en Allemagne, soit les deux conjoints avaient une nationalité étrangère, soit un époux avait la nationalité allemande et l'autre une nationalité étrangère. Dans ce chiffre il y avait au moins 34 000 couples mariés franco-allemands, le quatrième groupe le plus important après les couples germano-polonais, germano-italiens et germano-autrichiens (Hammes entre autres, WiSta 2010 p. 904/911 s.). Il s'y ajoutent les couples allemands qui vivent à l'étranger ainsi que les couples étrangers qui vivent en Allemagne. Comme les questions des effets juridiques du mariage se rattachent entre autres à la nationalité, les mariages avec un élément d'extranéité peuvent amener à des difficultés juridiques, notamment en ce qui concerne les questions du droit des régimes matrimoniaux. Le régime matrimonial légal en Allemagne est celui de la participation aux acquêts (Zugewinngemeinschaft). Les patrimoines des époux restent séparés, et c'est simplement à la dissolution du régime – par exemple en cas de divorce- que le profit produit pendant le mariage sera compensé. Le régime matrimonial légal en France est la communauté des biens réduite aux acquêts. Les acquêts pendant le mariage deviennent patrimoine commun. Si par exemple un couple vit en Allemagne sous le régime de communauté d'après le droit français, des problèmes apparaissent si les époux acquièrent un bien immobilier en Allemagne. Comme le régime matrimonial français n'est en règle générale pas connu, l'évaluation précise de la portée des droits pour chacun des époux lors de l'inscription du droit de propriété dans le livre foncier (Grundbuch) amène à d'importantes incertitudes. (pour une communauté réduite aux acquêts d'après le droit espagnol, comparer p.e. OLG Düsseldorf, FamRZ 2010, 1564 s.). Pour un établissement de crédit allemand il est particulièrement difficile de mesurer la portée exacte que des obligations d'un époux ou de sa faillite ont sur le patrimoine lié à une communauté de biens. La solution pratique la plus souvent

* Unofficial translation of Bundesrat Drucksache 67/11, of 4 February 2011, pp. 7–10, by Bernadette Chaussade-Klein.

choisie, consistant en ce que les époux choisissent le droit allemand pour le patrimoine situé en Allemagne d'après l'article 15 alinéa 2 de la loi d'introduction au BGB répond bien à la question mais les oblige à avoir un régime matrimonial scindé qui peut conduire lors des compensations matrimoniales à des difficultés de calcul. Les couples allemands en France rencontreront des problèmes semblables au vu des traditions entièrement différentes.

Le choix d'une solution par un traité bilatéral présente aux époux concernés l'avantage de proposer des solutions le plus rapidement possibles tandis qu'une harmonisation du contenu du droit de la famille de tous les Etats européens ne peut avancer que beaucoup plus lentement en raison de traditions juridiques différentes qui souvent sont formées durant des siècles et sont profondément implantées dans la population.

De plus il existe pour la République Française et la République Fédérale d'Allemagne une mission politique. Le désir d'harmoniser le droit français et le droit allemand de la famille provient d'une déclaration commune lors du quarantième anniversaire du traité de L'Elysée en 2003.

La possibilité d'adhérer au traité du 4 février 2010 entre la République Fédérale d'Allemagne et la République Française sur le régime matrimonial optionnel de la participation aux acquêts (par la suite: traité) est ouverte aux autres membres de l'Union Européenne. Dans ces pays également le droit du mariage et particulièrement les régimes matrimoniaux est nationalement très différemment organisé et amène à des problèmes semblables à ceux en Allemagne et en France.

2. BUT DES PROPOSITIONS DE MODIFICATION

En considération des incertitudes juridiques dans les mariages avec un élément d'extraneïté, avec un traité doit être créé un régime matrimonial optionnel (d'abord) binational qui contient des règlements identiques pour les deux systèmes juridiques et qui peut offrir aux personnes concernées clarté et sécurité juridiques. Pour pouvoir octroyer au nouveau régime matrimonial optionnel une certaine adhésion tant en France qu'en Allemagne, le traité prend en considération les particularités de régime matrimonial existant dans les deux droits. Dans sa structure de base, le régime matrimonial optionnel de participation aux acquêts correspond au régime allemand de participation aux acquêts (*Zugewinngemeinschaft*) mais présente aussi des modifications qui prennent en compte la tradition juridique française. Les époux dans les deux pays peuvent choisir ce régime à la place du régime légal, à côté des autres régimes nationaux optionnels quand leur régime matrimonial est soumis au droit matériel de l'un des Etats contractants. Les dispositions du droit international privé dans les deux Etats ne sont pas mises en cause. Un lien direct international n'est pas nécessaire, cependant le régime matrimonial optionnel de la participation aux acquêts n'offrira d'avantages qu'à des couples mariés avec un lien international.

Avec la modification proposée du Code civil allemand (BGB), le régime matrimonial optionnel est introduit dans le droit allemand de la famille. Les règlements d'impositions des successions et des donations correspondent aux dispositions de la participation aux acquêts d'après le droit allemand et doivent garantir que des époux ne prennent distance du choix du nouveau régime matrimonial pour des raisons fiscales.

3. COMPÉTENCE LÉGISLATIVE

La compétence législative de la fédération résulte de l'article 73 alinéa 1 numéro 1 (affaires étrangères), de l'article 74 alinéa 1 numéro 1 (droit civil) et de l'article 105 alinéa 2 deuxième alternative en relation avec l'article 72ème alinéa 2 de la loi fondamentale (droit fiscal).

Une loi fédérale est, d'après l'article 72 alinéa 2 de la loi fondamentale, nécessaire pour la sauvegarde de l'unité juridique dans l'intérêt de tout le territoire. Pour atteindre une uniformisation du droit en France et en Allemagne il est impératif qu'il y ait un droit uniforme dans la République fédérale allemande. Ceci n'est possible que par un règlement législatif fédéral. Des règlements différents dans les mesures fiscales produiraient de l'insécurité juridique en cas de succession lors des impôts sur les successions et en raison de la large dispersion des personnes bénéficiaires dans chaque cas de succession ils conduiraient à un éclatement du droit avec des conséquences problématiques qui dans l'intérêt aussi bien de la fédération que dans celui des Länder ne peuvent être acceptables.

L'accord du Bundesrat est nécessaire d'après l'article 105 alinéa 3 de la loi fondamentale parce que le produit des impôts sur les successions et donations revient aux Länder d'après l'article 106 alinéa 2 numéro 2 de la loi fondamentale.

B. PARTIE SPÉCIALE

Sur l'article 1 (Ratification)

Comme le traité se rapporte à des objets de la compétence législative fédérale, l'article 59 alinéa 2 phrase 1 est applicable.

Sur l'article 2 (Modification du code civil-BGB)

Sur le numéro 1 (modification de la table des matières)
Puisqu'un un nouveau chapitre 4 doit être ajouté au livre 4 – droit de la famille (Familienrecht) du code civil, la table des matières doit être également complétée.

Sur le numéro 2

a) Généralités

Avec l'introduction du nouveau chapitre 4 « régime matrimonial optionnel de participation aux acquêts» on veut mettre en avant que le régime matrimonial optionnel de la participation aux acquêts d'après le traité est un régime supplémentaire que l'on peut choisir par contrat de mariage et qui est sur le même niveau que les régimes matrimoniaux optionnels de la séparation de biens et de la communauté des biens nommés dans les chapitres 2 et 3.

b) § 1519 BGB – nouveau –

aa) Principe

Le § 1519 BGB – nouveau – prend en considération la limitation à la liberté de contracter du § 1409 du BGB. D'après les § 1408 s. du BGB, les époux peuvent choisir à la place du régime légal de la participation aux acquêts par contrat la séparation de biens ou la communauté de biens. Avec le nouveau § 1519, le régime matrimonial optionnel de la participation aux acquêts d'après le traité entre la République Fédérale d'Allemagne et la République Française sur le régime matrimonial optionnel de la participation aux acquêts s'y ajoute comme régime matrimonial supplémentaire choisi par contrat de mariage.

Les règlements particuliers identiques en Allemagne et en France se trouvent dans les articles 1 à 19 du traité. Pour les motifs il est renvoyé au mémoire qui intègre le rapport explicatif sur le traité et que la France et l'Allemagne ont harmonisé.

bb) Application des § 1368 et 1412 BGB

L'article 5 du traité règle la nullité des actes de disposition sur des objets du ménage et sur le logement de la famille. L'exécution d'un acte nul envers un tiers qui en devient ainsi bénéficiaire n'est pas réglée dans la disposition. Avec la référence au § 1368 du BGB dans la loi de ratification, l'époux qui est donc protégé contre une vente nulle par l'article 5 du traité, doit donc aussi obtenir la possibilité de faire valoir en justice l'inefficacité de l'acte de disposition contre un tiers des droits provenant des objets du ménage ou du logement de la famille.

L'application du § 1412 du BGB est par contre exclue. L'inefficacité d'un acte de disposition envers un tiers ne doit pas dépendre de ce que le contrat de mariage qui fonde la participation aux acquêts soit inscrit au registre des régimes matrimoniaux (Güterrechtsregister) ou qu'il soit connu du tiers. L'enregistrement dans le registre des régimes matrimoniaux serait en considération de son importance minime dans la pratique une formalité inutile qui n'apporterait aucune plus-value à la protection du commerce juridique. Particulièrement lors d'actes de disposition sur des immeubles les notaires à l'acte auront à prendre en considération dans l'avenir la possibilité d'une interdiction de disposer.

c) Délimitation par rapport au droit des régimes matrimoniaux spéciaux au sens large
Le nouveau régime matrimonial supplante dans son champ d'application la législation relative au droit du régime matrimonial.
aa) § 1357 du BGB
A côté du règlement spécifique dans l'art. 6 du traité qui règle l'obligation solidaire à la dette des époux pour l'entretien du ménage il n'y a plus de place pour l'application du § 1357 du BGB.
bb) § 1365 BGB
L'article 5 alinéa 1 du traité qui a un caractère limitatif empêche qu'à côté en plus le § 1365 du BGB puisse trouver application. C'est consciemment qu'une telle disposition de protection n'a pas été reprise dans le traité (voir le rapport explicatif sur l'article 5 alinéa 1 du traité).
cc) § 1382 du BGB
L'article 17 alinéa 2 du traité ne contient aucun règlement spécifique sur le montant du taux d'intérêt lors d'un paiement différé. Pourtant il n'a pas été prévu un renvoi au § 1382 alinéa 4 du BGB. C'est pourquoi s'applique le § 246 du BGB. Donc le taux d'intérêt est de 4 %. Si le débiteur de la créance de participation est en retard de paiement, le taux d'intérêt est de 5 % au dessus de l'intérêt de base (§ 288 alinéa1 phrase 2, § 247 du BGB). De même,un besoin particulier de reprendre la norme spéciale du § 1382 alinéa 5 du BGB d'après laquelle la demande de sursis ne peut être présentée que dans le cadre d'une procédure en cours sur la péréquation des acquêts, n'existe pas.
dd) § 1384 du BGB
A la dissolution du mariage par décision judiciaire la date d'introduction de la demande en justice est d'après l'article 13 du traité déterminante pour la recherche de l'accroissement. Ainsi on n'attache pas à la demande en cours – comme au § 1384 BGB – par la signification de la demande à l'adversaire – mais au moment de l'introduction de la demande devant le tribunal.
ee) Péréquation des pensions
Une créance de compensation de régime matrimonial n'a pas lieu pour les droits basés sur la caisse de prévoyance vieillesse, § 1587 du BGB en relation avec le § 2 alinéa 4 de la loi sur la péréquation des retraites. C'est valable aussi lors d'un régime optionnel de participation aux acquêts. Les époux peuvent régler en faisant un contrat de mariage la qualification différente du patrimoine de retraite en France et en Allemagne. Une solution à la différente qualification du patrimoine de prévoyance vieillesse aurait surchargé en considérant les spécificités de la péréquation des retraites allemande du nouveau régime matrimonial optionnel.

d) le règlement successoral du régime matrimonial
   A l'inverse du BGB qui contient dans le paragraphe 1371 une disposition spéciale pour le règlement du régime légal lors du décès d'un époux, le traité ne comporte aucun règlement particulier pour ce cas.
   Le § 1371 alinéa 1 augmente la part légale de l'époux survivant (§ 1931 alinéa 1 du BGB) d'un quart pour compenser l'accroissement de manière forfaitaire. La relation entre régime matrimonial et droit des successions qui est sans cesse critiquée en droit allemand est étrangère au traité. Par l'application du § 1371 alinéa 1 du BGB, une autre créance de participation reviendrait de droit matériel à l'époux survivant pour qui le droit allemand s'applique, qu'à l'époux survivant pour qui le droit français s'applique, ceci malgré le régime matrimonial convenu d'une communauté optionnel de participation aux acquêts. Ceci contredirait le but du traité de créer un régime matrimonial commun qui se ressemble le plus possible dans les pays participants. Au décès d'un époux les acquêts doivent donc être d'abord compensés.
e) Intégration du droit des communautés de vie
   Le nouveau régime matrimonial optionnel de la participation aux acquêts doit être ouvert aux partenaires de vie dans le sens de la loi sur les communautés de vie. D'après les § 6 et 7 de cette loi (LPartG), les règlements matrimoniaux applicables pour les époux leur sont déjà applicables. Une égalité complète avec le mariage est ainsi atteinte. Pour le régime optionnel de participation aux acquêts on ne doit en faire une exception. Le § 6 du LPartG autorise le choix d'un autre régime matrimonial dans la convention de partenariat que simplement le choix du régime légal de participation aux acquêts. Le § 7 phrase 2 de la loi, LParG déclare les § 1409 à 1563 du BGB comme applicables de manière analogue. Par ce renvoi, le nouveau § 1519 du BGB est ainsi déjà intégré.
f) Conséquence juridique de la dénonciation du traité
   Si l'Allemagne devait dénoncer le traité, les conséquences devraient en être réglées dans une loi annexe : soit le contenu matériel du traité est maintenu, soit des règlements de liquidation seront créés d'après l'exemple du contrat « Einigungsvertrag » (Article 234 § 4 de la loi d'introduction au BGB).
   Si la France devait dénoncer le contrat, le régime matrimonial est conservé en raison du renvoi statique aux dispositions du traité comme un régime matrimonial qui sera alors qu'allemand.

Sur l'article 3 (Modification de la loi sur les fonctionnaires-greffiers de justice)

Conformément à l'article 12 alinéa 2 phrase 2 du traité, le tribunal peut sur demande d'un époux ordonner que des biens du débiteur soient transférés au créancier pour un but de compensation quand ceci est équitable. En outre, le tribunal peut conformément à l'art. 17 du traité ordonner sur la demande du débiteur un délai de paiement de la créance de participation et la fourniture d'une mesure de sûreté. Ces actes du tribunal sont comparables à ceux que le droit national a déjà donné au fonctionnaire-greffier de justice dans les § 1382, 1383 BGB, tant qu'il n'y a pas de procès en cours sur la créance de participation (§ 1382 alinéa 5 BGB). La raison pour la délégation de ces tâches était que dans ces cas, en général, aucune difficulté juridique ne se présentait mais il y avait plutôt des questions de faits à éclaircir et des préoccupations économiques à soupeser. Ces considérations concernent également les cas réglés dans les articles 12 alinéa 2 phrase 2 et 17 du traité – d'autant plus qu'il existe une ressemblance de structure entre la participation aux acquêts optionnel convenue par contrat et la participation aux acquêts réglée par la loi.

Sur l'article 4 (Modification de la loi sur la procédure en droit de la famille et dans les affaires gracieuses)

Sur le numéro 1
Dans la table des matières le nouveau titre du § 264 de la loi sur la procédure dans les affaires de famille et les affaires gracieuses (FamFG) doit être actualisé.

Sur le numéro 2
Les créances résultant du traité et provenant du régime optionnel de participation aux acquêts sont des affaires de régime matrimonial d'après le § 261 alinéa 1 FamFG. Les procédures prévues dans les articles 5 alinéa 2, article 12 alinéa 2 phrase 2 et article 17 du traité sont comparables à celles du § 1369 alinéa 2 et des § 1382, 1383 du BGB. Par leur introduction dans le § 261 alinéa 2 de la FamFG ces matières procédurales sont déclarées également affaires de régime matrimonial.

Sur le numéro 3
Le § 264 alinéa 1 phrase 1 de la loi de la procédure dans les affaires de famille et les affaires gracieuses (FamFG) règle la procédure d'après les § 1382 et 1383 du BGB comme une exception au § 40 alinéa 2 de la FamFG qu'une décision du tribunal est exécutoire qu'avec l'autorité de la chose jugée. Comme le § 1383 du BGB lors du régime matrimonial de la participation aux acquêts, l'article 12 alinéa 2 phrase 2 du traité prévoit lors du régime optionnel de participation aux acquêts une liquidation de la créance de participation en nature comme cas d'exception à la demande d'une partie si cela correspond à des raisons d'équité. L'article 17 du traité prévoit la possibilité d'un délai de paiement judiciaire de la créance de participation pour laquelle il faut aussi, le cas échéant, fournir une sûreté et prend ainsi un règlement pour le régime matrimonial optionnel de participation aux acquêts similaire au § 1382 du BGB. Les règlements des articles 12 alinéa 2 phrase 2 et article 17 du traité sont semblables à ceux des § 1382 et 1383 du BGB et doivent être traités pareillement dans la procédure de

régime matrimonial. Et pour cette raison la décision du tribunal doit aussi dans les procédures de l'article 12 alinéa 2 phrase 2 et 17 du traité être exécutoire seulement au moment de l'autorité de la chose jugée.

Sur le numéro 4
Le § 269 alinéa 1 de la loi portant procédure des affaires de famille et des affaires gracieuses (FamFG) règle quelles procédures sont des affaires de pacte de vie. Y sont comprises d'après le § 269 alinéa 1 numéro 11 de la loi (FamFG) aussi les décisions d'après le § 6 LPartG en relation avec le § 1365 alinéa 2, avec le § 1369 alinéa 2, avec les § 1382 et1383 du BGB et d'après le § 269 alinéa 1 numéro 12 de la loi FamFG les décisions d'après le § 7 de la loi LPartG en relation avec les § 1426, 1430 et 1452 du BGB. Pour transposer l'égalité du pacte de vie avec le mariage également en procédure de régime matrimonial, égalité déjà décrite sous l'article 2 numéro 2 lettre e de la loi de ratification, le règlement dans le § 269 alinéa 1 numéro 12 de la FamFG doit poser clairement que des décisions dans ce sens sont aussi celles sur la base du § 1519 du BGB en relation avec l'article 5 alinéa 2, l'article 12 alinéa 2 phrase 2 et l'article 17du traité.

Sur l'article 5 (Modification de la loi sur les impôts sur les successions et les donations)

Les effets fiscaux sur les successions et les donations d'une dissolution du régime matrimonial optionnel de la participation aux acquêts doivent être harmonisés avec ceux de la dissolution du régime matrimonial légal du BGB. Une inégalité dans le traitement fiscal face au régime légal de la participation aux acquêts ferait sinon du nouveau régime matrimonial dans la pratique une alternative de deuxième catégorie. De manière analogue au § 5 alinéa 2 de la loi relative aux impôts sur les successions et les donations (ErbStG), la créance de participation d'après l'article 12 du traité ne doit pas constituer une acquisition (« Erwerb ») dans le sens des § 3 et 7 de la loi (ErbstG). Cela doit être applicable indépendamment du fait que le régime matrimonial optionnel de participation aux acquêts est dissous à cause du décès de l'un des époux ou que le régime a été dissous pendant la vie des époux. Donc la créance de participation aux acquêts, pour autant qu'elle ait été calculée et ait été la base d'un transfert de patrimoine, n'est pas soumise à l'imposition de la loi sur les impôts de successions et donations (ErbstG).

Une exemption de manière analogue au § 5 alinéa 1 ErbStG n'est pas nécessaire. Dans le cas d'une liquidation successorale de la péréquation des acquêts (§ 1371 alinéa 1 BGB), l'époux survivant est exempté de l'impôt sur les successions par la disposition sur l'acquisition dans le sens des § 3 et 7 ErbStG, du montant de la créance de participation fictive que celui-ci aurait pu faire valoir sous les conditions des § 1373 à 1383, 1390 du BGB. Puisque dans le régime matrimonial optionnel de la participation aux acquêts la péréquation des acquêts à la dissolution du régime matrimonial ne peut se faire que par la connaissance de la créance de participation réelle, il manque le champ d'application pour le § 5 alinéa 1 ErbStG.

De plus il n'y a pas la nécessité d'une application de manière analogue du § 29 alinéa 1 numéro 2 ErbStG. D'après le § 29 alinéa 1 numéro 2 ErbStG, l'impôt disparaît avec un effet rétroactif si dans les cas du § 5 alinéa 2ErbStG, des libéralités qui étaient imposables, sont déduites de la créance de participation conformément au § 1380 alinéa 1 du BGB. Comme le traité ne règle pas une telle déduction, il manque au § 29 alinéa 1 numéro 2 ErbStG le point de rattachement.

Sur l'article 6 (L'entrée en vigueur)

Les alinéas 1 et 2 règlent l'entrée en vigueur de la loi. Les stipulations sont conformes à l'exigence de l'article 82 alinéa 2 phrase 1 de la loi fondamentale (Grundgesetz). D'après l'alinéa 2 phrase 2, le moment auquel le traité entre en vigueur d'après son art. 20 doit être publié au journal officiel (Bundesgesetzblatt).

Remarques finales

Avec le traité entre la République Fédérale d'Allemagne et la République Française sur le régime optionnel de participation aux acquêts, les Etats signataires ont développé un nouveau modèle pour l'intégration des systèmes de droit civil en Europe. Le traité est ouvert en principe à l'adhésion de tout Etat membre de l'Union et élargit ainsi sous le régime de la liberté contractuelle les possibilités d'actions des citoyennes et des citoyens en créant un nouveau droit matériel. Le projet de loi de ratification et de transposition ici déposé rend, après l'entrée en vigueur du traité, cette nouvelle option accessible à ceux pour qui le droit matrimonial allemand est applicable,

Il n'y aura aucun frais supplémentaires pour les budgets publics ni pour l'économie, ni en particulier pour les petites et moyennes entreprises. Des effets de la loi sur les prix unitaires ou le niveau général des prix, en particulier sur le niveau des prix au consommateur ne sont pas à attendre.

Le projet de loi est en harmonie avec les idées directrices du gouvernement fédéral de développement durable dans le sens d'une stratégie nationale de durabilité. Les règlements voulus doivent contribuer à apporter plus de clarté dans les mariages comportant un élément d'extranéité.

Aucun devoirs d'information pour l'économie ni pour les citoyennes et les citoyens ou l'administration ne seront introduits, changés ou supprimés.

Le projet de loi est en accord avec le droit de l'Union Européenne et des traités de droit international public que la République Fédérale d'Allemagne a conclus. On ne doit pas attendre des conséquences concernant la politique d'égalité.

LOI FRANÇAISE DE RATIFICATION*

Loi n° 2013-98 du 28 janvier 2013 autorisant la ratification de l'accord entre la République française et la République fédérale d'Allemagne instituant un régime matrimonial optionnel de la participation aux acquêts

L'Assemblée nationale et le Sénat ont adopté, Le Président de la République promulgue la loi dont la teneur suit: Est autorisée la ratification de l'accord entre la République française et la République fédérale d'Allemagne instituant un régime matrimonial optionnel de la participation aux acquêts, signé à Paris le 4 février 2010, et dont le texte est annexé à la présente loi (2). La présente loi sera exécutée comme loi de l'Etat.

- Fait à Paris, le 28 janvier 2013.
- François Hollande
- Par le Président de la République:
- Le Premier ministre,
  - Jean-Marc Ayrault
  - Le ministre des affaires étrangères,
  - Laurent Fabius

(1) Travaux préparatoires: loi n° 2013-98. Sénat: Projet de loi n° 372 (2010-2011); Rapport de Mme Joëlle Garriaud-Maylam, au nom de la commission des affaires étrangères, n° 650 (2011-2012); Texte de la commission n° 651 (2011-2012); Discussion et adoption (procédure d'examen simplifiée) le 18 juillet 2012 (TA n° 128, 2011-2012). Assemblée nationale: Projet de loi, adopté par le Sénat, n° 102; Rapport de Mme Seybah Dagoma, au nom de la commission des affaires étrangères, n° 569; Avis de M. Pierre-Yves Le Borgn', au nom de la commission des lois, n° 308; Discussion et adoption (procédure d'examen simplifiée) le 17 janvier 2013 (TA n° 77). (2) Le texte sera publié ultérieurement au Journal officiel de la République française.

* JORF n° 0024 of 29 January 2013, p. 1721. Entry into force on 1 May 2013.

LOI ALLEMANDE DE RATIFICATION*

Loi sur le traité du 4 février 2010 entre la République Fédérale d'Allemagne et la République Française sur le régime matrimonial optionnel de participation aux acquêts du 15 mars 2012

Le Bundestag a voté avec le l'accord du Bundesrat la loi suivante :

Article 1. Ratification

Le traité signé à Paris le 4 février 2010 entre la République Fédérale d'Allemagne et la République Française sur le régime matrimonial optionnel de la participation aux acquêts est ratifié. Le traité est publié ci-dessous.

Article 2. Modification du BGB

Le BGB dans la version de la publication du 2 janvier 2002 (BGBl. I p. 42, 2909 ; 2003 I p. 738) ; dernièrement modifié par l'article 1 de la loi du 17 janvier 2011 (BGBl. I p. 1600) est modifié de la manière suivante :

1. Dans la table des matières est inséré après la mention livre 4 section 1 titre 6 sous-titre 2 chapitre 3 le texte suivant :
   « Chapitre 4
   Régime optionnel de participation aux acquêts »

2. Après le § 1518 est introduit le chapitre 4 suivant :
   « Chapitre 4
   Régime optionnel de Participation aux acquêts
   § 1519
   Convention par contrat de mariage
   Si les époux conviennent par contrat de mariage le régime matrimonial optionnel de participation aux acquêts, les dispositions du traité du 4 février 2010 entre la République Fédérale Allemande et la République Française sur le régime optionnel de la participation aux acquêts sont applicables. Le § 1368 est applicable de manière analogue. Le § 1412 ne doit pas être appliqué. »

* Unofficial translation of Bundesgesetzblatt, 2012, II, p. 178, by Bernadette Chaussade-Klein.

Article 3. Modification de la loi sur les fonctionnaires de justice (Rechtspflegergesetz)

Le paragraphe 25 numéro 3 de la loi sur les fonctionnaires de justice du 5 novembre 1969 (BGBl. I p. 2065) qui a été dernièrement modifié par l'article 5 de la loi du 7 décembre 2011 (BGBl. I p. 2582), est modifié de la manière suivante:

1. A la lettre b le point à la fin est remplacé par une virgule.

2. La lettre c suivante est ajoutée:
   « c) la décision sur le délai de paiement d'une créance de compensation et la remise de choses patrimoniales d'après le § 1519 BGB en relation avec l'article 12 alinéa 2 phrase 2 et l'article 17 du traité du 4 février 2010 entre la République fédérale d'Allemagne et la République Française sur le régime matrimonial optionnel de la participation aux acquêts, respectivement aussi en relation avec le § 7 de la loi sur le partenariat de vie (Lebenspartnerschaftsgesetz), tant qu' un litige n'est pas pendant concernant une créance de compensation. »

Article 4. Modification de la loi sur la procédure dans les affaires familiales et dans les affaires de la procédure en matière gracieuse

La loi sur la procédure des affaires familiales et des affaires de la procédure en matière gracieuse du 17 décembre 2008 (BGBl. I p. 2586, 2587), modifiée en dernier par l'article 2 alinéa 32 de la loi du 22 décembre 2011 (BGBl. I p. 3044) est modifiée de la manière suivante:

1. dans la table des matières la mention pour le § 264 est rédigé de la manière suivante:
   « § 264 procédure de délai de paiement et remise d'objets patrimoniaux ».

2. Le § 261 alinéa 2 est rédigé de la façon suivante:
   « (2) Sont des affaires de régime matrimonial également les procédures d'après le § 1365 alinéa 2, § 1369 alinéa 2, les § 1382, 1383, 1426, 1430 et 1452 du BGB ainsi que le § 1519 du BGB en relation avec l'article 5 alinéa 2, l'article 12 alinéa 2 phrase 2 et l'article 17 du traité du 4 février 2010 entre la République Fédérale d'Allemagne et la République Française sur le régime optionnel de la participation aux acquêts. »

3. Le § 264 est modifié comme suit:
   a) le titre est rédigé de la manière suivante:
      « § 264
      Procédure de délai de paiement et de remise d'objets patrimoniaux ».

   b) L'alinéa 1 phrase 1 est rédigé comme suit:
      « Dans les procédures d'après les § 1382 et 1383 du BGB ainsi que d'après le § 1519 du BGB en relation avec l'article 12 alinéa 2 phrase 2 et l'article 17 du

traité du 4 février 2010 entre la République Fédérale d'Allemagne et la République Française sur le régime matrimonial optionnel de participation aux acquêts, la décision du tribunal prend effet seulement avec l'autorité de la chose jugée.

4. Le § 269 alinéa 1 numéro 12 est rédigé comme suit:
   « 12. Décisions d'après le § 7 de la loi sur le partenariat de vie (Lebenspartnerschaftsgesetz) en relation avec les § 1426, 1430, 1452 du BGB ou avec le § 1519 du BGB et article 5 alinéa 2, article 12 alinéa 2 phrase 2 ou article 17 du traité du 4 février 2010 entre la République fédérale d'Allemagne et la République Française sur le régime matrimonial optionnel de la participation aux acquêts »

Article 5. Modification de la loi sur les impôts sur les successions et les donations

Est ajouté au § 5 de la loi sur l'impôt sur les successions et donations dans la version de la publication du 27 février 1997 (BGBl. I p. 378), qui a été modifié en dernier par l'article 11 de la loi du 7 décembre 2011 (BGBl. I p. 2592), l'alinéa 3 suivant:

> « (3) Si le régime matrimonial optionnel de la participation aux acquêts (§ 1519 BGB) est dissout et l'enrichissement est compensé, la créance de participation (article 12 alinéa 1 du traité du 4 février 2010 entre la République Fédérale d'Allemagne et la République Française sur le régime matrimonial optionnel de la participation aux acquêts ») ne rentre pas dans la catégorie « acquisition » (Erwerb) au sens des § 3 et 7.

Article 6. Entrée en vigueur

(1) Les articles 2 à 5 entrent en vigueur le jour où le traité du 4 février 2010 entre la République Fédérale d'Allemagne et la République Française sur le régime matrimonial optionnel de la participation aux acquêts entre en vigueur d'après son article 20 alinéa 2. Le jour de l'entrée en vigueur doit être publié dans le journal officiel (Bundesgesetzblatt).

(2) En outre cette loi entre en vigueur le jour après sa publication.
La loi ici présente est ainsi promulguée
Elle doit être publiée au journal officiel (Bundesgesetzblatt)
Berlin, le 15 mars 2012

Pour le Président de la République
Le Président du Bundesrat
Horst Seehofer
La Chancelière
Dr. Angela Merkel
La ministre de la Justice
S. Leutheusser-Schnarrenberger
Le ministre des Affaires Etrangères
Guido Westerwelle

ENGLISH*

CONTENTS

* Unofficial translations by Daniele Orlando. Revision by Marella Magris. Based on the German texts.

MEMORANDUM

I. GENERAL SECTION

1. BACKGROUND

International marriages are commonplace. In 2009 in 13% of the married couples living in Germany one or both spouses were foreign nationals. In addition, there are German couples living abroad and foreign couples living in Germany. Since the legal consequences of a marriage vary according to, among other things, the spouses' citizenship, international marriages may lead to legal difficulties, in particular with respect to property issues. The statutory matrimonial property regime in the Federal Republic of Germany is the community of accrued gains. The assets of the spouses remain separate and the gains accrued during the marriage are settled only at the termination of the property regime, e.g. in the case of divorce. The statutory matrimonial property regime in the French Republic is the community of acquisitions, under which all assets acquired during the marriage become common property. Given these divergent matrimonial property regimes, problems may arise. For example, if a couple lives in Germany under the community of property regime in accordance with French law and they acquire a plot of land in the Federal Republic of Germany. Since this French property regime is not generally known in German law, the precise valuation of the scope of each spouse's rights in the registration of a property right in the Land Register, for example, may lead to considerable uncertainties. For a German bank, the consequences of the liabilities of one spouse or his or her insolvency on the assets subject to community of property are particularly uncertain. The prevailing practical solution of choosing a German matrimonial property regime for assets situated in the Federal Republic of Germany in accordance with Article 15(2)(3) of the German *Einführungsgesetz zum Bürgerlichen Gesetzbuch* ('EGBGB') solves these problems, but imposes a split matrimonial regime which might bring about other problems in the calculation of the debt on the accrued gains. German couples may encounter similar problems in the French Republic, given the completely different traditions. Marriage law also varies considerably in the other states of the European Union.

This situation gives rise to the need to create provisions at an international level which are identical, or as closely comparable as possible, in order to provide the parties involved with legal clarity and certainty. At a European level there have been attempts to jointly answer the question of which national rights shall apply to international marriages and which judicial authority shall be competent. However, aligning the content of family law in all Member States is currently not on the European agenda, given the different, often centuries-old, legal traditions which are firmly rooted in each society. Therefore the approach adopted in this Agreement – to act bilaterally and on a limited area of law at first in order to offer solutions as quickly as possible to the spouses involved – seems to be effective. Moreover, the French Republic and the Federal Republic of Germany have a political mandate: the joint declaration on the 40th anniversary of the Élysée Treaty in 2003 indicated a desire to harmonize family law in Germany and France.

2. BASIC FEATURES OF APPLICABLE PRIVATE INTERNATIONAL LAW

The conflicts of laws provisions relating to property rights in the Federal Republic of Germany and in the French Republic are relatively similar. In particular, both allow spouses to choose the applicable law, in accordance with Article 15(2) of the EGBGB. The spouses can choose German law if at least one of them is a German national or has his or her habitual residence in the Federal Republic of Germany. German law can also be chosen where there are immovable property situated in the Federal Republic of Germany. In the French Republic, French law can be chosen with respect to the effects of the marriage on the matrimonial property in accordance with the Hague Convention on the law applicable to matrimonial property regimes of 14 March 1978. Besides the provisions of German law reflected in the Agreement, it contains an additional option: the spouses can choose French law if one of them established his or her first habitual residence in the French Republic after the marriage.

3. SUMMARY OF THE AGREEMENT

On 4 February 2010, during the Franco-German Council of Ministers in Paris, the Ministers of Justice of the two States signed the Agreement on the optional matrimonial property regime of the community of accrued gains, which should create, for the first time, unitary substantive laws in the area of family law for the Federal Republic of Germany and the French Republic, and which governs an identical optional matrimonial property regime for both states. In its structure, this matrimonial regime corresponds to the German community of accrued gains, albeit modified, taking account of the French legal tradition. Spouses in the two states can choose this property regime instead of the statutory property regime. This makes available to spouses an identical optional matrimonial property regime in both states and overcomes the difficulties that may arise with respect to unknown foreign matrimonial property rules.

II. SPECIFIC CONTENT

With regard to the history of the Agreement and the content of each provision reference is made to the Explanatory Report, which is attached to this Memorandum in German and French.

Article 1

Under Article 1, the optional matrimonial property regime of the community of accrued gains shall be available to spouses whose property regime is subject to the property law of one of the contracting states. Therefore, it can be chosen if either the German or the French law shall apply to the property regime of the spouses. A direct international element is not required, so spouses living in the Federal Republic of Germany without any connection to the French Republic can also choose this property regime by way of contract.

Article 2

Article 2 specifies that the assets of spouses under the optional matrimonial regime of the community of accrued gains remain separate and that "accrued gains" shall constitute the amount by which the final assets of a spouse exceed his or her initial assets. In principle, accrued gains shall be settled only upon termination of the matrimonial property regime.

Article 3

In accordance with the first paragraph of Article 3, this regime shall be agreed upon by way of marriage contract. The second paragraph of Article 3 specifies that the contract can be concluded prior to entering into marriage or while the spouses are married; it shall become effective at the earliest on the date of marriage.

Articles 4 to 6

Article 4 provides that in principle a spouse alone can only dispose of his or her assets. However, the first paragraph of Article 5 makes an exception for disposals by spouses pertaining to household items or rights which guarantee the family home, subjecting such dispositions to the prior consent of the other spouse. Moreover, in accordance with the first paragraph of Article 6, the spouses shall be jointly and severally liable for transactions pertaining to the management of the household and the needs of the children unless a spouse enters into payment obligations which are manifestly unreasonable with regard to the financial circumstances, of which the other contracting party is, or should have been, aware (Article 6(2)).

Articles 7 to 14

Under Article 7, the property regime shall be terminated by the death or declaration of death of one of the spouses, by a change of matrimonial property regime, or by a judgement of divorce or any other court decision which terminates the matrimonial property regime. In order to establish the debt on the accrued gains, comparison of the initial and final assets of each spouse is required. Articles 8 and 9 contain provisions relevant to the determination of the initial assets; the final assets shall be determined under Articles 10 and 11. The initial assets shall consist of the assets of each spouse on the date on which the matrimonial property regime became effective, while the final assets shall consist of the assets of each spouse on the date of termination of the matrimonial property regime; the liabilities of the spouses shall also be included in the final assets if they exceed the existing assets. Under Article 12, the spouse with the lower accrued gains can claim half of the surplus as debt on the accrued gains from the other spouse. Under Article 14, the debt on the accrued gains shall, however, be limited to half the value of the final assets of the debtor spouse.

Articles 15 to 18

Articles 15 to 18 contain provisions on the limitation of the claim to settlement, on the mutual duty of information of the spouses in establishing the debt on the accrued gains, and the deferral or premature settlement of the debt. The latter can be granted particularly in the case of malicious disposal by one of the spouses to the disadvantage of the debt on the accrued gains of the other spouse.

Articles 19 to 23

Article 19 provides that this Agreement shall only apply to marriage contracts that the spouses have concluded after its entry into force. Under the first paragraph of Article 20, the Agreement shall be subject to ratification by both states and under the second paragraph of Article 20 it shall enter into force on the first day following the exchange of the ratification instruments. The ratification instruments shall be deposited with the Government of the Federal Republic of Germany. Under Article 21, the Agreement shall be open to any Member State of the European Union. Article 22 contains a provision on the languages of the Agreement and Article 23 provides that the Federal Republic of Germany register this Agreement with the United Nations without delay after its entry into force.

ENCLOSURE TO THE MEMORANDUM

EXPLANATORY REPORT

A. GENERAL SECTION

1. BACKGROUND

Marriages between citizens of different states are no longer unusual. In approximately 13% of the marriages (in 2006) and divorces (in 2005) registered in Germany, the spouses had different nationalities. 14.59% of the marriages pronounced in France in 2006 were between binational couples. In addition, mixed marriages celebrated in France between French and German spouses in 2003 amounted to 2% of all binational marriages.

Matrimonial property regimes govern the legal consequences of a marriage on the assets of the spouses, the property relationships between the spouses, and the property relationships between the spouses and third parties. The determination of the property regime is not only important with regard to the issue of how the property relationships are concluded at the termination of the property regime, it also has consequences throughout the duration of the marriage, e.g. on the management and acquisition of assets, and on the liability of one of the spouses for liabilities incurred by the other spouse before and during the marriage.

In certain cases, the private international law of the states allows the spouses to designate the law applicable to the property regime. The spouses can choose to subordinate their property regime to the French or the German law in accordance with specific criteria. Thus, German private international law (Article 15(2) EGBGB – *Einführungsgesetz zum Bürgerlichen Gesetzbuche*) allows the spouses to subordinate their matrimonial regime to the German law, if:

- one of the spouses is a German national;
- one of the spouses has his or her habitual residence in Germany;
- one of the spouses owns immovable property in Germany, only for such property.

If the spouses did not designate the applicable law, the connecting factors provided for in Article 15(1) in conjunction with Article 14 of the EGBGB shall apply. German matrimonial law shall apply, for example, if both spouses are German nationals or if, throughout the duration of the marriage, they have their habitual residence in Germany.

As regards the French law, the Hague Convention on the law applicable to matrimonial property regimes of 14 March 1978 allows the spouses to subordinate their matrimonial property regime to the French law, if:

- one of the spouses is a French national;
- one of the spouses has his or her habitual residence in France;
- one of the spouses establishes his or her first habitual residence in France after the marriage.

In addition, spouses may designate the French law with regard to immovables situated in France (Article 3 of the aforementioned Hague Convention). If the spouses did not designate the applicable law, their matrimonial property regime shall be governed by the law of the state in which both spouses establish their first habitual residence after the marriage.

If the German or French law applies, the spouses may choose one of the regimes existing in Germany or in France.

a) German matrimonial property regimes
   German property law provides for three matrimonial regimes:
   - the community of accrued gains (*Zugewinngemeinschaft*);
   - the separation of property (*Gütertrennung*);
   - the community of property (*Gütergemeinschaft*).

   The community of accrued gains is the default statutory property regime. The other property regimes shall apply if chosen by the spouses by way of their marriage contract.
b) French matrimonial property regimes
   French property law provides for three matrimonial regimes:
   - the community of property (*communauté réduite aux acquêts*), community of personal and marital property (*communauté de meubles et acquêts*), universal community of property (*communauté universelle*);
   - the community of accrued gains (*participation aux acquêts*);
   - the separation of property (*séparation de biens*).

   The community of property is the default statutory property regime in France. The other property regimes shall apply if chosen by the spouses by way of their marriage contract.

The differences, notably between the two default statutory regimes are considerable.

Under the German law, the community of accrued gains corresponds to the separation of matrimonial property throughout the duration of the property regime with a settlement of the accrued gains after the termination of the property regime (§1363(2) BGB). The property regime by itself does not give rise to any common property between the spouses. Instead, each spouse retains his or her assets owned before and during the marriage and is only liable for his or her debts with his or her own assets. This also applies to an item owned by both spouses in defined shares (*Bruchteilsgemeinschaft*). Thus, for example, if the spouses have co-ownership of a house by equal shares, each spouse can dispose of his or her half. The community of property under the French law, instead, provides for three different sets of assets: the wife's personal property, the husband's personal property and the joint property. Under Article 1401 of the French Code Civil (CC), the joint property consists of the acquisitions made by the spouses jointly or separately throughout the duration of the marriage. The joint property also includes all acquisitions coming both from their personal activity and from savings made on the fruits and incomes of their personal property. In principle, each spouse alone can manage and dispose of the joint property. However, certain acts may only be entered into by both spouses jointly. For example, one of the spouses can only make an inter vivos gift of a joint property with the consent of the other spouse. Moreover, in France certain rules of the *régime primaire* applicable independent of the property regime may particularly restrict the right of the spouses to dispose of the joint property alone. Under these rules a spouse alone can neither dispose of the rights which guarantee the family home nor of the household items (termination of the rental agreement or alienation of the family home). This restriction would apply even if the family home were the personal property of that spouse.

2. SUITABILITY OF CREATING A JOINT PROPERTY REGIME

The creation of a joint property regime, which is set up, operated and terminated under the same provisions in the contracting states, represents significant judicial progress for couples, third parties and legal practitioners. As a matter of fact, this matrimonial regime constitutes a substantive law common to the contracting states.

The choice of this type of community by a couple does not lead to the difficulties which currently arise as a result of the adoption of the community of property under French law when the spouses acquire immovable property in Germany during the marriage. Since this French property regime does not exist in Germany, the registration of a property right on the Land Register does not enable third parties to assess the precise scope of the rights of each spouse. The prevailing practical solution of choosing a German matrimonial regime for assets situated in Germany (Article 15(2)(3) EGBGB) solves that problem, but imposes a split matrimonial regime which might bring about other problems in the calculation of the debt on the accrued gains.

Given these conditions and since the community of accrued gains exists in both the French and the German law (as statutory default regime in Germany and optional regime in France), it seemed appropriate to establish by way of a bilateral agreement an additional new optional matrimonial property regime, strongly based on the community of accrued gains already existing in both states and shaped under simple and modernised rules, identical in both France and Germany.

In order to allow later accession by other states of the European Union, the Agreement provides that every Member State of the European Union can accede to the Agreement after its entry into force (Article 21).

B. DESCRIPTION OF THE MATRIMONIAL REGIME

CHAPTER I. SCOPE OF APPLICATION AND DEFINITION

Article 1. Scope of Application

The optional matrimonial property regime of the community of accrued gains is open to all couples who are able to choose this property regime in a contracting state, even when the marriage is not binational. Thus, this optional property regime can be chosen by the spouses whose matrimonial regime is subject to French or German law under the applicable private international law, including those of a third country. For example, by application of French or German private international law, this shall apply to couples where:

- one of the spouses is a French or German national;
- one of the spouses has his or her habitual residence in France or in Germany;
- one of the spouses has established his or her first habitual residence in France;
- one of the spouses owns immovable property in France or in Germany, only for such property.

The optional matrimonial property regime of the community of accrued gains can, therefore, be applied, for example, to two German spouses living in France, two French spouses living in Germany, as well as two German spouses living in Germany and two French spouses living in France. The choice of this property regime does not require that the couple choose the law of a contracting state. Article 1 only requires that the property regime be subject to the property law of a contracting state. However, to avoid any doubt, in some cases it is advisable for the spouses to designate the law applicable to their property regime in their marriage contract, if permitted by private international law.

Article 2. Definition

Community of accrued gains means that throughout the duration of the property regime there is separation of matrimonial property. The adoption of this property regime does not affect the ownerships and liabilities of the spouses. Unlike under the community of property, there is no third set of assets shared by both spouses. Only on termination of the property regime are the gains generated throughout the duration of the property regime settled by a comparison of the assets of each spouse.

CHAPTER II. CREATION OF THE MATRIMONIAL PROPERTY REGIME

Article 3. Creation of the Matrimonial Property Regime

Paragraph 1:
The spouses may choose the optional matrimonial property regime of the community of accrued gains by way of a marriage contract. The form of the contract shall be governed by the law designated under the relevant private international law, i.e. the law in force in the place where the contract is concluded or the internal law applicable to property regimes.

Paragraph 2:
The spouses can agree by contract to choose the optional matrimonial property regime of the community of accrued gains either before or during the marriage. In the case of a marriage under French law, the option of concluding a contract before the marriage may, for example, prevent the initial entry into force of the community of property, which should then be liquidated before the adoption of a new property regime. The entry into force of the optional matrimonial property regime is evidently attached to the celebration of a marriage. Therefore, the optional matrimonial property regime of the community of accrued gains only takes effect if the marriage has been concluded. In Germany, this is not explicitly regulated, but may be derived from §1408 of the BGB, under which the parties to the contract must be the spouses. In France this is explicitly stated in Article 1395 of the Civil Code.

The joint property regime can also be adopted during the marriage. Under German law, the spouses can change their property regime at any time by way of marriage contract, including the option to opt out of the statutory regime of the community of accrued gains. The marriage contract, thus, takes effect after the conclusion of the contract. From that moment, the spouses are subject to the rules of the new property regime. Spouses under the French property regime can agree, in the interests of the family, to change their property regime after it has been in place for a period of two years (Article 1397 CC). Such a change becomes effective on the date of execution of the notarial instrument that provides for the change, if the spouses have no minor children and if their adult children or creditors do not oppose the change. Otherwise, in both cases, the change of the matrimonial regime becomes effective on the date of a ruling validating such change.

Paragraph 3:
The principle of freedom of contract under the third paragraph of Article 3 allows the spouses to deviate by contract from the provisions on the determination of the debt on the accrued gains. For example, the spouses may regulate the composition of the assets, the rules for the valuation of the assets, the amount of participation in the respective gains and the allocation of the accrued gains in alternative way. This option enables national specificities and the particular needs of the spouses to be taken into account. Insofar as the text states that the spouses may deviate from the provisions of Chapter V, they cannot deviate from those in Articles 5 and 6, which draw on the most important provisions of the French *régime primaire*. Precluding such deviation guarantees the identical application of the joint property regime in France and Germany.

CHAPTER III. MANAGEMENT, USE AND DISPOSAL OF ASSETS

The joint property regime is designed in such a way that throughout the duration of the marriage the spouses are subject to a separation of property. The separation of the assets has two consequences. First, the spouses retain the management, use and disposal of their own personal assets. In addition, each spouse is liable for debts incurred by him or her before or during the marriage. However, the separation of property is not complete as the spouses may not deviate from the application of specific mandatory provisions. Insofar as the provisions that restrict the effects of the separation of property in France and in Germany are not identical, the joint property regime adopts the essential elements of the French *régime primaire*, so that the matrimonial property regime may work in the same way in France and Germany (Articles 5 and 6).

Article 4. General Provisions on the Management, Use and Disposal of Assets

The aim of the optional matrimonial property regime of the community of accrued gains is to guarantee the complete independence of the spouses with regard to their own assets. Therefore, in principle, each spouse is able to manage, use and dispose of his or her assets alone, without the consent of the other spouse. In return, each spouse is liable for debts incurred by him or her before or during the marriage. This principle of the separation of property is dealt with in the German (§1364 BGB) and French (Article 1569 CC) regimes on the community of accrued gains. The independent management of assets also includes the right to acquire assets; for example, one of the spouses does not need the consent of the other to start a profession or to create, or enter into, a company.

However, this separation of property includes some restrictions, which are dealt with in Articles 5 and 6 of the regime. These restrictions are based on the mandatory rules of the French *régime primaire* (Articles 215 and 220 CC). These rules replace the corresponding provisions of the *régime primaire*, without prejudice to the other rules of this regime, which are applicable under the territorial principle.

Article 5. Restrictions on Disposal

General content:

In the legal systems of both states, the management of assets by one spouse alone may be restricted in exceptional cases to protect the other spouse. In Germany, as regards the statutory property regime of the community of accrued gains, §§1365 and 1369 of the BGB prohibit the disposal of the assets as a whole and of household items. A violation of this prohibition renders the transaction a nullity if the other spouse does not give consent. This occurs automatically and is enforceable against anybody.

French law also provides for restrictions on the disposal of the rights which guarantee the family home and the household items. This means, for example, that neither of the spouses can terminate the rental agreement of the main family home without the consent of the other spouse. However, unlike in Germany, a disposal without the consent of the other spouse is not automatically ineffective. Rather, the spouse must submit an application for annulment. The termination can, however, be approved by the spouse who had not given consent. In France, this restriction on the disposition of the rights which guarantee the family home and the household items is contained in Article 215 of the CC.

In order to avoid different restrictions applying in the two states with regard to the right to freely dispose of the family home and the household items in case of the adoption of the optional matrimonial property regime of the community of accrued gains, Article 5 of the joint property regime, which regulates the protection of the family home provided for in French law, also includes the protection of the household items, which is provided for in German law. The protection of the spouses under French law (Article 215 of the CC) is not as extensive as the protection of the household items under the German law. The joint property regime, therefore, adopts the German provision, which, for example, also applies to the vehicle necessary for the family.

An additional provision against the disposition of the assets as a whole, similar to §1365 of the BGB, did not seem necessary. In many cases, the family home constitutes a significant part of the assets. If a spouse cannot dispose of their property or their share of the immovable used as family home without the consent of the other, the protection of the other spouse is even stronger than in the German law, because it is irrelevant whether or not such property constitutes the total assets or just a significant part thereof (i.e. under the German law, 85% for smaller assets or less than 90% for greater assets).

Paragraph 1:

Paragraph 1 governs the restriction on the disposal of the rights on the family home and the household items. The family home includes all areas which the spouses use as a home, where they have lived together or which, in some circumstances, were designated as the family home, even if this did not actually happen. The family home may also include ancillary rooms (e.g. basement, attic, garage, gym). The aim of the provisions of Article 5 is to ensure extensive protection for the family with regard to the family home.

If one of the spouses disposes of the property or tenancy of the family home without the consent of the other spouse, such disposal is in principle ineffective. This means that the spouse who owns the house used as family home cannot sell the house without the consent of the other spouse. Similarly, the spouse who is a tenant in a flat where the family lives cannot terminate the rental agreement alone. The spouse who had not given consent can however authorize such termination. The protection of the family home is, therefore, very extensive and may also affect third party interests. The ineffectiveness of the termination of a rental agreement may be objected to the landlord of a flat used as the family home, even if he or she was unaware of the property regime of the spouses and, as a result, of the restrictions on disposal by the tenant spouse. The owner spouse cannot dispose alone of the household items either, whether they are in the flat or were already removed. The other spouse can, however, approve a transaction related to the family home or household items.

The consequences of the ineffectiveness of these transactions are regulated by the legal systems of the two states. In France, the invalidity must be asserted following an action for annulment, as determined in Article 215(3) of the CC, based on a provision of the French *régime primaire* which was not adopted in the joint property regime, but which applies to all spouses residing in France, irrespective of their property regime. On the contrary, in Germany a disposal without consent of the other spouse automatically becomes ineffective against anybody. Unlike under French law, it is not necessary to file an action for annulment and, in the event of a dispute, an action for recovery can be directly initiated. Court proceedings regarding the violation of the provisions of this Article are subject to the national legal systems. In France, therefore, Article 215(3) of the CC applies to the action for annulment.

Paragraph 2:

One of the spouses alone cannot dispose of the rights which guarantee the family home or the household items without the consent of the other. However, if the spouse is not in a position to provide such consent, for example, if prevented by sickness, or if his or her refusal is not justified by the interests of the family, the court can authorize the other spouse to enter alone into any legal transaction mentioned in paragraph 1. The authorization of the court in the case of the inability of the spouse to provide his or her consent for health reasons is similar to the right of management in the case of urgency provided for in §1454 of the BGB, but corresponds to a simplified procedure for the appointment of a guardian with the task of "authorising a specific legal transaction". This solution, aimed, above all, at preventing a spouse from arbitrarily refusing consent solely in order to adversely affect the other spouse, was adopted from the French *régime primaire* (Article 217(1) CC).

Article 6. Transactions Pertaining to the Management of the Household

Paragraph 1:
Paragraph 1 governs which transactions can be concluded by one spouse with an effect also for the other spouse. In accordance with the general principle of the separation of assets, each spouse alone may conclude transactions for the management of the household (e.g. acquiring household items). However, in a departure from the principle of the separation of assets, such transactions cause the other spouse, who was not originally a party to the contract and had not given consent to the contract, to be bound by the contract and to be jointly and severally liable for any resulting liabilities. This also applies to contracts which affect the needs of the children. For example, one of the spouses shall also be jointly and severally liable for liabilities resulting from a contract concluded by the other spouse with a private tutor.

Paragraph 2:
Paragraph 2 provides that the aforementioned joint and several liability is excluded if the following two conditions are met:

- the expenditure is disproportionate, and
- the contracting third party knows or should have known that the expenditure is disproportionate.

This limitation is required to protect the other spouse, who cannot be held liable for such excessive expenditure by the other spouse. Whether the expenditure is excessive is based on the lifestyle of the spouses. Thus, if the spouses earn a modest income, the acquisition of an expensive antique piece of furniture may be a manifestly excessive expenditure. In such a case, the other spouse is not liable for such a contract if the party to the contract was aware, or should have been aware, thereof.

This provision is a modernized version of Article 220 of the CC. Spouses residing in France who chose the joint property regime shall be subject to Article 6. The adopted provision does not conflict with German law, although it goes beyond §1357 of the BGB. The spouses, however, must accept it since they chose the optional matrimonial property regime of the community of accrued gains by way of contract. They thereby voluntarily adopt the provisions of Article 6, too.

CHAPTER IV. TERMINATION OF THE MATRIMONIAL PROPERTY REGIME

Article 7. Grounds for Termination of the Matrimonial Property Regime

The date of termination of the property regime is decisive here, since the debt on the accrued gains is established according to the composition and worth of the assets of the spouses at that point in time.
Article 7 provides that the matrimonial property regime shall end:

- with the death of, or declaration of death of, one of the spouses;
- with a change of matrimonial property regime, or
- when a divorce or another court decision which terminates the matrimonial property regime becomes final and binding.

The first provision makes it clear that a declaration of death will terminate the property regime even when such declaration is incorrect. The second provision makes it clear that a change of property regime will terminate the optional matrimonial property regime of the community of accrued gains. In Germany, the property regime can in fact be replaced by way of marriage contract. Similarly, spouses under a French property regime can agree to change their property regime in the interests of the family two years after its adoption. The third provision relates to other grounds for the termination of the marriage. In France, these grounds include legal separation, the annulment of the marriage in good faith by the spouses and the early settlement of the debt on the accrued gains. In Germany, these grounds include decisions pertaining to the early settlement of the debt on the accrued gains and on the termination of a marriage due to invalidity.

CHAPTER V. ESTABLISHING THE DEBT ON THE ACCRUED GAINS UPON TERMINATION OF THE MATRIMONIAL PROPERTY REGIME

PART 1. INITIAL ASSETS

Article 8. Creation of the Matrimonial Property Regime

Paragraphs 1 and 2:
Paragraphs 1 and 2 describe the assets comprising the initial assets.

The initial assets include three types of assets:

a) Assets owned by one of the spouses on the date on which the matrimonial property regime becomes effective.
The couple often agrees upon a marriage contract before the marriage. Therefore, under Article 3, as the date on which the marriage contract becomes effective is the date of the marriage at the earliest, the date on which the matrimonial property regime becomes effective is the date of the marriage at the earliest.
b) Assets acquired at a later date by one of the spouses by inheritance or gift.
In the legal systems of both states, gains resulting from a gift or inheritance are to be included in the initial assets (Germany: §1374(2) BGB; France: Article 1570 CC).
c) Assets acquired at a later date by one of the spouses as damages for pain and suffering.

French law includes damages for pain and suffering in the initial assets. This is not the case under the German statutory matrimonial property regime of the community of accrued gains, but is regularly the object of debate, given the personal nature of such claims. Even though an expansion of the privileged assets of a spouse to other facts is prohibited under the second paragraph of §1374 of the BGB, the parties are free to agree on such inclusion in the initial assets.

The community of accrued gains shall settle the gains acquired by each spouse throughout the duration of the regime. However, certain gains occur totally independent of the cooperation or activity of the other spouse, and should therefore not be settled. This will apply mostly to the assets mentioned in points (b) and (c), acquired by inheritance, gift or as damages for pain and suffering (non-pecuniary damages). Thus, in accordance with paragraph 2, these assets shall also be included in the initial assets and be excluded from the debt on the accrued gains.

By virtue of the freedom of contract, the parties are free to agree that gains other than those referred to in paragraph 1 will be included in the initial assets. The spouses can agree accordingly by way of marriage contract (see Article 3(3) of the regime). The initial assets shall consist of the assets of a spouse less his or her liabilities at the reference date. Initial assets do not correspond to a specific set of assets, but are rather one of the two parameters in a calculation to establish the accrued gains. The deduction of the liabilities may also exceed the existing assets. This means that the initial assets may even be negative. Similar provisions can be found in French law (Articles 1570 and 1571 CC) and in German law (§1374 BGB). Unlike the French provision, the German provision on the initial assets provides that such assets may not be negative and that liabilities may not be deducted in excess of the value of the assets. However, such provision has long been criticized. Negative initial assets have now been approved for the future with the reform of the community of accrued gains in 1 September 2009.

Paragraph 3:
Initial assets shall not include:

a) The fruits of these assets.
   This provision makes it clear that the fruits resulting from the initial assets, e.g. the income from the rent of a flat, shall not be included in the initial assets. These fruits shall constitute accrued gains. This notion is also found in the legal systems of both states (Germany: §1374(2) BGB; France: Article 1570 CC).
b) The initial assets transferred as a gift by one of the spouses to any of his or her lineal relatives throughout the duration of the property regime.
   If one of the spouses donated any of the initial assets to any of his or her lineal relatives throughout the duration of the property regime, such items shall be completely excluded from the calculation of the accrued gains in accordance with Paragraph 3(2). For this reason, such items shall be included neither in the final assets nor in the initial assets. This provision is based on French law. Any increase in value of such items by means independent of the initial assets shall be included in the final assets (see Article 10 on the composition of the final assets). This provision is a compromise between the German law, which includes assets gifted in such a way in the initial assets, and the French law, which allows gifting of the initial assets, which should not be included in the accrued gains, with the exception of the increase in value of such assets.

Paragraph 4:
In order to avoid disputes on the worth of the initial assets upon termination of the property regime, it is advisable to have a notary compile an inventory of the initial assets at the conclusion of the marriage contract. The spouses may also compile a private inventory in writing. Such an inventory is presumed to be correct if it is signed by both spouses. The notarial form is not compulsory. This presumption can be refuted if any incorrectness is proved. It can also be advisable to include in the inventory the value of the initial assets. The presumption of correctness shall also apply to this value, insofar as these items shall be valued on

the date on which the property regime becomes effective under the first point of Article 9(1) (or on the date of acquisition in the case of the assets referred to in Article 8(2)). The legal systems of both States provide for such inventories, which are presumed to be correct (Germany: §1377 BGB; France: Article 1570 CC).

Paragraph 5:
If the spouses compiled no inventory, initial assets shall be presumed to be non-existent. This presumption can also be rebutted.

Article 9. Valuation of the Initial Assets

General content:
As similar as the provisions on the property regime of the community of accrued gains are in principle in both states, they are very different with respect to a very important issue: the valuation of the initial assets. France bases the valuation of the initial assets on their value on the date of termination of the matrimonial regime (Article 1571 CC). By contrast, Germany focuses on their value on the date on which the property regime becomes effective (§1376(1) BGB). Any increase in value due to normal currency depreciation does not constitute accrued gains and will not be taken into consideration.

These different dates of valuation can produce, for example, the following lasting effects:

- Under the French provisions, in contrast to German law, the spouses face the risk of depreciation of the items of the initial assets.
  Example in Germany:
  One of the spouses enters into the property regime with assets consisting solely of a shares portfolio worth EUR 100,000 at the beginning of the regime. Upon termination of the property regime, the shares portfolio is only worth EUR 20,000. The final assets of that spouse amount in total to EUR 100,000 (including the shares portfolio). Thus, that spouse has achieved no accrued gains which the other spouse will participate in.
  Example in France:
  The initial situation is the same as in the previous example. The initial assets of one of the spouses amount to EUR 20,000. The final assets amount to EUR 100,000 (20,000 and 80,000). The spouse has, thus, achieved accrued gains worth EUR 80,000, which the other spouse will participate in with a debt worth EUR 40,000 (if the latter achieved no accrued gains).

- Under German law, in contrast with French law, the spouse participates in the increases in value of the initial assets which has occurred without his or her contribution (with the exception of changes in value due to currency fluctuations, which are not taken account of). Therefore, if, for example, a plot of land remains unchanged but its value increases over the course of time due to its location, such increase shall constitute accrued gains. This is not the case, though, under the French law.

Example in Germany:

One of the spouses enters into the property regime with a plot of land worth EUR 100,000 at the beginning of the regime. Upon termination of the property regime, the plot is worth EUR 200,000, because it was deemed suitable for building. Thus, the accrued gains which the other spouse will participate in amount to EUR 100,000. Therefore, the creditor spouse will be entitled to a debt of EUR 50,000 (if he or she achieved no accrued gains).

Example in France:

The initial situation is the same as in the previous example. The plot of land is worth EUR 200,000 both in the initial and final assets. Thus, the accrued gains in which the other spouse will participate are non-existent.

In order to take account of the provisions of both Germany and France, Article 11 presents a valuation model based on both legal systems:

Paragraph 1:

The first point of paragraph 1 is based on the German valuation model. All items in existence on the date on which the matrimonial property regime became effective shall be valued pursuant to their value at this point in time. This means that the spouse who is not the owner of those items participates in any increase in value of those items, even if this occurred without his or her contribution (with the exception of the changes in value due to currency fluctuations). The initial assets of a spouse would include, for example, a painting whose worth increased throughout the duration of the marriage because the artist had become increasingly famous; this increase constitutes accrued gains.

In the case of a spouse's privileged assets (gifts, inheritances or damages for pain and suffering) which have been acquired at a later date but belong to the initial assets in accordance with paragraph 8(2), the date of valuation is the date of acquisition of those assets, in accordance with paragraph 1(2).

Paragraph 2:

Paragraph 2 provides that all plots of land and equivalent rights included in the initial assets, with the exception of usufruct and dwelling entitlements, shall be valued on the date of termination of the property regime. The valuation model described in paragraph 2 shall therefore apply to the main less-than-lifetime property rights. Such assets shall be valued on the date of termination of the property regime or on the date of calculation in special cases in accordance with Article 13.

The objective of this provision is to exclude from the accrued gains the increases in value of immovables included in the initial assets that has occurred without the contribution of one of the spouses. Immovables usually constitute a significant proportion of the assets and can be subject to value fluctuations which are generally not due to the activity of the spouses. This is the case, for example, if the family home increased in value based solely on the appreciation of its location. For example, the worth of an immovable can increase considerably because an airport nearby was closed, thus stopping the noise nuisance. In such a case, it is in the interests of the parties not to share such improvements with the other spouse. By contrast, an immovable's increase in value due to the contribution of the spouse constitutes accrued gains and it shall not increase the worth of the initial assets.

Example:

One of the spouses enters into the property regime with a plot of land (worth EUR 50,000 at the beginning of the regime) where a house is built during the regime. Upon termination of the regime, the value of the bare land, excluding the house, amounts to EUR 100,000, as the location of the plot increased in value. Upon termination of the regime, the value of the plot including the house amounts to EUR 200,000. The valuation of the initial assets will only take account of the value of the bare land on the date of termination of the regime, i.e. EUR 100,000 (the location's increase in value of EUR 50,000 during the marriage shall not constitute accrued gains). The final assets of the spouse who owns the plot will include the plot of land with the house, i.e. EUR 200,000. The accrued gains, therefore, amount to EUR 100,000. If there are no other accrued gains, the debt on the accrued gains for the other spouse amounts to EUR 50,000.

If immovables and main less-than-lifetime property rights are alienated or substituted throughout the duration of the marriage, they shall be valued on the date of alienation or substitution.

Example:

The initial situation is the same as in the previous example (one of the spouses enters into the property regime with a plot of land where a house is built during the regime). The plot of land and the house are alienated during the marriage. At the time of the alienation, the plot of land is worth EUR 80,000 and the house is worth EUR 100,000. Only the value of the plot of land (EUR 80,000), which shall be adjusted in accordance with paragraph 3, shall be included in the initial assets. The final assets depend on the total assets still owned by the spouse. The proceeds of the alienation shall be included in the final assets only if they are still partly available. If, for example, upon termination of the regime the assets of the spouse only amount to EUR 80,000, he or she produced no accrued gains to be settled.

Usufruct and dwelling entitlements shall be exempted from this provision, as the spouses reduce the worth of these rights by using them.

Paragraph 3:

Depending on individual cases, a marriage can last many years. However, under paragraph 1, the initial assets shall be valued pursuant to their specific monetary value on the date on which the property regime became effective (or on the date of acquisition of the assets under Article 8(2)). Nevertheless, such monetary value can decrease over the years due to inflation. Mere increases in value occurring solely due to inflation shall not constitute accrued gains. Thus, paragraph 3 provides that the worth of the initial assets shall be adjusted for inflation.

Example:

(fictitious and without an actual average price change index, since the optional matrimonial property regime of the community of accrued gains can be applied at the earliest on the date of ratification of the Agreement):

At the beginning of the matrimonial regime, the assets of one of the spouses amount to EUR 100,000. The marriage lasts ten years. Upon termination of the property regime, the assets of that spouse amount to EUR 200,000. It is fictitiously assumed that the EUR 100,000 at the beginning of the regime ten years earlier correspond to EUR 150,000 upon termination of the regime. As a result, the initial assets are valued at EUR 150,000 and the final assets at EUR 200,000. Therefore, the accrued gains amount to EUR 50,000 so, if the other spouse accrued no gains, the debt on the accrued gains amounts to EUR 25,000.

France does not allow adjustment based on the general price level or the price of goods, products or services without any direct connection to the object of the agreement or the activity of the parties (Article L. 112–2(1) of the French *Code monétaire et financier* [Monetary and Finance Code]). However, insofar as Article 55 of the French Constitution provides for the principle of primacy of intergovernmental Agreements over the law, the selected adjustment mechanism can be legally applied to the joint property regime.

In the case of accession of other states, the average price change index shall be calculated from the price change indices of all contracting states.

Paragraph 4:

The valuation rules provided for in paragraphs 1 and 3 shall also apply to the valuation of liabilities.

Example:

(fictitious and without an actual average price change index, since the optional matrimonial property regime of the community of accrued gains is not yet in force):

At the beginning of the property regime, one of the spouses has debts amounting to EUR 10,000. The marriage lasts ten years. Upon termination of the property regime, the assets of that spouse amount to EUR 200,000. It is fictitiously assumed that the EUR 10,000 debts at the beginning of the regime correspond to EUR 14,000 upon termination of the regime ten years later. As a result, the initial assets are valued as debts and thus at a negative amount of EUR 14,000, and the final assets are valued at EUR 200,000. Hence, the accrued gains amount to EUR 214,000.

PART 2. FINAL ASSETS

Article 10. Composition of the Final Assets

Paragraph 1:
Paragraph 1 defines the final assets as the assets owned by each spouse on the date of termination of the property regime or on the reference date under Article 13, after the deduction of liabilities, including if they exceed the existing assets. Just like initial assets, the final assets can also be negative. Final assets do not correspond to a specific set of assets, but are rather a parameter in a calculation to establish the accrued gains. The legal systems of both states contain a similar provision in their property regimes of the community of accrued gains (Germany: §1375 BGB; France: Arts. 1572 and 1574 CC).

Paragraph 2:
Under specific conditions, certain assets shall be included in the final assets. This is to prevent one of the spouses from decreasing his or her accrued gains by way of disposal of certain assets, thus putting the other spouse at a disadvantage. The legal systems of both states provide for the inclusion in the final assets of asset reductions due to gifts without the consent of the other spouse and alienations with the intention to disadvantage (Germany: §1375(2) BGB; France: Article 1573 CC). The notional asset reduction due to squandering is only provided for by the German law, §1375(2)(2) of the BGB. In order to protect the other spouse, this provision is included in the optional matrimonial property regime of the community of accrued gains.

Point 1:
In principle, gifts shall be included in the final assets.

However, this shall not apply, if:

a) the gift is reasonable having regard to the lifestyle of the spouses (this is the case if the gift does not significantly exceed the budget of the spouses for daily expenses),
b) the gift is an item of the initial assets gifted to one of that spouse's lineal relatives (Article 8(3)(2)). However, any increase in value of such items that has occurred during the property regime by means independent of the initial assets shall be included in the final assets.

In addition, the value of the gift shall not be notionally included in the final assets if the other spouse had given consent or if the item was donated more than ten years prior to the termination of the property regime.

Point 2:
This relates to legal transactions entered into with the aim of reducing the other spouse's accrued gains or depriving the other spouse of the accrued gains. Such an intention to disadvantage must have been the principal motive. This includes, for example, selling a valuable item for a price significantly under its value, if the aim was to affect the accrued gains. The gain resulting from such alienation shall not be notionally included in the final assets if the other spouse had given consent or if the item was alienated more than ten years prior to the termination of the property regime.

Point 3:
This covers expenditures that are unnecessary and excessive having regard to the assets of the spouses. This would include, for example, a luxury cruise taken by one of the spouses, if the spouses earn a modest income. This also includes the destruction of an item by a spouse, whether or not the intent was to cause damage. The value of the squandered item shall not be notionally included in the final assets if the other spouse had given consent or if the item was squandered more than ten years prior to the termination of the property regime.

The time limit of ten years is provided for in the German community of accrued gains (§1375(3) BGB). The reason behind such time limit is that, after a certain time, it is no longer assumed that such action was aimed at disadvantaging the other spouse or it is assumed that the other spouse accepted it in the end. Moreover, this provision provides for legal certainty. For these reasons, the time limit of ten years has also been adopted in the optional matrimonial property regime of the community of accrued gains.

Article 11. Valuation of the Final Assets

Paragraph 1:
Final assets shall be valued pursuant to their value on the date of termination of the matrimonial property regime or on a date calculated in special cases in accordance with Article 13.

In France, subject to the special valuation rules in the case of divorce, separation or early settlement of the debt on the accrued gains, the value of the items that constitute the final assets shall be determined pursuant to their condition on the date of termination of the regime and to their worth on the date of liquidation of the property regime. The latter may occur many years after the former (Article 1574 CC).

In Germany, the accrued gains, and thus the initial and final assets of the spouses, are calculated, in principle, on the date of termination of the property regime. However, they may be calculated on an earlier date, such as the date of submission of a petition for the early settlement of the debt on the accrued gains or when the petition of divorce becomes pending (§§1378, 1384, 1387 BGB).

Paragraph 2:
Paragraph 2 specifies the date of valuation for the assets to be notionally included in the final assets, in accordance with Article 10(2).

- The value of the items under Article 10(2) shall be calculated on the date of the gift, alienation with the intention to disadvantage, or squandering.
- The increase in value of items from the initial assets gifted to any lineal relative of one spouse during the regime by means independent of the initial assets is calculated on the date of the gift.

Paragraph 3:
From the date of calculation, the values pursuant to paragraph 2 shall be adjusted by the average price-change rates for overall consumer prices in the contracting states.

PART 3. DEBT ON THE ACCRUED GAINS

Article 12. Claim to Settlement of the Debt on the Accrued Gains

Paragraph 1:
Paragraph 1 provides that the spouse who achieved the lower accrued gains throughout the duration of the property regime can claim, upon termination of the property regime, the settlement of a debt on the accrued gains from the other spouse amounting to half of the difference between the assets gained by each spouse during the marriage.

The initial and final assets of each spouse shall be compared to establish whether, and to what extent, each spouse achieved any gains during the marriage. The provisions on the composition and valuation of the initial and final assets, which are not identical, are contained in the articles of the regime that follow. If the final assets exceed the initial assets, the difference shall constitute the accrued gains of that spouse. There is no settlement of the losses, but only of the accrued gains. If the accrued gains of one spouse exceed the accrued gains of the other, he or she owes half of the difference to the other spouse.

Paragraph 2:
In principle, the debt on the accrued gains shall be a pecuniary claim. This is the same under the law of both Germany and France. While this is explicitly

governed in France in Article 1576 of the CC, in Germany there is no special provision. However, the pecuniary nature of the claim of settlement of the debt on the accrued gains results from the provisions of §§1372 et seq. of the BGB. For clarity, the French provision has been included in the optional matrimonial property regime of the community of accrued gains.

The legal systems of both states provide for the settlement in kind only in special cases (France: Article 1576 CC; Germany: §1383 BGB). For this reason, the optional matrimonial property regime of the community of accrued gains also provides that, upon petition of one of the parties, the court can order items of the debtor to be transferred to the creditor for the purposes of settling the debt if this is equitable. The court shall decide after weighing the interests of both spouses.

Paragraph 3:
Both in France and in Germany, the debt on the accrued gains shall not be transferable as long as the property regime has not been terminated. This shall apply regardless of whether the transfer was made free of charge or not. By contrast, the claim shall be transferable after the termination of the property regime and inheritable in the case of death (Germany: §1378(3) BGB; France: Article 1569 CC). A similar provision has thus been included in the optional matrimonial property regime of the community of accrued gains.

Article 13. Date of Calculation in Special Cases

In principle, the composition and value of the assets of the spouses can be calculated at the earliest when the regime is terminated. However, if a petition for divorce is submitted, it is not appropriate to wait for the judgment of divorce to become final and binding in order to decide on the debt on the accrued gains. It is preferable for the judge to decide on both the divorce and on the accrued gains during the divorce proceedings. In such cases the joint property regime provides that the date of termination of the property regime shall be substituted with the date of submission of the petition (and not the "*assignation en divorce*" as in France). In addition this provision, which applies even where the judge does not decide on the divorce and the settlement of the debt during the same proceedings, shortens the time period during which the debtor spouse can reduce his or her assets, thus also reducing the debt on the accrued gains for the other spouse.

The statutory property regime of the community of accrued gains under the German law provides for such mechanism (§1384 BGB). However, it differs in part from the mechanism in force in France. French law provides that the property regime shall be considered terminated on the date of submission of the petition aimed solely at establishing the composition of the assets (Article 1572 CC). This mechanism is effective not only in cases of divorce;

under the joint regime it applies equally when the regime is otherwise terminated by court order. This includes, for example, a decision on the early settlement of the debt on the accrued gains under Article 18. Also in these cases, it would be advisable to be able to calculate the accrued gains already during the proceedings for the early settlement of the debt on the accrued gains. In this case, the date of calculation shall be the date of submission of the petition to the court.

Article 14. Limitation of the Debt on the Accrued Gains

This provision guarantees that, even taking account of negative initial assets, no spouse shall give the other spouse more than 50% of the assets actually available on the reference date (date of calculation under Article 13 or actual termination of the regime). This restriction on the amount of the debt on the accrued gains corresponds to the basic principle of the property regime of the community of accrued gains, under which both spouses shall fairly participate in half of the assets acquired during the marriage.

Article 14 also guarantees that a debt on the accrued gains, apart from the case of the notional inclusion under Article 10(2) (with the exception of point 1(b)), shall only exist if there are positive assets on the date of calculation of the accrued gains. If, for example, during the regime both spouses only repaid their debts or if one spouse accrued no gains and the other repaid the debts, then no debt exists. In fact, there is no settlement of the losses.

This limitation only pertains to the debt on the accrued gains and not to other possible claims and liabilities between the spouses. However, the provision's aim of enabling the debtor spouse to at least keep half of his or her assets, is not justified if he or she decreased his or her assets disloyally (Article 10(2) with the exception of point 1(b)). To avoid limiting the amount of the debt if a spouse engaged in disloyal actions, resulting in a notional inclusion in the final assets, Article 14 provides that the limitation of the debt on the accrued gains shall amount to half of the amount to be included in the final assets in accordance with Article 10(2), with the exception of gifts at point 1(b). In case of gifts, it cannot be assumed that the spouse wanted to decrease his or her assets disloyally. Therefore, the dishonest spouse can be forced to use all of his or her assets and, even to incur debts, to settle the debt on the accrued gains after a notional inclusion.

Under Article 3(3), the spouses can derogate from the application of this provision by way of contract.

CHAPTER VI. MISCELLANEOUS

Article 15. Limitation

The claim to settlement of the debt on the accrued gains shall become statute barred three years after the termination of the property regime. This three-year limitation is also found in the legal systems of both states (Germany: §1378(4) BGB; France: Article 1578 CC). However, the beginning of the limitation period is different in the two states. While in Germany the emphasis is on the knowledge of the termination of the regime, in France the limitation period begins with the termination itself. To protect the creditor spouse, the joint regime has adopted the German approach. However, under certain circumstances, if the limitation period depends on the knowledge of the spouses, it may even commence many years after the termination of the regime. To provide legal certainty to the debtor spouse from a certain date, Article 15 provides for a limitation period of ten years from the termination of the regime, independent of the knowledge of the spouses.

Article 16. Duty of Information, Inventory

Paragraph 1:
If one spouse wishes to assert a claim to settlement of the debt, he or she has to know the value of the initial and final assets of the other spouse. Therefore, the spouses shall be entitled to information and to the submission of an inventory. The spouse requesting the information shall be granted, within his or her entitlement to information, the right to the presentation of supporting documents. Thereby, that spouse can better verify the information submitted by the other spouse and better defend his or her own interests. Moreover, litigation may be avoided if convincing evidence is presented. Each spouse has the right to an inventory to be compiled by a notary at his or her expense. A similar provision can be found in the German law (§1379 BGB). In the French provisions on the regime of the community of accrued gains, Article 1572 of the CC provides for the entitlement to the compilation of an inventory of the final assets; the entitlement to information is not explicitly provided for, but is recognized.

The right to information and to the compilation of an inventory provided for here enables the creditor spouse to pursue the claim to settlement of the debt on the accrued gains.

Paragraph 2:
The situation is the same if one of the spouses requests the termination of the marriage or the early settlement of the debt on the accrued gains. The entitlement in paragraph 1 shall also apply in this case.

Article 17. Deferral

Both German law (§1382 BGB) and French law (Article 1576 CC) provide for the possibility, on the one hand, to grant additional time for the settlement of the debt on the accrued gains under specific conditions and, on the other, to claim the provision of securities.

Paragraph 1:
Paragraph 1 governs the conditions under which deferral can be granted. Deferral shall be granted in the interests of the creditor spouse only in exceptional cases. The court shall decide in each case whether there is an undue hardship.

> *Example:*
> The debtor spouse must pay EUR 50,000 to the other spouse. However, the only asset owned by the debtor spouse is the house where he or she lives and conducts the business which constitutes his or her support base. In this case it would be iniquitous to expect that spouse to sell the house. A deferral would be considered.

Paragraph 2:
Interest must be paid on a deferred debt.

Paragraph 3:
Paragraph 3 provides that the court can order the debtor to provide security for a deferred debt. The court shall decide in its equitable discretion on the nature and scope of the security provided.

Article 18. Premature Settlement of Debt on the Accrued Gains

The legal systems of both states allow immediate assertion of the claim to settlement of the debt on the accrued gains under specific conditions if it is threatened (Germany: §§1385 and 1386 BGB; France: Article 1580 CC). Under German law, besides the petition for the termination of the regime (*Gestaltungsantrag*), a claim for benefits (*Leistungsantrag*) can be submitted, enabling the creditor spouse to directly claim the early settlement of the debt on the accrued gains in specific cases. Under French law, one spouse can claim the early settlement of the debt on the accrued gains if the other spouse's disorder in their affairs, improper management of assets or misconduct give rise to a concern that the continuation of the regime may affect the rights of the other spouse. In the case of such a petition, the provisions of the separation of matrimonial property regime shall apply. If the court grants the petition, the separation of property regime enters into force.

The option of demanding the early settlement of the debt on the accrued gains is also adopted in the optional matrimonial property regime of the community of accrued gains. Under Article 18, the early settlement of the debt on the accrued gains can be sought in the event that the management of assets by one spouse is such that it compromises the interests of the other spouse in the calculation of the debt. This shall apply in particular when one spouse commits any actions which, under Article 10(2) (with the exception of point 1(b)), can lead to a notional inclusion in the final assets. In contrast to Article 1580 of the CC, Article 18 also enables the debtor spouse to claim early settlement if the actions of the other spouse under Article 18(1) adversely affect the amount of the debt on the accrued gains at his or her expense.

If the debt is compromised, in many cases it will be useful to obtain provisional measures in court to secure the claim. Such procedural measures are not governed by the optional matrimonial property regime of the community of accrued gains. As such, the provisions of the state where the claim is submitted shall apply. In France, the application of the measures of Article 220-1 of the CC can be requested. In Germany, the debt on the accrued gains can be secured by way of provisional measures through a preventive seizure under §916 of the German *Zivilprozessordnung* (Code of Civil Procedure).

CHAPTER VII. FINAL PROVISIONS

Article 19. Temporal Application

This Agreement shall only apply to marriage contracts that the spouses have concluded after its entry into force.

Article 20. Ratification and Entry into Force

This Agreement shall be subject to ratification in accordance with the applicable provisions of the international law.

It shall enter into force as soon as possible.

It can be terminated.

Article 21. Accession

Due to the increasing mobility of married couples in the European Union, it is preferable to allow the other Member States to accede to the bilateral Agreement at a later date.

In the case of accession of one or more states, Germany shall act as depositary for the Agreement.

Article 22. Languages of the Agreement

In the case of accession, a further binding version of the Agreement can be produced in the official language of the acceding State.

Article 23. Registration

The registration of the Agreement is required under Article 102 of the Charter of the United Nations.

DRAFT LAW OF THE GERMAN FEDERAL GOVERNMENT

Draft law on the Agreement dated 4 February 2010 between the Federal Republic of Germany and the French Republic on the optional matrimonial property regime of the community of accrued gains

A. Problem and objective

In binational marriages, problems may arise with regard to the assets of the spouses, because the statutory matrimonial property regimes differ from State to State and may not be known in the legal system of another State. These problems are also of practical importance, because in approx. 13% of the married couples living in Germany in 2009, at least one of the spouses was a foreign national. Problems arise not only in the case of termination of the marriage, but also throughout the duration of the marriage, e.g. in the financing of real estate loans. In this context, a common regulation, with the necessary integration in the national law, shall provide more legal certainty and clarity.

B. Solution

The Federal Republic of Germany and the French Republic have decided to create a joint optional matrimonial property regime identical in both States, which corresponds, albeit modified, to the German community of accrued gains. This property regime can be chosen by spouses in both States instead of the statutory property regime and alongside the other optional regimes of that State. The possibility of acceding to the Agreement, originally created between Germany and France, is open to the other Member States of the European Union.

This Ratifying Law creates the necessary domestic premises for its ratification under Article 59(2)(1) of the German Constitution.

At the same time, the law governs the domestic implementation of the Agreement.

C. Alternatives

None.

D. Financial implications

The Federal State, the Länder and the local authorities will not be burdened with costs.

E. Other costs

The economy, especially small and medium firms, will not be burdened with additional costs. No effects of the law on individual prices or on the general price level, especially on the consumer price level, are expected.

F. Administrative costs

No information requirements for the economy, citizens and administration will be introduced, modified or dropped.

STATEMENT OF REASONS

A. GENERAL SECTION

1. FACTUAL AND LEGAL BACKGROUND

International marriages are very common. In 2009, in 13% of the married couples living in Germany, either both spouses were foreign nationals or one of them was a German national and the other a foreign national. Among them, the at least 34,000 French-German couples were the fourth-largest group, after the German-Polish, German-Italian and German-Austrian couples (Hammes et al., WiSta 2010 p.904/911 et seq.). There are also German couples who live abroad and foreign couples who live in Germany. Since the legal consequences of a marriage conform, among other things, to the spouses' citizenship, international marriages may lead to legal difficulties, in particular with respect to property issues. The statutory matrimonial property regime in Germany is the community of accrued gains. The assets of the spouses shall remain separate, and the gains accrued throughout the duration of the marriage shall be settled only at the termination of the property regime, e.g. in the case of divorce. In France, the statutory matrimonial property regime is the community of acquisitions, under which all assets acquired throughout the duration of the marriage shall become common property. For example, problems may arise if a couple lives in Germany under the regime of the community of property in accordance with the French law and the spouses acquire a land plot in Germany. Since in general the French property regime is not known in the German law, the precise assessment of the scope of the rights of each spouse upon registration of a property right in the Land Register may result in considerable uncertainties (on the community of property under the Spanish law, see e.g. OLG Düsseldorf, FamRZ 2010, p. 1564 et seq.). For a German bank, the consequences of the liabilities of one spouse or his or her insolvency on the assets subject to community of property are particularly uncertain. The prevailing solution of choosing a German matrimonial property regime for assets situated in Germany in accordance with Article 15(2)(3) of the *Einführungsgesetz zum Bürgerlichen Gesetzbuch* (EGBGB) solves that problem, but imposes a split matrimonial property regime which might result in other calculation problems in the case of settlement of the matrimonial property. German couples may encounter similar problems in France, given the completely different traditions.

The adoption of a bilateral solution agreed upon between states offers the advantage of providing solutions for the spouses as soon as possible, since aligning the content of the family law in all Member States of the European Union may necessarily only proceed at a slower pace, given the different, often centuries-old legal traditions which are firmly rooted in each state's society. Moreover, the French Republic and the Federal Republic of Germany have a political mandate. The joint declaration on the 40th anniversary of the Élysée Treaty in 2003 gave rise to the desire to align family law in Germany and France.

The opportunity to accede to the Agreement of 4 February 2010 between the Federal Republic of Germany and the French Republic on the optional matrimonial property regime of the community of accrued gains (hereinafter referred to as the "Agreement") is open to other Member States of the European Union. Also in these states, the marriage law – and in particular the matrimonial property regimes – varies considerably, thus giving rise to similar problems as in Germany and France.

2. OBJECTIVE OF THE PROPOSED AMENDMENTS

Given the legal uncertainties in the case of marriages with an international element, the Agreement shall create an (initially) binational optional matrimonial property regime, containing identical provisions for both legal systems and therefore able to offer legal clarity and certainty to the parties. In order to foster its acceptance both in France and Germany, the optional matrimonial property regime of the community of accrued gains includes features of the matrimonial regimes of both legal systems. In its basic structure, the optional matrimonial property regime of the community of accrued gains corresponds to the German community of accrued gains, albeit modified, taking account of the French legal tradition. Spouses in the two states can choose this property regime instead of the statutory property regime among the other optional matrimonial property regimes of the state, if their matrimonial property regime is subject to the property law of one of the contracting states. The provisions of the private international law in the two states are not affected. Though an international element is not required, the optional matrimonial property regime of the community of accrued gains will mainly benefit spouses in international marriages.

The proposed amendment to the German *Bürgerliches Gesetzbuch* (Civil Code, hereinafter BGB) will introduce such optional matrimonial property regime in German family law. The provisions related to the Inheritance Tax and Gift Tax correspond to the provisions on the community of accrued gains under German law and shall guarantee the spouses do not refrain from choosing the new matrimonial property regime for tax reasons.

3. LEGISLATIVE CAPACITY

The legislative capacity of the Federal State follows from Article 73(1)(1) (Foreign Affairs), Article 74(1)(1) (Civil Law) and Article 105(2)(second alternative) in conjunction with Article 72(2) (Tax Law) of the *German Grundgesetz* (Basic Law, hereinafter GG).

A federal law is required under Article 72(2) of the GG to guarantee legal uniformity in the national interest. In order to reach a harmonization of the law in France and Germany, it is crucial that a unitary set of laws shall apply in the Federal Republic of Germany. This can only be achieved by way of a federal regulation. Different provisions for inheritance tax would cause legal uncertainty in the case of succession and may result in legal fragmentation with problematic consequences – which cannot be tolerated in the interests of both the Federal State and the *Länder* – due to the range of possible beneficiaries in each inheritance case. The consent of the German *Bundesrat* is required under Article 105(3) of the GG, since the States are entitled to the revenues from inheritance tax and gift tax under Article 106(2)(2) of the GG.

B. SPECIAL SECTION

Article 1 (Consent)

Since the Agreement relates to matters of the Federal legislation, Article 59(2)(1) of the GG shall apply.

Article 2 (Amendment to the German *Bürgerliches Gesetzbuch*)

Point 1 (Amendment to the Table of Contents)
Since a new Chapter 4 will be added to Book 4 (Family Law) of the BGB, the Table of Contents shall be integrated as well.

Point 2

a) General section

   The new Chapter 4 "Optional Matrimonial Property Regime of the Community of Accrued Gains" shall clarify that the optional matrimonial property regime of the community of accrued gains, provided for by the Agreement, is an additional matrimonial property regime which can be chosen by way of marriage contract and takes its place on equal terms alongside the other matrimonial regimes of separation of property and community of property referred to in Chapters 2 and 3.

b) §1519 of the BGB – new –

aa) Principle

§1519 of the BGB – new – takes into account the limitations to contractual freedom in §1409 of the BGB. Under §§1408 et seq. of the BGB, the spouses can contractually choose the separation of property or the community of property instead of the statutory regime of the community of accrued gains. With the new §1519 of the BGB, the optional matrimonial property regime of the community of accrued gains, provided for by the Agreement between the Federal Republic of Germany and the French Republic, becomes an additional matrimonial property regime which can be chosen by way of marriage contract.

The single provisions identical in Germany and France are contained in Articles 1 to 19 of the Agreement. By way of explanation, see the Memorandum which encloses the Explanatory Report of the Agreement between France and Germany.

bb) Application of §§1368 and 1412 of the BGB

Article 5 of the Agreement governs the ineffectiveness of disposals on the household items and the family home. This provision shall not govern the enforcement of an ineffective legal transaction against any beneficiary third party. Therefore, with reference to §1368 of the BGB in the Ratifying Law, the spouse, who is protected from an unauthorized alienation by Article 5 of the Agreement, shall be granted the opportunity to assert the rights arising from the ineffectiveness of the disposal of the household items or the family home against a third party.

By contrast, the application of §1412 of the BGB is excluded. The ineffectiveness of a disposal against a third party shall not depend on whether the marriage contract designating the optional matrimonial property regime of the community of accrued gains is registered in the Matrimonial Regime Register or if the third party was aware thereof. The registration in the Matrimonial Regime Register would be an unnecessary formality, given its little practical importance, which provides no added value to the protection of transactions. In particular in the case of disposals of immovables, the certifying notaries will have to take account of the opportunity to prohibit the disposal.

c) Delimitation from other property regimes in a broad sense

In its application, the new property regime supersedes the matrimonial property regime.

aa) §1357 of the BGB

The special provision contained in Article 6 of the Agreement, which governs the spouses' joint and several liability for transactions of one of the spouses for the management of the household, leaves no room for the application of §1357 of the BGB.

bb) §1365 of the BGB

The first paragraph of Article 5 of the Agreement, which is exhaustive in nature, prevents the application of §1365 of the BGB. The Agreement has deliberately not adopted such protective provision (see the Explanatory Report on Article 5(1) of the Agreement).

cc) §1382 of the BGB

The second paragraph of Article 17 of the Agreement contains no specific provision on the amount of the interest to be paid in the case of deferred debt. Similarly, there is no reference to §1382(4) of the BGB. Hence, §246 of the BGB shall apply and the interest rate is 4 percent. If the debtor is in default, the interest rate is 5 percentage points above the base interest rate (§288(1)(2), §247 of the BGB). There is no particular need to adopt the special procedural provision of §1382(5) of the BGB, under which a petition for deferral may be submitted only in a pending lawsuit on the debt on the accrued gains.

dd) §1384 of the BGB

In the case of termination of the marriage by way of court decision, under Article 13 of the Agreement the date of submission of the petition to the court shall be decisive for the calculation of the accrued gains. The emphasis here is not – as in §1384 of the BGB – on the suit pending upon petition of the defendant, but rather on the point in time of the submission of the petition.

ee) Pension rights adjustment

Compensation for old-age pension rights which are subject to pension rights adjustment is not provided in compliance with §1587 of the BGB in conjunction with Article 2(4) of the German *Versorgungsausgleichsgesetz* (Pension Rights Adjustment Law). This shall also apply in the case of the optional matrimonial property regime of the community of accrued gains. The spouses can regulate the different allocation of the pension assets in Germany and France by way of marriage contract. The solution of the different allocation would have overloaded the new optional property regime, given the specificities of the German pension system.

d) Settlement of the matrimonial regime with respect to inheritance

In contrast with the BGB, which contains the special provision of §1371 for the settlement of the statutory matrimonial regime in the case of death of a spouse, the Agreement provides no particular provision for such case.

§1371(1) of the BGB increases the legal inheritance portion of the surviving spouse (§1931(1) of the BGB) by a quarter, in order to settle the debt on the accrued gains in a lump sum. The Agreement does not adopt the conjunction of matrimonial regime and inheritance law, which has long been criticized also in the German law. By applying §1371(1) of the BGB, despite the adoption of the optional matrimonial property regime of the community of accrued gains, a surviving spouse under the German law would be entitled to a different debt on the accrued gains compared to a surviving spouse under the French law. This would be contrary to the objective of the Agreement to create a unitary property regime, as identical as possible in all the participating states. Therefore, in the case of death of a spouse, the accrued gains should initially be settled.

e) Inclusion of civil partnerships
The new optional matrimonial property regime of the community of accrued gains shall also be open to civil partnerships within the terms of the German *Lebenspartnerschaftsgesetz* (Civil Partnership Act, hereinafter LPartG). Under §§6 and 7 of the LPartG, the same provisions on property rights that apply to spouses shall also apply to unmarried partners. Full equality with marriage is thereby achieved. No exception shall be made with respect to the optional matrimonial property regime of the community of accrued gains. §6 of the LPartG authorizes civil partners to choose a property regime other than the statutory regime of the community of accrued gains. §7(2) of the LPartG declares that §§1409 to 1563 of the BGB can be applied mutatis mutandis. The new §1519 of the BGB is already recognised by this reference.

f) Legal situation in the case of termination of the Agreement
If Germany terminates the Agreement, the consequences should be regulated in an Accompanying Law: either the substantive content of the Agreement is maintained or operational provisions should be created, e.g. along the lines of the Unification Treaty (Article 234 §4 EGBGB).
If France terminates the Agreement, the regime is maintained as an exclusively German property regime, thanks to the static reference to the provisions of the Agreement.

Article 3 (Amendment to the German *Rechtspflegergesetz*)

In accordance with Article 12(2)(2) of the Agreement, upon petition of one of the spouses, the court can order items of the debtor to be transferred to the creditor for the purposes of settling the debt if this is equitable. Moreover, upon petition the court can grant additional time for the debtor to settle the debt on the accrued gains and order the provision of securities, in accordance with Article 17 of the Agreement. These decisions of the court are similar to those that the national law has already delegated to court officials in §§1382, 1383 of the BGB, insofar as a petition for the debt on the accrued gains is not pending (§1382(5) BGB). The reason for delegating these tasks was that in such cases no legal difficulty occurs in general, but factual questions should be clarified and economic interests should be weighed. These considerations shall apply – not least because the basic structure of the optional matrimonial regime of the community of accrued gains contractually chosen and the community of accrued gains governed by the law are the same – also to the cases governed in Article 12(2)(2) and Article 17 of the Agreement.

Article 4 (Amendment to the German *Gesetz über das Verfahren in Familiensachen und in den Angelegenheiten der freiwilligen Gerichtsbarkeit*)

Point 1
In the Table of Contents, the new heading to §264 of the German *Gesetz über das Verfahren in Familiensachen und in den Angelegenheiten der freiwilligen Gerichtsbarkeit* (Act on Court Procedure in Family Matters and Non-Litigious Matters, hereinafter FamFG) shall be corrected.

Point 2
The claims resulting from the Agreement pertaining to the optional matrimonial property regime of the community of accrued gains are property rights cases under §261(1) of the FamFG. Court proceedings under Article 5(2), Article 12(2)(2) and Article 17 of the Agreement are comparable to those of §1369(2) and §§1382 and 1383 of the BGB. Through inclusion in §261(2) of the FamFG, these proceedings are also declared property rights cases.

Point 3
§264(1)(1) of the FamFG provides that a court decision shall only be effective when it becomes final and binding for the proceedings under §§1382 and 1383 of the BGB as an exception to §40(2) of the FamFG. Like §1383 of the BGB for the matrimonial property regime of the community of accrued gains, Article 12(2)(2) of the Agreement on the optional matrimonial property regime of the community of accrued gains provides for the settlement in kind only in special cases upon petition of a party, if equitable. Article 17 of the Agreement provides for the opportunity of judicially deferring the settlement of the debt on the accrued gains, for which securities should be provided, where appropriate, and is thus comparable – with respect to the optional matrimonial property regime of the community of accrued gains – to the provision of §1382 of the BGB. The provisions of Article 12(2)(2) and Article 17 of the Agreement are similar to those in §§1382 and 1383 of the BGB and should be equally handled in matrimonial legal proceedings. For this reason, a court decision shall only be effective when it becomes final and binding also in the proceedings under Article 12(2)(2) and Article 17 of the Agreement.

Point 4
§269(1) of the FamFG governs what kind of court proceeding civil partnerships cases are. In accordance with §269(1)(11) of the FamFG these also include decisions under §6 of the LPartG in conjunction with §1365(2), §1369(2), §§1382

and 1383 of the BGB, and in accordance with §269(1)(12) of the FamFG decisions under §7 of the LPartG in conjunction with §§1426, 1430 and 1452 of the BGB. In order to achieve equality between civil partnerships and marriages – already described in Article 2(2)(e) of the Ratifying Law – also in property rights cases, the provision of §269(1)(12) of the FamFG shall clearly provide that these also include the decisions under §1519 of the BGB in conjunction with Article 5(2), Article 12(2)(2) and Article 17 of the Agreement.

Article 5 (Amendment to the German *Erbschaftsteuer- und Schenkungsteuergesetz*)

The consequences related to the inheritance tax and gift tax of the termination of the optional matrimonial property regime of the community of accrued gains shall be aligned to those of the termination of the statutory matrimonial property regime of the BGB. In practice, an unequal tax treatment would otherwise make the new property regime of the community of accrued gains a rather second-rate alternative to the statutory property regime. In accordance with §5(2) of the German *Erbschaftsteuer- und Schenkungsteuergesetz* (Law on Inheritance Tax and Gift Tax, hereinafter ErbStG), the debt on the accrued gains under Article 12 of the Agreement shall not constitute an acquisition within the terms of §§3 and 7 of the ErbStG. This shall apply regardless of whether the optional matrimonial property regime of the community of accrued gains is terminated by the death of a spouse or during their lifetimes. The debt on the accrued gains is thus not subject to taxation under the ErbStG, as long as it was specifically calculated and is the basis of an assets transfer.

An exemption under §5(1) of the ErbStG is not required here. In the case of inheritance settlement of the community of accrued gains (§1371(1) BGB), through the provision on acquisitions within the terms of §§3 and 7 of the ErbStG, the surviving spouse is exempt from the Inheritance Tax in the amount of the notional debt on the accrued gains, which the spouse could have asserted under §§1373 to 1383, 1390 of the BGB. Since in the optional matrimonial property regime of the community of accrued gains, in the case of termination of the property regime the debt on the accrued gains can be asserted only by determining the actual debt, there is no room for the application of §5(1) of the ErbStG.

Moreover, there is no need to apply mutatis mutandis §29(1)(2) of the ErbStG. Under §29(1)(2) of the ErbStG, the tax expires with retroactive effect, insofar as in the cases of §5(2) of the ErbStG the free gifts, which were taxable, were included in the debt on the accrued gains, in accordance with §1380(1) of the BGB. Since this is not the case in the Agreement, there is no room for the application of §29(1)(2).

Article 6 (Entry into force)

Paragraphs 1 and 2 govern the entry into force of the law. The provisions comply with the requirements of Article 82(2)(1) of the GG.

In accordance with paragraph 2(2), the date of entry into force of the Agreement under its Article 20 shall be published in the German *Bundesgesetzblatt* (Law Gazette).

Closing remarks

Through the Agreement between the Federal Republic of Germany and the French Republic on the optional matrimonial property regime of the community of accrued gains, the states involved developed a new model for the integration of the civil laws in Europe. In principle the Agreement is open to any Member State of the European Union, thus expanding the options of the European citizens under the regime of private autonomy, by creating a new property law. The hereby presented draft of a ratification and implementation law makes this new option available to anyone subject to the German matrimonial property law after the entry into force of the Agreement.

The public finances and the economy, especially small and medium firms, will not be burdened with additional costs. No effects of the law on individual prices or on the general price level, in particular on the consumer price level, are expected.

The draft law is compatible with the guiding principles of the German Federal Government on sustainable development in line with the national sustainability strategy. The proposed provisions shall contribute to greater legal clarity in international marriages.

No information requirements for the economy, citizens and administration will be introduced, modified or dropped.

The draft law is compatible with the law of the European Union and with international treaties entered into by the Federal Republic of Germany.

Important effects with respect to gender equality are not expected.

GERMAN RATIFICATION ACT

Law on the Agreement dated 4 February 2010 between the Federal Republic of Germany and the French Republic on the optional matrimonial property regime of the community of accrued gains

The German *Bundestag*, with the consent of the German *Bundesrat*, has passed the following law:

Article 1. Consent

The Agreement signed in Paris on 4 February 2010 between the Federal Republic of Germany and the French Republic on the optional matrimonial property regime of the community of accrued gains is hereby approved. The Agreement is published hereafter.

Article 2. Amendment to the German *Bürgerliches Gesetzbuch*

The German *Bürgerliches Gesetzbuch* (Civil Code, hereinafter BGB) in the version published on 2 January 2002 (German *Bundesgesetzblatt* – Law Gazette, hereinafter 'BGBl.', I p. 42, 2909; 2003 I p. 738), last amended by Article 1 of the Act dated 17 January 2011 (BGBl. I p. 1600), shall hereby be amended as follows:

1. In the Table of Contents, the following indication shall be added after the indication of Book 4(1)(6)(2)(3):
   "Chapter 4 Optional matrimonial property regime of the community of accrued gains".

2. After §1518, Chapter 4 shall be added as follows:
   "Chapter 4 Optional matrimonial property regime of the community of accrued gains
   §1519
   Agreement by way of marriage contract
   If the spouses agree by way of marriage contract on the optional matrimonial property regime of the community of accrued gains, the provisions of the Agreement of 4 February 2010 between the Federal Republic of Germany and the French Republic on the optional matrimonial property regime of the community of accrued gains shall apply. §1368 shall apply accordingly. §1412 shall not apply."

Article 3. Amendment to the German *Rechtspflegergesetz*

§25 Number 3 of the *Rechtspflegergesetz* (Act on Senior Judicial Officers) of 5 November 1969 (BGBl. I p. 2065), last amended by Article 5 of the Act of 7 December 2011 (BGBl. I p. 582), shall hereby be amended as follows:

1. In letter (b), a comma shall replace the final full stop.

2. A new letter (c) shall be added as follows:
   "c) the decision on the deferral of the settlement of a debt and the transfer of assets pursuant to §1519 of the BGB in conjunction with Article 12(2)(2) and Article 17 of the Agreement of 4 February 2010 between the Federal Republic of Germany and the French Republic on the optional matrimonial property regime of the community of accrued gains, also in conjunction with §7 of the German *Lebenspartnerschaftsgesetz* (Civil Partnership Act), unless a lawsuit for the debt becomes pending."

Article 4. Amendment to the German *Gesetz über das Verfahren in Familiensachen und in den Angelegenheiten der freiwilligen Gerichtsbarkeit*

The German *Gesetz über das Verfahren in Familiensachen und in den Angelegenheiten der freiwilligen Gerichtsbarkeit* (Act on Court Procedure in Family Matters and Non-Litigious Matters, hereinafter FamFG) of 17 December 2008 (BGBl. I p. 2586, 2587), last amended by Article 2(32) of the Act dated 22 December 2011 (BGBl. I p. 3044), shall hereby be amended as follows:

1. In the Table of Contents, the indication of §264 shall read as follows:
   "§264 Court proceeding on the deferral of settlement and transfer of assets".

2. §261(2) shall read as follows:
   "(2) Property rights cases are also court proceedings pursuant to §1365(2), §1369(2), §§1382, 1383, 1426, 1430 and 1452 of the BGB, and pursuant to §1519 of the BGB in conjunction with Article 5(2), Article 12(2)(2) and Article 17 of the Agreement of 4 February 2010 between the Federal Republic of Germany and the French Republic on the optional matrimonial property regime of the community of accrued gains."

3. §264 shall be amended as follows:
   a) The heading shall read as follows:
      "§264
      Court proceeding on the deferral of settlement and transfer of assets".

   b) The first sentence of Article 264(1) shall read as follows:
      "(2) In court proceedings pursuant to §§1382 and 1383 of the BGB, and pursuant to §1519 of the BGB in conjunction with Article 12(2)(2) and Article 17 of the Agreement of 4 February 2010 between the Federal Republic of

Germany and the French Republic on the optional matrimonial property regime of the community of accrued gains, the decision of the court shall only be effective when it becomes final and binding."

4. Point 12 of §269(1) shall read as follows:
   "12. Decisions pursuant to §7 of the *Lebenspartnerschaftsgesetz* (Civil Partnership Act) in conjunction with §§1426, 1430 and 1452 of the BGB or with §1519 of the BGB and Article 5(2), Article 12(2)(2) or Article 17 of the Agreement of 4 February 2010 between the Federal Republic of Germany and the French Republic on the optional matrimonial property regime of the community of accrued gains".

Article 5. Amendment to the German *Erbschaftsteuer- und Schenkungsteuergesetz*

A new paragraph 3 shall hereby be added to §5 of the German *Erbschaftsteuer- und Schenkungsteuergesetz* (Law on Inheritance Tax and Gift Tax, hereinafter ErbStG) in the version published on 27 February 1997 (BGBl. I p. 378), last amended by Article 11 of the Act dated 7 December 2011 (BGBl. I p. 2592) as follows:

> "(3) If the optional matrimonial property regime of the community of accrued gains (§1519 of the BGB) is terminated and the accrued gains are settled, the debt on the accrued gains (Article 12(1) of the Agreement of 4 February 2010 between the Federal Republic of Germany and the French Republic on the optional matrimonial property regime of the community of accrued gains) shall not belong to acquisitions within the terms of §§3 and 7."

Article 6. Entry into force

(1) Articles 2 to 5 shall enter into force on the date on which the Agreement of 4 February 2010 between the Federal Republic of Germany and the French Republic on the optional matrimonial property regime of the community of accrued gains becomes effective. The date of entry into force shall be published in the BGBl.

(2) In all other regards, this law shall become effective on the day following its promulgation.

ITALIAN*

CONTENTS

* Unofficial translations by Maria Virginia Maccari and Elisa Sgutin. Revised by Marella Magris. Based on the German texts.

MOTIVAZIONI

I. PARTE GENERALE

1. SITUAZIONE INIZIALE

I matrimoni con elementi di internazionalità sono molto diffusi. Nel 2009, nel 13% ca. delle coppie di coniugi residenti in Germania, entrambi i coniugi avevano la cittadinanza straniera oppure un coniuge aveva la cittadinanza tedesca e l'altro una cittadinanza straniera. A ciò si aggiungono le coppie tedesche che vivono all'estero e le coppie straniere che vivono nella Repubblica Federale Tedesca. Poichè gli effetti giuridici del matrimonio dipendono, tra l'altro, dalla cittadinanza, i matrimoni tra cittadini di diversi Stati possono comportare difficoltà giuridiche, in particolare, con riferimento alle questioni patrimoniali. Nella Repubblica Federale Tedesca il regime legale dei beni è la comunione degli incrementi. I patrimoni dei coniugi rimangono separati e solo alla cessazione del regime dei beni – per esempio a causa di divorzio – viene compensato l'incremento patrimoniale prodotto in costanza di matrimonio. Nella Repubblica Francese il regime legale dei beni è la comunione dei beni limitata agli acquisti. Gli acquisti in costanza di matrimonio costituiscono patrimonio comune. Se, per esempio, una coppia vive in Germania in comunione limitata agli acquisti, secondo il diritto francese, sorgono dei problemi qualora i coniugi, in tale regime dei beni, acquistino un immobile nella Repubblica Federale Tedesca. Poiché il regime dei beni francese, di regola, non è conosciuto nella Repubblica Federale Tedesca, la precisa valutazione della portata dei diritti spettanti in capo ai singoli coniugi al momento della trascrizione di un diritto di proprietà nel libro fondiario conduce, per esempio, a considerevoli incertezze. Per un istituto di credito tedesco è particolarmente dubbio quali conseguenze abbiano i vincoli obbligatori o l'insolvenza di un coniuge sul patrimonio vincolato nella comunione degli acquisti. La soluzione spesso rinvenibile nella pratica, secondo cui i coniugi ai sensi dell'art. 15, comma 2, EGBGB scelgono il regime dei beni tedesco per i patrimoni situati nella Repubblica Federale Tedesca, risponde certamente a questa domanda, ma impone una scissione del regime dei beni che può condurre a difficoltà di calcolo nel caso di un conguaglio patrimoniale. In considerazione di tradizioni del tutto differenti, le coppie tedesche in Francia incontrano problemi analoghi. Anche negli altri Paesi dell'Unione Europea il diritto matrimoniale nazionale è disciplinato in modo diversificato.

Considerata questa situazione, esiste la necessità di creare regole internazionali possibilmente assimilabili o identiche, che offrano agli interessati chiarezza e sicurezza giuridica. Sul piano europeo vanno cercate risposte comuni alle domande concernenti la legge nazionale applicabile ai matrimoni con elementi di internazionalità e il foro competente. Viceversa è necessario un adeguamento sostanziale del diritto di famiglia negli Stati membri in ragione delle differenti tradizioni giuridiche, spesso nei secoli cresciute e profondamente radicate nella popolazione, attualmente non nell'agenda europea. L'impostazione seguita in questo accordo, di agire inizialmente bilateralmente e per un chiaro quadro giuridico, per offrire soluzioni il più possibile veloci per i coniugi coinvolti, si ripromette di essere un mezzo efficiente.

Inoltre per la Repubblica Francese e la Repubblica Federale Tedesca vi è anche un incarico politico. Dalla dichiarazione comune nella 40° ricorrenza del "Elysée-Vertrag" del 2003 scaturisce il desiderio di conformare il diritto di famiglia tedesco e francese.

2. LINEE GENERALI DEL DIRITTO PRIVATO INTERNAZIONALE VIGENTE

Le norme di conflitto del diritto del regime dei beni patrimoniale della Repubblica Federale Tedesca e della Repubblica Francese sono relativamente simili. Questo vale, in particolare, per le possibilità di scelta della legge ai sensi dell'art. 15, comma 2, EGBGB. Di conseguenza, i coniugi possono scegliere la legge tedesca quando almeno un coniuge possiede la cittadinanza tedesca o ha la sua dimora abituale nella Repubblica Federale Tedesca. Per il patrimonio immobiliare situato nella Repubblica Federale Tedesca può essere scelta, allo stesso modo, la legge tedesca.

Nella Repubblica Francese la legge francese può essere scelta per gli effetti patrimoniali del matrimonio ai sensi della Convenzione dell'Aja del 14 marzo 1978 sulla legge applicabile al regime dei beni matrimoniale. Questo accordo comprende, accanto alle ipotesi conosciute dal diritto tedesco, un'ulteriore fattispecie: i coniugi possono scegliere la legge francese quando uno dei coniugi stabilisce la sua dimora abituale nella Repubblica Francese dopo la celebrazione del matrimonio.

3. CONTENUTO SOSTANZIALE DELL'ACCORDO

Il 4 febbraio 2010, in occasione del Consiglio dei Ministri franco-tedesco a Parigi, i Ministri della Giustizia di entrambi gli Stati hanno sottoscritto l'accordo sul regime dei beni opzionale della partecipazione agli incrementi, con il quale, per la prima volta, si è inteso creare un diritto sostanziale uniforme nel settore del diritto di famiglia per la Repubblica Federale Tedesca e la Repubblica Francese, e nel quale viene regolato un regime dei beni opzionale identico nella Repubblica Tedesca e Francese. Questo regime dei beni corrisponde nella sua struttura di base al conguaglio degli incrementi tedesco; esso presenta però alcune differenze che tengono conto della tradizione giuridica francese. In entrambi gli Stati i coniugi possono scegliere questo regime dei beni in luogo del regime dei beni legale, accanto agli altri regimi dei beni opzionali nazionali. Con ciò viene messo a disposizione dei coniugi un regime dei beni opzionale identico sia in Germania sia in Francia e con il quale si eliminano in entrambi gli Stati le difficoltà giuridiche che possono sorgere in considerazione di regole straniere del regime dei beni non conosciute.

II. PARTE SPECIALE

Con riguardo alla storia dell'origine dell'accordo e al contenuto delle singole disposizioni si fa riferimento alla relazione esplicativa. La relazione è allegata a queste motivazioni nella versione linguistica tedesca e francese.

All'Articolo 1

Il regime dei beni opzionale della partecipazione agli incrementi può essere scelto dai coniugi il cui regime dei beni soggiace alla legge applicabile di uno Stato contraente. Esso può essere scelto qualora sia applicabile al regime dei beni dei coniugi o la legge tedesca o la legge francese. Non è necessario un collegamento internazionale diretto, anche una coppia di coniugi che vive nella Repubblica Federale Tedesca senza aver alcun collegamento con la Repubblica Francese può scegliere contrattualmente questo regime dei beni.

All'Articolo 2

L'art. 2, nel suo contenuto, stabilisce che nel regime dei beni opzionale della partecipazione agli incrementi il patrimonio dei coniugi resta separato e che "l'incremento patrimoniale" è l'importo per il quale il patrimonio finale di un coniuge supera il suo patrimonio iniziale. Di principio, il conguaglio dell'incremento patrimoniale viene effettuato solamente al momento della cessazione del regime dei beni.

All'Articolo 3

Ai sensi dell'articolo 3, comma 1, la convenzione del regime dei beni ha luogo tramite contratto matrimoniale. L'articolo 3, comma 2, stabilisce che il contratto può essere concluso prima della celebrazione del matrimonio o in costanza di matrimonio e che acquista efficacia non prima del giorno della celebrazione del matrimonio.

Agli Articoli da 4 a 6

L'articolo 4 stabilisce che ciascun coniuge, di principio, può disporre in maniera autonoma del proprio patrimonio. L'articolo 5, comma 1, esclude tuttavia da questo principio gli atti di diposizione posti in essere da un coniuge su beni dell'attività domestica o su diritti con i quali è garantita la casa familiare e li sottopone alla riserva di consenso dell'altro coniuge. Ai sensi dell'articolo 6, comma 1, i coniugi sono obbligati in solido dai contratti per la gestione dell'attività domestica e per i bisogni della prole, a meno che un coniuge assuma obbligazioni pecuniarie sproporzionate in rapporto al patrimonio, cosa che è nota alla controparte o che avrebbe dovuto esserlo (articolo 6, comma 2).

Agli Articoli da 7 a 14

Ai sensi dell'articolo 7 il regime dei beni cessa con la morte o con la dichiarazione di morte di uno dei coniugi, con il mutamento del regime dei beni o con la sentenza di divorzio o con ogni altra decisione giudiziale che pone fine al regime dei beni. Per determinare il credito di conguaglio dell'incremento patrimoniale, è necessario confrontare i relativi patrimoni iniziale e finale dei coniugi. Inoltre, gli articoli 8 e 9 contengono disposizioni rilevanti ai fini della determinazione del patrimonio iniziale; il patrimonio finale viene accertato sulla base degli articoli 10 e 11. Il patrimonio iniziale è il patrimonio di ciascun coniuge alla data di entrata in vigore del regime dei beni; il patrimonio finale è quello esistente alla cessazione del regime dei beni, nel quale vengono contemplati anche i vincoli obbligatori dei coniugi riferiti a quel periodo, anche se questi eccedono il patrimonio attivo. Ai sensi dell'articolo 12 il coniuge, il cui incremento patrimoniale sia inferiore, può pretendere dall'altro la metà dell'eccedenza quale credito di conguaglio. Ai sensi dell'articolo 14 il credito di conguaglio dell'incremento patrimoniale è limitato, tuttavia, alla metà del valore del patrimonio del coniuge obbligato al conguaglio.

Agli Articoli da 15 a 18

Gli articoli da 15 a 18 contengono disposizioni sulla prescrizione, sui reciproci obblighi informativi dei coniugi per la determinazione del credito di conguaglio dell'incremento patrimoniale, per la dilazione e per il conguaglio anticipato degli incrementi patrimoniali. Quest'ultimo è configurabile, in particolare, in caso di atti di disposizioni in mala fede di un coniuge a svantaggio del credito di conguaglio dell'incremento patrimoniale dell'altro.

Agli Articoli da 19 a 23

L'articolo 19 stabilisce che l'accordo si applica ai contratti matrimoniali stipulati dopo la sua entrata in vigore. Ai sensi dell'articolo 20, comma 1, l'accordo è soggetto a ratifica da parte di entrambi gli Stati e, ai sensi dell'articolo 20, comma 2, entra in vigore il primo giorno successivo allo scambio degli strumenti di ratifica. Gli strumenti di ratifica devono essere depositati presso il Governo della Repubblica Federale Tedesca. Ai sensi dell'articolo 21 l'adesione all'accordo resta aperta anche a tutti gli altri Stati Membri dell'Unione Europea. L'articolo 22 contiene una norma sul regime linguistico dell'accordo e l'articolo 23 contiene la disposizione in base alla quale la Repubblica Federale Tedesca registrerà l'accordo presso le Nazioni Unite immediatamente dopo l'entrata in vigore.

ALLEGATO ALLE MOTIVAZIONI

RELAZIONE ESPLICATIVA

A. PRESENTAZIONE GENERALE

1. SITUAZIONE INIZIALE

I matrimoni fra cittadini di diversi Stati non sono oggi più una rarità. Circa il 13% dei matrimoni celebrati (nel 2006) e dei divorzi pronunciati (nel 2005) in Germania ha interessato coniugi di nazionalità diversa.

Nel 2006 in Francia la percentuale dei matrimoni tra coppie miste è stata del 14,59%. Inoltre nel 2003 in Francia i matrimoni franco-tedeschi hanno rappresentato il 2% dei matrimoni bi-nazionali celebrati.

Il regime patrimoniale tra coniugi disciplina gli effetti giuridici del matrimonio sul patrimonio dei coniugi e sui rapporti patrimoniali dei coniugi fra loro e con i terzi. La individuazione del regime rileva primariamente per le modalità secondo le quali devono essere sciolti i vincoli di natura patrimoniale dei coniugi al momento della cessazione del regime dei beni. Il regime dei beni produce inoltre effetti anche in costanza di matrimonio, ad esempio sulla amministrazione del patrimonio e sull'acquisto dei beni, ed ancora sulla responsabilità di un coniuge per i vincoli obbligatori contratti dall'altro coniuge prima e durante il matrimonio.

Il diritto internazionale privato degli Stati consente ai coniugi, in determinati casi, la scelta della legge applicabile al regime patrimoniale.

I coniugi possono scegliere di sottoporre il loro regime patrimoniale, secondo precisi criteri, alla legge francese o alla legge tedesca.

Così, il diritto internazionale privato tedesco (art. 15, comma 2, EGBGB (*Einführungsgesetz zum Bürgerlichen Gesetzbuche*) consente ai coniugi di sottoporre gli effetti del regime dei beni del loro matrimonio alla legge tedesca, quando:

- uno dei coniugi ha la cittadinanza tedesca;
- uno dei coniugi ha la sua residenza abituale in Germania;
- alcuni beni immobili dei coniugi sono situati in Germania, limitatamente a questi beni.

Se i coniugi non hanno scelto la legge applicabile, valgono i criteri oggettivi di collegamento di cui all'art. 15, comma 1, in combinato disposto con l'art. 14 EGBGB. Il regime patrimoniale tedesco deve essere applicato, ad esempio, nel caso in cui entrambi i coniugi sono di nazionalità tedesca o se, durante il matrimonio, essi hanno la loro residenza abituale in Germania.

Secondo il diritto francese, la Convenzione dell'Aja sulla legge applicabile ai regimi patrimoniali dei coniugi del 14 marzo 1978 consente ai coniugi di sottoporre gli effetti del regime dei beni la legge francese quando:

- uno dei coniugi ha la cittadinanza francese;
- uno dei coniugi ha la sua residenza abituale in Francia;
- uno dei coniugi, dopo il matrimonio, stabilisce la sua prima residenza abituale in Francia.

Inoltre, i coniugi possono scegliere la legge francese per i beni immobili situati in Francia (art. 3 della sopracitata Convenzione dell'Aja).

Se i coniugi non hanno effettuato alcuna scelta, si applica al regime dei beni la legge dello Stato in cui essi hanno stabilito dopo il matrimonio la loro prima residenza abituale.

Qualora sia applicabile al regime dei beni la legge tedesca o quella francese, i coniugi hanno la possibilità di scegliere uno dei regimi esistenti in Germania o in Francia:

a) Regime patrimoniale tedesco
   Il regime patrimoniale tedesco conosce tre forme di regime dei beni:
   - la partecipazione agli incrementi;
   - la separazione dei beni;
   - la comunione dei beni.
     La partecipazione agli incrementi è il regime legale dei beni. Gli altri regimi trovano applicazione solo nel caso in cui i coniugi abbiano convenuto in tal senso in un contratto matrimoniale.
b) Regime patrimoniale francese
   Il regime patrimoniale francese conosce, ugualmente, tre tipi di regimi dei beni:
   - la comunione dei beni (o limitata agli acquisti; o comprensiva di acquisti di beni mobili; o quale comunione universale);
   - la partecipazione agli incrementi;
   - la separazione dei beni.

In Francia la comunione degli acquisti è il regime legale dei beni. Gli altri regimi trovano applicazione solo nel caso in cui i coniugi abbiano convenuto in tal senso in un contratto matrimoniale.

Le differenze, specificatamente tra i due regimi legali, sono notevoli.

La partecipazione agli incrementi secondo il diritto tedesco equivale a una separazione dei beni durante la vigenza del regime, con una compensazione degli incrementi alla cessazione del regime stesso (§1363, comma 2, del Bürgerliches Gesetzbuch (BGB)). Questo regime dei beni non conduce dunque di per sé ad una proprietà comune dei coniugi.[1] Ciascun coniuge conserva piuttosto la proprietà dei beni acquistati prima e durante il matrimonio e risponde, per contro, con il proprio patrimonio solo dei suoi debiti.[2] Questo vale anche per un bene che appartiene ad entrambi i coniugi per parti determinate (c.d. comunione per quote).[3] Così, ad esempio, nell'ipotesi in cui una casa appartenga in parti uguali ai coniugi, ciascun coniuge può disporre in linea di principio della sua metà.[4]

Il regime francese della comunione degli acquisti, invece, conosce tre masse patrimoniali distinte: il patrimonio della moglie, il patrimonio del marito e il patrimonio comune.

Ai sensi dell'art. 1401 del Code civil (CC), il patrimonio comune è costituito dagli acquisti fatti dai coniugi congiuntamente o disgiuntamente in costanza di matrimonio. Al patrimonio comune appartiene anche tutto ciò che viene acquistato in ragione del proprio lavoro o come frutti o redditi derivanti dai beni di ciascuno. In linea di principio, ciascun coniuge può amministrare disgiuntamente i beni comuni e disporne. Tuttavia, determinati atti possono essere compiuti solo congiuntamente dai coniugi. Così, ad esempio, ciascun coniuge può fare una donazione tra vivi avente ad oggetto un bene comune solo con il consenso dell'altro coniuge. Inoltre, in Francia, alcune regole del regime primario, che si applicano a prescindere dal regime matrimoniale dei beni, possono limitare, in particolare, il potere dei coniugi di disporre in maniera disgiunta dei beni comuni.

Un coniuge non può disporre quindi disgiuntamente né dei diritti tramite i quali è garantita la casa familiare né dei beni dell'attività domestica[5] (ad esempio, risoluzione del contratto di locazione o alienazione della casa familiare). Questa limitazione si applica anche se la casa familiare è bene personale di un coniuge.

2. OPPORTUNITÀ DI CREARE UN REGIME COMUNE DEI BENI

La creazione di un regime comune dei beni, che si costituisce, opera e si scioglie secondo regole identiche negli Stati contraenti, rappresenta un rilevante

1 "Alla creazione di una comunione dei beni o dei debiti tra i coniugi", nella versione francese.

2 "In questo modo, ciascun coniuge conserva l'amministrazione, il godimento e la libera disponibilità dei suoi beni personali, acquistati prima o durante il matrimonio. Per contro, ciascun coniuge è esclusivamente responsabile dei suoi debiti, sorti prima o durante il matrimonio", nella versione francese.

3 "Che è di proprietà indivisa dei coniugi", nella versione francese.

4 "I coniugi acquistino una casa in comproprietà, ciascuno di loro può disporre unicamente per la parte indivisa che gli appartiene", nella versione francese.

5 "Beni mobili di arredo", nella versione francese.

progresso giuridico per le coppie, i terzi e gli operatori giuridici. Di fatto, negli Stati contraenti, questa disciplina crea un diritto sostanziale comune.

Pertanto la scelta di questa forma di regime da parte della coppia non conduce alla difficoltà che attualmente sorgono con l'adozione della comunione degli acquisti regolata dal diritto francese, qualora i coniugi acquistino in costanza di matrimonio un bene immobile situato in Germania. Poiché il regime legale della comunione degli acquisti francese non è conosciuto in Germania, la trascrizione nel registro immobiliare di un diritto di proprietà[6] non consente ai terzi di valutare la precisa estensione dei diritti spettanti a ciascun coniuge. La soluzione, spesso ricorrente nella prassi, di scegliere, per un patrimonio situato in Germania, un regime patrimoniale tedesco (art. 15, comma 2, n. 3 EGBGB) risolve questo problema, ma impone ai coniugi un regime dei beni distinto, che può causare difficoltà nel calcolo del credito di conguaglio.

Considerata questa situazione iniziale, e poiché il regime della partecipazione agli incrementi (quale regime dei beni legale in Germania e regime dei beni opzionale in Francia) è presente nel diritto francese e nel diritto tedesco, è parso opportuno creare, attraverso un accordo bilaterale, un regime opzionale supplementare, ispirato ai regimi della partecipazione agli incrementi esistenti in ciascuno dei due paesi, che funzioni secondo delle regole semplici e moderne, identiche in Francia e in Germania.

Per consentire ad altri Stati dell'Unione Europea di aderire in seguito all'accordo, si prevede che dopo la sua entrata in vigore qualsiasi Stato membro dell'Unione europea possa aderirvi (art. 21).

B. PRESENTAZIONE DEL REGIME

CAPITOLO I. AMBITO DI APPLICAZIONE E DEFINIZIONE

Articolo 1. Ambito di applicazione

Il regime dei beni opzionale della partecipazione agli incrementi è aperto a tutti i coniugi per i quali è applicabile il regime patrimoniale di uno Stato contraente, senza che il matrimonio debba presentare un elemento di internazionalità. Di conseguenza questo regime dei beni opzionale può essere scelto da coniugi il cui regime matrimoniale dei beni è regolato dalla legge francese o dalla legge tedesca, secondo il diritto internazionale privato applicabile, anche di uno Stato terzo.

Questo vale, per esempio, in applicazione del diritto internazionale privato francese o tedesco, per coniugi:

- dei quali uno abbia la cittadinanza francese o tedesca;
- dei quali uno abbia la sua residenza abituale in Francia o Germania;

[6] "A nome dei coniugi in comunione dei beni", nella versione francese.

- dei quali uno stabilisca in Francia la sua prima residenza abituale;
- dei quali uno abbia beni immobili in Francia o in Germania, limitatamente a questi beni.

II regime dei beni opzionale della partecipazione agli incrementi può pertanto trovare applicazione,[7] ad esempio, per due tedeschi che vivono in Francia, per due francesi che vivono in Germania, ma anche per due tedeschi che vivono in Germania e per due francesi che vivono in Francia.

La scelta di questo regime dei beni non richiede che i coniugi scelgano la legge di uno Stato contraente. Secondo l'art. 1 è necessario soltanto che il regime dei beni soggiaccia alla legge sostanziale di uno Stato contraente. Ciò nonostante, al fine di evitare ogni ambiguità, in alcuni casi è consigliabile per i coniugi indicare nel loro contratto matrimoniale la legge applicabile al loro regime patrimoniale, ove questo sia ammesso secondo il diritto internazionale privato.

Articolo 2. Definizione

"Partecipazione agli incrementi" significa che, per la durata del regime dei beni, i patrimoni dei coniugi restano separati. La costituzione del regime dei beni non influisce sui regimi di proprietà e sui rapporti obbligatori. Di conseguenza non esiste una terza massa patrimoniale comune ad entrambi i coniugi come nel regime della comunione dei beni.

L'incremento patrimoniale realizzato durante il regime medesimo risulta dalla comparazione tra le masse patrimoniali di entrambi i coniugi solo alla cessazione del regime dei beni.[8]

CAPITOLO II. COSTITUZIONE DEL REGIME DEI BENI

Articolo 3. Costituzione del regime dei beni

Al comma 1:
I coniugi possono scegliere mediante contratto matrimoniale il regime dei beni opzionale della partecipazione agli incrementi. Per la forma di questo contratto vige la legge designata secondo il corrispondente diritto internazionale privato. Si tratta, al riguardo, delle legge applicabile nel luogo di conclusione del contratto o del diritto interno applicabile al regime dei beni.[9]

---

7 "Può essere scelto da", nella versione francese.

8 "Solo alla cessazione del regime, si confrontano gli acquisti realizzati da ciascun coniuge durante il regime al fine di determinare il credito di conguaglio dovuto da un coniuge all'altro", nella versione francese.

9 "Conformemente alle regole di diritto internazionale privato tedesco e francese, la forma del contratto deve rispettare o il diritto interno in vigore nel luogo di conclusione del contratto o

Al comma 2:
I coniugi possono convenire il regime dei beni opzionale della partecipazione agli incrementi prima della celebrazione del matrimonio o in costanza di matrimonio. La possibilità di concludere un contratto prima della celebrazione del matrimonio può impedire, ad esempio nel caso di matrimonio celebrato secondo il diritto francese,[10] che sorga inizialmente una comunione degli acquisti, la quale dovrebbe essere in seguito liquidata per poter adottare un altro regime.

Il vigore del regime dei beni opzionale è collegato alla celebrazione del matrimonio. Per questa ragione il regime dei beni opzionale della partecipazione agli incrementi può produrre effetti soltanto quando il matrimonio sia effettivamente celebrato. In Germania questo non è regolato espressamente ma risulta dal §1408 BGB, a norma del quale le parti contraenti devono essere coniugi. In Francia ciò risulta espressamente dall'art. 1395 CC.

Il regime dei beni comune può essere pattuito anche in costanza di matrimonio.

Secondo il diritto tedesco i coniugi possono modificare il regime dei beni in ogni momento mediante contratto matrimoniale, e in tal modo anche rinunciare al regime dei beni legale della partecipazione agli incrementi. Il contratto matrimoniale produce effetti dal momento della sua conclusione. A partire da questo momento trovano applicazione fra i coniugi le regole del nuovo regime dei beni.

I coniugi soggetti a un regime dei beni francese possono pattuire, nell'interesse della famiglia, di modificare il regime matrimoniale dei beni dopo un periodo di applicazione di due anni (art. 1397 CC). Questa modifica diviene efficace il giorno della formazione del certificato notarile[11] che prevede il mutamento, se i coniugi non hanno figli minorenni e se i figli maggiorenni o i creditori non si oppongono al mutamento. Nel caso contrario, in entrambe le predette ipotesi, il mutamento del regime dei beni diviene efficace con la sentenza[12] che lo omologa.

Al comma 3:
Il principio di libertà contrattuale di cui all'art. 3, comma 3, consente ai coniugi di derogare convenzionalmente alle norme sulla determinazione del credito di conguaglio dell'incremento patrimoniale. Ad esempio essi possono disciplinare diversamente la composizione dei patrimoni, le regole sulla valutazione dei beni, la quota di partecipazione ai relativi acquisti patrimoniali e la ripartizione degli incrementi. Dette facoltà di modifica consentono di tenere conto delle specificità nazionali o delle esigenze specifiche dei coniugi.

Atteso che il testo stabilisce che i coniugi possono derogare alle norme del Capitolo V, essi non possono quindi derogare alle regole inserite negli articoli 5 e

la legge interna applicabile al regime patrimoniale", nella versione francese.
10 "In Francia", nella versione francese.
11 "Alla data dell'atto notarile", nella versione francese.
12 "Alla data della sentenza", nella versione francese.

6, nei quali sono riprese le disposizioni più importanti del "*régime primaire*" francese. Con l'impossibilità di deroga si garantisce un'applicazione identica del regime dei beni comune in Francia e in Germania.

CAPITOLO III. AMMINISTRAZIONE, GODIMENTO E DISPOSIZIONE DEL PATRIMONIO

Il regime dei beni comune comporta che, per i coniugi, vige il regime della separazione dei beni. La separazione del patrimonio produce due conseguenze.

Innanzitutto i coniugi mantengono l'amministrazione, il godimento e la disposizione dei loro beni personali. Inoltre ciascun coniuge risponde per i debiti da lui contratti prima o in costanza di matrimonio.

Tuttavia la separazione dei patrimoni dei coniugi non è omnicomprensiva, in quanto essi non possono derogare all'applicazione di determinate norme imperative.

Nella misura in cui le disposizioni che limitano gli effetti della separazione del patrimonio dei coniugi non sono identiche in Francia e in Germania, il regime dei beni comune riprende le disposizioni essenziali del "*régime primaire*" francese, al fine di consentire al regime dei beni di funzionare in maniera identica in Francia e in Germania (artt. 5 e 6).

Articolo 4. Disposizioni generali su amministrazione, godimento e disposizione del patrimonio

Scopo del regime dei beni della partecipazione agli incrementi è quello di assicurare una completa autonomia dei coniugi in relazione al loro patrimonio. Ne deriva che ciascun coniuge deve poter amministrare, godere e disporre del proprio patrimonio in linea di principio autonomamente e senza il consenso dell'altro coniuge. Per contro ciascun coniuge risponde singolarmente per i debiti da lui contratti prima o in costanza di matrimonio.

Questo principio di separazione del patrimonio dei coniugi è previsto nelle discipline tedesca (§1364 BGB) e francese (art. 1569 CC) della partecipazione agli incrementi. Nell'amministrazione autonoma del patrimonio rientra anche il diritto di acquistare beni: nessun coniuge necessita del consenso dell'altro, per esempio, per intraprendere un'attività professionale, per creare una società o diventarne socio.

Questa separazione del patrimonio dei coniugi presenta tuttavia alcuni limiti, menzionati negli artt. 5 e 6 del regime dei beni.

Detti limiti sono ispirati alle norme imperative del "*régime primaire*" francese (artt. 215 e 220 CC). Le norme si sostituiscono alle corrispondenti disposizioni del "*régime primaire*", senza pregiudicare le altre norme di tale regime; queste ultime sono applicabili in ragione del principio territoriale.

Articolo 5. Limiti di disposizione

In generale:
Negli ordinamenti giuridici di entrambi i Paesi, l'amministrazione del patrimonio è limitata in casi eccezionali a tutela dell'altro coniuge.[13]

In Germania per il regime legale della partecipazione agli incrementi è previsto, nei §§1365, 1369 BGB, un divieto di disposizione del patrimonio nella sua interezza e di beni dell'attività domestica. Una violazione di questo divieto di disposizione comporta l'inefficacia[14] dell'atto giuridico, qualora l'altro coniuge non lo ratifichi. L'inefficacia[15] è automatica e opera *erga omnes.*

Anche la Francia conosce un limite di disposizione per i diritti che garantiscono la casa familiare e i beni mobili facenti parte dell'abitazione. Ciò significa, ad esempio, che un coniuge non può recedere[16] dal contratto di locazione relativo all'abitazione principale senza il consenso dell'altro coniuge. Un atto di diposizione senza il consenso dell'altro coniuge non è, tuttavia, automaticamente inefficace[17] come in Germania, piuttosto il coniuge deve esercitare un'azione di nullità.

Tale atto[18] può, tuttavia, essere ratificato dal coniuge che non ha prestato il suo consenso.

In Francia questo limite di disposizione volto ad assicurare la casa familiare e il mobilio, unitamente ai beni mobili facenti parte dell'abitazione, è previsto nell'art. 215 CC.

Per evitare che, in caso di adozione del regime dei beni opzionale della partecipazione agli incrementi, vigano nei due Paesi diversi limiti al diritto di disporre liberamente della casa familiare e dei beni dell'attività domestica, l'art. 5 del regime dei beni comune, che prevede la tutela della casa familiare conosciuta nel diritto francese, estende la tutela ai beni dell'attività domestica, ai quali ci si riferisce nel diritto tedesco.[19]

La disciplina francese sui beni mobili facenti parte dell'abitazione (art. 215 CC) non tutela il coniuge in modo tanto ampio quanto la disciplina tedesca sui beni dell'attività domestica. Il regime dei beni comune riprende perciò la norma

---

13 "Il diritto di un coniuge di gestire in via autonoma il suo patrimonio può essere limitato in casi eccezionali per proteggere l'altro coniuge", nella versione francese.

14 "Nullità", nella versione francese.

15 "Nullità", nella versione francese.

16 "Risoluzione", nella versione francese.

17 "Nulla", nella versione francese.

18 "Atto di recesso da un contratto di durata", nella versione tedesca.

19 "Per evitare che l'adozione del regime opzionale della partecipazione agli incrementi implichi nei due Paesi dei diversi limiti di disposizione riguardo al diritto di disporre liberamente dell'abitazione coniugale e dei beni dell'attività domestica, l'art. 5 del regime dei beni comune, che prevede la tutela dell'abitazione coniugale conosciuta nel diritto francese, estende la tutela ai beni dell'attività domestica, ai quali ci si riferisce nel diritto tedesco", nella versione francese.

di protezione tedesca che, ad esempio, si applica anche all'autovettura necessaria per i bisogni della famiglia.

Non è parsa necessaria un'ulteriore norma di protezione contro le disposizioni del patrimonio nella sua interezza, analoga al §1365 BGB. In molti casi la casa familiare dovrebbe già costituire una parte rilevante del patrimonio. Se un coniuge non può disporre del propio diritto di proprietà o di comproprietà sull'immobile adibito a casa familiare senza il consenso dell'altro coniuge, si garantisce a quest'ultimo una tutela ancora più efficace rispetto al diritto tedesco, poiché è irrilevante che tale proprietà corrisponda all'intero patrimonio o solo ad una parte cospicua di esso (ovvero, secondo la giurisprudenza tedesca, l'85% per i piccoli patrimoni o meno del 90% per i patrimoni più ingenti).

Al comma 1:
Nel comma 1 è regolato il limite di disposizione di diritti su una casa familiare e sui beni dell'attività domestica.

La casa familiare include tutti i locali che i coniugi utilizzano come abitazione, o nei quali abbiano vissuto insieme o che, secondo le circostanze, fossero stati destinati a divenire casa familiare, anche qualora ciò non si sia verificato. Alla casa familiare possono appartenere, dunque, anche i locali annessi (ad esempio la cantina, la soffitta, il garage, i locali per lo sport e per il fitness).

Scopo della norma dell'art. 5 è quello di assicurare un'ampia tutela della famiglia con riferimento alla casa familiare.

Se un coniuge dispone del diritto di proprietà o dei rapporti di locazione relativi alla casa familiare, un tale atto di disposizione è in via di principio inefficace senza il consenso dell'altro coniuge. Ciò significa che il coniuge proprietario di una casa utilizzata come casa familiare non può alienare efficacemente la casa senza il consenso dell'altro coniuge. Anche il coniuge conduttore di un'abitazione in cui vive la famiglia non può da solo recedere efficacemente dal contratto di locazione. Il coniuge che non ha acconsentito ad una tale condotta può però ratificare il recesso.

La tutela della casa familiare è dunque molto ampia e può anche coinvolgere interessi di terzi. Al locatore di un'abitazione adibita a casa familiare può essere opposta l'inefficacia del recesso da un contratto di locazione, anche se egli non era a conoscenza del regime dei beni dei coniugi e, dunque, del limite di disposizione del coniuge conduttore.

Nemmeno dei beni dell'attività domestica – indifferentemente che questi si trovino nell'abitazione o che siano già stati rimossi – il proprietario può disporre disgiuntamente. Tuttavia, l'altro coniuge può ratificare il negozio giuridico riguardante la casa familiare o i beni dell'attività domestica.

La disciplina delle conseguenze di questa inefficacia[20] è rimessa agli ordinamenti giuridici di entrambi i Paesi.

---

[20] "Nullità", nella versione francese.

In Francia la nullità deve essere fatta valere mediante azione in giudizio. Ciò risulta dall'art. 215, comma 3, CC derivante da una norma del "*régime primaire*" francese, non recepita nel regime dei beni comune, ma che trova comunque applicazione per tutti i coniugi residenti in Francia, indipendentemente dal loro regime dei beni matrimoniale.

In Germania, invece, qualora manchi il consenso dell'altro coniuge, una corrispondente disposizione conduce automaticamente all'inefficacia *erga omnes*. Diversamente dal diritto francese non è necessario esperire un'azione volta a far valere l'inefficacia. In caso di controversia può agirsi direttamente per la restituzione.

I procedimenti diretti a far valere le conseguenze giuridiche collegate alla violazione della norma introdotta con questo articolo sono disciplinati dai relativi ordinamenti giuridici nazionali. In Francia trova dunque applicazione l'art. 215, comma 3, CC sull'azione di nullità.

Al comma 2:
Un coniuge non può disporre senza l'altro dei diritti che garantiscono la casa familiare o dei beni dell'attività domestica. Se però un coniuge non è in grado di esprimere il suo consenso, perché, ad esempio, il suo stato di salute non glielo permette, o nega il suo consenso senza che gli interessi della famiglia giustifichino il suo rifiuto, il giudice può autorizzare l'altro coniuge a compiere da solo gli atti giuridici menzionati al comma 1.

L'autorizzazione del giudice, in caso d'incapacità del coniuge di esprimere il proprio consenso per causa di malattia, presenta similitudini con la disciplina dell'amministrazione d'urgenza del §1454 BGB, essa tuttavia corrisponde in sostanza a una procedura semplificata di nomina di un curatore, incaricato "di prestare il consenso per un atto giuridico determinato".

Questa soluzione, volta in particolare a evitare che un coniuge rifiuti arbitrariamente il suo consenso al solo fine di arrecare danno all'altro coniuge, si ispira al "*régime primaire*" francese (art. 217, c. 1 CC).

Articolo 6. Atti di gestione dell'attività domestica

Al comma 1:
Nel comma 1 sono disciplinati i negozi giuridici che possono essere conclusi con efficacia anche per l'altro coniuge.

Ciascun coniuge può, secondo il principio generale della separazione patrimoniale, concludere da solo contratti per la gestione dell'attività domestica (egli può, ad esempio, acquistare beni dell'attività domestica). In deroga a tale principio questi contratti comportano però che il coniuge originariamente non parte contrattuale, e che non ha nemmeno acconsentito alla conclusione del contratto, sia tuttavia vincolato al medesimo contratto e risponda in solido per le obbligazioni da esso derivanti.

Questo vale anche per i contratti riguardanti i bisogni della prole. Ne consegue, per esempio, che un coniuge risponde in solido anche per le obbligazioni nascenti da un contratto concluso dall'altro coniuge con un insegnante che fornisce ripetizioni.

Al comma 2:
Il comma 2 prevede che la summenzionata responsibilità solidale sia esclusa se esistono cumulativamente due presupposti:

- si tratta di spese non congrue[21] e
- il terzo contraente era a conoscenza della non congruità[22] delle spese o avrebbe dovuto esserlo.

Il limite alla responsibilità solidale è necessario per tutelare un coniuge che non può essere obbligato per le spese non congrue[23] dell'altro coniuge. La valutazione del carattere eccessivo dipende dalle condizioni di vita di entrambi i coniugi. Ad esempio l'acquisto di un costoso mobile antico può costituire una spesa manifestamente eccessiva qualora entrambi i coniugi dispongano solo di un esiguo reddito. In tale caso l'altro coniuge non può essere vincolato dal contratto, se la controparte ne era a conoscenza o avrebbe dovuto esserlo.[24]

Questa disposizione riprende in forma modernizzata l'art. 220 CC. I coniugi residenti in Francia che abbiano pattuito il regime dei beni comune sono soggetti all'art. 6.

La disciplina accolta non è in contraddizione con il diritto tedesco. Invero, essa va oltre il §1357 BGB, ma i coniugi devono rispettarla se hanno scelto, mediante contratto, il regime dei beni opzionale della partecipazione agli incrementi. In tal modo essi hanno accolto[25] liberamente anche la disciplina dell'art. 6.

CAPITOLO IV. CESSAZIONE DEL REGIME DEI BENI

Articolo 7. Cause di cessazione del regime dei beni

La data della cessazione del regime dei beni è derimente. In questo momento ha luogo, infatti, l'accertamento del credito di conguaglio dell'incremento patrimoniale sulla base della composizione e del valore del patrimonio dei coniugi.

21 "Manifestamente eccessive", nella versione francese.
22 "Manifesta eccessività", nella versione francese.
23 "Irragionevoli", nella versione francese.
24 "In tal caso l'altro coniuge non sarà obbligato solidalmente se il terzo era a conoscenza del carattere manifestamente eccessivo", nella versione francese.
25 "Accettato", nella versione francese.

L'articolo 7 prevede che il regime dei beni comune cessi:

- con la morte o con la dichiarazione di morte presunta[26] di uno dei coniugi;
- con il mutamento del regime dei beni;
- con la sentenza di divorzio o con ogni altra decisione giudiziale passata in giudicato che pone fine al regime dei beni.

Con la prima disposizione si precisa che una dichiarazione di morte presunta porta alla cessazione del regime dei beni, anche quando questa dichiarazione è erronea.

Con la seconda disposizione si precisa che anche il mutamento del regime dei beni comporta la cessazione del regime dei beni opzionale della partecipazione agli incrementi. In Germania, infatti, il regime dei beni può essere mutato in un altro regime dei beni mediante contratto matrimoniale. Parimenti, i coniugi che vivono in un regime dei beni francese possono concordare, nell'interesse della famiglia, di modificare il regime dei beni due anni dopo la sua applicazione.

La terza disposizione comprende altre cause di cessazione del regime dei beni.[27]

In Francia questo corrisponde alle fattispecie della separazione senza scioglimento del matrimonio, dell'annullamento del matrimonio in caso di buona fede dei coniugi e della liquidazione anticipata del credito di conguaglio.

In Germania sono da ricomprendere fra queste cause le decisioni sul conguaglio anticipato dell'incremento patrimoniale e sullo scioglimento di un matrimonio a seguito di nullità.

CAPITOLO V. DETERMINAZIONE DEL CREDITO DI CONGUAGLIO DELL'INCREMENTO PATRIMONIALE AL MOMENTO DELLA CESSAZIONE DEL REGIME DEI BENI

SEZIONE 1. PATRIMONIO INIZIALE

Articolo 8. Composizione del patrimonio iniziale

Ai commi 1 e 2:
Nei commi 1 e 2 sono descritti i beni del patrimonio facenti parte del patrimonio iniziale.

Il patrimonio iniziale comprende tre categorie di beni patrimoniali:

a) i beni che appartengono ad un coniuge alla data di entrata in vigore del regime.

26 "Dichiarazione di assenza", nella versione francese.

27 "Di scioglimento del matrimonio", nella versione tedesca.

Di frequente le coppie di coniugi concludono un contratto matrimoniale prima della celebrazione del matrimonio. Atteso che, ai sensi dell'art. 3, il contratto matrimoniale diviene efficace non prima della celebrazione del matrimonio, il primo termine per l'entrata in vigore del regime dei beni è la data della celebrazione del matrimonio.

b) i beni che un coniuge acquista successivamente per effetto di successione o donazione.

Nell'ordinamento giuridico di entrambi i Paesi, gli incrementi patrimoniali per donazione o per successione sono da includere nel patrimonio iniziale (Germania: §1374, comma 2, BGB; Francia: art. 1570 CC).

c) il patrimonio[28] che un coniuge acquista successivamente a titolo di risarcimento dei danni non patrimoniali.

Nel diritto francese il risarcimento dei danni non patrimoniali viene conteggiato nel patrimonio iniziale. In Germania non è così nel regime legale della partecipazione agli incrementi, ma questo è spesso fonte di dibattiti che muovono dal carattere altamente personale di tale credito. Anche se si respinge un ampliamento del patrimonio personale, comprensivo di altre fattispecie nell'art. 1374, c. 2, BGB,[29] le parti possono pattuire liberamente di comprendere tali somme nel patrimonio iniziale.

Il conguaglio patrimoniale deve compensare gli incrementi patrimoniali conseguiti da entrambi i coniugi nel vigore del regime dei beni. Vi sono però incrementi patrimoniali che vengono conseguiti in maniera assolutamente indipendente dalla partecipazione o dalla prestazione dei coniugi e, perciò, non devono essere compensati. Questo vale, in particolare, per i valori patrimoniali che sono stati menzionati nelle sopra descritte lettere b) e c) e che un coniuge ha acquistato per effetto di successione, donazione o come ristoro per le sofferenze subite (risarcimento dei danni non patrimoniali). Perciò, ai sensi del comma 2, questi valori patrimoniali sono da computare al patrimonio iniziale e, sono quindi, da sottrarre dal conguaglio dell'incremento patrimoniale.

Le parti sono libere di pattuire, nella loro autonomia privata, che anche altri incrementi patrimoniali, oltre a quelli menzionati al comma 1, siano computati al patrimonio iniziale. I coniugi possono concordare una simile pattuizione nel contratto matrimoniale (cfr. art. 3, comma 3, della disciplina del regime dei beni).

Il patrimonio iniziale è il patrimonio che, detratti i vincoli obbligatori, appartiene ad un coniuge alla data stabilita per la determinazione. Il patrimonio iniziale non è una particolare massa patrimoniale, bensì una delle due grandezze di calcolo per l'accertamento dell'incremento patrimoniale.

---

28 "Le indennità", nella versione francese.

29 "Anche se l'art. 1347, comma 2, BGB non permette di ampliare ad altre fattispecie l'attivo riservato", nella versione francese.

I vincoli obbligatori possono essere dedotti anche in una misura che supera l'ammontare del patrimonio attivo. Ciò significa che il patrimonio iniziale può anche essere negativo.

Norme analoghe si rinvengono nel diritto francese (artt. 1570, 1572 CC) e nel diritto tedesco (§1374 BGB). In realtà, la disciplina tedesca sul patrimonio iniziale prevedeva, in contrasto con la disciplina francese, che questo non potesse essere negativo, e ammetteva la detrazione di vincoli obbligatori solo nel limite dell'ammontare del patrimonio. Tuttavia, questa disciplina è stata a lungo criticata e, con la riforma del diritto di conguaglio dell'incremento patrimoniale del 1° settembre 2009, il patrimonio iniziale negativo è stato ammesso per il futuro.

Al comma 3:
Al patrimonio iniziale non sono computati:

a) I frutti di questo patrimonio.
   Con questa regola si precisa che i frutti prodotti dal patrimonio iniziale, come ad esempio il reddito locativo di un'immobile di proprietà, non sono da computare al patrimonio iniziale. Di conseguenza si tratta di incremento patrimoniale.
   Questo principio generale è rinvenibile anche negli ordinamenti giuridici di entrambi i Paesi (Germania: §1374(2) BGB; Francia: art. 1570 CC).
b) I beni del patrimonio iniziale che sono stati donati da un coniuge ai parenti in linea retta in costanza di regime dei beni.
   Se in costanza di regime dei beni un coniuge dona beni del patrimonio iniziale a parenti in linea retta, ai sensi dell'art. 3, comma 2, questi beni devono essere del tutto esclusi dal calcolo dell'incremento patrimoniale. Per questa ragione, essi non vengono compresi né nel patrimonio iniziale né nel patrimonio finale. Questa disposizione si ispira al diritto francese.
   Gli eventuali incrementi di valore apportati ad uno di questi beni e che non abbiano origine nel patrimonio iniziale vengono computati nel patrimonio finale[30] (cfr. art. 10 sulla composizione del patrimonio finale).

Questa disciplina rappresenta un compromesso fra il diritto tedesco, che comprende nel patrimonio iniziale i beni che sono stati così donati, e il diritto francese, il quale ammette donazioni dal patrimonio iniziale senza che queste vengano computate nell'incremento patrimoniale, con eccezione degli incrementi di valore che il patrimonio donato abbia avuto.[31]

---

30 "Tuttavia rientrerà nel patrimonio finale il plusvalore apportato a tali beni se il plusvalore non è stato prodotto dai frutti derivanti dal patrimonio iniziale", nella versione francese.

31 "Il quale prevede che i beni donati siano computati nel patrimonio iniziale, e il diritto francese, il quale prevede che i beni del patrimonio iniziale possano essere donati a chiunque, senza che ciò implichi, fatta riserva dei plusvalori realizzati su questi beni, effetti sul calcolo degli incrementi", nella versione francese.

Al comma 4:
Per evitare controversie sull'ammontare del patrimonio iniziale al momento della cessazione del regime dei beni, è opportuno far redigere da un notaio un inventario del patrimonio iniziale già al momento della conclusione del contratto matrimoniale. Tuttavia, i coniugi possono redigere un inventario anche mediante scrittura privata.

Un tale inventario del patrimonio iniziale si presume corretto se sottoscritto da entrambi i coniugi. La forma notarile non è prescritta. La presunzione di correttezza può essere superata con la prova della sua non correttezza. Può anche essere opportuno inserire il valore dei beni del patrimonio iniziale nell' inventario già al momento della sua redazione. In questo caso la presunzione di correttezza vale anche per detto valore, qualora questi beni patrimoniali vengano valutati, ai sensi dell'art. 9, comma 1, n. 1, alla data dell'entrata in vigore del regime dei beni (o alla data del loro acquisto in relazione ai beni patrimoniali di cui all'art. 8, comma 2).

Gli ordinamenti giuridici di entrambi i Paesi conoscono tali inventari, la cui correttezza viene presunta (Germania: §1377 BGB; Francia: art. 1570 CC).

Al comma 5:
Se i coniugi non hanno redatto alcun inventario del patrimonio, si presume che non esista un patrimonio iniziale. Anche questa presunzione può essere superata.

Articolo 9. Valutazione del patrimonio iniziale

In generale:
Per quanto le discipline dei due Paesi sul regime della partecipazione agli incrementi siano fondamentalmente molto simili, esse differiscono in un punto essenziale: la valutazione del patrimonio iniziale.

La Francia pone alla base della valutazione dei beni che compongono il patrimonio iniziale il valore che questi hanno al momento della cessazione del regime dei beni (art. 1571 CC).

In Germania, al contrario, ci si basa sul valore che il patrimonio aveva al momento dell'entrata in vigore del regime dei beni (§1376, comma 1, BGB). Gli aumenti di valore che dipendono dalla normale inflazione non rappresentano però, secondo la giurisprudenza, un incremento patrimoniale e rimangono pertanto esclusi.

Questi differenti momenti di riferimento per la valutazione possono avere, ad esempio, le seguenti persistenti conseguenze:[32]

---

32 "Negative", nella versione francese.

- Secondo la disciplina francese, al contrario di quella tedesca, i coniugi sopportano il rischio di una diminuzione di valore dei beni del patrimonio originario.
  Esempio Germania:
  Un coniuge apporta al regime dei beni, come unico valore patrimoniale, un deposito azionario, il cui valore all'entrata in vigore del regime è pari a € 100.000. Al momento della cessazione del regime dei beni il deposito azionario vale soltanto € 20.000. Il patrimonio finale del coniuge ammonta complessivamente a € 100.000 (comprensivi del deposito azionario). Dunque il coniuge non ha realizzato alcun incremento patrimoniale, del quale l'altro coniuge debba essere reso partecipe.
  Esempio Francia:
  Medesima situazione di partenza dell'esempio di cui sopra. Il patrimonio iniziale del coniuge viene stimato in € 20.000, il patrimonio finale in € 100.000 (20.000 e 80.000). Dunque il coniuge ha realizzato un incremento patrimoniale di € 80.000, del quale l'altro coniuge dovrebbe essere reso partecipe con un credito di conguaglio dell'incremento patrimoniale di € 40.000 (se quest'ultimo non ha realizzato alcun incremento patrimoniale).

- Secondo il diritto tedesco, in contrapposizione alla disciplina francese, il coniuge partecipa agli aumenti di valore del patrimonio iniziale che si verificano senza il suo intervento (ad eccezione delle variazioni di valore basate su fluttuazioni monetarie, le quali non vengono prese in considerazione). Di conseguenza si determina un incremento patrimoniale se, per esempio, un terreno rimane immutato, ma acquista valore con il decorrere del tempo in virtù della sua ubicazione. Secondo il diritto francese, al contrario, questo non porta ad un incremento patrimoniale.
  Esempio Germania:
  Un coniuge apporta al regime dei beni un terreno che, al momento dell'entrata in vigore del regime, ha un valore pari a € 100.000. Alla cessazione del regime dei beni il bene ha un valore di € 200.000, poiché è stato dichiarato terreno edificabile. L'incremento patrimoniale di cui deve essere reso partecipe l'altro coniuge ammonta, dunque, a € 100.000. Il coniuge legittimato al conguaglio riceve, quindi, € 50.000 (se egli stesso non ha realizzato alcun incremento patrimoniale).
  Esempio Francia:
  Medesima situazione iniziale dell'esempio di cui sopra. Il terreno viene valutato sia nel patrimonio iniziale che in quello finale € 200.000. In tal caso non è sorto alcun incremento patrimoniale di cui si debba rendere partecipe l'altro coniuge.
  Per tener conto della disciplina nazionale sia tedesca che francese, nell'art. 11 è stato concepito un modello di valutazione ispirato a entrambi gli ordinamenti giuridici.

Al comma 1:
Il comma 1, numero 1, si ispira al modello di valutazione tedesco. I beni del patrimonio che esistevano alla data di entrata in vigore del regime dei beni vengono valutati secondo il valore che possedevano in quella data.

Questo significa che il coniuge a cui non appartiene il bene partecipa agli aumenti di valore di questo bene, anche se questi si realizzano senza il suo intervento (ad eccezione delle variazioni di valore che dipendono da fluttuazioni della moneta). Se al patrimonio iniziale di un coniuge appartiene, ad esempio, un quadro che acquista valore nel corso degli anni di matrimonio, poiché l'artista diventa sempre più noto, questo aumento di valore conffluisce nell'incremento patrimoniale.

Per il patrimonio privilegiato[33] (donazioni, successioni, risarcimento danni non patrimoniali[34]) vale a dire per il patrimonio che viene acquistato successivamente, ma che secondo l'art. 8, comma 2, appartiene al patrimonio iniziale, il momento della valutazione è secondo il comma 1, n. 2, il giorno in cui questo patrimonio è stato acquistato.

Al comma 2:
Il comma 2 precisa che il diritto di proprietà immobiliare e gli altri diritti reali immobiliari del patrimonio iniziale, ad eccezione del diritto di usufrutto e del diritto di abitazione, vengono valutati il giorno della cessazione del regime dei beni. Il metodo di valutazione descritto al comma 2 è applicabile, dunque, ai diritti reali principali che non hanno durata vitalizia (rendita vitalizia). Queste componenti del patrimonio vengono valutate con il loro valore al momento della cessazione del regime dei beni o, in casi particolari, al giorno di riferimento per il calcolo, ai sensi dell'art. 13.

L'obiettivo di tale norma è di escludere dall'incremento patrimoniale gli incrementi di valore degli immobili del patrimonio iniziale che si sono verificati senza l'intervento di uno dei coniugi. Gli immobili rappresentano, di regola, una parte essenziale del patrimonio e possono essere soggetti a variazioni di valore che, in generale, non dipendono dalla prestazione dei coniugi. Questa fattispecie ricorre, per esempio, quando interviene un aumento di valore di una casa familiare inclusa nel patrimonio iniziale, che dipende soltanto dall'aumento di valore dell'ubicazione. Per esempio gli immobili possono acquistare considerevole valore qualora venga chiuso un aeroporto situato nelle vicinanze e, di conseguenza, cessi l'inquinamento acustico. In un caso del genere, appare del tutto conforme[35] agli interessi coinvolti non rendere partecipe il coniuge di tali incrementi di valore.

---

33 "Riservato", nella versione francese.
34 "Somme versate quali indennità del pregiudizio subito", nella versione francese.
35 "Logico", nella versione francese.

Gli aumenti di valore di immobili che dipendono dalla prestazione comune dei coniugi rappresentano invece un incremento patrimoniale. Essi non accrescono, dunque, il valore del patrimonio iniziale.

Esempio:

Un coniuge ha apportato al regime dei beni un terreno (il cui valore all'entrata in vigore del regime dei beni è, ad esempio, € 50.000) su cui, in costanza di regime, viene costruita una casa. Alla cessazione del regime dei beni, il solo terreno, senza la casa, ha un valore di € 100.000, poiché l'ubicazione del terreno ha acquistato valore.[36] Alla cessazione del regime dei beni, il terreno con la casa ha un valore di € 200.000. Per la valutazione del patrimonio iniziale viene preso in considerazione solo il mero terreno con il valore che questo ha al momento della cessazione dei beni: € 100.000 (l'aumento di valore di € 50.000 conseguito in costanza di matrimonio e in ragione dell'ubicazione non comporta un incremento patrimoniale). Nel patrimonio finale, il terreno comprensivo della casa è conteggiato per il coniuge al quale esso appartiene: € 200.000.[37] L'incremento patrimoniale ammonta, dunque, a € 100.000. In assenza di altri incrementi patrimoniali, il credito di conguaglio dell'incremento patrimoniale ammonta a € 50.000.

Se durante il matrimonio vengono alienati o sostituiti immobili o diritti reali principali non vitalizi, il valore del patrimonio deve essere computato con il valore esistente il giorno dell'alienazione o della sostituzione.

Esempio:

Medesima situazione di cui sopra (un terreno viene apportato al regime dei beni e, in costanza di regime, vi viene costruita una casa). In costanza di matrimonio viene alienato il terreno comprensivo della casa. Al momento dell'alienazione il terreno ha un valore di € 80.000 e la casa un valore di € 100.000. Per il patrimonio iniziale viene computato solo il valore del terreno nell'ammontare di € 80.000, da adeguare ai sensi del comma 3. Per il patrimonio finale di esso è determinante quel che il coniuge ha ancora complessivamente del proprio patrimonio.[38] Il ricavo della vendita si ritrova nel patrimonio finale solo se di questo residua ancora un valore. Se, ad esempio, al momento della cessazione del regime dei beni il coniuge non ha più di € 80.000, egli non ha ottenuto alcun incremento che deve essere compensato.

L'usufrutto e il diritto di abitazione sono esclusi da questa disciplina poiché i coniugi, mediante l'utilizzo, ne hanno diminuito il valore.

---

36 "Maggior valore", nella versione francese.

37 "Nel patrimonio finale si terrà conto del terreno con la casa, per un valore di 200.000", nella versione francese.

38 "E' la totalità dell'attivo ancora rimasto al coniuge", nella versione francese.

Al comma 3:
Un matrimonio può durare, a seconda del caso, molti anni. Ai sensi del comma 1, il patrimonio iniziale viene tuttavia indicato con un determinato valore monetario al momento dell'entrata in vigore del regime dei beni (o al momento dell'acquisto dei beni patrimoniali menzionati nell'art. 8, comma 2). Questo valore monetario può però diminuire negli anni a causa dell'inflazione. I meri aumenti di valore dovuti semplicemente all'inflazione non costituiscono però alcun incremento patrimoniale. Con il comma 3 viene perciò creata una norma secondo cui il valore del patrimonio iniziale deve essere corretto in base all'inflazione.

Esempio:
(fittizio e senza tasso reale medio di inflazione, poiché il regime dei beni opzionale della partecipazione agli incrementi può applicarsi solo dal giorno della ratifica dell'accordo):
All'inizio del regime dei beni un coniuge ha un patrimonio di € 100.000. Il matrimonio dura dieci anni. Al momento della cessazione del regime dei beni il coniuge ha un patrimonio finale di 200.000 €. Si presume fittiziamente che i 100.000 € dell'inizio del regime dei beni, dieci anni prima, corrispondano a un valore monetario di 150.000 € alla cessazione del regime dei beni. Da ciò consegue che il patrimonio iniziale deve essere conteggiato in 150.000 € e il patrimonio finale in 200.000 €. L'incremento patrimoniale ammonta perciò a 50.000 €, il credito di conguaglio dell'incremento patrimoniale ammonta a 25.000 €, se l'altro coniuge non ha conseguito alcun incremento patrimoniale.
La Francia non permette le indicizzazioni che si basano sul livello generale dei prezzi o sul prezzo di beni, prodotti o prestazioni di servizio e che non presentano alcun collegamento immediato con l'oggetto dell'accordo o con l'attività di una delle parti (Art. L 112-2, para. 1, del Code monétaire et financier). Tuttavia, poiché l'art. 55 della Costituzione francese prevede il principio della primazia di convenzioni fra Stati sulle leggi, il meccanismo di indicizzazione monetaria prescelto può trovare validamente applicazione nel quadro del regime dei beni comune.
Se altri Stati aderiscono all'accordo, il tasso medio di variazione monetaria si computa in base al tasso di variazione monetaria di tutti gli Stati contraenti.

Al comma 4:
Le regole di valutazione previste ai commi 1 e 3 valgono anche per la valutazione dei vincoli obbligatori.

Esempio:
(esempio fittizio, senza tasso reale medio di inflazione, poiché il regime dei beni opzionale della partecipazione agli incrementi non è ancora entrato in vigore):
All'inizio del regime dei beni, il coniuge ha solo debiti per un ammontare di 10.000 €. Il matrimonio dura dieci anni. Alla cessazione del regime dei beni il

coniuge ha un patrimonio finale di 200.000 €. Si presume fittiziamente che i 10.000 € di debiti dell'inizio del regime dei beni, dieci anni prima, corrispondano a un valore monetario di 14.000 € alla cessazione del regime dei beni. Da ciò consegue che il patrimonio iniziale è stimato in debiti e perciò con un passivo di 14.000 € e il patrimonio finale in 200.000 €. L'incremento patrimoniale ammonta perciò a 214.000 €.

SEZIONE 2. PATRIMONIO FINALE

Articolo 10. Composizione del patrimonio finale

Al comma 1:
Il comma 1 definisce che cos'è il patrimonio finale ovvero il patrimonio che, detratti i vincoli obbligatori, appartiene a un coniuge al momento della cessazione del regime dei beni oppure al giorno di riferimento della determinazione ex art. 13, anche quando i vincoli obbligatori superano il patrimonio attivo. Il patrimonio finale, così come il patrimonio iniziale, può anche essere negativo. Non è una particolare massa patrimoniale, ma una delle misure di calcolo per la determinazione dell'incremento.

Gli ordinamenti giuridici di entrambi gli Stati conoscono per il proprio regime dei beni della partecipazione agli incrementi una disciplina corrispondente (Germania: §1375 BGB; Francia: artt. 1572 e 1574 CC).

Al comma 2:
In presenza di determinati presupposti nel patrimonio finale vengono inclusi valori patrimoniali. Con questo si vuole evitare che un coniuge, attraverso atti di disposizione del patrimonio, diminuisca il proprio incremento e penalizzi l'altro coniuge.

Riduzioni patrimoniali dovute a donazioni senza il consenso del coniuge o con intento di pregiudizio, che sono da computare nel patrimonio finale, sono conosciute dagli ordinamenti giuridici di entrambi i Paesi (Germania: §1375, c. 2, BGB: Francia: art. 1573 CC). La riduzione patrimoniale[39] dovuta a sperpero si ritrova solo in Germania, §1375, comma 2, n. 2, BGB. A tutela dell'altro coniuge, questa disposizione viene incorporata anche nel regime opzionale della partecipazione agli incrementi.

Al numero 1:
In linea di principio, le donazioni sono da computare nel patrimonio finale.

Questo tuttavia non vale, quando:

---

[39] "Riprovevole", nella versione tedesca.

a) la donazione è congrua al tenore di vita dei coniugi (questa fattispecie ricorre quando la donazione non eccede in maniera rilevante la disponibilità economica dei coniugi per la vita quotidiana);
b) la donazione viene effettuata a un parente in linea retta con sostanze del patrimonio iniziale di un coniuge (art. 8, comma 3, n. 2). Gli incrementi di valore di questi beni donati, sorti nel vigore del regime dei beni con sostanze che non appartengono al patrimonio iniziale, vengono tuttavia conteggiati nel patrimonio finale.[40]

Inoltre, il valore della donazione non deve essere incluso fittiziamente nel patrimonio finale, se l'altro coniuge ha acconsentito alla donazione o se la donazione ha avuto luogo più di dieci anni prima della cessazione del regime dei beni.

Al numero 2:
Sono qui inclusi gli atti giuridici finalizzati a diminuire l'incremento dell'altro coniuge o a privarlo dell'incremento. L'intento di pregiudizio deve essere stato il motivo determinante. Tra questi atti ricadrebbe, per esempio, la vendita di un oggetto prezioso ad un valore considerevolmente inferiore, qualora il fine perseguito sia stato quello di influire sull'incremento patrimoniale.

L'incremento di valore derivante da tali alienazioni non deve essere incluso fittiziamente nel patrimonio finale, se l'alienazione è avvenuta con il consenso dell'altro coniuge o più di dieci anni prima della cessazione del regime dei beni.

Al numero 3:
Nel numero 3 ricadono le spese superflue ed eccessive[41] in rapporto al patrimonio. Tra queste rientrerebbe, per esempio, una crociera di lusso effettuata da un coniuge, qualora i coniugi abbiano soltanto un esiguo reddito. Rientra qui anche la distruzione di un bene da parte di un coniuge, indipendentemente da un intento lesivo.

Il valore dei beni oggetto di sperpero non deve essere incluso fittiziamente nel patrimonio finale, se l'altro coniuge ha acconsentito allo sperpero o se questo è avvenuto più di dieci anni prima della cessazione del regime dei beni.

La disciplina tedesca sul conguaglio dell'incremento patrimoniale prevede un termine di preclusione[42] di dieci anni (§1375(3) BGB). La ragione risiede nella circostanza che, una volta decorso un determinato periodo di tempo, non può più ritenersi che l'azione volta a diminuire il patrimonio abbia avuto luogo con lo

---

40 "La donazione riguarda un bene del patrimonio iniziale donato a un parente in linea retta (art. 8, c. 3, n. 2). Tuttavia, converrà riunire il valore dell'incremento prodotto con i miglioramenti realizzati, durante la vigenza del regime, su tale bene con sostanze che non derivano dal patrimonio iniziale", nella versione francese.

41 "Manifestatamente eccessive", nella versione francese.

42 "Prescrizione", nella versione francese.

scopo di pregiudicare l'altro coniuge o che l'atto non sia stato infine accettato dall'altro coniuge. Questa disciplina tende inoltre alla certezza dei rapporti giuridici.

Per queste ragioni, il limite temporale di dieci anni viene accolto anche qui nel regime dei beni opzionale della partecipazione agli incrementi.

Articolo 11. Valutazione del patrimonio finale

Al comma 1:
Nel comma 1 viene disciplinata la valutazione del patrimonio finale: il patrimonio finale deve essere basato sul valore che il patrimonio aveva alla cessazione del regime dei beni o al momento di valutazione in casi particolari secondo l'art. 13.

In Francia, salvo le regole specifiche di valutazione in caso di separazione, divorzio o di conguaglio anticipato dell'incremento patrimoniale, il valore dei beni patrimoniali disponibili, che formano il patrimonio finale, viene determinato secondo il loro stato alla data di cessazione del regime dei beni e secondo il loro valore alla data di liquidazione del regime dei beni. Quest'ultima può essere posteriore anche di molti anni rispetto al momento dello scioglimento (art. 1574 CC).

In Germania l'incremento patrimoniale, e con esso il patrimonio iniziale e finale dei coniugi, vengono determinati nel momento della cessazione del regime dei beni. Essi possono essere determinati in un momento precedente, ovvero nel momento in cui è stata proposta domanda di conguaglio anticipato dell'incremento patrimoniale o alla data di pendenza della domanda di divorzio (§§1378, 1384, 1387 BGB).

Al comma 2:
Il comma 2 disciplina il momento in cui devono valutatarsi i beni fittiziamente aggiunti al patrimonio finale ai sensi dell'art. 10, comma 2.

- Il valore dei beni di cui all'art. 10, comma 2, è calcolato alla data della donazione, dell'alienazione con intento di pregiudizio o dello sperpero.
- L'entità degli incrementi di valore apportati durante la vigenza del regime dei beni ad un bene del patrimonio iniziale, donato a parenti in linea retta, con mezzi che non appartengono al patrimonio iniziale, si calcola al momento della donazione.

Al comma 3:
I valori da includere secondo il comma 2 sono da adeguare, a partire dal momento del calcolo, in base alla variazione media dell'indice generale dei prezzi al consumo degli Stati contraenti.

SEZIONE 3. CREDITO DI CONGUAGLIO DELL'INCREMENTO PATRIMONIALE

Articolo 12. Pretesa[43] al conguaglio dell'incremento patrimoniale

Al comma 1:
Nel comma 1 si prevede che il coniuge, il quale ha ottenuto l'incremento patrimoniale minore nel vigore del regime dei beni, alla cessazione di questo può pretendere dall'altro coniuge il conguaglio dell'incremento patrimoniale nell'ammontare della metà della differenza tra le masse patrimoniali che i due coniugi hanno acquistato durante il matrimonio.

Il patrimonio iniziale e il patrimonio finale di ciascun coniuge vengono raffrontati fra di loro per stabilire in quale misura ciascun coniuge abbia registrato un incremento patrimoniale durante il matrimonio. Le norme concernenti la composizione e la valutazione del patrimonio iniziale e del patrimonio finale, che non sono identiche, sono precisate negli articoli seguenti del regime dei beni. Se il patrimonio finale supera quello iniziale, questa eccedenza è l'incremento patrimoniale del coniuge. Non vi è alcun conguaglio delle perdite del patrimonio (acquisti patrimoniali negativi), ma solo un conguaglio dell'incremento. Quando l'incremento patrimoniale di un coniuge supera quello dell'altro, il coniuge che ha ottenuto l'incremento patrimoniale più elevato deve all'altro coniuge la metà della differenza.

Al comma 2:
Di principio, il credito di conguaglio dell'incremento patrimoniale è una pretesa pecuniaria. Questo vale in modo indifferenziato in entrambi gli Stati, Germania e Francia, in virtù del diritto vigente.

Mentre in Francia questo è espressamente disciplinato nell'art. 1576 CC, non esiste in Germania alcuna disposizione specifica, ma emerge dalle disposizioni di cui ai §§1372 ss. BGB che il credito di conguaglio dell'incremento patrimoniale configuri una pretesa pecuniaria. Per finalità di chiarezza, nel regime dei beni opzionale della partecipazione agli incrementi è stata accolta la disciplina francese.

Entrambi gli ordinamenti giuridici conoscono la compensazione in natura solo come fattispecie particolare (Francia: art. 1576 CC; Germania: §1383 BGB). Per questa ragione, anche il regime dei beni opzionale della partecipazione agli incrementi prevede che ai fini di tale pagamento il giudice possa ordinare, su domanda di una o dell'altra parte, il trasferimento di beni patrimoniali al creditore, se ciò corrisponde ad equità. Il giudice deve decidere avuto riguardo agli interessi di entrambi i coniugi.

---

43 "Diritto", nella versione francese.

Al comma 3:
In Francia come in Germania, il credito di conguaglio dell'incremento patrimoniale non è cedibile finché il regime dei beni matrimoniale non sia cessato. Questo vale indipendentemente dalla circostanza che la cessione avvenga a titolo oneroso o gratuito. La pretesa è invece cedibile dopo la cessazione del regime dei beni ed è trasmissibile *mortis causa* (Germania: §1378, c. 3 BGB; Francia: art. 1569 CC). Una disciplina conforme è stata perciò accolta anche nel regime dei beni opzionale della partecipazione agli incrementi.

Articolo 13. Momento del calcolo in casi particolari

Fondamentalmente, la composizione e il valore del patrimonio dei coniugi possono essere determinati solo quando il regime dei beni è cessato.

Se, tuttavia, è stata presentata una domanda di divorzio, è poco opportuno decidere prima su tale domanda e di seguito, ovvero dopo il giudicato della decisione di divorzio, sulla pretesa al credito di conguaglio. È più sensato che, in connessione al procedimento di divorzio davanti al giudice, si decida anche riguardo all'incremento patrimoniale.[44] Per poter determinare la composizione e il valore del patrimonio dei coniugi, il regime dei beni comune prevede che al posto della data di cessazione del regime subentri, in questi casi, il momento della presentazione della domanda innanzi al giudice (e non la "*assignation en divorce*" in Francia). Anche qualora il giudice non decida contestualmente sul conguaglio e sul divorzio, questa disciplina permette di ridurre il periodo di tempo in cui il coniuge obbligato al conguaglio dell'incremento patrimoniale può diminuire il suo patrimonio e, dunque, ridurre la pretesa al conguaglio dell'altro coniuge.

Il regime dei beni legale della comunione degli incrementi regolato dal diritto tedesco conosce tale meccanismo (§1384 BGB). Per contro, esso deroga parzialmente al meccanismo vigente in Francia. Il diritto francese prevede che il regime matrimoniale è da intendersi cessato dal giorno della presentazione della domanda finalizzata alla sola determinazione della composizione del patrimonio (art. 1572 cc).

Questo meccanismo non opera solo in caso di divorzio, ma anche quando il regime dei beni cessa in altro modo per decisione giudiziale. Tra queste ipotesi rientra, ad esempio, la decisione sul conguaglio anticipato dell'incremento patrimoniale ai sensi dell'art. 18. Anche in questi casi è sensato poter calcolare già in pendenza della procedura sul conguaglio anticipato dell'incremento patrimoniale, anche l'incremento medesimo. Riguardo a ciò il momento del calcolo è l'introduzione della domanda innanzi al giudice.

---

44 "È preferibile che il giudice possa decidere sull'importo del credito dell'incremento patrimoniale e sul divorzio nella medesima procedura", nella versione francese.

Articolo 14. Limitazione del credito di conguaglio dell'incremento patrimoniale

Con questa disposizione si vuole assicurare che, anche in considerazione di un patrimonio iniziale negativo, nessuno debba cedere al coniuge più del 50% del proprio patrimonio finale effettivamente esistente alla data di riferimento per il calcolo (momento del calcolo di cui all'art. 13 o effettiva cessazione del regime dei beni).

La limitazione dell'ammontare del credito di conguaglio dell'incremento patrimoniale corrisponde all'idea di fondo del diritto di conguaglio dell'incremento patrimoniale, in base alla quale i due coniugi partecipano equamente, ciascuno per la metà, a ciò che essi hanno acquistato durante il matrimonio.

L'art. 14 assicura, altresì, che un credito di conguaglio, a prescindere dai casi di inclusione fittizia ai sensi dell'art. 10, comma 2 (ad eccezione del numero 1 lettera b), sorga soltanto qualora sussista effettivamente un patrimonio attivo nel giorno di riferimento per il calcolo dell'incremento patrimoniale. Ad esempio, se nel vigore del regime dei beni entrambi i coniugi hanno solamente estinto debiti o un coniuge non ha ottenuto alcun incremento patrimoniale e solo l'altro ha estinto debiti, non sorge alcun credito di conguaglio dell'incremento patrimoniale. Non vi è infatti alcun conguaglio degli acquisti patrimoniali negativi.

Questa limitazione riguarda soltanto il credito di conguaglio dell'incremento patrimoniale e non le altre possibili pretese e obbligazioni esistenti tra i coniugi. Il fine della disciplina, volta a consentire al coniuge obbligato al conguaglio dell'incremento patrimoniale di conservare almeno metà del suo patrimonio, non è però giustificato qualora tale coniuge abbia diminuito in maniera sleale il suo patrimonio (art. 10, comma 2, con eccezione del n. 1, lett. b).

Per non limitare l'ammontare del credito di conguaglio, qualora un coniuge abbia tenuto comportamenti sleali che cagionano una inclusione fittizia nel patrimonio finale, l'art. 14 prevede che il limite del credito di conguaglio dell'incremento patrimoniale sia accresciuto della metà dell'ammontare da conteggiarsi nel patrimonio finale in applicazione dell'art. 10, c. 2. Sono fatte salve le donazioni di cui all'art. 10, c. 2, n. 1, lett. b. In tal caso, non si può supporre che un coniuge abbia voluto diminuire slealmente il suo patrimonio.

Il coniuge disonesto può pertanto essere obbligato ad utilizzare il suo intero patrimonio e addirittura ad indebitarsi per adempiere al credito di conguaglio integrato dell'importo fittiziamente incluso.

Ai sensi dell'art. 3, comma 3, i coniugi possono derogare convenzionalmente all'applicazione di tale norma.

CAPITOLO VI. ALTRE DISPOSIZIONI

Articolo 15. Prescrizione

Il credito di conguaglio dell'incremento patrimoniale si prescrive in tre anni dalla conoscenza da parte del coniuge della cessazione del regime dei beni. La regola di prescrizione triennale corrisponde alle disposizioni degli ordinamenti giuridici nazionali (Germania: §1378(4) BGB; Francia: art. 1578 CC).

Tuttavia, il termine iniziale di decorrenza differisce nei due Paesi. Mentre in Germania esso viene riferito alla conoscenza della cessazione del regime dei beni, in Francia il termine decorre dalla cessazione stessa del regime dei beni. A tutela del coniuge legittimato al conguaglio dell'incremento patrimoniale viene adottata la regola tedesca per la determinazione del termine iniziale. In presenza di determinate circostanze, tuttavia, essendo la decorrenza del termine subordinata alla conoscenza, la prescrizione può verificarsi anche dopo molti anni dalla cessazione del regime dei beni. Per garantire al coniuge obbligato al conguaglio dell'incremento patrimoniale certezza giuridica a partire da un preciso momento temporale, l'art. 15 prevede anche un termine di prescrizione, indipendente dalla conoscenza, di dieci anni dalla cessazione del regime dei beni.

Articolo 16. Obbligo di informazione, inventario

Al comma 1:

Se un coniuge vuole far valere il credito di conguaglio dell'incremento patrimoniale, egli deve conoscere l'ammontare[45] del patrimonio iniziale e del patrimonio finale dell'altro coniuge. Perciò viene riconosciuta al coniuge una pretesa all'informazione e alla presentazione di un inventario. Al coniuge legittimato all'informazione viene attribuito, nell'ambito della sua pretesa all'informazione, un diritto alla presentazione di documenti giustificativi. In tal modo, il legittimato all'informazione può verificare le indicazioni dell'obbligato all'informazione e far valere al meglio i propri interessi. Inoltre, se vengono esibiti documenti giustificativi convincenti, possono essere evitati, del caso, conflitti tra le parti. Ciascun coniuge può pretendere che l'inventario sia predisposto da un notaio a spese del coniuge richiedente. Una disciplina corrispondente si ritrova nel diritto tedesco al §1379 BGB. Anche nelle norme francesi sul regime dei beni della comunione degli incrementi è disciplinata, nell'art. 1572 CC, una pretesa alla presentazione di un inventario del patrimonio finale; la pretesa all'informazione, sebbene non espressamente regolata, è riconosciuta.

Per consentire al coniuge legittimato al conguaglio la realizzazione del credito di conguaglio dell'incremento patrimoniale, viene qui prevista una pretesa all'informazione e alla presentazione di un inventario.

---

45 "La composizione e il valore", nella versione francese.

Al comma 2:
La medesima composizione di interessi si configura quando un coniuge voglia chiedere lo scioglimento del matrimonio o presentare domanda per il conguaglio anticipato dell'incremento patrimoniale. Di conseguenza, la pretesa di informazione di cui al comma 1 vale anche in questo caso.

Articolo 17. Dilazione di pagamento

Sia il diritto tedesco (§1382 BGB) sia il diritto francese (art. 1576 CC) conoscono la possibilità, da un lato, di dilazionare il credito di conguaglio dell'incremento patrimoniale alla ricorrenza di determinate circostanze, e, dall'altro, di pretendere la prestazione di garanzie.

Al comma 1:
Il comma 1 disciplina i presupposti in presenza dei quali può essere disposta una dilazione. Una dilazione può essere disposta, nell'interesse del coniuge legittimato al conguaglio, solo in casi eccezionali. Il giudice deve decidere se nel singolo caso sussista una eccessiva iniquità.

> *Esempio:*
> Il coniuge obbligato al conguaglio deve liquidare all'altro coniuge € 50.000. Il solo valore patrimoniale di proprietà del coniuge obbligato è la casa, in cui egli vive e in cui ha ubicato la propria attività, da cui ricava i mezzi di sostentamento. In questo caso sarebbe iniquo[46] pretendere dal coniuge l'alienazione della casa. In tale ipotesi potrebbe configurarsi una dilazione.

Al comma 2:
Un credito di conguaglio dilazionato produce interessi.

Al comma 3:
Il comma 3 precisa che il giudice può ordinare che il debitore fornisca garanzia per un credito dilazionato. Sulla natura e sull'ammontare della garanzia decide il giudice secondo equo apprezzamento.

Articolo 18. Conguaglio anticipato dell'incremento patrimoniale

Gli ordinamenti giuridici di entrambi gli Stati conoscono la facoltà, nel caso in cui il credito di conguaglio dell'incremento patrimoniale sia messo in pericolo, di far valere anticipatamente questo credito in presenza di determinati presupposti (Germania: §§1385, 1386 BGB; Francia: art. 1580 CC).

Nel diritto tedesco, accanto alla domanda costitutiva ("*Gestaltungsantrag*"), può essere proposta una domanda esecutiva ("*Leistungsantrag*") che consente, in

---

46 "Ingiusto", nella versione francese.

determinati casi, di pretendere anticipatamente e direttamente il credito di conguaglio dell'incremento patrimoniale.[47]

Nel diritto francese un coniuge può pretendere il conguaglio anticipato dell'incremento patrimoniale se, a causa del disordine dell'altro coniuge nei suoi affari, della sua cattiva amministrazione del patrimonio o della sua condotta sconveniente, è da temere che la continuazione del regime dei beni pregiudichi i diritti dell'altro coniuge. Nel caso in cui venga presentata una domanda si applicano le disposizioni sulla separazione dei beni. Se il giudice accoglie la domanda, per i coniugi subentra il regime della separazione dei beni.

La facoltà di pretendere il conguaglio anticipato dell'incremento patrimoniale viene prevista anche per il regime dei beni opzionale della partecipazione agli incrementi. Ai sensi dell'art. 18, può essere fatto valere un conguaglio anticipato dell'incremento patrimoniale se un coniuge non amministra adeguatamente il suo patrimonio e pregiudica in tal modo i diritti dell'altro coniuge nel calcolo del credito di conguaglio dell'incremento patrimoniale. Questo vale in particolare quando un coniuge compie azioni che, in applicazione dell'art. 10, comma 2 (con eccezione dell'art. 10, c. 2, n. 1, lett. b), conducano ad aggiunte fittizie nel patrimonio finale.

A differenza dell'art. 1580 CC, l'art. 18 consente anche al coniuge obbligato al conguaglio di pretendere il conguaglio anticipato dell'incremento patrimoniale, qualora la condotta dell'altro coniuge, ai sensi dell'art. 18, comma 1, pregiudichi a suo sfavore l'ammontare del credito di conguaglio dell'incremento patrimoniale.

Se il credito di conguaglio dell'incremento patrimoniale è a rischio, in molti casi è sensato ottenere dal giudice provvedimenti provvisori a garanzia della pretesa. I provvedimenti processuali non sono regolati autonomamente nell'ambito del regime dei beni opzionale della partecipazione agli incrementi. Nella materia si applicano le disposizioni dello Stato in cui il provvedimento viene fatto valere.

In Francia possono essere richiesti i provvedimenti di cui all'art. 220-1 CC. In Germania soccorre la garanzia della pretesa al credito di conguaglio dell'incremento patrimoniale tramite lo strumento di tutela provvisoria del sequestro conservativo, secondo il §916 del codice di procedura civile (ZPO).

CAPITOLO VII. DISPOSIZIONI FINALI

Articolo 19. Applicazione temporale

L'accordo si applicherà solo ai contratti matrimoniali conclusi dai coniugi dopo la sua entrata in vigore.

---

[47] "Nel diritto tedesco una richiesto di indennizzo proposta contestualmente alla domanda di sciogliemnto del regime permette in alcuni casi di richiedere direttamente e in via anticipatoria la liquidazione del credito di partecipazione", nel testo francese.

Articolo 20. Ratifica ed entrata in vigore

Il presente accordo è soggetto a ratifica secondo le norme di diritto internazionale vigenti.

Deve entrare in vigore il prima possibile.

È revocabile.

Articolo 21. Adesione

Considerata la crescente mobilità di coppie di coniugi all'interno dell'Unione Europea, è auspicabile rendere possibile anche ad altri Stati membri una adesione all'accordo.

In caso di adesione di uno o più Stati, la Germania è designata quale depositaria dell'accordo.

Articolo 22. Regime linguistico dell'accordo

In caso di adesione può essere redatta una nuova versione linguistica vincolante dell'accordo nella lingua ufficiale dello Stato aderente.

Articolo 23. Registrazione

Il dovere di registrazione dell'accordo si basa sull'art. 102 della Carta delle Nazioni Unite.

PROGETTO DI LEGGE DEL GOVERNO FEDERALE TEDESCO

Progetto di legge sull'Accordo del 4 febbraio 2010 fra la Repubblica Federale Tedesca e la Repubblica Francese sul regime dei beni opzionale della partecipazione agli incrementi

A. Problema e obiettivo

Nell'ipotesi di matrimoni binazionali possono sorgere problemi riguardo al patrimonio dei coniugi, poiché nei diversi Paesi i regimi legali dei beni sono differenti e, di regola, non sono conosciuti negli altri Paesi. Questi problemi hanno anche specifica rilevanza pratica perché in Germania, nel 2009, in circa il 13% dei matrimoni almeno uno dei coniugi possedeva cittadinanza straniera. Problemi non sorgono solo al momento dello scioglimento del matrimonio, ma anche in costanza di matrimonio, per esempio nel caso di finanziamento di investimenti immobiliari. Di fronte a questo scenario, un accordo internazionale fra Stati con la necessaria integrazione nel diritto nazionale si pone l'obiettivo di creare maggiore sicurezza e chiarezza giuridica.

B. Soluzione

La Repubblica Federale Tedesca e la Repubblica Francese hanno deciso di creare un regime dei beni comune, identico in entrambi gli Stati, che corrisponda, in forma modificata, al conguaglio dell'incremento patrimoniale tedesco. Questo regime dei beni può essere scelto dai coniugi in entrambi i Paesi in sostituzione del rispettivo regime legale dei beni e accanto ai rispettivi regimi dei beni opzionali nazionali. La possibilità di aderire all'accordo di matrice franco-tedesca resta aperta anche agli altri Stati membri dell'Unione Europea.

Con la presente legge di ratifica si creano i presupposti nazionali per la ratifica, ai sensi dell'art. 59, comma 2, frase 1, del Grundgesetz.

Allo stesso tempo, la legge disciplina l'attuazione nazionale dell'Accordo.

C. Alternative

Nessuna.

D. Conseguenze finanziarie

Lo Stato federale, i Länder e i comuni non saranno gravati da costi.

E. Altri costi

Per l'economia, in particolare per le piccole e medie imprese, non sorgono costi ulteriori. Non si attendono conseguenze della legge su costi unitari e sul livello generale dei prezzi, in particolare sul livello dei prezzi al consumo.

F. Costi burocratici

Non sono introdotti, modificati o revocati obblighi di informazione per l'economia, i cittadini o l'amministrazione.

MOTIVAZIONE ALLA LEGGE DI RATIFICA

A. PARTE GENERALE

1. SITUAZIONE INIZIALE DI FATTO E DI DIRITTO

I matrimoni con elementi di internazionalità sono molto diffusi. Nell'anno 2009, nel 13% ca. delle coppie di coniugi residenti in Germania, entrambi i coniugi avevano cittadinanza straniera oppure un coniuge aveva la cittadinanza tedesca e l'altro una cittadinanza straniera. Tra questi vi erano almeno 34.000 coppie franco-tedesche, il quarto gruppo più numeroso dopo le coppie tedesco-polacche, tedesco-italiane e tedesco-austriache (Hammes e altri, WiSta 2010 pp. 904/911 ss.). A ciò si aggiungono le coppie tedesche che vivono all'estero e le coppie straniere che vivono in Germania. Poichè gli effetti giuridici del matrimonio dipendono, tra l'altro, dalla cittadinanza, i matrimoni tra cittadini di diversi Stati possono condurre a complicanze giuridiche, in particolare, con riferimento alle questioni patrimoniali. In Germania, il regime legale dei beni è la partecipazione agli incrementi. I patrimoni dei coniugi rimangono separati e solo alla cessazione del regime dei beni – per esempio a causa di divorzio – viene compensato l'incremento patrimoniale prodotto in costanza di matrimonio. In Francia, il regime legale dei beni è la comunione dei beni limitata agli acquisti. Gli acquisti in costanza di matrimonio costituiscono patrimonio comune. Se per esempio una coppia vive in Germania in regime di comunione limitata agli acquisti, secondo il diritto francese, sorgono dei problemi se i coniugi acquistano, in tale regime dei beni, un immobile in Germania. Poiché il regime dei beni francese, di regola, non è conosciuto in Germania, la precisa valutazione della portata dei diritti spettanti in capo ai singoli coniugi al momento della trascrizione di un diritto di proprietà nel libro fondiario conduce, per esempio, a considerevoli incertezze (sulla comunione degli acquisti nel diritto spagnolo si veda, per esempio, OLG Düsseldorf, FamRZ 2010, 1564 ss.). Per un istituto di credito tedesco è particolarmente dubbio quali conseguenze abbiano i vincoli obbligatori o l'insolvenza di un coniuge sul patrimonio vincolato nella comunione degli acquisti. La soluzione spesso rinvenibile nella pratica, secondo cui i coniugi ai sensi dell'art. 15, comma 2, EGBGB (*Einführungsgesetz zum Bürgerlichen Gesetzbuch*) scelgono il regime dei beni tedesco per i patrimoni situati in Germania, risponde certamente a questa domanda, ma impone una scissione del regime dei beni che può condurre a difficoltà di calcolo nel caso di un conguaglio patrimoniale. In considerazione di tradizioni del tutto differenti, le coppie tedesche in Francia incontrano problemi analoghi.

La scelta di un accordo bilaterale presenta il vantaggio di poter offrire soluzioni il più possibile tempestive per i coniugi coinvolti, poiché un'armonizzazione del diritto di famiglia in tutti gli Stati membri dell'Unione Europea può procedere necessariamente solo molto lentamente, a causa di tradizioni giuridiche diverse, spesso sviluppatesi nei secoli e profondamente radicate nella popolazione. In tal senso esiste anche un mandato politico per la Repubblica Francese e la Repubblica Federale Tedesca. L'intento di armonizzare il diritto di famiglia tedesco e francese discende dalla dichiarazione comune per il "40° anniversario del Trattato dell'Eliseo 2003". La possibilità di aderire all'Accordo del 4 febbraio 2010 fra la Repubblica Federale Tedesca e la Repubblica Francese sul regime dei beni opzionale della partecipazione agli incrementi (di seguito: Accordo) è aperta ad altri Stati membri dell'Unione Europea. Anche in questi Stati il diritto matrimoniale, specialmente il diritto del regime dei beni, è disciplinato in maniera molto diversa e conduce a problemi analoghi a quelli presenti in Germania e in Francia.

2. SCOPO DELLE PROPOSTE DI RIFORMA

In considerazione delle incertezze giuridiche nei matrimoni con elementi di internazionalità, con l'Accordo si vuole creare un regime dei beni opzionale (inizialmente) bi-nazionale, che contiene norme identiche per entrambi gli ordinamenti giuridici offrendo così agli interessati chiarezza e sicurezza giuridica. Per garantire consenso al nuovo regime dei beni opzionale della partecipazione agli incrementi sia in Francia sia in Germania, esso tiene conto di particolarità di diritto patrimoniale dei beni derivanti da entrambi gli ordinamenti giuridici. Nella sua struttura di base la partecipazione opzionale agli incrementi corrisponde alla partecipazione agli incrementi tedesca, ma presenta anche modifiche riconducibili alla tradizione giuridica francese. In entrambi gli Stati, i coniugi possono scegliere questo regime dei beni al posto del regime dei beni legale, in aggiunta agli altri regimi opzionali nazionali, qualora il loro regime dei beni soggiaccia al diritto sostanziale di uno degli Stati contraenti. In entrambi gli Stati non vengono alterate le disposizioni del diritto internazionale privato. Non è necessario un elemento diretto di internazionalità, tuttavia il regime dei beni opzionale della partecipazione agli incrementi offre vantaggi specialmente nei matrimoni con elementi di internazionalità.

Con la riforma proposta del BGB, il regime dei beni opzionale viene inserito nel diritto di famiglia tedesco. Le norme sulle imposte di successione e di donazione corrispondono alle disposizioni sulla partecipazione agli incrementi del diritto tedesco e devono garantire che i coniugi non evitino di scegliere il nuovo regime dei beni per ragioni fiscali.

3. COMPETENZA LEGISLATIVA

La competenza legislativa federale deriva dall'art. 73, comma 1, n. 1 (affari esteri), dall'art. 74, comma 1, n. 1 (diritto civile) e dall'art. 105, comma 2, seconda alternativa, in combinato disposto con l'art. 72, comma 2 (diritto tributario), del Grundgesetz.

Ai sensi dell'art. 72, comma 2, del Grundgesetz, è necessaria una legge federale per la tutela dell'unità giuridica nell'interesse nazionale. Per ottenere un'uniformazione del diritto in Francia e in Germania, è presupposto imperativo che nella Repubblica Federale Tedesca viga un diritto uniforme. Questo si può ottenere solo mediante una disciplina legislativa federale. Infatti regole diverse genererebbero incertezza giuridica nelle imposte di successione per causa di morte e condurrebbero, in ragione della variabilità di possibili beneficiari nei singoli casi di successione, ad una frammentazione giuridica con dubbie conseguenze, che non possono essere tollerate nell'interesse sia dello Stato federale che dei *Länder.*

L'approvazione del Consiglio Federale è necessaria ai sensi dell'art. 105, comma 3 del Grundgesetz, poiché l'imposizione fiscale delle successioni e delle donazioni compete ai *Länder*, ai sensi dell'art. 106, comma 2, n. 2, Grundgesetz.

B. PARTE SPECIALE

All'Articolo 1 (Approvazione)

Poiché l'Accordo si riferisce a materie della legislazione federale, si applica l'art. 59, comma 2, frase 1, del Grundgesetz.

All'Articolo 2 (Modifica del BGB)

Al comma 1 (*Modifica dell'indice*)
Poiché si introduce un nuovo Capitolo 4 nel Libro 4 – Diritto della famiglia – del BGB, si integra anche l'indice.

Al comma 2

a) In generale
   Con l'introduzione del nuovo Capitolo 4 "Regime opzionale della partecipazione agli incrementi" si chiarisce che il regime dei beni opzionale della partecipazione agli incrementi secondo l'Accordo è un regime dei beni

ulteriore adottabile mediante contratto matrimoniale, che si affianca in via paritetica ai regimi opzionali della separazione e della comunione dei beni, contemplati nei Capitoli 2 e 3.

b) §1519 BGB – nuovo –

aa) Principio fondamentale

Il §1519 BGB – nuovo – tiene conto della limitazione della libertà contrattuale di cui al §1409 BGB. Ai sensi dei §§1408 e ss. BGB, i coniugi possono scegliere convenzionalmente la separazione dei beni o la comunione dei beni al posto del regime dei beni legale della partecipazione agli incrementi. Con il nuovo §1519 BGB, in conformità all'Accordo fra Repubblica Federale Tedesca e Repubblica Francese sul regime dei beni opzionale della partecipazione agli incrementi, il regime dei beni opzionale della partecipazione agli incrementi viene introdotto quale ulteriore regime adottabile mediante contratto matrimoniale.

Le singole disposizioni identiche in Germania e in Francia sono contenute negli articoli da 1 a 19 dell'Accordo. Per le motivazioni si rinvia al corrispondente allegato, contenente la relazione illustrativa dell'Accordo approvato da Francia e Germania.

bb) Applicazione dei §§1368 e 1412 BGB

L'art. 5 dell'Accordo regola l'inefficacia di disposizioni su beni dell'attività domestica e sull'abitazione familiare. La disposizione non disciplina l'opponibilità di un atto giuridico inefficace nei confronti di un terzo che ne tragga vantaggio. Con il riferimento nella legge di ratifica al §1368 BGB, anche il coniuge che, nell'ipotesi di alienazione illegittima viene tutelato dall'art. 5 dell'Accordo, deve avere la possibilità di far valere contro un terzo i diritti derivanti dall'inefficacia dell'atto di disposizione di beni dell'attività domestica o dell'abitazione familiare.

L'applicazione del §1412 BGB è per contro esclusa. L'inefficacia di un atto di disposizione nei confronti di un terzo non deve dipendere dalla circostanza che il contratto matrimoniale a fondamento della partecipazione opzionale agli incrementi sia registrato nel registro del regime dei beni o sia conosciuto dal terzo. La trascrizione nel registro del regime dei beni, in considerazione della sua scarsa rilevanza pratica, sarebbe una formalità superflua, che non porterebbe alcun valore aggiunto per la tutela dei traffici giuridici. In particolare, in caso di atti di disposizione su beni immobili, i notai roganti dovranno considerare in futuro la possibilità di un divieto di disposizione.

c) Delimitazione in senso ampio da altro regime dei beni

Il nuovo regime dei beni si sostituisce, nel suo campo di applicazione, al regime patrimoniale fra i coniugi.

aa) §1357 BGB

Accanto alla norma speciale nell'art. 6 dell'Accordo, che disciplina la responsabilità solidale dei coniugi per gli atti di un coniuge per la gestione dell'attività domestica, non vi è spazio per un'applicazione del §1357 BGB.

bb) §1365 BGB

L'art. 5, comma 1, dell'Accordo, che ha carattere esaustivo, impedisce che il §1365 BGB possa trovare applicazione accanto al medesimo. Una tale norma di tutela non è stata volutamente accolta nell'Accordo (vedi la relazione esplicativa all'art. 5, comma 1, dell'Accordo).

cc) §1382 BGB

L'art. 17, comma 2, dell'Accordo non contiene alcuna disposizione speciale sulla entità del tasso di interesse in caso di dilazione. Tuttavia, non è previsto un rinvio al §1382, comma 4 BGB. Si applica perciò, ove richiesto, il §264 BGB. Il tasso di interesse ammonta dunque al 4%. Se il debitore del conguaglio è in mora, il tasso di interesse ammonta a 5 punti percentuali oltre il tasso base di interesse (§288, comma 1, frase 2, §247 BGB). Non esiste nemmeno una particolare esigenza di includere la norma processuale speciale del §1382, comma 5, BGB, secondo la quale una richiesta di dilazione può essere presentata solo in un procedimento pendente avente ad oggetto il credito di conguaglio.

dd) §1384 BGB

In caso di scioglimento del matrimonio per atto del giudice, per l'accertamento dell'incremento patrimoniale, ai sensi dell'art. 13 dell'Accordo, è determinante il momento della presentazione della domanda in giudizio. Pertanto – come ai sensi del §1384 BGB – non si ha riguardo alla litispendenza a seguito di notifica della domanda al convenuto. Determinante è il momento in cui la domanda è presentata al Tribunale.

ee) Conguaglio delle aspettative previdenziali

Per i diritti alle aspettative previdenziali per anzianità, soggetti al conguaglio, delle aspettative previdenziali non ha luogo un conguaglio patrimoniale, §1587 BGB in combinato disposto con il §2, comma 4, della legge sul conguaglio delle aspettative previdenziali. Questo vale anche in caso di regime opzionale della partecipazione agli incrementi. Mediante la conclusione di un contratto matrimoniale, i coniugi possono disciplinare una diversa imputazione del patrimonio previdenziale assistenziale in Germania e Francia. In considerazione delle particolarità del conguaglio delle aspettative previdenziali tedesco, una soluzione alla diversa imputazione del patrimonio previdenziale assistenziale avrebbe reso eccessivamente complesso il nuovo regime dei beni opzionale.

d) Liquidazione del regime dei beni secondo il diritto successorio

Contrariamente al BGB, che contiene la disposizione speciale del §1371 BGB per la liquidazione del regime legale dei beni in caso di morte di uno dei coniugi, l'Accordo non prevede per questa ipotesi alcuna disciplina distinta.

Il §1371, comma 1, BGB aumenta la quota ereditaria legittima del coniuge superstite (§1931, comma 1, BGB) di un quarto, quale conguaglio forfettario dell'incremento patrimoniale. Il collegamento fra diritto patrimoniale dei beni e diritto successorio, che nel diritto tedesco è oggetto di continue critiche, è estraneo all'Accordo. A seguito dell'applicazione del §1371, comma 1, BGB, al coniuge superstite per il quale trovi applicazione la legge tedesca spetterebbe sul piano sostanziale, nonostante il regime dei beni prescelto della comunione opzionale degli incrementi, un conguaglio degli incrementi diverso rispetto al coniuge superstite per il quale trovi applicazione il diritto francese. Questo contrasterebbe con la finalità dell'Accordo di creare un regime dei beni uniforme, il più possibile identico negli Stati aderenti. Pertanto, alla morte di un coniuge, dovrà essere compensato innanzitutto l'incremento patrimoniale.

e) Inclusione del diritto delle unioni civili tra persone dello stesso sesso (*Lebenspartnerschaftsrecht*)
Il nuovo regime dei beni opzionale della partecipazione agli incrementi deve poter essere applicato anche ai conviventi ai sensi della legge sulle unioni civili tra persone dello stesso sesso (LPartG). Sulla base dei §§6 e 7 LPartG si applicano già ai conviventi le disposizioni del regime dei beni che trovano applicazione per i coniugi. In tal modo è raggiunta una completa equiparazione con il matrimonio. Per il regime dei beni opzionale della partecipazione agli incrementi non sarà fatta alcuna eccezione. Il §6 LPartG consente di optare nel contratto di unione civile tra persone dello stesso sesso per un regime dei beni diverso dal regime dei beni legale della comunione degli incrementi. Il §7, frase 2 LPartG dichiara pertanto applicabili i §§da 1409 a 1563 BGB conformemente. Il nuovo §1519 BGB è con ciò già ricompreso in questo rinvio.

f) Stato di diritto in caso di risoluzione dell'Accordo
Se la Germania dovesse risolvere l'Accordo, le conseguenze sarebbero da disciplinare in una legge di attuazione: o viene mantenuto il contenuto materiale dell'Accordo o vengono create norme di attuazione, ad esempio, secondo il modello del Trattato di Riunificazione (art. 234, §4 della legge introduttiva al BGB).
Se la Francia dovesse risolvere l'Accordo, il regime dei beni resterebbe quale regime dei beni esclusivamente tedesco, a causa del rinvio fisso alle disposizioni dell'Accordo.

All'Articolo 3 (Modifica della legge sull'amministrazione della giustizia)

Ai sensi dell'art. 12, comma 2, frase 2, dell'Accordo il giudice, su domanda di uno dei coniugi, può ordinare che i beni del debitore siano trasferiti al creditore al fine di compensazione, se ciò corrisponde ad equità. Inoltre ai sensi dell'art. 17

dell'Accordo il giudice, su domanda, può dilazionare al debitore il credito di conguaglio dell'incremento patrimoniale e disporre la prestazione di una garanzia. Queste attività del giudice sono paragonabili a quelle che il diritto nazionale ha attribuito al cancelliere già nei §§1382, 1383 BGB, sempre che non penda una causa sul credito di conguaglio (§1382, comma 5, BGB). Fondamento dell'attribuzione di queste mansioni era che, in questi casi, non sorgono, in generale, difficoltà di natura giuridica, ma occorre chiarire questioni di fatto e bilanciare interessi economici. Queste considerazioni riguardano anche i casi regolati dall'art. 12, comma 2, frase 2 e dall'art. 17 dell'Accordo – non da ultimo per l'identica struttura di fondo della partecipazione opzionale agli incrementi convenuta convenzionalmente e della comunione alle partecipazioni regolata dalla legge.

All'Articolo 4 (Modifica della legge sul procedimento in materia di diritto della famiglia e sulle questioni di volontaria giurisdizione)

Al comma 1
Nell'indice deve essere adeguata la nuova formulazione della rubrica del §264 della legge sul procedimento di diritto della famiglia e sulle questioni di volontaria giurisdizione (FamFG).

Al comma 2
Le pretese risultanti ai sensi dell'Accordo del regime dei beni opzionale della partecipazione agli incrementi sono questioni di diritto patrimoniale dei beni ai sensi del §261, comma 1, FamFG. I procedimenti previsti secondo l'art. 5, comma 2, l'art. 12, comma 2, frase 2, e l'art. 17 dell'Accordo sono paragonabili a quelli del §1369, comma 2, e dei §§1382, 1383 BGB. Con l'introduzione nel §261, comma 2, FamFG, queste materie del procedimento vengono dichiarate parimenti questioni di diritto patrimoniale dei beni.

Al comma 3
Il §264, comma 1, frase 1, FamFG regola per i procedimenti conformi ai §§1382 e 1383 BGB in via di eccezione al §40, comma 2, FamFG, che una decisione del Tribunale diviene efficace solo con il passaggio in giudicato. Come il §1383 BGB in caso di regime dei beni della comunione agli incrementi, l'art. 12, comma 2, frase 2, dell'Accordo prevede, in caso di regime dei beni opzionale della partecipazione agli incrementi e su domanda di una delle parti, una attribuzione del credito di conguaglio in natura quale ipotesi speciale, se ciò corrisponde ad equità. L'art. 17 dell'Accordo prevede la possibilità di una dilazione giudiziale del credito di conguaglio, per la quale è da prestare se del caso anche garanzia, e dispone pertanto per il regime dei beni opzionale della partecipazione agli incrementi una norma analoga al §1382 BGB. Le norme dell'art. 12, comma 2, frase 2, e l'art. 17 dell'Accordo sono simili a quelle dei §§1382 e 1383 BGB e devono essere applicate conformemente in procedimenti patrimoniali dei beni.

Per questa ragione, anche nei procedimenti secondo l'art. 12, comma 2, frase 2, e l'art. 17 dell'Accordo, la decisione del giudice diviene efficace solo con il passaggio in giudicato.

Al comma 4

Il §269, comma 1, FamFG regola quali procedimenti siano questioni di diritto delle unioni civili fra persone dello stesso sesso. Tra questi, ai sensi del §269, comma 1, n. 11 FamFG, si annoverano anche le decisioni secondo il §6 LPartG in combinato disposto con il §1365, comma 2, §1369, comma 2, §§1382 e 1383 BGB e, ai sensi dell'art. 269, comma 1, n. 12 FamFG le decisioni secondo il §7 LPartG in combinato disposto con i §§1426, 1430 e 1452 BGB. Per attuare l'equiparazione delle unioni civili fra persone dello stesso sesso al matrimonio, descritta all'art. 2, n. 2, lett. e, della legge di ratifica, la disposizione nel §269, comma 1, n. 12, FamFG deve chiarire che sono decisioni in questo senso anche quelle sulla base del §1519 BGB in combinato disposto con l'art. 5, comma 2, l'art. 12, comma 2, frase 2, e l'art. 17 dell'Accordo.

All'Articolo 5 (Modifica della legge sull'imposta di successione e donazione)

Le conseguenze di una cessazione del regime dei beni opzionale della partecipazione agli incrementi ai fini dell'imposta di successione e donazione devono essere uniformate a quelle per la cessazione del regime legale dei beni del BGB. Altrimenti una disparità di trattamento fiscale rispetto al regime legale dei beni della comunione agli incrementi renderebbe nella prassi il nuovo regime dei beni un'alternativa di seconda classe. Conformemente al §5, comma 2, della legge sull'imposta di successione e donazione (ErbStG), il credito di conguaglio dell'incremento patrimoniale ex art. 12 dell'Accordo non deve configurare un acquisto ai sensi dei §§3 e 7 ErbStG. Questo deve valere indipendentemente dalla circostanza che il regime dei beni opzionale della partecipazione agli incrementi sia cessato alla morte di un coniuge o già quando i coniugi erano in vita. Il credito di conguaglio dell'incremento patrimoniale non soggiace perciò all'imposizione fiscale ai sensi del ErbStG, qualora esso sia stato concretamente calcolato e costituisca il fondamento di un trasferimento patrimoniale.

Non è necessaria un'esenzione conforme al §5, comma 1, ErbStG. In caso di liquidazione successoria del conguaglio dell'incremento patrimoniale (§1371, comma 1, BGB), il coniuge superstite viene esentato, mediante la norma relativa ad un acquisto ai sensi dei §§3 e 7 ErbStG, dall'imposta di successione nell'ammontare del credito di conguaglio fittizio che egli avrebbe potuto far valere nei presupposti dei §§ da 1373 a 1383, 1390 BGB. Poiché nel regime dei beni opzionale della partecipazione agli incrementi il conguaglio dell'incremento patrimoniale può essere fatto valere alla cessazione del regime dei beni solo con la determinazione dell'effettivo credito di conguaglio dell'incremento patrimoniale, per il §5, comma 1, ErbStG viene meno l'ambito di applicazione.

Inoltre non occorre alcuna conforme applicazione del §29, comma 1, n. 2, ErbStG. Ai sensi del §29, comma 1, n. 2, ErbStG, l'imposta si estingue con efficacia retroattiva nella misura in cui, nei casi del §5, comma 2 ErbStG, le attribuzioni a titolo gratuito, che erano soggette ad imposta, siano state conteggiate al credito al conguaglio ex §1380, comma 1 BGB. Poichè l'Accordo non disciplina una tale imputazione, manca il criterio di collegamento per il §29, comma 1, n. 2, ErbStG.

All'Articolo 6 (Entrata in vigore)

I commi 1 e 2 regolano l'entrata in vigore della legge. Le disposizioni sono conformi al requisito dell'art. 82, comma 2, frase 1 del Grundgesetz.

Secondo il comma 2, frase 2, la data in cui l'Accordo entra in vigore secondo il suo art. 20 deve essere pubblicata sulla Gazzetta Ufficiale del Governo Federale.

Considerazioni conclusive

Con l'Accordo fra la Repubblica Federale Tedesca e la Repubblica Francese sul regime dei beni opzionale della partecipazione agli incrementi, gli Stati parte hanno sviluppato un nuovo modello per l'integrazione degli ordinamenti civili in Europa. L'Accordo resta aperto, di principio, all'adesione di qualsiasi Stato Membro dell'Unione Europea ed estende in tal modo, sotto il regime dell'autonomia privata, le opzioni negoziali di cittadine e cittadini, creando un nuovo diritto sostanziale. Il progetto qui proposto di una legge di ratifica e di recepimento rende accessibile, dopo l'entrata in vigore dell'Accordo, questa nuova opzione a coloro per i quali vige il regime dei beni tedesco.

Per il bilancio pubblico e per l'economia, in particolare per le piccole e medie imprese, non sorgono costi ulteriori. Non si attendono effetti della legge sui prezzi unitari e sul livello generale dei prezzi, in particolare sul livello dei prezzi al consumo.

Il progetto di legge si accorda con il pensiero guida del Governo Federale in materia di sviluppo sostenibile, nel senso della strategia nazionale di sostenibilità. Le norme progettate intendono contribuire ad una maggiore chiarezza giuridica nei casi di matrimoni con elementi di estraneità.

Non sono introdotti, modificati o revocati obblighi di informazione per l'economia, le cittadine e i cittadini e l'amministrazione.

Il progetto di legge è compatibile con il diritto dell'Unione Europea e i Trattati di diritto internazionale stipulati dalla Repubblica Federale Tedesca.

Non sono attesi effetti di significato per le pari opportunità.

LEGGE TEDESCA DI RATIFICA

Legge sull'Accordo del 4 febbraio 2010 fra la Repubblica Federale Tedesca e la Repubblica Francese sul regime dei beni opzionale della partecipazione agli incrementi del 15 marzo 2012

Il Parlamento Federale ha approvato, con il consenso del Consiglio Federale, la seguente legge:

Articolo 1. Approvazione

E' approvato l'Accordo sottoscritto a Parigi il 4 febbraio 2010 fra la Repubblica Federale Tedesca e la Repubblica Francese sul regime dei beni opzionale della partecipazione agli incrementi. L'Accordo viene pubblicato di seguito.

Articolo 2. Modifica del BGB

Il BGB, nella versione pubblicata il 2 gennaio 2002 (BGBl. I p. 42, 2909, 2003 I p. 738), da ultimo modificato dall'art. 1 della l. 17 gennaio 2011 (BGBl. - Bundesgesetzblatt (Gazzetta federale) – I p. 1600), è modificato come segue:

1. Nell'indice, dopo l'indicazione del Libro 4, Parte 1, Titolo 6, Sottotitolo 2, Capitolo 3, è inserita la seguente indicazione:
   "Capitolo 4
   Regime dei beni opzionale della partecipazione agli incrementi".

2. Dopo il §1518 viene inserito il seguente Capitolo 4:
   "Capitolo 4
   Regime dei beni opzionale della partecipazione agli incrementi".
   §1519
   Stipulazione mediante contratto matrimoniale
   Se i coniugi convengono mediante contratto matrimoniale il regime dei beni opzionale della partecipazione agli incrementi, si applicano le disposizioni dell'Accordo del 4 febbraio 2010 fra la Repubblica Federale Tedesca e la Repubblica Francese sul regime dei beni opzionale della partecipazione agli incrementi. Il §1368 si applica in modo conforme. Il §1412 non si applica."

Articolo 3. Modifica della legge dell'amministrazione della giustizia

Il §25, n. 3, della legge dei funzionari giudiziari del 5 novembre 1969 (BGBl. I p. 2065), da ultimo modificato con l'art. 5 della legge del 7 dicembre 2011 (BGBl. I p. 2474), è modificato come segue:

1. alla lettera b, il punto è sostituito da una virgola.

2. viene aggiunta la seguente lettera c:
   "c) la decisione sulla dilazione di un credito di conguaglio e sul trasferimento di beni patrimoniali secondo il §1519 BGB in combinato disposto con l'art. 12, comma 2, frase 2, e l'art. 17 dell'Accordo del 4 febbraio 2010 fra la Repubblica Federale Tedesca e la Repubblica Francese sul regime dei beni opzionale della partecipazione agli incrementi, ciascuno anche in combinato disposto con il §7 della legge sulla convivenza registrata (*Lebenspartnerschaftsgesetz*), qualora sul credito di conguaglio non penda una controversia."

Articolo 4. Modifica della legge sui procedimenti in materia di diritto della famiglia e sulle questioni di volontaria giurisdizione

La legge sui procedimenti in materia di famiglia e sulle questioni di volontaria giurisdizione del 17 dicembre 2008 (BGBl. I p. 2586, 2587), da ultimo modificata con l'art. 2, c. 32 della legge del 22 dicembre 2011 (BGBl. I p. 3044), è modificata come segue:

1. Nell'indice, la rubrica del §264 viene formulata come segue:
   "§264 Procedimento sulla dilazione e sul trasferimento di beni patrimoniali".

2. Il §261, c. 2, viene formulato come segue:
   "(2) Le questioni sul regime patrimoniale sono anche procedimenti ai sensi del §1365, comma 2, del §1369, comma 2, dei §§1382, 1383, 1426, 1430 e 1452 del BGB, così come ai sensi del §1519 del BGB in combinato disposto con l'art. 5, comma 2, l'art. 12, comma 2, frase 2, e l'art. 17 dell'Accordo del 4 febbraio 2010 fra la Repubblica Federale Tedesca e la Repubblica Francese sul regime dei beni opzionale della partecipazione agli incrementi".

3. Il §264 è modificato come segue:
   a) L'intestazione viene formulata come segue:
      "§264
      Procedimento sulla dilazione e sul trasferimento di beni patrimoniali".

   b) Il c. 1, frase 1, viene formulata come segue:
      "Nei procedimenti ai sensi dei §§1382 e 1383 del BGB, come anche ai sensi del §1519 del BGB in combinato disposto con l'art. 12, comma 2, frase 2, e l'art. 17

dell'Accordo del 4 febbraio 2010 fra la Repubblica Federale Tedesca e la Repubblica Francese sul regime dei beni opzionale della partecipazione agli incrementi, la decisione del Tribunale è efficace solo con il passaggio in giudicato."

4. Il §269, comma 1, n. 12, viene formulato come segue:

   "12. Decisioni ai sensi del §7 della legge sulla convivenza registrata in combinato disposto con i §§1426, 1430, 1452 del BGB o con il §1519 del BGB e l'art. 5, comma 2, l'art. 12, comma 2, frase 2 o l'art. 17 dell'Accordo del 4 febbraio 2010 fra la Repubblica Federale Tedesca e la Repubblica Francese sul regime dei beni opzionale della partecipazione agli incrementi".

Articolo 5. Modifica della legge sull'imposta di successione e sull'imposta di donazione

Al §5 della legge sull'imposta di successione e di donazione nella versione pubblicata il 27 febbraio 1997 (BGBl. I p. 378), da ultimo modificata dall'art. 14 della legge dell'7 dicembre 2011 (BGBl. I p. 2592), viene aggiunto il seguente comma 3:

> "(3) Se cessa il regime dei beni della partecipazione opzionale agli incrementi (§1519 BGB) e viene compensato l'incremento patrimoniale, il credito di conguaglio (Art. 12 c. 1 dell'Accordo del 4 febbraio 2010 fra la Repubblica Federale Tedesca e la Repubblica Francese sul regime dei beni opzionale della partecipazione agli incrementi) non rientra negli acquisti ai sensi dei §§3 e 7".

Articolo 6. Entrata in vigore

(1) Gli artt. da 2 a 5 entrano in vigore il giorno in cui l'Accordo del 4 febbraio 2010 fra la Repubblica Federale Tedesca e la Repubblica Francese sul regime dei beni opzionale della partecipazione agli incrementi entra in vigore secondo il suo art. 20, comma 2. Il giorno dell'entrata in vigore sarà pubblicato sulla Gazzetta Ufficiale Federale.

(2) Per il rimanente, questa legge entra in vigore il giorno successivo alla promulgazione.

SPANISH*

CONTENTS

* Unofficial translations by Thomas Feige and Michaela Kolb. Revision by Helena Lozano Miralles. Based on the German texts.

MEMORANDO

I. GENERALIDADES

1. SITUACIÓN DE PARTIDA

Los matrimonios con cónyuges de distinta nacionalidad son muy comunes. En el año 2009, en el 13 por ciento de los casos de matrimonios residentes en Alemania, los dos cónyuges tenían nacionalidad extranjera o un cónyuge tenía nacionalidad alemana y el otro nacionalidad extranjera. A ellos se suman los matrimonios alemanes que viven en el extranjero y los matrimonios extranjeros que viven en la República Federal de Alemania. Dado que las consecuencias legales del matrimonio se determinan entre otras circunstancias por la nacionalidad, los matrimonios con cónyuges de distinta nacionalidad pueden causar problemas jurídicos especialmente en lo que se refiere al régimen económico matrimonial. El régimen legal supletorio en la República Federal de Alemania es el régimen de participación en las ganancias. El patrimonio de cada cónyuge es privativo y solo con la disolución del régimen matrimonial – por ejemplo, por motivo de divorcio – se compensan las ganancias obtenidas durante el matrimonio. El régimen legal supletorio en la República Francesa es la comunidad de gananciales. Las ganancias obtenidas durante el matrimonio se convierten en patrimonio común. Por ejemplo, si un matrimonio en comunidad de gananciales, conforme al derecho francés, vive en la República Federal de Alemania, podrán surgir problemas cuando los cónyuges con este régimen matrimonial adquieran un inmueble en la República Federal de Alemania. Dado que el régimen matrimonial francés no suele ser conocido en la República Federal de Alemania, la estimación precisa, por ejemplo, del alcance de los derechos correspondientes a los respectivos cónyuges al inscribir un título de propiedad en el Registro de la Propiedad lleva a considerables incertidumbres. Para una institución de crédito alemana resulta especialmente dudoso determinar cuáles son las consecuencias de las obligaciones o de la insolvencia de un cónyuge para el patrimonio vinculado a la comunidad de gananciales. La solución por la que se suele optar en la práctica y que consiste en elegir el régimen legal alemán para el patrimonio localizado en la República Federal de Alemania, conforme al artículo 15, apartado 2, de la Ley de Introducción al Código Civil

(EGBGB), da respuesta a esta pregunta, pero les exige soportar un fraccionamiento del régimen matrimonial que puede llevar a dificultades de cálculo a la hora de la disolución del régimen económico matrimonial. Las tradiciones completamente diferentes con las que se encuentran las parejas alemanas en la República Francesa les plantearán problemas similares. También en los otros países de la Unión Europea el derecho matrimonial nacional tiene formas muy diferentes.

Ante esta situación es necesario crear regulaciones a nivel internacional que sean lo más comparables o idénticas posible y que proporcionen claridad y seguridad jurídica a los afectados. Por esta razón, se buscan respuestas comunes a nivel europeo a las preguntas de cuál es el derecho nacional aplicable a matrimonios con cónyuges de distinta nacionalidad y cuáles son los tribunales competentes. En cambio, dadas las diferentes tradiciones jurídicas, que a menudo son el resultado de un proceso evolutivo de varios siglos y que cuentan con un profundo arraigo en la población, actualmente no está en la agenda europea una armonización de los contenidos del derecho de familia en los Estados miembros.

Por este motivo, el enfoque utilizado en este Acuerdo, o sea, el de actuar primero de forma bilateral y para un marco jurídico limitado a fin de conseguir lo antes posible soluciones para los cónyuges afectados, promete ser un camino eficiente.

Para esta armonización existe también un mandato político para la República Francesa y la República Federal de Alemania. De la declaración conjunta con motivo del 40 aniversario del Tratado del Elíseo en el año 2003 surge la voluntad de armonizar el derecho de familia alemán y francés.

2. LÍNEAS GENERALES DEL VIGENTE DERECHO INTERNACIONAL PRIVADO

Las normas de conflicto en materia de regímenes económicos matrimoniales (*die güterrechtlichen Kollisionsvorschriften*) de la República Federal de Alemania y de la República Francesa son relativamente parecidas, especialmente en lo que se refiere a las posibilidades de elección del Derecho aplicable, conforme al artículo 15, apartado 2, EGBGB, que dispone que los cónyuges podrán elegir el derecho alemán si al menos un cónyuge tiene nacionalidad alemana o reside de forma habitual en la República Federal de Alemania. Para bienes inmuebles que se encuentren en la República Federal de Alemania también se puede elegir el derecho alemán.

En la República Francesa se puede elegir el derecho francés para los efectos económicos del matrimonio, conforme al Convenio de La Haya del 14 de marzo de 1978 sobre la Ley aplicable a los regímenes matrimoniales. Además de los requisitos conocidos en el derecho alemán, este convenio contiene otro supuesto:

los cónyuges pueden elegir el derecho francés si uno de los cónyuges establece su residencia habitual en la República Francesa después de la celebración del matrimonio.

3. CONTENIDO SUSTANCIAL DEL ACUERDO

Con motivo del Consejo de Ministros franco-alemán que se celebró el 4 de febrero de 2010 en París, las ministras de Justicia de ambos países firmaron el Acuerdo sobre el régimen opcional de participación en las ganancias. Con este Acuerdo se pretendía crear por primera vez un Derecho sustantivo uniforme en el ámbito del derecho de familia para la República Federal de Alemania y la República Francesa con el que se normalizaría un régimen matrimonial opcional idéntico en la República Federal de Alemania y en la República Francesa. En su estructura básica, este régimen opcional se corresponde con el régimen alemán de participación en las ganancias, aunque también comporta modificaciones que tienen en consideración la tradición jurídica francesa. Los cónyuges en ambos países podrán elegir este régimen matrimonial en lugar del régimen legal supletorio o de alguno de los otros regímenes opcionales. Con ello se persigue ofrecer a los cónyuges un régimen económico matrimonial opcional idéntico tanto en la República Francesa como en la República Federal de Alemania que elimina así, en ambos Estados, las dificultades jurídicas que puedan surgir respecto a normas de regímenes matrimoniales extranjeros desconocidos.

II. DETALLES

En lo que concierne a la génesis del Acuerdo y al contenido de sus disposiciones individuales, remitimos al informe explicativo. Este informe se adjunta al presente memorando en los idiomas alemán y francés.

Sobre el artículo 1

Conforme al artículo 1, el régimen opcional de participación en las ganancias puede ser elegido por los cónyuges cuyo régimen económico matrimonial se rija por el derecho sustantivo de uno de los Estados contratantes. Puede ser elegido, por lo tanto, siempre y cuando sea de aplicación el derecho francés o el derecho alemán al régimen matrimonial de los cónyuges. No es necesario que uno o ambos cónyuges sean de distinta nacionalidad: un matrimonio que vive en la República Federal de Alemania sin vínculo alguno con la República Francesa podrá estipular este régimen en capitulaciones matrimoniales.

Sobre el artículo 2

El artículo 2 dispone que el patrimonio de los cónyuges en el régimen opcional de participación en las ganancias se mantiene separado y las "ganancias" están constituidas por el montante resultante de la diferencia entre el patrimonio final de un cónyuge y su patrimonio inicial. Por principio, las ganancias se compensan sólo en el momento de la disolución del régimen matrimonial.

Sobre el artículo 3

El establecimiento del régimen matrimonial se lleva a cabo, conforme al artículo 3, apartado 1, mediante capitulaciones matrimoniales. El artículo 3, apartado 2, dispone que las capitulaciones podrán otorgarse antes o después de celebrado el matrimonio; pero los efectos no pueden producirse con anterioridad a la fecha de la celebración del matrimonio.

Sobre los artículos 4 a 6

El artículo 4 establece que cada cónyuge puede disponer libremente de su patrimonio. Pero el artículo 5, apartado 1, excluye de este principio la capacidad de un cónyuge de disponer sobre objetos del ajuar doméstico y sobre derechos por medio de los cuales se garantiza la vivienda familiar, y somete esta disposición al consentimiento del otro cónyuge. Además, conforme al artículo 6, apartado 1, los contratos relativos al mantenimiento del hogar familiar y a la educación de los hijos obligan solidariamente a los cónyuges, salvo que un cónyuge contraiga obligaciones pecuniarias manifiestamente excesivas con respecto al nivel de vida de los cónyuges, y ello sea conocido o debería ser conocido por la otra parte contratante (artículo 6, apartado 2).

Sobre los artículos 7 a 14

Conforme al artículo 7, el régimen matrimonial se disuelve con la muerte o la declaración de fallecimiento de uno de los cónyuges, con el cambio del régimen matrimonial o con la sentencia de divorcio o cualquier otra disposición judicial que motive la disolución del régimen matrimonial. Para el cálculo de la participación se requiere la comparación entre los respectivos patrimonios iniciales y finales de los cónyuges. Los artículos 8 y 9 contienen las disposiciones relevantes para la valoración del patrimonio originario; el patrimonio final se calcula conforme a los artículos 10 y 11. El patrimonio originario es el patrimonio de cada uno de los cónyuges en la fecha de entrada en vigor del régimen matrimonial, el patrimonio final es el patrimonio en la fecha de disolución del régimen matrimonial. Las obligaciones de cada cónyuge se tendrán en cuenta aunque su importe exceda del importe del activo. Conforme al artículo 12, el cónyuge que haya experimentado menor incremento podrá exigir del otro cónyuge la mitad de la diferencia como participación. No obstante, y conforme al artículo 14, la participación está limitada a la mitad del valor del patrimonio final del cónyuge deudor.

Sobre los artículos 15 a 18

Los artículos 15 a 18 contienen disposiciones sobre la prescripción, la obligación mutua de los cónyuges de informar para el cálculo de la participación, el aplazamiento y la participación anticipada en las ganancias. Esta última podría darse especialmente en los casos de actos de disposición fraudulentos de un cónyuge en perjuicio de la participación del otro.

Acerca de los artículos 19 a 23

El artículo 19 establece que el Acuerdo solo será aplicable a capitulaciones matrimoniales que se otorguen después de su entrada en vigor. Conforme al artículo 20, apartado 1, el Acuerdo requiere la ratificación de ambos Estados y conforme al artículo 20, apartado 2, entrará en vigor al día siguiente al intercambio de los instrumentos de ratificación. Los documentos de ratificación se depositarán ante el Gobierno de la República Federal de Alemania. Conforme al artículo 21, el Acuerdo está abierto a la adhesión del resto de los Estados miembros de la Unión Europea. El artículo 22 contiene una disposición acerca de los idiomas del Acuerdo y el artículo 23 regula que la República Federal de Alemania registrará el Acuerdo inmediatamente después de su entrada en vigor ante las Naciones Unidas.

INFORME EXPLICATIVO

A. PRESENTACIÓN GENERAL

1. SITUACIÓN DE PARTIDA

Los matrimonios entre personas de diferentes nacionalidades ya no son raros hoy en día. En Alemania, en aproximadamente el 13% de los matrimonios (en 2006) y de los divorcios (en 2005) los cónyuges tenían nacionalidades distintas.

En el año 2006, en Francia el porcentaje de matrimonios con cónyuges de distinta nacionalidad era del 14,59%. Además, en el año 2003, en Francia los matrimonios franco-alemanes constituían el 2% de todos los matrimonios de distinta nacionalidad.

El régimen económico matrimonial regula los efectos jurídicos del matrimonio sobre el patrimonio de los cónyuges, las relaciones jurídico-patrimoniales de los cónyuges entre ellos y las relaciones jurídico-patrimoniales de los cónyuges con terceros. La determinación del régimen matrimonial no es relevante solamente en lo que concierne a las relaciones jurídico-patrimoniales de los cónyuges cuando se disuelve el régimen matrimonial. El régimen económico matrimonial también tiene efectos constante el matrimonio, por ejemplo sobre la administración y adquisición de bienes, así como sobre la responsabilidad de uno de los cónyuges con respecto a las obligaciones contraídas por el otro cónyuge antes o durante el matrimonio.

El derecho internacional privado de los Estados concede a los cónyuges, en determinados casos, la elección del derecho aplicable a su régimen matrimonial.

Los cónyuges pueden elegir someter su régimen económico matrimonial al derecho francés o alemán, según determinados criterios.

Así el derecho internacional privado alemán (artículo 15, apartado 2, EGBGB, *Einführungsgesetz zum Bürgerlichen Gesetzbuche*) concede a los cónyuges la posibilidad de someter los efectos de su régimen matrimonial al derecho alemán en los siguientes casos:

- uno de los cónyuges posee la nacionalidad alemana;
- uno de los cónyuges tiene su residencia habitual en Alemania;
- los cónyuges poseen bienes inmuebles en Alemania, exclusivamente en lo que concierne a estos bienes.

Si los cónyuges no han elegido ningún derecho aplicable, se aplican los criterios objetivos del artículo 15, apartado 1, en relación al artículo 14 EGBGB. Conforme a ello, se aplicará el régimen legal alemán si ambos cónyuges son alemanes o si tienen su residencia habitual en Alemania durante el matrimonio.

Conforme al derecho francés, el Convenio de La Haya del 14 de marzo de 1978 sobre la Ley aplicable a los regímenes matrimoniales permite a los cónyuges someter los efectos de su régimen matrimonial al derecho francés en los siguientes casos:

- uno de los cónyuges posee la nacionalidad francesa;
- uno de los cónyuges tiene su residencia habitual en Francia;
- uno de los cónyuges, después de la celebración del matrimonio, establece su primera residencia habitual en Francia.

Además, los cónyuges pueden elegir el derecho francés para su bienes inmuebles situado en este país (artículo 3 del mencionado Convenio de La Haya).

De no elegirse un derecho aplicable por parte de los cónyuges, se aplicará a su régimen económico matrimonial el derecho del Estado en que hayan establecido su primera residencia habitual después de la celebración del matrimonio.

Si puede aplicarse al régimen económico matrimonial tanto el derecho alemán como el derecho francés, los cónyuges pueden elegir entre los siguientes regímenes existentes en Alemania o en Francia:

a) Régimen económico matrimonial alemán
   El régimen económico matrimonial alemán conoce tres regímenes matrimoniales:
   - La participación en las ganancias;
   - La separación de bienes;
   - La sociedad de gananciales.

   El régimen de participación en las ganancias es el régimen legal supletorio. Los otros regímenes matrimoniales sólo se aplican si los cónyuges así lo estipulan en capitulaciones matrimoniales.
b) Régimen económico matrimonial francés
   El régimen económico matrimonial francés también conoce tres tipos de regímenes matrimoniales:
   - La sociedad de gananciales (comunidad de bienes gananciales; comunidad de bienes muebles y ganancias; comunidad universal de bienes);
   - La participación en las ganancias;
   - La separación de bienes.

   El régimen legal supletorio en Francia es la sociedad de gananciales. Los otros regímenes matrimoniales sólo se aplican si los cónyuges así lo estipulan en capitulaciones matrimoniales.

Las diferencias entre los dos regímenes legales supletorios son considerables:

La participación en las ganancias conforme al derecho alemán supone la separación de bienes durante la vigencia del régimen matrimonial con compensación de la participación después de la disolución del régimen (§1363, apartado 2, del Código Civil alemán, BGB). El régimen económico matrimonial como tal, por lo tanto, no lleva a un patrimonio común de los cónyuges.[1] Más bien, cada cónyuge mantiene su patrimonio adquirido antes o durante el matrimonio como propiedad privativa, y como contrapartida sólo responde de sus deudas con su patrimonio propio.[2] En última instancia, ello se aplica también a un bien que pertenezca a ambos cónyuges en proporción a su cuota (la llamada comunidad por cuotas, *Bruchteilsgemeinschaft*).[3] Así, por ejemplo, en el caso de una casa que pertenezca a ambos cónyuges a partes iguales, cada cónyuge puede disponer en principio de su mitad.[4]

La sociedad de gananciales conforme al derecho francés, por otro lado, conoce tres masas de bienes diferentes: los bienes privativos de la esposa, los bienes privativos del esposo y los bienes comunes.

Conforme al artículo 1401 del Código Civil francés (CC) los bienes comunes se componen de los bienes gananciales que los cónyuges han adquirido durante el matrimonio, bien solos, bien en común. También forma parte todo aquello que se ha adquirido a través del propio trabajo y lo que se ha obtenido como fruto o beneficio de los bienes propios. Es cierto que cada cónyuge a priori puede administrar y disponer solo y por sí mismo de los bienes comunes, pero determinados actos únicamente pueden ser realizados conjuntamente por los dos cónyuges. Así, las donaciones entre vivos de bienes comunes sólo son posibles con el consentimiento del otro cónyuge. Adicionalmente, en Francia, conforme a normas del "*régime primaire*" que se aplican con independencia del régimen matrimonial, se puede limitar en especial la facultad de los cónyuges de disponer por sí solos de los bienes comunes.

De este modo, un cónyuge no puede disponer por sí solo de los derechos por medio de los cuales se garantiza la vivienda familiar, ni del ajuar doméstico[5] (denuncia del contrato de arrendamiento o venta de la vivienda familiar). Estas limitaciones se aplicarían incluso si la vivienda familiar fuera un bien privativo del cónyuge.

---

1 En la versión francesa: "No lleva a la creación de una sociedad de gananciales de los bienes o de las deudas".

2 En la versión francesa: "Por lo tanto, cada cónyuge conserva la administración, el goce y la libre disposición de sus bienes personales, adquiridos antes o constante el matrimonio. Por el contrario, cada cónyuge es responsable exclusivamente de sus deudas, contraídas antes o constante el matrimonio".

3 En la versión francesa: "Que es de propiedad indivisa de los cónyuges".

4 En la versión francesa: "Los cónyuges adquieran una casa en copropiedad, cada uno de ellos puede disponer únicamente de la parte indivisa que le pertenece".

5 En la versión francesa: "Bienes muebles mobiliarios".

2. CONVENIENCIA DE LA CREACIÓN DE UN RÉGIMEN MATRIMONIAL COMÚN

La creación de un régimen matrimonial común que se establece, funciona y se disuelve conforme a unas normas idénticas para los Estados contratantes, supone un progreso jurídico significativo para las parejas, para terceros y para quienes aplican el derecho. Con esta regulación del régimen matrimonial, en suma, se crea un derecho sustantivo común en los Estados contratantes.

Si los cónyuges eligen esta forma de comunidad, no surgirán las dificultades que actualmente resultan de la adopción de la sociedad de gananciales conforme al derecho francés, cuando los cónyuges adquieren durante su matrimonio un inmueble en Alemania. Dado que este régimen legal supletorio francés no es conocido en Alemania, la inscripción de un derecho de propiedad[6] en el Registro no permite a terceros estimar el alcance preciso de los derechos correspondientes a cada uno de los cónyuges. La solución que solemos encontrar en la práctica y que consiste en la elección del régimen legal alemán para el patrimonio localizado en Alemania (artículo 15, apartado 2, número 3, EGBGB), da una respuesta a esta cuestión, pero exige que los cónyuges soporten un fraccionamiento del régimen matrimonial que puede llevar a dificultades de cálculo a la hora de la liquidación del crédito de participación.

A la vista de esta situación de partida y dado que el régimen de participación en las ganancias existe tanto en el derecho francés como en el alemán (como régimen legal supletorio en Alemania y como régimen matrimonial opcional en Francia), parece oportuno crear mediante acuerdo bilateral un nuevo régimen matrimonial opcional adicional, que se asemeje mucho al régimen de participación en las ganancias ya existente en ambos Estados y que esté estructurado conforme a normas sencillas y modernas idénticas en Francia y en Alemania.

Para facilitar que otros Estados de la Unión Europea se adhieran con posterioridad, el Acuerdo prevé que, después de su entrada en vigor, cualquier Estado miembro de la Unión Europea pueda adherirse al Acuerdo (artículo 21).

B. PRESENTACIÓN DEL RÉGIMEN MATRIMONIAL

CAPÍTULO I. ÁMBITO DE APLICACIÓN Y DEFINICIÓN

Artículo 1. Ámbito de aplicación

El régimen opcional de participación en las ganancias estará abierto a todos los cónyuges cuyo régimen económico matrimonial se rija por el derecho de un

[6] En la versión francesa: "A nombre de los cónyuges en sociedad de gananciales".

Estado contratante, sin que sea necesario que uno o ámbos cónyuges tengan distinta nacionalidad. Por tanto, este régimen opcional podrá ser elegido por cónyuges cuyo régimen matrimonial esté sujeto al derecho francés, al alemán o al de un país tercero, conforme al derecho internacional privado aplicable.

Lo anterior vale, por ejemplo, en aplicación del derecho internacional privado francés o alemán para cónyuges

- cuando uno de ellos sea ciudadano francés o alemán;
- cuando uno de ellos tenga su residencia habitual en Francia o en Alemania;
- cuando uno de ellos establezca su primera residencia habitual en Francia;
- cuando uno de ellos tenga bienes inmuebles en Francia o en Alemania, por lo que concierne a dichos bienes.

Conforme a ello, el régimen opcional de participación en las ganancias puede ser aplicado,[7] por ejemplo, en los casos de dos alemanes que vivan en Francia o de dos franceses que vivan en Alemania, pero también de dos alemanes que vivan en Alemania y de dos franceses que vivan en Francia.

La elección de este régimen matrimonial no exige que los cónyuges elijan el derecho de un Estado contratante. Conforme al artículo 1 sólo es necesario que el régimen matrimonial se rija por el derecho sustantivo de un Estado contratante. En algunos casos, para evitar dudas por parte de los cónyuges, será recomendable que se especifique el derecho aplicable a su régimen matrimonial en sus capitulaciones matrimoniales, si lo permite el derecho internacional privado.

Artículo 2. Definición

"Participación en las ganancias" significa que durante la vigencia del régimen matrimonial existe una separación de bienes. El establecimiento del régimen económico matrimonial no afecta a las relaciones de propiedad ni a las obligaciones de los cónyuges. Por consiguiente, no existe una tercera masa de bienes común a ambos cónyuges que sí existe en los casos de comunidades de bienes.

Sólo con la disolución del régimen matrimonial se compensan entre los dos cónyuges los incrementos obtenidos en ambas masas de bienes durante el régimen matrimonial.[8]

7 En la versión francesa: "Puede ser elegido".

8 En la versión francesa: "Sólo con la disolución del régimen, se comparan las ganancias realizadas por cada uno de los cónyuges durante el régimen para determinar el crédito de participación que un cónyuge debe al otro".

CAPÍTULO II. ESTABLECIMIENTO DEL RÉGIMEN MATRIMONIAL

Artículo 3. Establecimiento del régimen matrimonial

Sobre el apartado 1:
Los cónyuges podrán convenir mediante capitulaciones matrimoniales que su régimen económico matrimonial será el régimen opcional de participación en las ganancias. Para la forma de estas capitulaciones se aplicará el derecho correspondiente conforme al respectivo derecho internacional privado. Es decir, el derecho aplicable en el lugar de otorgamiento de las capitulaciones o el derecho nacional aplicable al régimen matrimonial.[9]

Sobre el apartado 2:
Los cónyuges podrán pactar antes o después de la celebración del matrimonio que su régimen matrimonial sea el del régimen opcional de la participación en las ganancias. La posibilidad de otorgar capitulaciones antes del matrimonio puede evitar, por ejemplo, en el caso de la celebración de un matrimonio conforme al derecho francés,[10] que exista una sociedad de gananciales que habrá de ser liquidada posteriormente para poder establecer un nuevo régimen matrimonial.

Para la entrada en vigor del régimen opcional es condición necesaria que el matrimonio se celebre. Por esta razón, el régimen matrimonial opcional de participación en las ganancias puede surtir efecto sólo cuando el matrimonio se celebre. En Alemania no hay normas expresas para ello: resulta del §1408 BGB conforme al cual las partes contratantes han de ser cónyuges. En Francia resulta expresamente del artículo 1395 CC.

El régimen matrimonial común también podrá ser acordado durante el matrimonio.

Conforme al derecho alemán, los cónyuges pueden cambiar su régimen matrimonial en cualquier momento mediante capitulaciones matrimoniales, para así también prescindir del régimen legal supletorio de participación en las ganancias. Las capitulaciones matrimoniales surten efecto con la firma del contrato. A partir de ese momento se aplican entre los cónyuges las normas del nuevo régimen matrimonial.

En el interés de su familia, los cónyuges sujetos a un régimen matrimonial francés pueden acordar cambiar el régimen matrimonial después de un tiempo de aplicación de dos años (artículo 1397 CC). Este cambio surtirá efecto a partir

---

9 En la versión francesa: "Conforme a las reglas de derecho internacional privado alemán y francés, la forma del contrato debe respetar o el derecho interno vigente en el lugar de celebración del contrato o la ley interna aplicable al régimen económico matrimonial".

10 En la versión francesa: "En Francia".

de la fecha de la formalización del documento notarial[11] que prevé el cambio, siempre que los cónyuges no tengan hijos menores de edad y los hijos mayores de edad o los acreedores no se opongan al cambio. Por contra, en los dos casos mencionados anteriormente, el cambio de régimen matrimonial surtirá efecto desde que se dicte sentencia[12] firme.

Sobre el apartado 3:
El principio de la libertad contractual conforme al artículo 3, apartado 3, facilita a los cónyuges la posibilidad de apartarse, mediante contrato, de las normas para la determinación del crédito de participación. Les permite, por ejemplo, regular de otra manera la composición de los patrimonios, las reglas para la valoración de los bienes, la cuota de participación en el incremento patrimonial respectivo y la distribución de las ganancias. Con esta posibilidad de cambio se podrán tener en cuenta particularidades nacionales o las necesidades específicas de los cónyuges.

En la medida en que el texto establece que los cónyuges pueden dejar sin efecto las reglas del Capítulo V los cónyuges no pueden dejar sin efecto las reglas recogidas en los artículos 5 y 6, en los que se enumeran las principales disposiciones del "régime primaire" francés. Mediante la imposibilidad de esta derogación se garantiza una aplicación idéntica del régimen económico matrimonial común en Francia y en Alemania.

CAPÍTULO III. ADMINISTRACIÓN, GOCE Y DISPOSICIÓN DEL PATRIMONIO

El régimen matrimonial común está estructurado de tal forma que a los cónyuges se les aplica el régimen matrimonial de la separación de bienes. La separación de bienes tiene dos consecuencias.

Ante todo, los cónyuges mantienen la administración, el goce y la disposición de sus bienes personales. Además, cada cónyuge es responsable de las deudas asumidas por él o ella, antes o constante el matrimonio.

Aun así, la separación de los bienes de los cónyuges no es completa, ya que no pueden prescindir de la aplicación de determinadas disposiciones obligatorias.

En la medida en que las disposiciones que limitan los efectos de la separación de bienes de los cónyuges no son idénticas en Francia y en Alemania, el régimen matrimonial común acoge las principales disposiciones del "régime primaire" francés, para que el régimen matrimonial pueda funcionar de la misma manera en Francia y en Alemania (artículos 5 y 6).

---

11 En la versión francesa: "En la fecha del acto notarial".
12 En la versión francesa: "En la fecha de la sentencia".

Artículo 4. Disposiciones generales en materia de administración, goce y disposición del patrimonio

El objetivo del régimen matrimonial de participación en las ganancias es garantizar la independencia completa de los cónyuges en lo que a su patrimonio se refiere. Por lo tanto, cada uno de los cónyuges en principio deberá administrar, gozar y también disponer de sus bienes por sí solo y sin que sea necesario el consentimiento del otro cónyuge. Como contrapartida, cada cónyuge por sí solo será responsable de las deudas asumidas por él antes o durante el matrimonio.

Este principio de la separación de los patrimonios de los cónyuges está establecido en las normas alemanas de participación en las ganancias (§1364 BGB) y en las francesas (artículo 1569 CC). La administración autónoma del patrimonio incluye el derecho a adquirir bienes: por ejemplo, para comenzar una actividad profesional, para constituir una sociedad o para convertirse en socio, ningún cónyuge requiere el consentimiento del otro.

No obstante, esta separación de los patrimonios de los cónyuges contiene algunas limitaciones que se recogen en los artículos 5 y 6 de las normas del régimen matrimonial.

Dichas limitaciones se deben a las normas obligatorias del "*régime primaire*" francés (artículos 215 y 220 CC). Estas normas sustituyen al "*régime primaire*", sin perjuicio de las demás disposiciones de este régimen; éstas últimas se aplicarán conforme al principio de territorialidad.

Artículo 5. Limitaciones a la disposición

Generalidades:

En los ordenamientos jurídicos de ambos países, la administración de los bienes queda limitada en casos excepcionales para proteger al otro cónyuge.[13]

Para el régimen legal supletorio alemán de la participación en las ganancias, se prevé en los §§1365, 1369 BGB una prohibición de disponer del patrimonio por entero y de objetos del ajuar doméstico. Una vulneración de esta prohibición de disponer conlleva la ineficacia[14] del acto de disposición, si el otro cónyuge no presta su consentimiento. La ineficacia[15] entra en vigor automáticamente y es eficaz *erga omnes*.

Francia también conoce una prohibición de disponer en el caso de los derechos que garantizan la vivienda familiar y el ajuar doméstico. Eso significa, por ejemplo, que un cónyuge no puede denunciar[16] el contrato de arredamiento de la vivienda principal sin el consentimiento del otro cónyuge. Sin embargo,

---

13 En la versión francesa: "El derecho de un cónyuge a administrar de forma autónoma su patrimonio puede ser limitado en casos excepcionales para proteger al otro cónyuge".

14 En la versión francesa: "Nulidad".

15 En la versión francesa: "Nulidad".

16 En la versión francesa: "Rescindir".

una disposición que no cuente con el consentimiento del otro cónyuge no será automáticamente ineficaz,[17] tal y como lo sería en Alemania. Más concretamente, el cónyuge deberá interponer una demanda de nulidad.

La denuncia[18] también puede ser ratificada por el cónyuge que no había prestado su consentimiento.

En Francia, esta prohibición de disponer, que garantiza la vivienda conyugal y el ajuar doméstico con sus objetos, está recogida en el artículo 215 CC.

Para evitar que, si se elige el régimen matrimonial opcional de participación en las ganancias, se apliquen en ambos países diferentes prohibiciones por lo que atañe al derecho a la libre disposición sobre la vivienda familiar y los objetos del ajuar doméstico, el artículo 5 del régimen matrimonial común, que prevé la protección de la vivienda familiar conocida en el derecho francés, amplía la protección a los objetos del ajuar doméstico, a los que hace referencia el derecho alemán.[19]

La norma francesa sobre el ajuar doméstico (artículo 215 CC) no protege a los cónyuges tan ampliamente como el derecho alemán respecto a los objetos del ajuar doméstico. Por lo tanto, el régimen matrimonial común adopta la norma protectora alemana que se aplica, por ejemplo, también al vehículo necesario para las necesidades de la familia.

Una norma protectora adicional contra actos de disposición del patrimonio por entero, parecido al §1365 BGB, no parecía necesaria. Es de suponer que en muchos casos la vivienda familiar ya constituye la mayor parte del patrimonio. Si un cónyuge no puede disponer de su propiedad o de su copropiedad en el inmueble utilizado como vivienda familiar sin el consentimiento del otro cónyuge, la protección de este último está garantizada aún mejor que en el derecho alemán, ya que no depende de si esta propiedad constituye todo el patrimonio o sólo una parte conspicua (conforme a la jurisprudencia alemana, el 85% si se trata de patrimonios pequeños y menos del 90% si se trata de patrimonios más importantes).

Sobre el apartado 1:

El apartado 1 regula la limitación de la libre disposición de derechos sobre la vivienda familiar y los objetos del ajuar doméstico.

Forman parte de la vivienda familiar todas las habitaciones que los cónyuges usen como vivienda, en las que hayan vivido juntos o que, conforme a las

---

17 En la versión francesa: "Nula".

18 En la versión alemana: "El acto de rescisión de un contrato de ejecución duradera".

19 En la versión francesa: "Para evitar que la adopción del régimen opcional de la participación en las ganacias implique en los dos países diferentes límites de disposición por lo que concierne al derecho de disponer libremente de la vivienda familiar y de los objetos del ajuar doméstico, el artículo 5 del régimen de participación en las ganancias, que prevé la protección de la vivienda familiar conocida en el derecho francés, extiende esa protección a los objetos del ajuar doméstico, aludidos en el derecho alemán".

circunstancias, estaban destinadas a convertirse en domicilio familiar, aunque ello no haya llegado a realizarse. Por lo tanto, las habitaciones accesorias podrán ser parte de la vivienda familiar (por ejemplo sótano, desván, garaje, gimnasio).

El objetivo de la disposición del artículo 5 es la garantía integral de la protección de la familia en lo que a la vivienda familiar se refiere.

Actos de disposición sobre la propiedad o sobre la relación arrendaticia de la vivienda familiar sin el consentimiento del otro cónyuge en principio serán nulos. Eso significa que un cónyuge que sea propietario de la vivienda utilizada como domicilio familiar no puede vender la vivienda de forma eficaz sin el consentimiento del otro cónyuge. Tampoco el cónyuge que sea inquilino de un piso en el que viva su familia podrá rescindir el contrato de arrendamiento de forma eficaz sin el consentimiento del otro cónyuge, aunque el cónyuge que no haya consentido tal comportamiento sí podrá ratificar la rescisión.

La protección de la vivienda familiar, por la tanto, es muy amplia y también puede afectar los intereses de terceros. El arrendador de una vivienda que es domicilio familiar puede ser confrontado con la ineficacia de la rescisión del contrato de arrendamiento, aunque no haya tenido conocimiento del régimen matrimonial de los cónyuges y por tanto de la limitación de la libre disposición del cónyuge arrendatario.

Tampoco podrá disponer el propietario por sí solo de los objetos del ajuar doméstico, tanto si se encuentran dentro de la vivienda como si ya han sido retirados de ella. No obstante, el otro cónyuge podrá ratificar los actos de disposición de la vivienda familiar o de los objetos del ajuar doméstico.

Los efectos de la ineficacia[20] dependerán de los ordenamientos jurídicos de ambos países.

En Francia, la ineficacia tendrá que ser reclamada mediante demanda de nulidad. Así resulta del artículo 215, apartado 3, CC que parte de una norma del "*régime primaire*" francés, que no se ha incorporado al régimen matrimonial común, pero que sigue aplicándose a todos los cónyuges residentes en Francia, independientemente de su régimen matrimonial.

En Alemania, por el contrario, tal disposición conllevará automáticamente la ineficacia *erga omnes,* si falta el consentimiento del otro cónyuge. Contrariamente al derecho francés, no es necesaria una demanda para la reclamación de la ineficacia. En caso de conflicto se podrá interponer directamente una acción reivindicatoria.

Los procedimientos que supongan la reclamación de consecuencias legales relacionadas con la vulneración de la regla introducida mediante este artículo estarán sujetos a los respectivos ordenamientos nacionales. Por consiguiente, en Francia se aplicará a la demanda de nulidad el artículo 215, apartado 3, CC.

[20] En la versión francesa: "Nulidad".

Sobre el apartado 2:
Un cónyuge no podrá disponer sin el otro sobre derechos que garanticen la vivienda familiar u objetos del ajuar doméstico. Pero si el cónyuge no puede manifestar su voluntad, por ejemplo, porque su salud no se lo permite, o si niega su consentimiento sin que necesidades de la familia justifiquen su negativa, un Juzgado podrá autorizar al cónyuge a realizar por sí solo los actos contenidos en el apartado 1.

La autorización del Juzgado en caso de incapacidad por enfermedad del cónyuge a presentar su consentimiento se parece al derecho de administración en caso de necesidad del §1454 BGB, pero corresponde, en el fondo, a un procedimiento simplificado de nombramiento de un curador encargado de dar el "consentimiento para un determinado negocio jurídico".

Esta solución, cuyo objetivo principal es el de impedir que un cónyuge niegue su consentimiento arbitrariamente, sólo para perjudicar al otro cónyuge, se ha adoptado del "régime primaire" francés (artículo 217, apartado 1, CC).

Artículo 6. Negocios referentes al mantenimiento del hogar familiar

Sobre el apartado 1:
El artículo 1 regula cuáles son los negocios que se podrán realizar y que también tendrán efectos para el otro cónyuge.

Así, conforme al principio general de la separación de patrimonios, cada uno de los cónyuges podrá celebrar por sí solo los contratos para el mantenimiento del hogar (por ejemplo, podrá adquirir objetos para el ajuar doméstico). No obstante, apartándose del principio de la separación de bienes, estos contratos determinan que el cónyuge, que en principio no es parte del contrato y no ha consentido la firma del mismo, aún así quedará vinculado por el contrato y responderá solidariamente de las obligaciones resultantes del mismo.

Lo mismo se aplicará a los contratos relacionados con las necesidades de los hijos. De este modo, por ejemplo, el otro cónyuge también responderá solidariamente de las obligaciones del contrato de un cónyuge con un profesor particular.

Sobre el apartado 2:
El apartado 2 prevé que la obligación común anteriormente mencionada quedará excluida si los dos siguientes requisitos se encuentran presentes a la vez:

- Que se trate de gastos desproporcionados[21] y
- Que el tercero contratante conociera los gastos desproporcionados[22] o debiera haberlos conocido.

---

21 En la versión francesa: "Manifiestamente excesivos".
22 En la versión francesa: "Manifiestamente excesivos".

Esta limitación de la obligación común es necesaria para proteger al otro cónyuge que no deberá ser responsable de los gastos desproporcionados[23] de su cónyuge. La valoración del carácter desproporcionado se regirá por el nivel de vida de ambos cónyuges. Así por ejemplo, la adquisición de un costoso mueble antiguo puede ser un gasto a todas luces desproporcionado, si ambos cónyuges disponen solo de pocos ingresos. En un caso así, el otro cónyuge no estará vinculado por el contrato, si la otra parte contratante lo sabía o debería haberlo sabido.[24]

Esta disposición es una adopción modernizada del artículo 220 CC. Los cónyuges residentes en Francia, que hayan pactado el régimen matrimonial común, estarán sujetos al artículo 6.

La norma adoptada no es contraria al derecho alemán. Es cierto que va más allá del §1357 BGB: pero los cónyuges la tendrán que aceptar si ellos mismos han elegido mediante capitulaciones el régimen matrimonial opcional de participación en las ganancias. Con ello, también han adoptado[25] voluntariamente la disposición del artículo 6.

CAPÍTULO IV. DISOLUCIÓN DEL RÉGIMEN MATRIMONIAL

Artículo 7. Causas de disolución del régimen matrimonial

El momento de la disolución del régimen económico matrimonial es decisivo, porque a partir de este momento se llevará a cabo la determinación del crédito de participación conforme a la composición y al valor del patrimonio de los cónyuges.

El artículo 7 prevé que el régimen matrimonial se extingue en los siguientes casos:

- con la muerte o la declaración de fallecimiento[26] de uno de los cónyuges;
- con el cambio del régimen matrimonial;
- con la sentencia de divorcio o cualquier otra decisión judicial que motive la disolución del régimen matrimonial.

Con la primera disposición se deja claro que una declaración de fallecimiento terminará el régimen matrimonial también en los casos en los que esta declaración sea incorrecta.

Con la segunda disposición se deja claro que también un cambio de régimen matrimonial extinguirá el régimen matrimonial opcional de participación en las

---

23 En la versión francesa: "No razonables".

24 En la versión francesa: "En ese caso, el otro cónyuge no se estará obligado solidariamente si el tercero no tenía conocimeinto del carácter manifiestamente excesivo".

25 En la versión francesa: "Aceptado".

26 En la versión francesa: "Declaración de ausencia".

ganancias. En efecto, en Alemania el régimen matrimonial puede ser cambiado mediante la elección de otro régimen en capitulaciones matrimoniales. Asimismo, los cónyuges que tienen establecido un régimen matrimonial francés pueden acordar cambiar, en el interés de la familia, el régimen matrimonial dos años después de su aplicación.

La tercera disposición recoge otros motivos para la disolución del régimen económico matrimonial.[27]

En Francia ello se corresponde con la separación sin disolución del vínculo matrimonial, la declaración de la nulidad del matrimonio en el caso de cónyuges de buena fe y de la liquidación anticipada del crédito de participación.

En Alemania comprende decisiones sobre el crédito de participación anticipado y sobre la disolución del matrimonio por causa de nulidad.

CAPÍTULO V. DETERMINACIÓN DEL CRÉDITO DE PARTICIPACIÓN EN EL MOMENTO DE LA DISOLUCIÓN DEL RÉGIMEN MATRIMONIAL

SECCIÓN 1. PATRIMONIO INICIAL

Artículo 8. Composición del patrimonio inicial

Sobre los apartados 1 y 2:

En los apartados 1 y 2 se describen los bienes que serán parte del patrimonio originario.

El patrimonio originario comprenderá tres tipos de bienes:

a) Los bienes que pertenecen al cónyuge en el momento en el que entra en vigor el régimen matrimonial.
   En muchos casos, los cónyuges otorgarán capitulaciones matrimoniales antes de celebrar el matrimonio. Dado que, conforme al artículo 3, la fecha más temprana para la eficacia de las capitulaciones matrimoniales es la celebración del matrimonio, la fecha más temprana para la entrada en vigor del régimen matrimonial será la fecha de la celebración del matrimonio.
b) Los bienes que un cónyuge adquiera más tarde a título de herencia o donación. Los ordenamientos jurídicos de ambos países disponen que los aumentos del patrimonio por donación o por herencia han de sumarse al patrimonio inicial (Alemania: §1374 apartado 2 BGB; Francia: artículo 1570 CC).
c) El patrimonio[28] posteriormente adquirido por un cónyuge en concepto de reparación de daños materiales o morales.

---

27 En la versión alemana: "Disolución del matrimonio".

28 En la versión francesa: "Las indemnizaciones".

En el derecho francés, las indemnizaciones son parte del patrimonio inicial. En Alemania, en el régimen legal supletorio de la participación en las ganancias no lo son, pero sí se discute una y otra vez acerca de la naturaleza personalísima de este crédito. Incluso si se rechaza una ampliación del patrimonio privativo por otros supuestos en el §1374, apartado 2, BGB,[29] las partes están libres de convenir tal inclusión en el patrimonio inicial.

El objetivo de la participación en las ganancias es igualar el incremento del patrimonio conseguido por ambos cónyuges durante la vigencia del régimen económico matrimonial. Por otro lado, hay incrementos patrimoniales que se han conseguido independientemente de la participación o de los esfuerzos de los cónyuges y que, por lo tanto, no han de ser compensados. Lo dicho se aplica especialmente a los bienes mencionados en los anteriores puntos b) y c) y a los bienes que un cónyuge haya adquirido por herencia, donación o como indemnizaciones de daños sufridos (*pretium doloris*). Por todo ello, estos bienes conforme al apartado 2 se sumarán al patrimonio inicial y se excluirán del crédito de participación.

En su autonomía privada, las partes serán libres de convenir que otros incrementos de patrimonio, no mencionados en el apartado 1, también sean imputados al patrimonio inicial. Los cónyuges podrán incluir un pacto a este respecto en sus capitulaciones matrimoniales (ver artículo 3, apartado 3, de la regulación del régimen matrimonial).

El patrimonio inicial es el patrimonio que pertenece a un cónyuge, después de restar sus obligaciones, en la fecha establecida para su determinación. El patrimonio inicial no es ninguna masa de bienes concreta, sino uno de los dos parámetros de cálculo para la determinación de las ganancias.

Las obligaciones podrán ser restadas incluso si superan el volumen del activo. Eso significa que el patrimonio inicial también podrá ser negativo.

Las disposiciones correspondientes se encuentran en el derecho francés (artículos 1570, 1571 CC) y en el derecho alemán (§1374 BGB). Al contrario que la normativa francesa, la normativa alemana vigente preveía que el patrimonio no podía ser negativo y permitía la deducción de obligaciones sólo hasta el montante del activo. Pero esta normativa llevaba siendo criticada mucho tiempo. Con la reforma del régimen de participación del 1 de septiembre de 2009 se estableció que el patrimonio inicial negativo sería admitido en el futuro.

Sobre el apartado 3:
Bienes excluidos del patrimonio inicial:

a) Los frutos de este patrimonio.

---

[29] En la versión francesa: "Aunque el artículo 1347, apartado 2, BGB, no permite ampliar el activo reservado a otros supuestos ".

Con esta disposición se deja claro que los frutos del patrimonio inicial, por ejemplo, los ingresos del alquiler de una vivienda en propiedad, no serán incluidos en el patrimonio inicial, sino que constituirán bienes gananciales.
Esta idea básica también se encuentra en los ordenamientos jurídicos de ambos países (Alemania: §1374 apartado 2 BGB; Francia: Artículo 1570 CC).

b) Los bienes del patrimonio inicial donados por un cónyuge a parientes en línea recta durante la vigencia del régimen matrimonial.
Si un cónyuge ha donado bienes del patrimonio inicial a parientes en línea recta durante la vigencia del régimen matrimonial, conforme al apartado 3, número 2, éstos quedarán completamente excluidos en el momento del cálculo del crédito de participación. Por esta razón no se tendrán en cuenta ni para el patrimonio inicial, ni para el patrimonio final. Esta disposición se apoya en el derecho francés.
Los posibles aumentos de valor por mejoras que se realicen en tal bien y que no procedan del patrimonio inicial, serán tenidos en cuenta para el patrimonio final[30] (véase el artículo 10 sobre la composición del patrimonio final).

Esta normativa constituye un compromiso entre el derecho alemán, que atribuye de esta manera bienes donados al patrimonio inicial, y el derecho francés, que permite donaciones del patrimonio inicial sin que se tengan en cuenta para la determinación de las ganancias, con la excepción de los aumentos de valor experimentados por el patrimonio donado.[31]

Sobre el apartado 4:
Para evitar controversias sobre el montante del patrimonio en el momento de la disolución del régimen matrimonial, parece oportuno encargar a un notario la realización de un inventario del patrimonio inicial en el momento del otorgamiento de las capitulaciones matrimoniales. Pero también es posible que los cónyuges realicen un inventario en un documento privado.

Este inventario del patrimonio inicial se considerará exacto si ha sido firmado por ambos cónyuges. No es preceptiva la forma notarial. La presunción de exactitud podrá ser refutada probando su inexactitud. También puede ser oportuno incorporar el valor de los bienes del patrimonio inicial a la hora de elaborar el inventario. En este caso la presunción de exactitud se extiende también a ese valor, siempre que conforme al artículo 9, apartado 1, número 1, estos bienes hayan sido valorados en la fecha de la entrada en vigor del régimen

30 En la versión francesa: "Sin embargo, se calculará en el patrimonio final la plusvalía aportada por esos bienes si la plusvalía no ha sido producida por frutos que derivan del patrimonio inicial".

31 En la versión francesa: "Esta normativa constituye un compromiso entre el derecho alemán, que prevé que los bienes donados se calculen en el patrimonio inicial, y el derecho francés, que prevé que los bienes del patrimonio inicial puedan ser donados a cualquiera, sin que ello implique, prescindiendo de las plusvalías realizadas con estos bienes, efectos en el cálculo de las ganancias".

matrimonial (o en la fecha de su adquisición cuando se trate de bienes conforme al artículo 8, apartado 2).

Los ordenamientos jurídicos de ambos países conocen tales inventarios, cuya exactitud se presume (Alemania: §1377 BGB; Francia: Artículo 1570 CC).

Sobre el apartado 5:
Si los cónyuges no han realizado un inventario del patrimonio, se presumirá que el patrimonio inicial no existe. También esta presunción podrá ser refutada.

Artículo 9. Valoración del patrimonio inicial

Generalidades:
Por parecidas que sean en principio las disposiciones de ambos países acerca de sus respectivos regímenes matrimoniales de participación en las ganancias, hay un punto muy importante en el que son muy diferentes: la valoración del patrimonio inicial.

A la hora de valorar los bienes del patrimonio inicial, Francia siempre aplica el valor que estos bienes tienen en el momento de la disolución del régimen económico matrimonial (artículo 1571 CC).

En cambio, Alemania se basa en el valor que el patrimonio tenía en el momento de la entrada en vigor del régimen matrimonial (§1376, apartado 1, BGB). Ahora bien, conforme a la jurisprudencia, los aumentos de valor que se deban a la inflación normal no constituyen ganancias y, por lo tanto, no se tendrán en cuenta.

Estos momentos de valoración diferentes pueden tener, por ejemplo, las siguientes consecuencias duraderas:[32]

- Conforme a la normativa francesa y en contra de la normativa alemana, los cónyuges soportan el riesgo de la depreciación de bienes del patrimonio inicial.
  Ejemplo Alemania:
  Un cónyuge aporta al régimen matrimonial, como único elemento patrimonial, una cartera de acciones. Al comienzo del régimen matrimonial tiene un valor de 100.000 euros. En el momento de la disolución del régimen matrimonial la cartera de acciones solo vale 20.000 euros. El patrimonio final del cónyuge es de un total de 100.000 euros (incluida la cartera de acciones). Por lo tanto, el cónyuge no habrá obtenido ganancias en las que el otro cónyuge tendría que participar.
  Ejemplo Francia:
  Situación de partida igual que en el ejemplo de arriba. El patrimonio inicial del cónyuge se tasa en 20.000 euros. El patrimonio final en 100.000 euros

32 En la versión francesa: "Negativas".

(20.000 y 80.000). Por lo tanto, el cónyuge ha obtenido una ganancia de 80.000 euros en la que el otro cónyuge participará con un crédito de participación de 40.000 euros (si el otro cónyuge no ha obtenido ninguna ganancia).

- Según el derecho alemán, en contra de la normativa francesa, el cónyuge participará en incrementos de valor del patrimonio inicial que se produzcan sin su contribución (con la excepción de cambios de valor que se deban a fluctuaciones monetarias, que no se tendrán en cuenta). De este modo, se produce una ganancia, por ejemplo, cuando una propiedad inmobiliaria permanece sin cambios pero, a causa de su ubicación, gana en valor a lo largo del tiempo. Conforme al derecho francés, en cambio, no se producen ganancias.
  Ejemplo Alemania:
  Un cónyuge aporta una finca al régimen matrimonial, que al comienzo del régimen tiene un valor de 100.000 euros. En el momento de la disolución del régimen matrimonial la finca tiene un valor de 200.000 euros porque el terreno ha sido recalificado. La ganancia en la que habrá de participar el otro cónyuge, por lo tanto, es de 100.000 euros. Con ello, el cónyuge con derecho a compensación recibirá 50.000 euros (si el mismo no ha obtenido ninguna ganancia).
  Ejemplo Francia:
  Situación de partida igual que en el ejemplo de arriba. La finca será valorada en 200.000 euros tanto en el patrimonio inicial como en el patrimonio final. No se habrá producido ninguna ganancia en la que el otro cónyuge habría de participar.

Para tener en cuenta tanto las normas nacionales alemanas como las francesas, en el artículo 11 se ha concebido un modelo de valoración que se inspira en los dos ordenamientos jurídicos:

Sobre el apartado 1:
El apartado 1, número 1, entronca con el modelo de valoración alemán. Los bienes existentes en la fecha de inicio del régimen económico matrimonial se valoran en esta fecha.

Eso significa que el cónyuge, al que no pertenece un bien, participará en los incrementos de valor de estos bienes, aunque éstos se produzcan sin su intervención (con la excepción de cambios de valor que se deban a fluctuaciones monetarias). Por ejemplo, si el patrimonio inicial de un cónyuge incluye un cuadro que aumenta de valor durante los años de duración del matrimonio, porque el artista es cada vez más conocido, el incremento de valor se incorpora a las ganancias.

Para los bienes privativos[33] (donaciones, herencias, indemnizaciones de daños no patrimoniales),[34] que hayan sido adquiridos posteriormente, pero que conforme al artículo 8, apartado 2, son parte del patrimonio inicial, la fecha de valoración conforme al apartado 1 número 2 es la fecha en la que se haya adquirido este patrimonio.

Sobre el apartado 2:
El apartado 2 dispone que los inmuebles y otros derechos reales inmobiliarios del patrimonio inicial, excepto los derechos de usufructo, uso y habitación, sean valorados en la fecha de la disolución del régimen matrimonial. Por lo tanto, el método de valoración descrito en el apartado 2 se aplicará a los derechos reales relevantes, que no estén constituidos de por vida (renta vitalicia). Estos elementos patrimoniales se valorarán con su valor en la fecha de la disolución del régimen matrimonial o en la fecha establecida en los casos especiales conforme al artículo 13.

El *sentido y finalidad* de esta norma es excluir de las ganancias el incremento de valor de los inmuebles del patrimonio inicial que se haya producido sin la intervención de uno de los cónyuges. Los inmuebles a menudo representan una parte significativa del patrimonio y pueden estar sujetos a variaciones de valor, que por regla general no se deben a los esfuerzos de los cónyuges. Ello sucede, por ejemplo, cuando el valor de una vivienda familiar del patrimonio inicial sube y el incremento se debe exclusivamente a la revalorización de su ubicación. Así, el valor de un inmueble puede subir de forma significativa porque, por ejemplo, se cierra un aeropuerto cercano y, por lo tanto, ya no hay contaminación acústica. En un caso como este, sí está justificado[35] no permitir participar al otro cónyuge en tales incrementos de valor.

Los incrementos de valor de inmuebles que se deben a esfuerzos comunes de los cónyuges, en cambio, sí representan una ganancia. Por consiguiente, no aumentarán el valor del patrimonio inicial.

Ejemplo:

Un cónyuge ha aportado al régimen matrimonial un terreno (valor al comienzo del régimen matrimonial de, por ejemplo, 50.000 euros) en el que se ha construido una casa constante el régimen. En el momento de la disolución del régimen matrimonial, el terreno solo, sin casa, tiene un valor de 100.000 euros, porque la ubicación del terreno ha hecho aumentar su valor.[36] El terreno con casa tiene un valor de 200.000 euros al finalizar el régimen matrimonial. A la hora de valorar el patrimonio inicial, se aplicará solo el valor del terreno con su importe en el momento de la disolución del

[33] En la versión francesa: "Reservados".
[34] En la versión francesa: "Sumas abonadas como indemnización de los perjuicios".
[35] En la versión francesa: "Es lógico".
[36] En la versión francesa: "Habiendo aumentado el terreno su valor".

régimen matrimonial: 100.000 euros. (El incremento de valor de 50.000 euros que se ha producido durante el matrimonio a causa de la ubicación no significa una ganancia). A la hora de determinar el patrimonio final se tiene en cuenta el terreno con la casa para el cónyuge propietario: 200.000 euros.[37] La ganancia, por lo tanto, es de 100.000 euros. Sin otras ganancias, el crédito de participación del otro cónyuge es de 50.000 euros.

Si se han vendido o sustituido inmuebles u otros derechos reales significativos no constituidos de forma vitalicia durante los años de matrimonio, éstos se contabilizarán con su valor en la fecha de su venta o sustitución.

Ejemplo:

Situación de partida como arriba (se aporta un terreno al régimen económico matrimonial y durante la existencia de dicho régimen se construye una casa en el mismo). Durante el matrimonio se vende el terreno con la casa. En el momento de la venta, el terreno tiene un valor de 80.000 euros y la casa un valor de 100.000 euros. Para el patrimonio inicial, sólo se contabilizará el valor del terreno por un importe de 80.000, cuyo valor ha de ser actualizado conforme al apartado 3. Para el patrimonio final será determinante el resto del patrimonio total que el cónyuge tenga.[38] El resultado de la venta solo se reflejará en el patrimonio final si todavía queda algo de los beneficios generados por dicha venta. Por ejemplo: si el cónyuge, al finalizar el régimen matrimonial, no tiene más de 80.000 euros, entonces no ha obtenido ninguna ganancia que tenga que compensar.

Los derechos de usufructo, uso y habitación estarán exentos de esta regla porque los cónyuges habrán disminuido el valor de estos derechos mediante su utilización.

Sobre el apartado 3:

Según el caso, un matrimonio puede durar muchos años. Sin embargo, conforme al apartado 1, el patrimonio inicial se valorará con un determinado valor monetario en el momento del comienzo del régimen matrimonial (o en la fecha de la adquisición de los bienes mencionados en el artículo 8, apartado 2). No obstante, este valor monetario puede disminuir a lo largo de los años a causa de la inflación. Pero simples incrementos de valor, que solo se producen a causa de la inflación, no deberán constituir una ganancia. Por ello, en el apartado 3 se crea una norma conforme a la cual el valor monetario del patrimonio inicial habrá de ser ajustado por la inflación.

---

37 En la versión francesa: "En el patrimonio final se tendrá en cuenta el terreno con la casa, por un valor de 200.000 euros".

38 En la versión francesa: " Para el patrimonio final será determinante la totalidad del activo que aún le queda al cónyuge".

Ejemplo:

(ficticio y sin tasas de variaciones de precios promediadas concretamente, ya que el régimen opcional de participación en las ganancias solo podrá ser aplicado a partir de la fecha de la ratificación del Acuerdo):

Al comienzo del régimen matrimonial el cónyuge tiene un patrimonio de 100.000 euros. El matrimonio dura diez años. Al finalizar el régimen matrimonial, el cónyuge tiene un patrimonio final de 200.000 euros. De forma ficticia, se supone que los 100.000 euros al comienzo del régimen matrimonial diez años antes, se corresponden con un valor monetario de 150.000 euros al finalizar el régimen. Como consecuencia, el patrimonio inicial habrá de fijarse en 150.000 euros y el patrimonio final en 200.000 euros. Las ganancias, por tanto, son de 50.000 euros, el crédito de participación es de 25.000 euros, si el otro cónyuge no ha obtenido ganancias propias.

Francia no permite actualizaciones que se basen en el índice general de precios o en el precio de bienes, productos y servicios y no tengan ninguna conexión inmediata con el objeto del Acuerdo o con la actividad de una de las partes (artículo L. 112–2, apartado 1, del Código monetario y financiero francés, *Code monétaire et financier*). No obstante, en tanto en cuanto el artículo 55 de la Constitución francesa prevé el principio de la primacía de los acuerdos interestatales sobre las leyes, el mecanismo de actualización elegido podrá aplicarse de forma válida en el marco del régimen económico matrimonial común.

Cuando otros Estados se adhieran al Acuerdo, la tasa de variación media de precios se determinará con las tasas de variación de precios de todos los Estados contratantes.

Sobre el apartado 4:

Las normas de valoración previstas en los apartados 1 y 3 también se aplicarán a la valoración de las obligaciones.

Ejemplo:

(ejemplo ficticio sin tasas de variación de precios promediadas concretamente, ya que el régimen opcional de participación en las ganancias todavía no ha entrado en vigor)

Al comienzo del régimen matrimonial, el cónyuge solo tiene deudas por importe de 10.000 euros. El matrimonio dura diez años. Al extinguirse el régimen matrimonial, el cónyuge tiene un patrimonio final de 200.000 euros. De forma ficticia, se supone que los 10.000 euros de deuda al comienzo del régimen matrimonial diez años antes se corresponden con un valor monetario de 14.000 euros al finalizar el régimen. Como consecuencia de ello, el patrimonio inicial habrá de estimarse con deudas y por lo tanto con un pasivo de 14.000 euros y el patrimonio final en 200.000 euros. La ganancia, por consiguiente, es de 214.000 euros.

SECCIÓN 2. PATRIMONIO FINAL

Artículo 10. Composición del patrimonio final

Sobre el apartado 1:
El apartado 1 define qué es el patrimonio final: el patrimonio después de restar las obligaciones que un cónyuge posea en el momento de la finalización del régimen matrimonial o en la fecha establecida conforme al artículo 13, aunque su importe exceda el montante del activo. Igual que el patrimonio inicial, el patrimonio final también podrá ser negativo. No es ninguna masa de bienes concreta, sino uno de los parámetros de cálculo para la determinación de las ganancias.

Los ordenamientos jurídicos de ambos países conocen de una norma en este sentido para su respectivos regímenes de participación en las ganancias (Alemania: §1375 BGB; Francia: artículos 1572 y 1574 CC).

Sobre el apartado 2:
En determinadas circunstancias hay que sumar bienes al patrimonio final. Con ello, se pretende evitar que un cónyuge reduzca sus ganancias mediante determinados actos dispositivos de su patrimonio, perjudicando al otro cónyuge.

Reducciones de patrimonio mediante disposiciones a título gratuito sin el consentimiento del cónyuge o con la intención de perjudicarle son conocidas en los ordenamientos jurídicos de ambos países y han de ser añadidas al patrimonio final (Alemania: §1375, apartado 2, BGB; Francia: artículo 1573 CC). La disminución del patrimonio[39] a causa de dilapidación solo se encuentra en Alemania, §1375, apartado 2, número 2, BGB. Para proteger al otro cónyuge, esta disposición también se incorpora al régimen opcional de participación en las ganancias.

Sobre el número 1:
Las donaciones, a priori, se suman al patrimonio final. Pero ello no se aplicará en los siguientes casos:

a) La donación no es excesiva en consideración al nivel de vida del matrimonio (este será el caso si no supera de forma significativa la disponibilidad económica de los cónyuges para su vida diaria);
b) La donación se realiza con bienes del patrimonio inicial de un cónyuge a un pariente en línea recta (artículo 8, apartado 3, número 2). Las mejoras realizadas en estos bienes donados durante la vigencia del régimen

39 En la versión alemana: "Disminución reprobada del patrimonio".

matrimonial con medios, que no formaban parte del patrimonio inicial, sí serán tenidas en cuenta para el patrimonio final.[40]

Además, el valor de la donación no será añadido de forma ficticia al patrimonio final, si el otro cónyuge ha prestado su consentimiento a la donación o si la donación se ha producido en una fecha que exceda los diez años anteriores a la disolución del régimen matrimonial.

Sobre el número 2:
Aquí se incluyen los negocios jurídicos cuyo objetivo es la disminución de la ganancia del otro cónyuge o la exclusión de su ganancia. Es necesario que la intención de perjudicar haya sido su motivo principal. Aquí se puede incluir, por ejemplo, la venta de un bien valioso muy por debajo de su valor, si el objetivo pretendido es el de incidir en las ganancias.

El incremento de valor de semejantes ventas no será añadido de forma ficticia al patrimonio final, si la venta se realizó con el consentimiento del otro cónyuge o si se produjo más de diez años antes de la disolución del régimen matrimonial.

Sobre el número 3:
En el número 3 se incluyen los gastos que sean inútiles y excesivos[41] en relación al patrimonio. Se incluiría, por ejemplo, un crucero de lujo de un cónyuge, cuando los cónyuges dispongan solo de pocos ingresos. También se incluye aquí la destrucción de un bien por parte de un cónyuge, independientemente de la intención de perjudicar.

El valor de los bienes dilapidados no será añadido de forma ficticia al patrimonio final, si el otro cónyuge ha prestado su consentimiento a la dilapidación o si la dilapidación se ha producido en una fecha que exceda los diez años anteriores a la disolución del régimen matrimonial.

Las disposiciones alemanas sobre la participación prevén un plazo de preclusión[42] de diez años (§1375, apartado 3, BGB). El motivo de ello es que transcurrido un cierto tiempo ya no se supone que el acto tendente a la disminución del patrimonio se haya realizado con la intención de perjudicar al otro cónyuge o que, finalmente, haya sido aceptado por éste. Esta norma además sirve como garantía de la seguridad jurídica.

Por estas razones, el límite temporal de diez años ha sido incorporado también en el régimen opcional de participación en las ganancias.

---

40 En la versión francesa: "La donación concierne a un bien del patrimonio originario donado a un pariente en línea directa (artículo 8, apartado 3, número 2). Sin embargo, será conveniente reunir el valor del crédito de participación alcanzado con las mejoras realizadas sobre ese bien, durante la vigencia del régimen, con sustancias que no derivan del patrimonio originario".

41 En la versión francesa: "Manifiestamente excesivos".

42 En la versión francesa: "Prescripción".

Artículo 11. Valoración del patrimonio final

Sobre el apartado 1:
El apartado 1 regula la valoración del patrimonio final: El patrimonio final se basa en el valor que el patrimonio tiene en el momento de la disolución del régimen matrimonial o, en los casos específicos conforme al artículo 13, en el momento establecido para el cálculo.

En Francia, sin perjuicio de las normas de valoración específicas para los casos de divorcio, separación o de liquidación anticipada de las ganancias, se determina el valor de los bienes existentes que constituyan el patrimonio final conforme a su estado en la fecha de disolución del régimen matrimonial y conforme a su valor en la fecha de la liquidación del régimen matrimonial. Esta última podrá suceder varios años después de la fecha de la disolución (artículo 1574 CC).

En Alemania, el incremento patrimonial y, por lo tanto, el patrimonio inicial y el patrimonio final de los cónyuges se determina en la fecha de la disolución del régimen matrimonial. Podrán ser calculados en una fecha anterior, por ejemplo, en la fecha en la que se presentó la solicitud del crédito de participación anticipada o en la que la solicitud de divorcio se convirtió en objeto de litigio (§§1378, 1384, 1387 BGB).

Sobre el apartado 2:
El apartado 2 fija la fecha en la que se valorará el patrimonio que, de forma ficticia, se ha de añadir al patrimonio final conforme al artículo 10, apartado 2.

- El valor de los bienes se calculará conforme al artículo 10, apartado 2, en la fecha de su donación, enajenación fraudulenta o dilapidación.
- El valor de las mejoras que hayan sido realizadas, con medios que no pertenezcan al patrimonio inicial, constante el régimen matrimonial, en un bien del patrimonio inicial donado a un pariente en línea directa, será calculado en el momento de la donación.

Sobre el apartado 3:
Los valores que habrán de añadirse conforme al apartado 2 deberán ajustarse, a partir de la fecha de cálculo a las tasas de variación experimentadas por el índice general de precios de consumo de los Estados contratantes.

SECCIÓN 3. CRÉDITO DE PARTICIPACIÓN

Artículo 12. Prétensión a la participación[43]

Sobre el apartado 1:
El apartado 1 dispone que el cónyuge que obtenga el menor incremento patrimonial durante la existencia del régimen matrimonial pueda, al finalizar el

---

43 En la versión francesa: “Derecho de participación”.

mismo, exigir del otro cónyuge la compensación de las ganancias en forma de la mitad del importe de la diferencia entre los montantes de patrimonio que ambos cónyuges hayan acumulado durante el matrimonio.

Se compararán los patrimonios iniciales y finales de cada cónyuge para determinar hasta qué punto cada uno de los cónyuges ha obtenido o no un aumento de patrimonio durante el matrimonio. Las disposiciones, respecto a la composición y valoración del patrimonio inicial y final que no sean idénticos, se detallan en los siguientes artículos del régimen matrimonial. Si el patrimonio final es mayor que el patrimonio inicial, esta diferencia constituye la ganancia de un cónyuge. No hay compensación por pérdidas de patrimonio (adquisición patrimonial negativa), sino solo de las ganancias. Si las ganancias de un cónyuge son mayores que las del otro cónyuge, el cónyuge que haya obtenido la ganancia mayor debe al otro cónyuge la mitad de la diferencia.

Sobre el apartado 2:
A priori, el crédito de participación es una pretensión dineraria. Conforme al derecho vigente, esto es igual en ambos países, Alemania y Francia.

Pero mientras ello está expresamente regulado en Francia, en el artículo 1576 CC, en Alemania no hay ninguna disposición específica. El hecho de que la participación sea una pretensión dineraria se deduce de los requisitos de los §§1372 y siguientes BGB. Para mayor claridad, en el régimen opcional de participación en las ganancias se ha adoptado la norma francesa.

Ambos ordenamientos jurídicos conocen la compensación en especie solo como caso excepcional (Francia: artículo 1576 CC; Alemania: §1383 BGB). Por esta razón, el régimen opcional de participación en las ganancias prevé que el tribunal, a solicitud de una parte o de la otra, pueda ordenar, con la finalidad de este pago, el traspaso de bienes del deudor, si ello responde al principio de equidad. El tribunal ha de decidir ponderando los intereses de ambos cónyuges.

Sobre el apartado 3:
El crédito de participación no es transmisible ni en Francia ni en Alemania hasta que no quede disuelto el régimen económico matrimonial. Ello es válido independientemente de si la transmisión es a título oneroso o gratuito. Por contra, este derecho sí es transmisible después de la disolución del régimen matrimonial y transmisible por herencia en caso de fallecimiento (Alemania: §1378, apartado 3, BGB; Francia: artículo 1569 CC). Por lo tanto, la correspondiente norma ha sido incorporada también en el régimen opcional de la participación en las ganancias.

Artículo 13. Fecha de cálculo en casos especiales

A priori, la composición y el valor del patrimonio de los cónyuges sólo se podrá calcular después de la disolución del régimen matrimonial.

No obstante, si se presenta una solicitud de divorcio es poco conveniente decidir primero sobre esta solicitud y posteriormente, es decir, después de la firmeza de la sentencia de divorcio, sobre el crédito de participación. Es más sensato tomar la decisión sobre las ganancias[44] conjuntamente con el procedimiento judicial de divorcio. Para poder determinar la composición y el valor del patrimonio conyugal, el régimen matrimonial común prevé que en estos casos la fecha de la disolución del régimen matrimonial sea sustituida por la fecha de la presentación de la solicitud en el juzgado (y no la "assignation en divorce" en Francia). Incluso, si el juez no dictamina a la vez sobre el crédito de participación y el divorcio, esta norma permite que el plazo del que dispone el cónyuge deudor de la participación para disminuir su patrimonio, y con ello reducir el crédito de participación del otro cónyuge, sea más corto.

El régimen legal supletorio de participación en las ganancias conforme al derecho alemán conoce este mecanismo (§1384 BGB). Por contra, difiere en parte del mecanismo vigente en Francia. El derecho francés prevé que el régimen matrimonial se considere disuelto desde la fecha en la que se presente la solicitud cuyo único objetivo sea la determinación de la composición del patrimonio (artículo 1572 CC).

Este mecanismo no solo se aplicará en los casos de divorcio. También se aplicará si el régimen matrimonial termina de otra manera por una decisión judicial, por ejemplo, por una decisión sobre la liquidación anticipada de las ganancias conforme al artículo 18. También en estos casos es conveniente que la liquidación anticipada pueda calcularse durante el procedimiento correspondiente. La fecha de cálculo, en este caso, es la presentación de la solicitud en el juzgado.

Artículo 14. Limitación del crédito de participación

Con esta disposición deberá garantizarse que nadie tenga que entregar más del 50% de su patrimonio final realmente existente en la fecha de cálculo (fecha de cálculo conforme al artículo 13 o disolución real del régimen matrimonial) a su cónyuge, incluso teniendo en cuenta un patrimonio inicial negativo.

Esta limitación del importe de la participación se corresponde con la intención fundamental del derecho de participación en las ganancias, conforme al cual ambos cónyuges participan a partes iguales en lo conseguido durante el matrimonio.

Mediante el artículo 14 se garantizará también que el crédito de participación solo se produce si en la fecha establecida parael cálculo de las ganancias hay un patrimonio positivo, omitiendo los casos de adiciones ficticias conforme al artículo 10, apartado 2 (con excepción del número 1, letra b). Por ejemplo, si ambos cónyuges durante la existencia del régimen matrimonial solo han pagado

44 En la versión francesa: "Es preferible que el juez pueda decidir sobre el importe del crédito de participación y sobre el divorcio en el mismo procedimiento".

deudas o un cónyuge no ha obtenido ganancias y el otro solo ha pagado deudas, entonces no se produce ningún crédito de participación. No hay compensación de la adquisición patrimonial negativa.

Esta limitación sólo se aplicará a la participación y no a otros derechos y obligaciones que puedan existir entre los cónyuges. El objetivo de esta norma, es decir, que el cónyuge deudor de la participación pueda quedarse con al menos la mitad de su patrimonio, no está justificado si el cónyuge deudor ha disminuido su patrimonio de forma desleal (artículo 10, apartado 2, con la excepción del número 1, letra b).

Para no limitar el importe de la participación cuando un cónyuge haya cometido actos desleales que causen una adición ficticia al patrimonio final, el artículo 14 prevé que la limitación de la participación se aumente por la mitad del importe que en aplicación del artículo 10, apartado 2, deberá sumarse al patrimonio final. Esta disposición no se aplicará a donaciones en el sentido del artículo 10, apartado 2, número 1, letra b. En estos casos no se podrá suponer que el cónyuge haya querido mermar su patrimonio de forma desleal.

Por ello, el cónyuge desleal podrá ser forzado a emplear la totalidad de su patrimonio e incluso a contraer deudas, para pagar el crédito de participación con el importe adicionado de forma ficticia.

Conforme al artículo 3, apartado 3, los cónyuges podrán derogar la aplicación de esta disposición en sus capitulaciones.

CAPÍTULO VI. OTRAS DISPOSICIONES

Artículo 15. Prescripción

El crédito de participación prescribirá a los tres años de la fecha en que el cónyuge tenga conocimiento de la disolución del régimen matrimonial. Una prescripción de la participación a los tres años se corresponde con la normativa de los ordenamientos jurídicos nacionales (Alemania: §1378 apartado 4 BGB; Francia: artículo 1578 CC).

No obstante, el inicio del plazo es diferente en ambos países. Mientras en Alemania se inicia con el conocimiento de la disolución del régimen matrimonial, en Francia el plazo comienza con la disolución misma del régimen matrimonial. Para la protección del cónyuge acreedor de la participación se adopta el inicio del plazo alemán. No obstante, en ciertas circunstancias, si el comienzo del plazo depende del conocimiento, podrá ocurrir que la prescripción tenga lugar muchos años después de la disolución del régimen matrimonial. Para dar seguridad jurídica al cónyuge deudor de la participación a partir de una determinada fecha, el artículo 15 prevé también un plazo de prescripción de diez años a partir de la disolución del régimen matrimonial, independientemente de su conocimiento.

Artículo 16. Obligación de informar, inventario

Sobre el apartado 1:
Si un cónyuge quiere reclamar su crédito de participación, entonces tendrá que saber a cuánto ascienden[45] el patrimonio inicial y el patrimonio final del otro cónyuge. Por todo ello se concede a los cónyuges un derecho a recibir información y a exigir la presentación de un inventario. Al que tenga el derecho a recibir información se le concede, en el mismo ámbito,[46] el derecho a recibir justificantes. Así, al cónyuge que tenga el derecho a la información le será más fácil controlar las declaraciones del cónyuge que esté obligado a informar, y podrá realizar mejor sus intereses. Además, si se presentan justificantes convincentes, se podrán evitar litigios. Cada cónyuge podrá solicitar que un notario realice el inventario, corriendo con los gastos el cónyuge que lo solicite. Una disposición correspondiente se encuentra en el derecho alemán en el §1379 BGB. En las disposiciones francesas sobre el régimen matrimonial de la participación en las ganancias, en el artículo 1572 CC, también se regula la pretensión[47] a recibir un inventario del patrimonio final; la pretensión[48] a la información no está expresamente regulado, pero sí reconocido.

Para posibilitar al cónyuge con derecho a la participación el ejercicio de su reclamación, está prevista una pretensión[49] a recibir información y un inventario.

Sobre el apartado 2:
La misma situación de intereses existe si un cónyuge solicita la disolución del matrimonio o si quiere presentar una demanda para la liquidación anticipada de su crédito de participación en las ganancias. Por ello la pretensión[50] a recibir información del apartado 1 se aplicará también en este caso.

Artículo 17. Aplazamiento

Tanto el derecho alemán (§1382 BGB) como el derecho francés (artículo 1576 CC) conocen la posibilidad de, por un lado, aplazar el crédito de participación bajo determinadas circunstancias y, por otro, ordenar la constitución de garantías.

Sobre el apartado 1:
El apartado 1 regula los requisitos por los cuales se podrá disponer un aplazamiento. En el interés del cónyuge con derecho al crédito de participación,

45 En la versión francesa: "La composición y el valor del patrimonio inicial".
46 En la versión francesa: "Derecho".
47 En la versión francesa: "Derecho".
48 En la versión francesa: "Derecho".
49 En la versión francesa: "Un derecho".
50 En la versión francesa: "El derecho".

el aplazamiento se deberá ordenar sólo en casos excepcionales. Un tribunal decidirá si en el caso particular existe falta de equidad.

Ejemplo:

El cónyuge obligado a pagar el crédito de participación tiene que entregar al otro cónyuge 50.000 euros. Pero el único bien patrimonial, que el cónyuge obligado a pagar posee, es la casa en la que vive y en la que se desarrolla la actividad que constituye su medio de subsistencia. En este caso, sería contrario al principio de equidad[51] que el cónyuge tuviera que vender su casa. Podría tomarse en consideración un aplazamiento.

Sobre el apartado 2:
Un aplazamiento del pago de la participación devengará intereses legales.

Sobre el apartado 3:
El apartado 3 determina que el tribunal podrá ordenar al deudor constituir una garantía para la deuda aplazada. El tribunal decidirá el tipo y el volumen de la garantía de forma equitativa.

Artículo 18. Liquidación anticipada del crédito de participación

Los ordenamientos jurídicos de ambos países conocen la posibilidad de reclamar el crédito de participación de forma anticipada, bajo determinadas circunstancias y si dicho derecho se encuentra en peligro (Alemania: §§1385, 1386 BGB; Francia: artículo 1580 CC).

En el derecho alemán no solo se puede presentar una solicitud potestativa ("*Gestaltungsantrag*"), sino también una solicitud de prestación ("*Leistungsantrag*") que facilite poder exigir la liquidación de la participación de forma anticipada y directa en determinados casos.[52]

En el derecho francés, el cónyuge podrá exigir el crédito anticipado de la participación atendiendo a las siguientes causas: el desorden en los asuntos del otro cónyuge, su mala administración del patrimonio o su conducta indebida, que hagan temer que una prolongación del régimen matrimonial perjudique los derechos del otro cónyuge. En caso de una solicitud de este tipo, se aplicarán las disposiciones sobre la separación de bienes. Si el tribunal estima la solicitud, los cónyuges pasarán al régimen de separación de bienes.

Esta posibilidad de poder exigir la liquidación anticipada de la participación se propone también para el régimen opcional de participación en las ganancias. Conforme al artículo 18, se podrá reclamar la liquidación anticipada de la

---

51 En la versión francesa: "Injusto".

52 En la versión francesa: "En el derecho alemán una demanda de indemnización, presentada en paralelo a la demanda de disolución del régimen, en ciertos casos permite solicitar directamente y de forma anticipada la liquidación de la participación en las ganancias."

participación en las ganancias si un cónyuge no administra su patrimonio de forma debida y con ello perjudica los derechos del otro a la hora del cálculo del crédito de participación. Se aplicará especialmente si un cónyuge comete actos que conforme al artículo 10, apartado 2 (con la excepción del artículo 10, apartado 2, número 1, letra b) provoquen adiciones ficticias al patrimonio final.

A diferencia del artículo 1580 CC, el artículo 18 permite también al cónyuge compensador exigir la liquidación anticipada, si los actos de su cónyuge en el sentido del artículo 18, apartado 1, disminuyen el montante de la participación en su perjuicio.

Si el crédito de participación está en peligro, en muchos casos será oportuno obtener medidas cautelares del tribunal para asegurar este derecho. Las medidas procesales no se regulan de forma independiente en el marco del régimen opcional de participación en las ganancias. Se aplicarán las normas del país en el que se reclamen las medidas cautelares.

En Francia, se podrán solicitar las medidas conforme al artículo 220-1 CC. En Alemania, se podrá considerar la garantía de la participación mediante la protección jurídica cautelar del embargo preventivo conforme al §916 de la Ley de Enjuiciamiento Civil (ZPO).

CAPÍTULO VII. DISPOSICIONES FINALES

Artículo 19. Aplicación temporal

El Acuerdo solo se aplicará a capitulaciones matrimoniales otorgadas por los cónyuges después de su entrada en vigor.

Artículo 20. Ratificación y entrada en vigor

Este Acuerdo requiere de su ratificación conforme a las normas vigentes del Derecho internacional.

Deberá entrar en vigor tan pronto como sea posible.

Es revocable.

Artículo 21. Adhesión

Debido a la cada vez mayor movilidad de los matrimonios en la Unión Europea es deseable facilitar también a otros países miembros la adhesión a este Acuerdo.

En el caso de la adhesión de uno o más estados, Alemania se designará como depositaria del Acuerdo.

Artículo 22. Régimen lingüístico del Acuerdo

En el caso de la adhesión de un estado, se podrá realizar una nueva versión igualmente auténtica en el idioma oficial de este estado.

Artículo 23. Registro

El deber de registrar el Acuerdo se basa en el artículo 102 de la Carta de las Naciones Unidas.

PROYECTO DE LEY DEL GOBIERNO DE LA REPÚBLICA FEDERAL DE ALEMANIA

Proyecto de Ley sobre el Acuerdo de 4 de febrero de 2010 entre la República Federal de Alemania y la República Francesa sobre el régimen matrimonial opcional de participación en las ganancias

A. Problema y objetivo

En el caso de matrimonios de cónyuges de distinta nacionalidad pueden surgir problemas relacionados con el patrimonio de los mismos, debido a que los regímenes económicos matrimoniales son diferentes en los distintos países y suelen ser desconocidos en el otro país. Estos problemas también tienen relevancia práctica, puesto que en el año 2009, de aproximadamente el 13 por ciento de los matrimonios en Alemania, al menos uno de los cónyuges poseía una nacionalidad que no era la alemana. Los problemas no surgen sólo en el momento de la disolución del matrimonio sino también constante el matrimonio, por ejemplo, a la hora de financiar créditos inmobiliarios. Ante esta situación, una regulación a nivel de tratado internacional con su necesario desarrollo en el derecho nacional debe proporcionar más seguridad y claridad jurídica.

B. Solución

La República Federal de Alemania y la República Francesa han acordado crear un régimen económico matrimonial opcional común e idéntico en ambos Estados, que se corresponda con modificaciones con el derecho alemán de participación en las ganancias. Los cónyuges en ambos países podrán elegir este régimen económico matrimonial en lugar del respectivo régimen legal o de los otros regímenes económicos matrimoniales opcionales nacionales. La posibilidad de adherirse al Acuerdo de origen franco-alemán estará abierta a los demás países miembros de la Unión Europea.

Con la presente Ley de Ratificación se crean los requisitos nacionales que conforme al artículo 59, apartado 2, inciso 1, de la Ley Fundamental (*Grundgesezt*) son necesarios para su ratificación.

Al mismo tiempo, la Ley regula la aplicación nacional del Acuerdo.

C. Alternativas
Ninguna.

D. Consecuencias económico-financieras
No supondrá gastos para el Estado federal, los Estados federados (*Länder*) o los municipios.

E. Otros costes
No supondrá costes adicionales para la economía, en especial para las pequeñas y medianas empresas. No se espera que esta Ley influya en precios individuales o en el índice general de precios, en especial en el índice de precios de consumo.

F. Costes burocráticos
No se introducirán, modificarán o suprimirán deberes de información para la economía, las ciudadanas y los ciudadanos o la administración.

FUNDAMENTACIÓN DE LA LEY DE RATIFICACIÓN

A. PARTE GENERAL

1. SITUACIÓN INICIAL REAL Y JURÍDICA

Los matrimonios con entre personas de diferente nacionalidad están bastante extendidos. En el año 2009, en el 13 por ciento de los casos de matrimonios residentes en Alemania, o ambos cónyuges tenían nacionalidad extranjera o un cónyuge tenía nacionalidad alemana y el otro nacionalidad extranjera. Entre ellos había al menos 34.000 matrimonios franco-alemanes, lo cual representaba el cuarto grupo más numeroso detrás de los matrimonios entre alemanes y polacos, alemanes e italianos, y alemanes y austriacos (Hammes et al., WiSta 2010 p. 904/911 y siguientes). A ellos se suman los matrimonios alemanes que viven en el extranjero y los matrimonios extranjeros que viven en Alemania. Dado que las consecuencias legales del matrimonio se rigen, entre otras cosas, por la nacionalidad, los matrimonios entre personas con distintas nacionalidades pueden causar problemas jurídicos, especialmente en lo que se refiere al régimen económico matrimonial. El régimen legal supletorio en Alemania es el régimen de participación en las ganancias. El patrimonio de los cónyuges es privativo y solo con la disolución del régimen matrimonial – por ejemplo, por motivo de divorcio – se compensan las ganancias obtenidas durante el matrimonio. El régimen legal supletorio en Francia es la comunidad de gananciales. Las ganancias obtenidas durante el matrimonio se convierten en patrimonio común. Por ejemplo, si un matrimonio en comunidad de gananciales conforme al derecho francés vive en Alemania, surgen problemas cuando los cónyuges con este régimen matrimonial adquieren un inmueble en Alemania. Dado que el régimen matrimonial francés por lo general no se conoce en Alemania, la estimación precisa, por ejemplo, del alcance de los derechos correspondientes a los respectivos cónyuges a la hora de la inscripción del título en el Registro de la Propiedad lleva a una considerable inseguridad (sobre la sociedad de gananciales conforme al derecho español ver, p.ej., OLG Düsseldorf, FamRZ 2010, 1564 y siguientes). Para un institución de crédito alemán resulta especialmente dudoso determinar cuáles son las consecuencias de las deudas o de la insolvencia de un cónyuge para el patrimonio vinculado a la comunidad de gananciales. La solución que nos encontramos a menudo en la práctica y que consiste en que los cónyuges elijan el régimen legal alemán para su patrimonio localizado en Alemania, conforme al artículo 15, apartado 2, de la Ley de Introducción al Código Civil (EGBGB), da respuesta a esta pregunta, pero les exige soportar un fraccionamiento del régimen matrimonial que puede llevar a dificultades de cálculo a la hora de la liquidación de la participación. Ante las grandes diferencias entre las respectivas tradiciones, las parejas alemanas en Francia se encontrarán con problemas parecidos.

La elección de una solución en forma de tratado bilateral presenta la ventaja de poder ofrecer lo antes posible soluciones para los cónyuges afectados, ya que la armonización del derecho de familia de todos los países miembros de la Unión Europea necesariamente avanzará mucho más despacio, dadas las tradiciones jurídicas diferentes, a menudo desarrolladas a través de los siglos y muy arraigadas en la población. Para esta armonización existe también un mandato político para la República Francesa y la República Federal de Alemania, puesto que, de la declaración conjunta con motivo del 40 aniversario del Tratado del Elíseo en el año 2003 (*40. Jahrestag des Elysée-Vertrages 2003*) surge la voluntad de armonizar el derecho de familia alemán y francés. La posibilidad de adherirse al Acuerdo de 4 de febrero 2010 entre la República Federal de Alemania y la República Francesa sobre el régimen matrimonial opcional de participación en las ganancias (en lo sucesivo: el Acuerdo) está abierta a otros Estados miembros de la Unión Europea. También en estos Estados, el derecho matrimonial y en especial el derecho económico matrimonial presentan formas muy diferentes y llevan a problemas parecidos a los indicados para los casos de Alemania y Francia.

2. OBJETIVO DE LAS ENMIENDAS

Ante la inseguridad jurídica en los casos de matrimonios entre personas de distintas nacionalidades, el objetivo del Acuerdo es la creación de un régimen económico matrimonial opcional, en un principio binacional, que incluya idénticas disposiciones para ambos ordenamientos jurídicos y que, por lo tanto, pueda proporcionar claridad y seguridad jurídica a los afectados. Para promover la aceptación del nuevo régimen matrimonial opcional de participación en las ganancias tanto en Francia como en Alemania se han tomado en cuenta particularidades originarias de los regímenes matrimoniales de ambos ordenamientos jurídicos.

En su estructura básica, el régimen matrimonial opcional de participación en las ganancias se corresponde con el régimen de participación en las ganancias alemán, aunque también comporta modificaciones que tienen en consideración la tradición jurídica francesa. Los cónyuges en ambos países podrán elegir este régimen matrimonial en lugar del régimen legal supletorio o de alguno de los otros regímenes nacionales opcionales si su régimen matrimonial está sujeto al derecho material de uno de los Estados contratantes.

Las disposiciones del derecho internacional privado en ambos países no se verán afectadas. No es necesario un reenvío internacional directo; el régimen matrimonial opcional de participación en las ganancias reportará ventajas para los cónyuges especialmente en los casos de matrimonios entre personas con distintas nacionalidades.

Con la propuesta de modificación del Código Civil (BGB), el régimen matrimonial opcional será introducido en el Derecho de familia alemán. Las disposiciones en materia de Derecho de sucesiones y de donaciones se corresponden con las normas del régimen de participación en las ganancias conforme al Derecho alemán, y su objetivo es asegurar que los cónyuges no desistan de la elección del nuevo régimen matrimonial por causas fiscales.

3. COMPETENCIA LEGISLATIVA

La competencia legislativa del Gobierno Federal resulta de los artículos 73, apartado 1, número 1 (Asuntos exteriores), 74, apartado 1, número 1 (Derecho civil), y del 105, apartado 2,segunda alternativa, en relación con el artículo 72, apartado 2, de la Ley Fundamental (Derecho fiscal).

Conforme al artículo 72, apartado 2, de la Ley Fundamental es necesaria una ley federal para salvaguardar la unidad jurídica en aras del interés nacional. Para la unificación del derecho en Francia y Alemania es imprescindible la aplicación de un derecho unificado en la República Federal de Alemania. Ello sólo se podrá conseguir mediante una regulación legal federal. La existencia de regulaciones diferentes para el impuesto sobre sucesiones crearía inseguridad jurídica en el caso de fallecimiento; asimismo, a causa de la dispersión de las personas beneficiadas en cada sucesión, regulaciones diferentes llevarían a una fragmentación del derecho con consecuencias problemáticas, lo cual resultaría inaceptable tanto en el interés del Estado federal como en el de los Estados federados (*Länder*).

Conforme al artículo 105, apartado 3, de la Ley Fundamental, es necesaria la aprobación por parte de la Cámara Alta (*Bundesrat*), ya que conforme al artículo 106, apartado 2, número 2,de la Ley Fundamental, los ingresos de los impuestos sobre sucesiones y donaciones corresponden a los Estados federados (*Länder*).

B. PARTE ESPECIAL

Sobre el artículo 1 (Aprobación)

Dado que el Acuerdo se refiere a materias de legislación federal, se aplicará el artículo 59, apartado 2, inciso 1, de la Ley Fundamental.

Sobre el artículo 2 (Modificación del Código Civil)

Sobre el número 1 (Modificación del índice)
Dado que se introduce el nuevo capítulo 4 en el libro 4 – Derecho de familia – del Código Civil, también se integrará el índice.

Sobre el número 2

a) General
   Con la introducción del nuevo capítulo 4 “Régimen matrimonial opcional de participación en las ganancias” se pretende dejar claro que el régimen económico matrimonial opcional de participación en las ganancias es, conforme al Acuerdo, otro régimen matrimonial susceptible de ser elegido mediante capitulaciones matrimoniales, que se suma de forma paritaria a los demás regímenes matrimoniales opcionales de la separación de bienes y de la comunidad de bienes, mencionados en los capítulos 2 y 3.
b) §1519 BGB – nuevo –
   aa) Principio fundamental
      El §1519 BGB – nuevo – tiene en consideración la limitación de la libertad contractual conforme al §1409 BGB. De acuerdo al §§1408 y ss. del BGB, los cónyuges, mediante capitulaciones, pueden elegir la separación de bienes o la comunidad de bienes en lugar del régimen legal supletorio de participación en las ganancias. Con el nuevo §1519 BGB, el régimen matrimonial opcional de participación en las ganancias conforme al Acuerdo entre la República Federal de Alemania y la República Francesa sobre el régimen matrimonial opcional de participación en las ganancias se suma como otro régimen económico matrimonial susceptible de ser escogido mediante capitulaciones matrimoniales.
      Las disposiciones individuales, idénticas en Alemania y en Francia, se encuentran en los artículos 1 a 19 del Acuerdo. Para su fundamentación, se remite al memorando que contiene el informe explicativo del Acuerdo aprobado por Francia y Alemania.
   bb) Aplicación de los §§1368 y 1412 BGB
      El artículo 5 del Acuerdo regula la ineficacia de disposiciones sobre elementos del ajuar doméstico y sobre la vivienda habitual de los cónyuges. No queda afectada por esta disposición la ejecución de un negocio jurídico ineficaz frente a un tercero favorecido por este. Con referencia al §1368 BGB en la Ley de Ratificación, el cónyuge, protegido por el artículo 5 del Acuerdo en caso de una enajenación no autorizada, tendrá por tanto la posibilidad de hacer valer frente a terceros los derechos que resulten de la ineficacia de disposiciones sobre elementos del ajuar doméstico o sobre la vivienda familiar.

Por otro lado, se excluirá la aplicación del §1412 BGB. La ineficacia de una disposición frente a un tercero no dependerá de que las capitulaciones matrimoniales del régimen matrimonial opcional de participación en las ganancias estén inscritas en el registro del matrimonio o sean conocidas por el tercero. A la vista de su escasa importancia práctica, su inscripción en el registro del matrimonio sería una formalidad superflua que no aportaría ningún valor añadido para la protección de las relaciones jurídicas. En concreto, en el supuesto de disposiciones sobre bienes inmuebles, los notarios fedatarios tendrán que tener en cuenta en el futuro la posibilidad de una prohibición de disponer de los referidos bienes.

c) Delimitación con el resto del Derecho patrimonial en sentido amplio

En su ámbito de aplicación, el nuevo régimen económico matrimonial sustituye al régimen patrimonial entre cónyuges.

aa) §1357 BGB

A la vista de las disposiciones especiales del artículo 6 del Acuerdo que regulan la responsabilidad solidaria de los cónyuges en los actos de un cónyuge para el mantenimiento del hogar familiar, no hay lugar para una aplicación del §1357 BGB.

bb) §1365 BGB

El artículo 5, apartado 1, del Acuerdo, que tiene carácter de norma de cierre conclusivo, impide que se pueda aplicar también el §1365 BGB. De forma deliberada no se ha incorporado tal disposición protectora en el Acuerdo (ver informe explicativo acerca del artículo 5, apartado 1, del Acuerdo).

cc) §1382 BGB

El artículo 17, apartado 2, no contiene ninguna regulación especial del tipo de interés en caso de aplazamiento. Aún así, no está prevista ninguna referencia al §1382, apartado 4, BGB. Por lo tanto, en este sentido se aplicará el §246 BGB. En consecuencia, el tipo de interés será del 4 por ciento. Si el deudor entra en mora, el tipo de interés será el tipo de interés básico más el 5 por ciento (§288, apartado 1, inciso 2, §247 BGB). Tampoco existe necesidad concreta de incorporar la norma procesal especial del §1382, apartado 5, BGB, por la cual una solicitud de aplazamiento sólo podrá ser presentada en un procedimiento pendiente sobre la participación.

dd) §1384 BGB

Conforme al artículo 13 del Acuerdo, en caso de disolución del matrimonio por decisión judicial, la fecha determinante para el cálculo de las ganancias será la de la interposición de la demanda judicial. Con ello no se tiende a la litispendencia – como en el §1384 BGB – tras presentar la demanda al oponente. La fecha de presentación de la demanda en el juzgado es determinante.

ee) Pensión compensatoria

No se realizará una compensación económico-patrimonial de los derechos a la pensión de jubilación sujetos a la pensión compensatoria, §1587 BGB en relación al §2, apartado 4, de la Ley de Pensiones Compensatorias. Lo mismo se aplica al régimen matrimonial opcional de participación en las ganancias. La adscripción del patrimonio de la pensión de jubilación es diferente en Alemania y en Francia. Los cónyuges podrán regular la adscripción mediante el otorgamiento de capitulaciones matrimoniales. A la vista de las particularidades de la pensión compensatoria alemana, una solución a las diferentes adscripciones del patrimonio de la pensión de jubilación hubiera sobrecargado el nuevo régimen económico matrimonial opcional.

d) Liquidación del régimen económico matrimonial en el marco del Derecho sucesorio

Al contrario que el Código Civil, que contiene la disposición especial del §1371 BGB para la liquidación del régimen legal supletorio en el caso del fallecimiento de un cónyuge, el Acuerdo no prevé ninguna regulación particular para este caso.

El §1371, apartado 1, BGB aumenta en un cuarto la parte hereditaria del cónyuge supérstite (§1931, apartado 1, BGB) como compensación de las ganancias a tanto alzado. La conexión entre el Derecho patrimonial y el Derecho sucesorio, a menudo criticada en el Derecho alemán, es ajena al Acuerdo. Mediante la aplicación del §1371, apartado 1, BGB, conforme al Derecho sostantivo, al cónyuge supérstite, si estuviera sujeto al Derecho alemán, le correspondería una participación distinta de la que le correspondería si este mismo cónyuge supérstite estuviera sujeto al Derecho francés, a pesar de haber elegido el régimen matrimonial opcional de participación en las ganancias. Esto sería contrario al objetivo del Acuerdo, que no es otro que el de crear un régimen económico matrimonial unificado que se parezca lo más posible en los países participantes. Por lo tanto, a la muerte de un cónyuge ante todo deberán compensarse las ganancias.

e) Incorporación del derecho de uniones civiles entre personas del mismo sexo (*Lebenspartnerschaftsrecht*)

El nuevo régimen matrimonial opcional de participación en las ganancias también debe estar abierto a parejas del mismo sexo en el sentido de la Ley de Uniones Civiles entre Personas del Mismo Sexo (LPartG). Conforme a los §§6 y 7 LPartG, las disposiciones del derecho patrimonial aplicables a cónyuges ya se aplican también a parejas del mismo sexo en uniones civiles. Con ello, se ha conseguido la plena igualdad con el matrimonio. Para el régimen matrimonial opcional de participación en las ganancias no se debe hacer ninguna excepción. El §6 LPartG permite la elección de otro régimen legal que no sea la participación en las ganancias en el contrato de unión civil entre personas del mismo sexo. En este sentido, el §7, inciso 2, LPartG, declara aplicables de la forma correspondiente los §§de 1409 a 1563 BGB. Por lo tanto, el nuevo §1519 BGB ya está incluido en esta referencia.

f) Situación legal en caso de terminación del Acuerdo
Si Alemania diera por terminado el Acuerdo, las consecuencias habrían de regularse en una ley de acompañamiento: o bien se mantiene el contenido material del Acuerdo o bien se crearán disposiciones de liquidación, p.ej. siguiendo el modelo del Tratado de Unificación (artículo 234, §4, de la Ley de Introducción al Código Civil, *Einführungsgesetz zum Bürgerlichen Gesetzbuch*).
Si Francia diera por terminado el Acuerdo, a causa de la referencia estática a las disposiciones del Acuerdo, el régimen económico matrimonial quedaría como un régimen económico matrimonial exclusivamente alemán.

Sobre el artículo 3 (Modificación de la ley de secretarios judiciales)

Conforme al artículo 12, apartado 2, inciso 2, del Acuerdo, a petición de uno de los cónyuges, el tribunal podrá ordenar la transferencia de bienes del deudor al acreedor con la finalidad de la liquidación si ello responde al principio de la equidad. Además, conforme al artículo 17 del Acuerdo, a petición del deudor el tribunal puede conceder un aplazamiento del pago de la participación y ordenar la aportación de garantías. Estas actuaciones del tribunal son comparables a las que el derecho nacional en los §§1382, 1383 BGB ya ha transmitido al secretario judicial, siempre que no esté pendiente ningún litigio sobre la participación (§1382, apartado 5, BGB). La razón de la transmisión de estas tareas era consecuencia de que, en estos casos, no suele haber problemas jurídicos: únicamente hay que aclarar dudas concretas y valorar cuestiones económicas. Estas consideraciones también son válidas para los casos regulados en el artículo 12, apartado 2, inciso 2, y en el artículo 17 del Acuerdo – especialmente por la idéntica estructura básica del régimen matrimonial opcional de participación en las ganancias y el régimen legal supletorio de participación en las ganancias.

Sobre el artículo 4 (Modificación de la ley sobre el procedimiento en asuntos del derecho de familia y en asuntos de la jurisdicción voluntaria)

Sobre el número 1
En el índice se adaptará la nueva versión del epígrafe del §264 de la Ley sobre el Procedimiento en Asuntos del Derecho de Familia y en Asuntos de la Jurisdicción Voluntaria (FamFG)

Sobre el número 2
Las pretensiones resultantes del Acuerdo del régimen matrimonial opcional de participación en las ganancias son asuntos de derecho patrimonial conforme al

§261, apartado 1, FamFG. Los procedimientos previstos conforme al artículo 5, apartado 2; artículo 12, apartado 2, inciso 2, y artículo 17 del Acuerdo son comparables con los de los §1369, apartado 2, y §§1382, 1383 BGB. Con su introducción en el §261, apartado 2, FamFG, estas materias de procedimiento son declaradas asuntos de derecho patrimonial.

Sobre el número 3

El §264, apartado 1, inciso 1, FamFG dispone, para procedimientos conforme a los §§1382 y 1383 BGB como excepción al §40, apartado 2, FamFG, que una decisión del tribunal sólo tendrá efecto en el momento en que sea firme. Al igual que el §1383 BGB en el caso del régimen matrimonial de participación en las ganancias, el artículo 12, apartado 2, inciso 2, del Acuerdo del régimen matrimonial opcional de participación en las ganancias prevé como caso particular y a petición de uno de los interesados el pago de la participación en especie si ello responde al principio de equidad. El artículo 17 del Acuerdo prevé la posibilidad de un aplazamiento judicial del pago de la participación, para el que, en su caso, también habría que constituir una garantía. Con ello adopta una disposición para el régimen matrimonial opcional de participación en las ganancias que es comparable al §1382 BGB. Las disposiciones del artículo 12, apartado 2, inciso 2, y del artículo 17 del Acuerdo se parecen a las de los §§1382 y 1383 BGB y en los procedimientos de derecho patrimonial matrimonial deberán tratarse de la misma manera. Esta es también la razón por la que, en los procedimientos conforme al artículo 12, apartado 2, inciso 2, y al artículo 17 del Acuerdo, la decisión del tribunal sólo tendrá efecto en el momento en que sea firme.

Sobre el número 4

El §269, apartado 1, FamFG dispone qué procedimientos son asuntos de uniones civiles entre personas del mismo sexo. Entre ellos se contarán conforme al §269, apartado 1, número 11, FamFG también las decisiones conforme al §6 LPartG en relación a los §1365, apartado 2; §1369, apartado 2; §§1382 y 1383 BGB y conforme al §269, apartado 1, número 12, FamFG así como decisiones conforme al §7 LPartG en relación a los §§1426, 1430 y 1452 BGB. Para aplicar, también en el Derecho procesal del régimen económico matrimonial, la igualdad entre la unión civil de personas del mismo sexo y el matrimonio, ya descrita bajo el artículo 2, número 2, letra e, de la Ley de Ratificación, las disposiciones del §269, apartado 1, número 12, FamFG deberán dejar claro que las decisiones conforme al §1519 BGB en relación a los artículos 5, apartado 2; 12, apartado 2, inciso 2, y al artículo 17 del Acuerdo también son decisiones en este sentido.

Sobre el artículo 5 (Modificación de la ley del impuesto sobre sucesiones y donaciones)

Las consecuencias del derecho de impuestos sobre sucesiones y donaciones en el caso de la disolución del régimen matrimonial opcional de participación en las ganancias se ajustan a las de la disolución del régimen legal supletorio del Código Civil. De no ser así, el trato jurídico-fiscal desigual frente al régimen legal supletorio de participación en las ganancias convertiría al nuevo régimen matrimonial en una alternativa más bien secundaria en la práctica. Conforme al §5, apartado 2, de la Ley de Impuestos sobre Sucesiones y Donaciones (ErbStG), la participación conforme al artículo 12 del Acuerdo no constituirá una adquisición en el sentido de los §§3 y 7 ErbStG. Ello se aplicará independientemente de si el régimen matrimonial opcional de participación en las ganancias finalizara por el fallecimiento de un cónyuge o en vida de ambos cónyuges. La participación, por lo tanto, no está sujeta a la imposición conforme al ErbStG, siempre que haya sido calculada de forma concreta y sea la base de una transferencia patrimonial.

No se requiere ninguna exención conforme al §5 apartado 1 ErbStG. En el caso de la liquidación de la participación en el marco del derecho sucesorio (§1371, apartado 1, BGB), las disposiciones para adquisiciones en el sentido de los §§3 y 7 ErbStGel determinan que el cónyuge supérstite queda exento del impuesto sucesorio por el montante de la participación ficticio que el cónyuge supérstite hubiera podido reclamar con los requisitos de los §§de 1373 a 1383, 1390 BGB. Dado que, en el régimen matrimonial opcional de participación en las ganancias, la participación a la finalización del régimen matrimonial sólo se podrá reclamar mediante el cálculo de la participación real, no existe ningún campo de aplicación para el §5, apartado 1, ErbStG.

Además, no se requiere ninguna aplicación correspondiente del §29, apartado 1, número 2, ErbStG. Conforme al §29, apartado 1, número 2, ErbStG, el impuesto se extinguirá con efecto retroactivo, en tanto que, en los casos del §5, apartado 2, ErbStG, las donaciones gratuitas sujetas a la obligación tributaria hayan sido imputadas a la participación conforme al §1380, apartado 1, BGB. Dado que el Acuerdo no regula tal imputación, falta la base de vinculación con el §29, apartado 1, número 2, ErbStG.

Sobre el artículo 6 (Entrada en vigor)

Los apartados 1 y 2 regulan la entrada en vigor de la Ley. Las disposiciones cumplen con los requisitos del artículo 82, apartado 2, inciso 1, de la Ley Fundamental.

Conforme al apartado 2, inciso 2, la fecha en la que el Acuerdo entra en vigor conforme a su artículo 20, se publicará en el Boletín Oficial del Estado alemán (*Bundesgesetzblatt*).

Conclusiones

Con el Acuerdo entre la República Federal de Alemania y la República Francesa sobre el régimen matrimonial opcional de participación en las ganancias, los países contratantes han desarrollado un nuevo modelo para la integración de los ordenamientos del derecho civil en Europa. De un modo general, el Acuerdo está abierto al ingreso de cada uno de los Estados miembros de la Unión Europea y así, al crear un nuevo derecho sustantivo, amplía las opciones de actuación de las ciudadanas y ciudadanos bajo el régimen de la autonomía privada. El proyecto de una Ley de Ratificación y Aplicación presentado aquí hace accesible a los que están sujetos al derecho matrimonial patrimonial alemán esta nueva opción después de la entrada en vigor del Acuerdo.

No habrá costes adicionales para los erarios públicos y la economía, en especial para las pequeñas y medianas empresas. No se espera que esta Ley influya en los precios individuales o en el índice general de precios, en especial, en el índice de precios de consumo.

El proyecto de ley está en consonancia con la idea dominante del Gobierno federal del desarrollo sostenible en el sentido de la estrategia nacional de sostenibilidad. La intención de las disposiciones es contribuir a una mayor claridad jurídica en matrimonios entre personas de distinta nacionalidad.

No se introducirán, modificarán o suprimirán deberes de información para la economía, las ciudadanas y los ciudadanos o la administración.

El proyecto de ley es compatible con el Derecho de la Unión Europea y los tratados internacionales que la República Federal de Alemania ha firmado.

No se esperan consecuencias de relevancia para la política de igualdad.

ACTO DE RATIFICACIÓN DE LA REPÚBLICA FEDERAL DE ALEMANIA

Ley sobre el Acuerdo de 4 de febrero de 2010 entre la República Federal de Alemania y la República Francesa sobre el régimen matrimonial opcional de participación en las ganancias de 15 de marzo de 2012
Con la aprobación de la Cámara Alta Federal, el Parlamento Federal ha aprobado la siguiente Ley:

Artículo 1. Aprobación

Se aprueba el Acuerdo entre la República Federal de Alemania y la República Francesa sobre el régimen matrimonial opcional de participación en las ganancias, firmado en París el 4 de febrero de 2010. El Acuerdo se publica a continuación.

Artículo 2. Modificación del BGB (Código Civil)

El BGB (Código Civil) en la redacción de lo publicado el 2 de enero de 2002 (BGBl. I p. 42, 2909; 2003 I P. 738), modificado por última vez por el artículo 1 de la Ley de 17 de enero de 2011 (BGBl. I p. 1600), se modifica de la siguiente forma:

1. En el índice se introducirá, conforme a la indicación sobre el libro 4, apartado 1, título 6, subtítulo 2, capítulo 3, la siguiente indicación:
   "Capítulo 4
   Régimen matrimonial opcional de participación en las ganancias".

2. Detrás del §1518 se introducirá el siguiente capítulo 4:
   "Capítulo 4
   Régimen matrimonial opcional de participación en las ganancias.
   §1519
   Estipulación en capitulaciones matrimoniales
   Cuando los cónyuges estipulen en capitulaciones matrimoniales el régimen matrimonial opcional de participación en las ganancias, se aplicarán las disposiciones del Acuerdo de 4 de febrero de 2010 entre la República Federal de Alemania y la República Francesa sobre el régimen matrimonial opcional de participación en las ganancias. El §1368 se aplicará mutatis mutandis. El §1412 no se aplicará."

Artículo 3. Modificación de la ley de secretarios judiciales

El §25, número 3, de la Ley de Secretarios Judiciales de 5 de noviembre de 1969 (BGBl. I p. 2065), modificado por última vez por el artículo 5 de la Ley de 7 de diciembre de 2011 (BGBl. I p. 582), se modifica de la siguiente forma:

1. En la letra b se sustituye el punto final por una coma.

2. Se añade la siguiente letra c:
   "c) la decisión sobre el aplazamiento del pago de una participación y la transmisión de bienes conforme al §1519 del BGB (Código Civil) en relación al artículo 12, apartado 2, inciso 2, y al artículo 17 del Acuerdo de 4 de febrero de 2010 entre la República Federal de Alemania y la República Francesa sobre el régimen matrimonial opcional de participación en las ganancias; también en relación al §7 de la Ley de Uniones Civiles entre Personas del Mismo Sexo (*Lebenspartnerschaftsgesetz)* siempre que no penda un litigio sobre la participación."

Artículo 4. Modificación de la ley de procedimientos en asuntos del derecho de familia y en asuntos de la jurisdicción voluntaria

La Ley de Procedimientos en Asuntos del Derecho de Familia y en Asuntos de la Jurisdicción Voluntaria, de 17 de diciembre de 2008 (BGBI. I p. 2586, 2587), modificada por última vez por el artículo 2, apartado 32, de la Ley de 22 de diciembre de 2011 (BGBl. I p. 3044) se modifica de la siguiente forma:

1. En el índice, el título del §264 queda redactado de la siguiente forma:
   "§264 Procedimiento para el aplazamiento y la transferencia de bienes patrimoniales".

2. El §261 apartado 2 queda como sigue:
   "(2) Las controversias de régimen patrimonial también son procedimientos conforme al §1365, apartado 2; §1369, apartado 2; §§1382, 1383, 1426, 1430 y 1452 del BGB (Código Civil) así como conforme al §1519 del BGB (Código Civil) en relación al artículo 5, apartado 2, artículo 12, apartado 2, inciso 2, y al artículo 17 del Acuerdo de 4 de febrero de 2010 entre la República Federal de Alemania y la República Francesa sobre el régimen matrimonial opcional de la participación en las ganancias."

3. El §264 se modifica de la siguiente forma:
   a) El título queda redactado de la siguiente forma:
      "§264
      Procedimiento para el aplazamiento y la transmisión de bienes patrimoniales".

   b) El apartado 1, inciso 1, queda como sigue:
      "En los procedimientos conforme a los §§1382 y 1383 del BGB (Código Civil) así como conforme al §1519 del Código Civil en relación al artículo 12,

apartado 2, inciso 2, y al artículo 17 del Acuerdo de 4 de febrero de 2010 entre la República Federal de Alemania y la República Francesa sobre el régimen matrimonial opcional de participación en las ganancias, la decisión del tribunal sólo tendrá efecto en el momento en que sea firme la decisión judicial."

4. El §269 apartado 1 número 12 queda como sigue:
   "12. Decisiones conforme al §7 de la Ley de uniones civiles entre personas del mismo sexo en relación a los §§1426, 1430, 1452 del BGB (Código Civil) o al §1519 del BGB (Código Civil) y al artículo 5, apartado 2; artículo 12, apartado 2, inciso 2, o al artículo 17 del Acuerdo de 4 de febrero de 2010 entre la República Federal de Alemania y la República Francesa sobre el régimen matrimonial opcional de participación en las ganancias".

Artículo 5. Modificación de la ley del impuesto sobre sucesiones y donaciones

Al §5 de la Ley del Impuesto sobre Sucesiones y Donaciones en la redacción de lo publicado el 27 de febrero de 1997 (BGBl. I p. 378), modificada por última vez por el artículo 11 de la Ley de 7 de diciembre de 2011 (BGBl. I p. 2592), se añade el siguiente apartado 3:

"(3) Cuando se disuelva el régimen matrimonial opcional de participación en las ganancias (§1519 del BGB (Código Civil)) y se compensen las ganancias, la participación (artículo 12, apartado 1, del Acuerdo de 4 de febrero de 2010 entre la República Federal de Alemania y la República Francesa sobre el régimen matrimonial opcional de la participación en las ganancias) no será considerada adquisición a los efectos de los §§3 y 7."

Artículo 6. Entrada en vigor

(1) Los artículos 2 a 5 entrarán en vigor en la misma fecha en la que entre en vigor el Acuerdo de 4 de febrero de 2010 entre la República Federal de Alemania y la República Francesa sobre el régimen matrimonial opcional de participación en las ganancias conforme a su artículo 20, apartado 2. La fecha de la entrada en vigor se publicará en el Boletín Oficial del Estado alemán (*Bundesgesetzblatt*).

(2) En todo lo demás, la ley entrará en vigor el día después de su publicación.

RECOMMENDATIONS FOR FURTHER READING

AMANN H., *Die Verfügungsbeschränkung über die Familienwohnung im Güterstand der Wahl-Zugewinngemeinschaft, DNotZ* 2013, 252

BECKER E., *Das deutsch-französische Abkommen über den Güterstand der Wahl-Zugewinngemeinschaft*, www.europarl.europa.eu/studies

ID., *Ein europäischer Güterstand? Der deutsch-französische Wahlgüterstand, Era Forum* 12, 1 (2011) 103

ID., *Auf dem Weg ins BGB: Die deutsch-französische Wahl-Zugewinngemeinschaft, FF* 2012, 199

BOELE-WOELKI K./FERRAND F./GONZALEZ BEILFUSS C./JÄNTERÄ-JAREBORG M./ LOWE N./ MARTINY M./PINTENS W., *Principles of European Family Law Regarding Property Relations Between Spouses*, Intersentia, Cambridge – Antwerp – Portland 2013

BRAEUER M., *Der neue deutsch-französische Wahlgüterstand, Forum Familienrecht* 2010, 113

BRAUN S., *Die Wahl-Zugewinngemeinschaft: Ein neuer Güterstand im deutschen (und französischen) Recht, MittBayNot* 2012, 89

CUBEDDU M.G./HENRICH D., *Due modelli di regime patrimoniale dei beni in Europa?, Riv. dir. civ.*, I, 2010, 563

DELERUE K.S., *Der neue deutsch-französische Wahlgüterstand – Für und Wieder eines bilateralen Abkommens, FamRBint-Beratungspraxis* 2010, 70

DETHLOFF N., *The Franco-German Optional Matrimonial Property Regime – A Trailblazer for the Alignement of Family Law? Der deutsch-französische Wahlgüterstand – Wegbereiter für eine Angleichung des Familienrechts, RabelsZ* 2012, 509

FÖTSCHL A., *The Common Matrimonial Property Regime (COMP) of Germany and France: Epoch-Making in the Unification of Law, Yb. Priv. Int. L.* 2009, 395; *European Review of Private Law* 2010, 881

FUGARDO ESTIVILL J.M., *Regimes económicas del matrimonio y de la pareja*, Bosch, Barcelona 2011

GONZÁLEZ BEILFUSS C., *El acuerdo franco-alemán instituyendo un régimen económico matrimonial común, Anuario español de derecho internacional privado*, 10, 2010, 317–496

ID., *The Franco-German Treaty Instituting a Common Matrimonial Regime of Participation in the Acquisitions: How Could Catalonia Opt in?, Liber amicorum Walter Pintens*, Intersentia, Cambridge – Antwerp – Portland, 2012, 623

GOTTWALD P., *Die versteckte Perle oder "Much ado about nothing"? Gedanken zum neuen Güterstand der Wahl-Zugewinngemeinschaft, Liber amicorum Walter Pintens*, Intersentia, Cambridge – Antwerp – Portland, 2012, 651

HEINEMANN J., *Die Wahl-Zugewinngemeinschaft als neuer Güterstand, FamRB* 2012, 129

KLIPPSTEIN T., *Der deutsch-französische Güterstand der Wahl-Zugewinngemeinschaft, FPR* 2010, 510

KRAUSE L., *Der vorläufige Rechtsschutz im neuen Güterrecht, ZFE* 2010, 247

JÄGER T., *Der neue deutsch-französische Güterstand der Wahl-Zugewinngemeinschaft – Inhalt und seine ersten Folgen für die Gesetzgebung und Beratungspraxis, DNotZ* 2010, 804

MARTINY D., *Der neue deutsch-französische Wahlgüterstand – Ein Beispiel optionaler bilateraler Familienrechtsvereinheitlichung, ZEuP* 11 (2011), 577

MECKE C.E., *Güterrechtliche Grundsatzfragen, AcP* 211 (2011), 886–916

MEYER T., *Der neue deutsch-französische Wahlgüterstand, FamRZ* 2010, 612

ROLLAND W., *Anmerkung zum deutsch-französischen Güterstand der Wahl-Zugewinngemeinschaft vor dem Hintergrund der Entwicklung des internationalen Güterrechts, Festschrift Brudermüller*, Beck, München, 2014, 571

SCHAAL D., *Der neue Güterstand der Wahl-Zugewinngemeinschaft, ZNotP* 2010, 162

SEEVOGEL J.C., *Der Wahlgüterstand der Gütertrennung für die Europäische Ehe*, Giesking, Bielefield, 2011

SIMLER P., *Le nouveau régime matrimonial optionnel franco-allemand de partecipations aux acquêts, Droit de la famille*, n. 5, mai 2010, étude 8.

STEER C., *Die neue deutsch-französische Wahl-Zugewinngemeinschaft – eine interessante Option auch für Inlandssachverhalte?, Notar* 2010, 119

STÜRNER M., *Der deutsch-französische Wahlgüterstand als Modell für die europäische Rechtsvereinheitlichung, JZ* 2011, 545

SÜSS R., *Der deutsch-französische Güterstand der Wahl-Zugewinngemeinschaft als erbrechtliches Gestaltungsmittel, ZErb* 2010, 281